PAUL HOWARD

I READ THE NEWS TODAY, OH BOY

The short and gilded life of Tara Browne,
the man who inspired The Beatles' greatest song

PICADOR

First published 2016 by Picador

First published in paperback 2016 by Picador

This edition published 2017 by Picador
an imprint of Pan Macmillan
20 New Wharf Road, London N1 9RR
Associated companies throughout the world
www.panmacmillan.com

ISBN 978-1-5098-0004-9

1 3 5 7 9 8 6 4 2

A CIP catalogue record for this book is available from the British Library.

Typeset by Ellipsis, Glasgow
Printed and bound by CPI Group (UK) Ltd, Croydon, CR0 4YY

Visit **www.picador.com** to read more about all our books
and to buy them. You will also find features, author interviews and
news of any author events, and you can sign up for e-newsletters
so that you're always first to hear about our new releases.

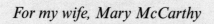

For my wife, Mary McCarthy

Contents

PROLOGUE

It was a never-to-be-forgotten night. And true to the Sixties cliché, hardly anyone who was there can remember anything about it. Or at least they recall it in little broken shards of memory. It was one of those parties that would define a moment in time. There was drink and there were drugs. There were wispishly thin girls in miniskirts with geometrically cut hair, and groovy young men in impeccably tailored suits who spoke in short, staccato sentences: 'Yeah, cool, man!'

Mick Jagger and Chrissie Shrimpton were there. So were Brian Jones and Anita Pallenberg. And a black man in native African robes who kept performing a peculiar toast: 'Ob-la-di, ob-la-da, – I drink again, I die,' before pouring a finger of whiskey onto a drawing-room carpet that cost more than an average family car.

And there was half a Magritte. Mick Jagger couldn't stop laughing when he saw it. Years later, others thought they might have imagined it. Was it something they smoked? But no. It was there, on the wall. The legend had it that an elderly housemaid noticed what she thought was dust on the modern masterpiece but was in fact a cluster of stars. She gave the canvas a rub with a chamois and, hey presto – a humble domestic's ironic twist on the work of an artist who set out to challenge people's preconditioned observations of reality. There was something about it that was so of the moment, so wacky and satirical, so surreally surreal. And, of course, very, very funny, especially if you'd dropped enough acid or smoked enough grass, which many of the guests most assuredly had.

On Saturday, 23 April 1966, there was a party at Luggala, the

Guinness family's exquisite Gothic house, set in the heart of a 5,000-acre estate, which plunged dizzyingly down a steep valley in the Wicklow Mountains. The occasion was the twenty-first birthday of Tara Browne, the Dublin-born brewery heir, music lover, style icon, racing car driver and sometime *Vogue* model, who was one of the most famous faces in what *Time* magazine had very recently called 'Swinging London'.

For one weekend, the world capital of cool was transplanted to a remote corner of the Irish countryside. The party guests were driven to the house on a narrow road that stared down precipitously on the deathly dark Lough Tay and its beach of fine white sand. One or two may have remarked, as visitors often do, on its resemblance to the porter that made the family's name and fortune. The journey took them several hundred feet down into the valley, then along the edge of the water, past a low meadow spotted with rabbits and sika deer, before the snow-white walls of Luggala Lodge – his mother Oonagh's fairytale home – revealed themselves through an embrasure in the trees.

A large marquee had been fixed to the side of the house by David Mlinaric, the London society decorator, to accommodate a dance floor. A buffet, prepared by two French chefs, was laid out along the length of the dining room, amid the period furniture and ancestral portraits. And from the arms of ancient trees, planted two centuries earlier by the house's original owners, hung coloured lights that flashed in time to the music of The Lovin' Spoonful, Tara's favourite band. Oonagh, a brewery heiress with film-star looks, paid $10,000 to fly them to Ireland from New York – her gift to her son, her miracle baby, to celebrate his coming of age.

Rich, handsome and effortlessly cool, Tara seemed to be at the centre of everything that was hip and happening during those handful of years in the 1960s when Britain gave up mourning its lost empire and became once again the cultural focus of the world. He was the living, breathing quintessence of Swinging London, a dandy with the air of a young prince. The hippest of hip cats, he always seemed to be right on the heartbeat of the moment in everything he did, whether introducing Paul McCartney to the mind-expanding possibilities of LSD in his Belgravia flat, turning heads in his psychedelically coloured AC Cobra, or gadding about London's West End with a Beatle or a Rolling Stone or perhaps Peter Sellers or Roman Polanski by his side.

In the context of the decade, he wasn't as vital a figure as Mick Jagger, or Mary Quant, or Michael Caine, or David Bailey, or Robert Fraser, or Terence Stamp, or John Lennon, or Vidal Sassoon. He didn't write a song, or star in a movie, or take a photograph, or design an item of clothing, or invent a haircut, or discover a guitar riff that defined the era in which he lived. In fact, he didn't produce anything more enduring than the memory of him as a young man who seemed unusually in harmony with the spirit of the times, a social butterfly who fluttered prettily across Sixties London and then was suddenly gone.

Fifty years on, he is familiar to many as John Lennon's lucky man who made the grade, only to blow his mind out in a car. But while 'A Day in the Life' immortalized the life of Tara Browne, it also succeeded in reducing it, for he was more than just another slumming aristocrat who lived too fast and died too young.

Swinging London, much like any popular social movement, was built on a serendipitous coming together of unique individuals. Some were unique for what they did. Others, like Tara, were unique for simply being themselves. Part of what gave the city its extraordinary creative energy in the 1960s was a new spirit of class unconsciousness that was embraced by Tara and many of his young blueblood friends. Just over a decade and a half after the Second World War, the hidebound social divisions that had been a feature of British life for centuries suddenly seemed not to matter. A new generation of confident young men and women gave the class system a vigorous shake, and for a few years, until the sediment settled again, no one cared if you were Penny from Kensington or Penniless from Hull.

The Guinnesses were aristocrats, but not snobs. At least not all of them. Tara had grown up in the space where royalty and bohemia intersected. He was an impossibly worldly sixteen-year-old at the dawn of the 1960s, when the old aristocracy of princes, princesses, lords and ladies were beginning to mix with a new aristocracy of pop musicians, clothes designers, movie directors, artists, photographers, ad men and hairdressers. The right honourables were rubbing shoulders with 'right-on-orables' and quite often it was Tara making the introductions.

One of the other great social shifts that allowed London to swing with such abandon was a general and widespread loosening of morals among Britain's youth. The country became more permissive. A generation that had grown up with National Service and post-war rationing suddenly started breaking out. The Guinnesses had never really been in. Tara's mother had been one of the Bright Young People, an earlier youth scene whose antics between the wars were a cultural precursor of what was to come three decades later. In many ways, the Sixties merely democratized the way that England's upper classes had always lived. Tara was raised not to give a hoot what anyone thought of him – and wasn't that after all the *leitmotif* of London during its renaissance years, when hair became longer and hemlines shorter and young people no longer had to be who their parents wanted them to be?

Tara grew up liberated from the concerns of ordinary children. At the age of eleven, he walked out of his posh Dublin boarding school and told his parents that he was finished with formal education. Instead, he received a different kind of schooling, as he chaperoned his peripatetic mother between homes in Dublin, London, New York, Venice, Paris and the south of France, crossing trajectories along the way with Salvador Dali, John Huston, Brendan Behan, Igor Stravinsky, Humphrey Bogart, Norman Mailer, Lucian Freud and a host of others.

As a teenager, he was sophisticated to a degree that disarmed people. Socially, he was fearless. In fact, he thrilled to danger of any kind, whether it was experimenting with the newest hallucinogenic drugs, shooting the breeze with the East End villains who popped into his motor repair shop in London, or tearing up the King's Road in a low-slung sports car, a record player built into its dash, maybe a bit of Oscar Brown Junior, up high, the needle skipping across the vinyl as he weaved through the traffic flow.

It was how many of his friends would still remember him fifty years after his final birthday party: in a hurry. Nicki Browne – the postman's daughter he married at eighteen while she was pregnant with the first of their two sons – said her husband never expected to live for long, which explained his apparent eagerness to cram so many experiences into whatever time he had.

He had an uncanny, barometric ability to always be at the centre of the current excitement. When he was in his mid-teens, he lived in Paris, a Billy Budd figure in a velvet suit escorting his wealthy Irish mother and his gigolo stepfather with the shady Nazi past. At sixteen, he was a habitué of all of the city's best-known jazz dives, where he would sit, Gauloise burning between his knuckles, watching the legendary musicians perform. 'He appeared in our lives almost fully formed, as if from an egg,' recalled his friend Martin Wilkinson, who met Tara shortly after he arrived back in London, just as the city was beginning to swing.

As the city blossomed through the early years of the decade, so Tara blossomed as an unnaturally with-it young man about town. Sixties London wasn't one single scene. It was a collection of different ones. Yet, somehow, he seemed to be at the centre of most of them, a first-hand witness to many of the events and trends that shaped and coloured the decade.

The guest list for his twenty-first birthday party reflected the mix of people who made up his social circle and captured Swinging London in perfect microcosm. Hereditary peers and baronets shared David Mlinaric's dance floor with pretty, stick-thin models and members of the avowedly anti-Establishment Stones.

Sir Alfred Beit was there. And Jane, Julian and Victoria Ormsby-Gore, the impossibly hip children of Lord Harlech, the British Ambassador to the United States during the Cuban Missile Crisis. David Dimbleby and Derek Hart of the BBC chatted with the Irish sculptor Eddie Delaney about Nelson's Pillar, the monument on Dublin's main thoroughfare that had recently been blown up by the IRA. Yul Brynner's son, Rock, was there and John Betjeman's daughter, Candida, as well as John Paul Getty, the son of reputedly the richest man on the planet, and his socialite girlfriend, Talitha Pol, all members of Tara's far-reaching social circle. All human life was there. A great big social stew of pop stars, aristos, debbie girls, artists, chancers, billionaires, models, scenesters and titled hangers-on. 'If you asked me to sum up the Sixties in a single moment,' said Joe Butler of The Lovin' Spoonful, 'then I would just describe the weekend of Tara Browne's twenty-first birthday party.'

While the band played a set that included 'Daydream' – a number two that spring in both the UK and US charts – Tara's guests partied through the night until the sun showed its face over the top of the valley and breakfast time was announced by the placing of a large tureen of vodka and tomato juice, the Luggala morning tipple, in the middle of the dining-room table.

His mother's photographs from the night capture the decade at its sunny, hopeful height. Tara and Nicki, their marriage straining at the seams, sit behind a set of bongos, sharing a laugh on what would be one of their last truly happy times together. Brian Jones, tripping on acid, tackles a slice of birthday cake with a dessert fork, while Anita Pallenberg stares into the camera, her head resting adoringly on his shoulder. With their identical pudding bowl haircuts, they resemble twins more than doomed lovers. Oonagh, in a pink ballgown, shares a laugh with Patrick Cummins, the Luggala butler who could have stepped from the pages of a P. G. Wodehouse novel, while a young Mick Jagger shares a large pink armchair with his soon-to-be ex-girlfriend on the night when, she later remembered, their relationship began to go off the rails.

Tara – wearing one of his signature black velvet suits, a blue shirt with a purple collar and blue brocade tie – looks the epitome of Swinging London cool: young and stylish, with an undeniable air of never-had-it-so-good contentedness. With a cigarette in one hand and a knowing smile tugging at his lips, it's not difficult to see why he is remembered as part of the popular iconography of the times.

For many of those who knew him, his death in a car crash later that year was the demarcation line between the Sixties when they were good and the Sixties when they turned bad. 'While he was alive,' said his friend the poet Hugo Williams, 'it was the miniskirt and the Twist and "I Wanna Hold Your Hand". And after he died, it was more about long hair and drugs and psychedelia and Altamont and horrible things like that.'

So when his friends remember that time, they think about Tara on the night of his birthday party. They remember John Sebastian singing 'Do You Believe in Magic?' and Brian Jones and Mick Jagger enjoying a night together before the diabolical internal dynamics of the Stones drove a fatal wedge between them. They remember the cloying grass they smoked and the acid trip they went on up in the Wicklow Mountains the day after the party. They remember half a Magritte and laughing so hard at it that it hurt. They remember Tara in the happy, optimistic prime of his life, a young aristocratic gadabout who was John Lennon's muse on a record that would become the musical high watermark of the decade. A happy, fun-loving, Sixties peacock. A lucky man who made the grade.

1: GUINNESS FOR STRENGTH

Two miles south of Claremorris, close to where the N17 motorway cuts a swathe through County Mayo, there is an old abandoned mansion that stands as a lonely remnant of Ireland's aristocratic past. Behind its boarded-up windows and flaking yellow outer walls are the echoes of a more colourful era and a largely forgotten way of life. Walking through the vast emptiness of the house today, it's not difficult to summon up a time when its rooms and passageways pulsed with life: the master of the house, in dinner jacket or plus-fours, moving from room to room with the easy propriety of the landed gentleman, while housemaids and footmen scuttle about the place, conducting the business of the house. It was here, amid the old-world splendour of Castle Mac Garrett, that Tara Browne – icon of Swinging London – spent his early childhood.

Life in the house moved to the rhythm of the seasons, much like the world of the Anglo-Irish aristocracy into which he was born. At various times of the year, there was pheasant and snipe shooting, hunting, trout fishing and point-to-point racing. Assorted European royals and members of the English gentry with absurdly rococo titles visited regularly to enjoy the sport. It was the era, too, of the great country house party and Castle Mac Garrett, with its seventeen bedrooms, was built for entertaining on a lavish scale.

Even now, in its current dilapidated state, it's easy to imagine the house as it was in the years of Tara's childhood: the walls of the main entrance hall and impressive staircase wainscoted with family coats of arms set in plaster and portrait paintings of his mutton-chopped, ermine-swathed forebears.

Everywhere, there are reverberations of what life here must have been like. Each door gives way to a big empty room that once served a function in the daily life of the house. There is a pantry and a large kitchen, where a team of chefs laboured to keep the household fed. There is a long drawing room and a short drawing room, both with elaborate, neoclassical stucco ceilings, where guests, in evening dress, enjoyed cocktails before a gong signalled the start of dinner. There is a large formal dining room, whose walls were once painted robin's egg blue, and a library with a beamed ceiling and mahogany shelves once lined with leather-bound books. There is a walk-in vault where the family silver was stored and a laundry room where the morning newspapers – the *Daily Telegraph* and the *Irish Times* – were ironed by a member of staff before they were presented with breakfast.

There are servant quarters and a butler's room. There is a smoking room and, off the main ballroom, a boudoir, where the lady of the house could take a moment out from entertaining to powder her nose and perhaps exchange tittle-tattle about the guests. In the voluminous albums of photographs collected by his mother, there is one of Tara, aged four, sitting on the little tricycle that he liked to ride very fast around the house's courtyard. With his awkward smile and mane of straw-coloured hair, he looks like any ordinary little boy, and not the well-born son of two aristocratic dynasties.

•

Tara was the youngest son of Dominick Geoffrey Edward Browne, the fourth Lord Oranmore and Browne – or Dom, as he was more familiarly known – and Oonagh Guinness, a granddaughter of the first Earl of Iveagh and a glamorous society beauty. Their marriage produced two boys, whose births bookended the years of the Second World War. Garech, the elder, was born in 1939, just weeks before Britain declared war on Germany, while Tara arrived six years later, just as the Allies were advancing on Berlin.

Dom was, by most accounts, a lovably rakish figure who had

a keen eye for women and excused his frequent romantic wanderings with a simple line in reasoning: 'What do you expect? I'm an
Edwardian!'

'Our father,' recalled Judith Haslam, a daughter from his first
marriage, 'was what they called NSIT. It stood for Not Safe In
Taxis. It meant that, if the occasion arose, he might behave like
something less than a gentleman. When he was with my mother,
she used to jump out of the window of the car to get away from
him. He was very good-looking in his youth. Women fell in love
with him. He was very, very charming. Too charming really. No
one ever said no to him. He had this way of getting around
people.'

At the age of thirty-seven, he was, by the standards of the
time, relatively advanced in years when he began what was his
second family. He already had five children, including Judith, from
his first marriage to Mildred Egerton, the granddaughter of the
third Earl of Ellesmere. Similarly, Oonagh Guinness, who was
eight years his junior, had a son and a daughter from her marriage
to the London stockbroker Philip Kindersley.

Dom was born in Dublin on 21 October 1901, into a way of
life that was in its twilight. The Brownes were once the biggest
landowners in the province of Connacht and one of the famous
Tribes of Galway, a group of fourteen merchant families who
dominated the political, commercial and social life in the city from
medieval to early modern times.

The first member of the family to be ennobled was Dom's
great-grandfather, who was also called Dominick, in 1836. As an
MP for Mayo, he campaigned for the restoration of Catholic
property rights removed by the Penal Laws. Daniel O'Connell,
who led the fight for Catholic Emancipation, once wrote to him,
saying, 'The country never wanted men of your constitutional
principles more than it does at present.'

When he was raised to the peerage, he chose the rather
unwieldy titles of Baron Oranmore of Carrabrowne Castle in the
County of the Town of Galway and Baron Browne of Castle Mac
Garrett in the County of Mayo. But, within a decade, he was on

the verge of bankruptcy. The Potato Famine of 1845 to 1852 ruined him, just as it did many other large Irish landowners. He managed to hold on to Castle Mac Garrett but he was forced to sell all of his other estates, including Ashford Castle, also in Mayo. By the time Dom was born, the Browne family fortune had dwindled away to almost nothing.

Born, as he was, into Ireland's Protestant ascendancy, political events at the beginning of the century always threatened to upset the happy equilibrium of Dom's childhood. The Easter Rising of 1916, in which armed rebels took over key buildings in Dublin and declared Ireland's independence from Britain, made him an effective prisoner in Mayo during his Easter holidays from Eton.

Castle Mac Garrett managed to escape the ritual burnings of the homes of the gentry that was a feature of the War of Independence that followed the Rising. According to family legend, Dom's father had shown great kindness to a young footman who became an IRA commander and ordered that the Browne house be spared. But the Irish Civil War, which resulted from the disputed treaty with Britain, did manage to upset the genteel rhythm of life in the house. In 1923 it was requisitioned by the army of the new Irish Free State for use as a barracks and the family was forced to leave. They moved to England, where they had recently inherited Mereworth Castle in Kent. When Dom's father returned to Castle Mac Garrett the following year, he was devastated to see the damage that had been done during its occupation. He wrote in his diary: 'I don't think it will ever be possible to go back and live at home.'

Dom's early life followed the classic trajectory of a member of the British aristocracy. He was schooled at Eton, then he studied, briefly, at Oxford. 'He was thrown out for having too good a time,' according to his eldest son, Dominick. 'He was out all night and not behaving himself. He had an enormously strong constitution for everything – gambling, women, drinking.'

Equally brief was his career in the military. He served with the Grenadier Guards, where he earned a reputation as a fine shot, before his interest in pursuing the sybaritic pleasures of the night did for him again. 'He was what they call bowler-hatted out,' said his son. 'Handed his bowler hat and told he was no use to the army, thanks all the same.'

Even marriage in his mid-twenties to Mildred Egerton failed to curb his louche ways. However, his life was turned upside down in June 1927 when his mother and father were killed – just as his son would be killed almost forty years later – in a car accident. Their chauffeur-driven Daimler was involved in a collision with a bus on the main road between Tonbridge and Tunbridge Wells in Kent. Lady Oranmore was pronounced dead at the scene. Lord Oranmore sustained catastrophic internal injuries and died three weeks later.

At the age of twenty-six – not long married, and still reeling from the sudden loss of his parents – Dom entered the House of Lords, where he would have a seat for seventy-two years, without ever speaking, until hereditary peerages were abolished in 1999.

He also inherited two castles – one in England and one in Ireland. Dom had always longed to return to the Mayo of his childhood. Despite the political and economic uncertainty surrounding the newly independent Irish state, he decided to make his permanent home at Castle Mac Garrett.

'He didn't fancy spending his life hanging about with other Old Etonians,' according to Dominick. 'He wanted to be his own king, which is how he felt when he was in Ireland.'

Dom wrote to William T. Cosgrave, the first leader of the Irish Free State, seeking an assurance that the castle and its 3,000-acre demesne would not be confiscated by the Land Commission, which had been set up to compulsorily purchase, then redistribute, land owned by non-Irish citizens in the wake of independence. Cosgrave gave him the assurance he sought. In 1930, Dom sold his father's English estate to set up a permanent home with his first wife and their young family in the west of Ireland.

The decision to offload Mereworth was forced on him. It took a considerable amount of money to maintain and run one major country house, let alone two. Few upper-class families emerged from the Great War, and the hard decade that followed it, with their fortunes intact. Punitive post-war taxation, as well as the worldwide economic crisis triggered by the Wall Street Crash, fatally weakened the financial and social position of many of the aristocracy, whose numbers had been ravaged anyway by the war.

Even families like the Guinnesses, who had an industrial fortune to support them – 'trade', as it was snootily referred to by the idle rich – discovered that big country houses were becoming increasingly impractical and financially draining. In England, as well as Ireland, an era was coming to an end. As Noel Coward put it in his song 'The Stately Homes of England', the big house and all it represented was 'rather in the lurch'.

Dom's answer to this crisis was to go to work. After selling Mereworth, he attempted to make his one remaining estate self-sufficient, turning Castle Mac Garrett into a working farm and becoming a major food producer in the west of Ireland.

'There were huge greenhouses,' recalled Philomena Flatley, who worked as his secretary from 1950. 'There was everything in there. Every fruit and vegetable you could think of. They had vines with grapes. They had figs. They had orchards. They sold an awful lot of tomatoes in season. Smith the gardener would load it all up and bring it off to the market and to local shops. They made feed for cows. They sold garden produce. There was a dairy and they sold milk to the creamery. They churned as well to make butter. And eggs. They had hens. Free range.'

Land was reclaimed, reseeded and stocked with a herd of Aberdeen Angus cattle. Suffolk and Galway sheep were cross-bred in order to provide the 'perfect' lamb. Some 1,200 pheasants were raised every year for shoots. Eels were caught in the eel weir, then shipped to the markets of London, where they were a popular dish. Castle Mac Garrett even had a sawmill that provided the country's nascent Electricity Supply Board with the wooden poles used in the electrification of rural Ireland.

'There were horses here as well,' Philomena said. 'Prince d'Ardia Caracciolo and also Lord Harrington sent their mares to

Castle Mac Garrett for service. There were so many things happening. His plan was that the estate would be entirely self-sufficient and that the income would pay for the maintenance of the house and the salaries of the staff.'

Despite the demands of trying to make the estate pay for itself, he still found time to indulge his hobbies. He hosted regular shooting parties, at which members of venerable European families would come to shoot pheasant, snipe or whatever happened to be in season.

His responsibilities as a farm-owner and family man did nothing to dissuade him from his pursuit of attractive women. By 1934 – married and with five children under the age of ten – his eye had been taken by a woman who was reputed to be one of the most beautiful women in Ireland.

•

Oonagh Guinness was the youngest of Ernest Guinness's three blonde, blue-eyed daughters. She was a member of the sixth generation of the brewing dynasty, whose surname was as famous as Ireland itself. Over the course of the previous 150 years, the family had built what was once a small business into one of the world's most identifiable brands and one of the world's biggest fortunes. The Guinnesses used the political, commercial and financial clout that accompanied their success to rise to the ranks of the British aristocracy, in defiance of traditional class snobbishness towards fortunes earned through industry.

Irish by birth, but British by manners and political affiliation, the family expertly steered through the choppy political waters of the late nineteenth and early twentieth century, managing to be from both countries and neither country at exactly the same time. The Guinnesses were opposed to every Irish nationalist movement from Home Rule to land reform to political rights for the country's Catholic majority. The same Daniel O'Connell who praised the Brownes said: 'With contemptuous pity, I dismiss the Guinnesses.'

And yet the people of Ireland retained a deep sentimental attachment to them, thanks to their enlightened employment practices and acts of philanthropy, which included building new accommodation for families living in Dublin's overcrowded and notoriously squalid tenements and gifting St Stephen's Green to the people of the city.

The writer Brendan Behan, who was a close friend of both Oonagh and her children, regarded the family as the closest thing the country had to royalty. 'The Guinnesses,' he said, summing up an age-old paradox, 'are the only English aristocrats who have remained truly Irish.'

Contrary to popular belief, they didn't invent the highly distinctive dark beer which made them, at one point, the wealthiest family in Britain and Ireland. They were, in fact, relative late comers to the business of brewing. Porter was first produced in Shoreditch in the East End of London in 1722 and was so named because of its popularity among manual labourers – porters – in the markets of early eighteenth-century London.

The first Arthur Guinness, whose signature remains part of the iconography of the brand founded his brewery at St James's Gate, on the banks of the River Liffey, in 1759. Its grey walls, giant vats and confusion of piping would become as recognizable a part of Dublin as the smell of toasted hops that still hangs over the city in the early morning to this day.

His son, the second Arthur Guinness, was behind two business decisions that helped turn the family brewery into the most dominant Irish company of the nineteenth and early twentieth century. The first, taken with his father and their brewing partner, John Purser, was to concentrate on only one product. The second was to brew it so well that porter and Guinness would come to mean one and the same thing.

But it was Oonagh's grandfather, Edward, and his older brother, Sir Arthur – immortalized as the Cunning Brothers in James Joyce's *Ulysses* – who completed the family's ascent to the very heights of British society, where they could count the

British royal family amongst their friends. These fourth-generation Guinnesses initially ran the business as partners, although, in time, one brother proved to be more cunning than the other. Edward persuaded Sir Arthur, who was more interested in pursuing a peerage than running a brewery, to sell the business to him at what proved to be a knockdown price. The dissolution was announced on 1 January 1877, when Oonagh's grandfather became the sole owner of what was then the world's largest brewery. He was still only twenty-nine.

By his late thirties, he was an incredibly wealthy man, earning somewhere in the region of £100,000 per year at a time when only 4,000 people in Britain had an annual income of over £5,000.

The uncertain political and economic future of Ireland was probably behind his surprise decision in the late nineteenth century to cash in his inheritance and to make England his permanent home. In 1887, Guinness was floated on the stock market. The public was invited to buy a piece of Ireland's most successful business, although the family would remain the biggest shareholder, retaining 33 per cent of the stock.

Having achieved his business ambitions, he set about making his own mark in high society. His brother had become the first Guinness admitted to the ranks of the aristocracy when he was made a peer by Benjamin Disraeli in his 1880 resignation Honours List, in recognition of his services to the Conservative Party. Sir Arthur acquired the title Lord Ardilaun. In 1890, Edward, too, was ennobled. He chose the title Lord Iveagh and retired to Elveden, a vast estate in Suffolk.

When he died in 1927, Lord Iveagh left his shares and the job of managing the brewery to his three sons, Rupert, Ernest and Walter. All three were in their middle years and two of them were happily ensconced in careers that had nothing to do with brewing porter. Rupert, the eldest, succeeded his father as chairman of the company, but he had little interest in the day-to-day running, preferring to concentrate on farming. Walter, the youngest – and the future Lord Moyne – was the Minister for Agriculture and

Fisheries in Britain. So it was Oonagh's father, Ernest, who became the de facto head of the brewery at the age of fifty-one.

Ernest steered the business successfully through the difficult years between the wars and was a key player in the decision that turned Guinness into one of the most iconic brands of the twentieth century: the decision to advertise. Ernest's father had considered the notion of promoting the company's product through billboard and newspaper advertising to be vulgar. But Ernest's cousin, Kenelm Lee Guinness, a Guinness director, motor racing driver and later a role model to the teenage Tara, offered the company the benefit of his experience marketing the KLG spark plug, which he had invented. The famous Guinness toucan, the zoo keeper and sea lion, and the farmer pulling a horse in a cart soon featured in the company's ads and crossed quickly into the media mainstream.

Ernest married Marie Clotilde Russell – or Chloe, as she was popularly known – in 1903. The couple spent their time between Glenmaroon, their Dublin home; Holmbury House, their mansion on 300 acres in Surrey; and, as if to emphasize the Guinness family's propinquity to royalty, their house in London's Grosvenor Place, at the western perimeter of Buckingham Palace Gardens.

Together, they had three daughters, all of whom were given Irish names. Aileen, the eldest, was born in 1904, Maureen in 1907 and Oonagh in 1910. All three were considered to be extraordinary beauties in their time. They were part of a new wave of Guinnesses who would make newspaper headlines for reasons other than the business of brewing porter. Anticipating the Swinging Sixties by an entire generation, their permissive lifestyles and outrageous behaviour would earn them the prurient fascination of the gossip writers, who dubbed them the Golden Guinness Girls.

'The sisters are all witches,' the movie director John Huston, a close friend of Oonagh's, once said. 'Lovely ones, to be sure. But witches nonetheless. They are all transparent-skinned, with pale hair and light-blue eyes. You can nearly see through them. They are quite capable of changing swinish folk into real swine before your very eyes, and turning them back again without their even knowing it.'

The girls received little by way of a conventional school education, much like Tara later on. Homework, Oonagh would later tell Tara's eldest son, Dorian, was something that governesses did. They were born into a world of wealth and privilege but one which could also be cold and remote. It was a social norm among the upper classes that children saw their parents only intermittently: often for half an hour in the morning and half an hour in the evening. The Guinness girls were no different in that regard. The nannies that supervised their upbringing were capable of the most awful cruelty. 'My mother told me that if she was sick,' Garech recalled, 'she was forced to eat her vomit for her next meal.'

Ernest was determined to keep his daughters out of the politically turbulent Ireland of their childhood and they spent much of their early lives in England. In 1922, however, while holidaying in Ireland, they were witnesses to one of the defining moments of the Irish Civil War: the burning of the Four Courts, which they watched from the top of a turret in Glenmaroon, their vast Dublin home, a short distance from the brewery.

Oonagh was regarded as one of the most desirable young women in London by the time of her 'coming out' – the elaborate, 200-year-old ritual in which England's well-born daughters were presented to the Queen before the start of the summer social season. She was considered by many to be the most attractive of Ernest's daughters, sharing none of Aileen's grandiosity, and none of the pretensions to royalty that would later drive a wedge between Maureen and her own daughter, the writer Caroline Blackwood.

Oonagh was tiny, almost elfin, standing barely five feet tall in her stockinged feet, which were so slight that she wore children's shoes all her life. While Maureen was a born comedienne – she was the model for Osbert Lancaster's Maudie Littlehampton cartoons and bore more than a passing resemblance to Dame Edna Everage – Oonagh was demure. That's not to say she lacked assertiveness.

She once dared to tell King George V that he was 'pompous and boring'.

'Oonagh,' according to Martin Wilkinson, one of Tara's friends who knew her later on, 'was a strange mixture of very spoiled and very sweet and very fucked-up and very kind and very open. She was a convent girl crossed with this extremely sophisticated product of the Hollywood, Paris and literary worlds that she moved in. She had the air of a Fifties actress.'

In the established Guinness tradition, all three girls chose partners with money and impeccable breeding, although none of their marriages would prove to be happy. Aileen married her cousin, the Honourable Brinsley Plunkett – or Brinny, as he was known. They set up home in the spectacular Luttrelstown Castle, built on a 500-acre estate seven miles north-west of Dublin. Maureen married the ostentatiously named Basil Sheridan Hamilton-Temple-Blackwood, who very shortly afterwards inherited the title of Marquess of Dufferin and Ava when his father was killed in an aeroplane crash. With it came the spectacular Clandeboye house and estate, twelve miles north of Belfast. Oonagh was the youngest when she married. In 1929, just five days after celebrating her nineteenth birthday, she exchanged vows with a twenty-two-year-old stockbroker named Philip Kindersley. It seemed like a match made in Debrett's heaven. Philip was the youngest son of the successful financier Sir Robert Kindersley, a director of the Bank of England, who had been knighted for his work as president of the National Savings Committee.

Philip met Oonagh at a ball in London in 1928. Tall and dark, he was every young debutante's dream. A year later, they married at St Margaret's, Westminster. And, very quickly, they discovered they had almost nothing in common. 'My father and mother weren't suited at all,' recalled their son, the champion amateur jockey Gay Kindersley. 'My father was sort of hunting and shooting. My mother liked the company of intellectuals. It's a wonder they ever hit it off. I mean, in those days, the men used to go to these debs' dances and just cling on to the lady they were dancing with. There wasn't very much in the way of conversation. And then one night, they said, "Will you marry me?"'

Philip's intention in marrying Oonagh, according to Gay, was simply to produce a son and heir.

Gay was born on 2 June 1930 and named after an American playboy called Gaylord, whose tragic death in a speedboat accident Philip had recently read about while holidaying in the south of France. Two years later, in January 1932, Oonagh gave birth to a daughter. Like Gay, Tessa was delivered by caesarean section. Both births took a heavy toll on the delicately built Oonagh, as all of her experiences of labour would.

The newly married Kindersleys set up home at Rutland Gate, Hyde Park, from where Philip commuted each morning to the City of London, while Oonagh was seldom seen without her children – at least in the daytime. Weekends were spent in the country, usually at Plaw Hatch Hall, the Kindersley family home in Sussex, where Philip's enthusiasm for riding, shooting and other country pursuits served to emphasize the lack of compatibility between him and his more sophisticated wife.

•

For Oonagh and Philip, getting married and starting a family didn't mean settling down. In fact, none of the Guinness girls let domesticity come between them and their enjoyment of a full and active social life. The 1920s was a time of carefree hedonism and raucous exuberance for London's young upper-class set. There was widespread relief that the Great War was over. The waste of an entire generation of men lost in the trenches of the Western Front – including Philip's brother, Bow – brought about a new attitude among young people, characterized by a studied lack of seriousness, a tendency towards excess and the elevation of triviality above everything else. And no one pulled it off with as much high-decibel enthusiasm as the raffish, fast-living and forever-capering set that posterity remembers as the Bright Young People.

The Guinness sisters became adults at the centre of this

pleasure-seeking, incessantly giggling demi-monde. Its habitués were characterized in *Bright Young People*, D. J. Taylor's authoritative biography of the set, as 'idle young men living in Mayfair mewses, blooming specimens of aristocratic girlhood from Pont Street and Lowndes Square (and) Tatterdemalion "artists" hunkered down in Chelsea basements'.

In the popular imagination, the lifestyle associated with the set was an endless round of cocktails, jazz, licentiousness, headline-grabbing stunts and fancy-dress parties that tried to outdo each other in the manner of theme and outrageousness. In his 1930 satirical novel, *Vile Bodies*, the writer Evelyn Waugh lampooned this louche and frivolous world, of which he himself was a part. 'Masked parties,' he wrote. 'Savage parties. Victorian parties. Greek parties. Wild West parties. Russian parties. Circus parties. Parties where one had to dress as somebody else, almost naked parties in St John's Wood, parties in flats and houses and shops and hotels and night clubs, in windmills and swimming baths . . . All that succession and repetition of mass humanity – Those vile bodies.'

Waugh dedicated the book to Oonagh's cousin, Bryan Guinness, and his wife, Diana Mitford, his close friends who were the first torchbearers of the set. Bryan and Diana were among the originators of the treasure hunt, the 1920s youth cult in which partygoers were given a series of cryptic clues that sent them dashing around London in open two-seater automobiles. These, in turn, grew into scavenger parties, at which guests were challenged to bring back random items, such as a policeman's helmet or the pipe of Stanley Baldwin, the Prime Minister, whose daughter Betty was a member of the set.

The old conservative stablishment, which had led Britain into a ruinous war, regarded them with exasperation.

'I don't understand them and I don't want to,' declared Waugh's fictional Lord Metroland, reflecting a commonly held attitude in Britain. 'They had a chance after the war that no generation has ever had. There was a whole civilization to be saved and remade. And all they seem to do is play the fool.'

Oonagh and Philip were dedicated members of the set. They were pictured in the 21 June 1933 edition of *Tatler* at a 'Come and Be Crazy Party' at London's Dorchester Hotel, surrounded by fellow revellers wearing pyjamas, false beards, public school blazers, top hats, shorts with garters and Harrow caps.

It was the Guinnesses, *Fortune*, the global business magazine reported, who started the fashion of driving to Cuckoo Weir, the swimming hole at Eton, for midnight bathing parties, and Kenelm Lee Guinness – the brewery director and racing driver – who drove a steamroller over an enormous pile of tin cans to find out how it would sound.

All of these antics coincided with the emergence of a new type of press, aimed at Britain's middle classes. Positioned somewhere between the stiff newspapers of record and the lower-brow tabloids, this new market was defined by Lord Northcliffe, the founder and publisher of the *Daily Mail*, as news that the thousand pound a year man is interested in reading. The new 'society journalism' was concerned not only with news, but with gossip and personalities. Oonagh and her sisters – rich, beautiful and fun-loving – fitted Lord Northcliffe's criteria for newsworthiness perfectly.

In 1931, to celebrate his wife's twenty-first birthday, Philip commissioned the royal portrait artist Philip de László to paint her. The portrait, capturing Oonagh in a white ballgown and an emerald necklace, with one hand placed demurely on her clavicle, cost £1,575 and was later exhibited in a retrospective of the Hungarian's work in Paris. While Oonagh was thrilled with the portrait, the picture of happy marital contentment that she and Philip presented was at sharp odds with the reality.

Adultery was almost institutionalized among the upper classes in Edwardian and post-Edwardian Britain. Extramarital affairs were socially permissible as long as they were conducted discreetly. According to Gay, his father remained faithful to his mother for barely a year of their married life. Then, he embarked on a relationship with her best friend and bridesmaid, Valerie French, the granddaughter of the first Earl of Ypres. Valsie, as she was known, had only recently become married herself, to Victor Brougham, the fourth Lord Brougham and Vaux. According to Gay, Oonagh knew about the affair and professed not to care until Valsie was photographed with Philip at a function, wearing her bridesmaid's dress.

While her husband found happiness in the arms of her best friend, Oonagh too had found love outside their marriage. It's not known exactly when her affair with Dom began. Discretion was important as they were both still married to other people. In her divorce petition, Dom's first wife, Mildred, suggested that it started early in 1934.

In the tight, socially incestuous world of the Anglo-Irish aristocracy, it's likely that Dom and Oonagh had met many times before they ever became lovers. Dom had known the Guinness family most of his life. His home of Castle Mac Garrett was just twenty miles away from Ashford Castle, which his great-grandfather had sold to Oonagh's great-grandfather back in the 1850s. He was invited there regularly to shoot woodcock and snipe and was also an occasional visitor to Ernest's London home at 17 Grosvenor Place.

With her marriage as good as over, Oonagh spent a great deal of that autumn and winter in Ireland. The social pages from the time suggest that Oonagh crossed paths with the Oranmore and Brownes at a number of shoots, race meetings and hunt balls through the latter half of 1933. By the summer of 1934, Dom and Oonagh were in the first flush of love.

As they prepared to move on to the next chapter of their lives, Oonagh and her first husband seemed to reach an unusually dignified accommodation with one another's lovers. In August 1934, Oonagh, Dom, Philip and Valsie all holidayed together in the south and south-west of Ireland. With their mutual friend, the writer Edward Lindsay-Hogg, they spent a weekend at the Tramore Races in Waterford. They then travelled together to Kerry, enjoying the scenic Lakes of Killarney before riding on horseback through the Gap of Dunloe, the spectacular mountain pass that lies in the shadow of Ireland's highest peak.

By then, Valsie had already divorced her husband, who was in serious financial difficulty as a result of his gambling debts. Philip told Oonagh that he wanted to marry Valsie, while Oonagh told Philip that she wanted to marry Dom.

'It suited everyone,' according to her son Garech. 'It was rather fortunate, really, that everyone fell in love with someone else at around the same time.'

Rumours of their unusual extramarital arrangement eventually reached the ears of the press. In the early months of 1935, the society writers began dropping hints about something that was already the subject of gossip in social circles in London. *The Bystander* began to refer to Valsie rather pointedly as Oonagh's 'erstwhile' friend. Earlier in the year, without using names, the same magazine reported that 'London's only really happy couple' were breaking up: 'Far be it from us to take sides, as we like them both enormously, but we consider the present situation constitutes one more instance of the close proximity of fire when we see a lot of smoke. We girls are tremendous believers in platonic relationships, but we do think they have their limitations, and when a husband is seen exclusively with another woman, it usually means it's ripened into something stronger. Similarly, when the wife stays on at the same house party as her boyfriend without her husband, we trust we are not being unduly suspicious if we wonder what it's all about.' In a reference to Dom's wife, Mildred, the column said, 'The one with whom we sympathize deeply is the boyfriend's wife. She seems to have had very little fun.'

While Mildred was aware of Dom's unfaithfulness, she was shocked to her core when he told her that he was leaving her and their five children for another woman. 'She was absolutely devastated,' remembered Dominick. 'We all were. You've lived together all your lives as a family and then you're suddenly separated. I was only six years old. We were all required to leave this castle in Ireland where we'd lived all our lives and suddenly we're staying in digs in London, near Marble Arch.'

Under English law a divorce was attainable only if one partner could prove adultery on the part of the other. And proof required at least one independent witness. The customary arrangement, in the case where a split was amicable, was to contrive a situation in which one or both parties would be 'caught' committing the act by an independent third party. But Oonagh and Dom's efforts to stage-manage an act of infidelity turned into a farce worthy of Oscar Wilde. They travelled to France to stay at a hotel, owned by a cousin of Oonagh's. However, the hotel manager refused to give evidence to support Philip's petition for divorce in what he believed was an act of loyalty to his employer. The act of infidelity was eventually staged in Austria.

The Oranmores and Kindersleys were divorced on the same day and in the same court in November 1935, but they managed to keep the news a secret for a while. Within days, Oonagh and Dom sailed to New York on a Cunard liner, the RMS *Aquitania*. Their presence in America was covered extensively in the national press, although they went to lengths to give the impression that they were travelling separately.

They married the following spring, at Marylebone Register Office, on 29 April 1936. It was a far more muted occasion than Oonagh's first wedding, which had been a 1929 society event of the year. The bride wore a mauve-blue ensemble with a matching hat, the groom a navy pin-striped suit with a red carnation in the button, and they exchanged their vows in front of half a dozen guests. The *Daily Express* reported that they made three unsuccessful attempts to leave the registry office and that their efforts to evade press photographers resulted in a car chase.

Ernest Guinness made Oonagh a wedding gift of an exquisite eighteenth-century house, tucked into a cleft on a 5,000-acre estate in the Wicklow Mountains. 'Luggala has been given to me by my kind father,' Oonagh wrote in the visitors' book. It was the home where, thirty years later, their younger son would celebrate his coming of age in the company of Brian Jones and

Mick Jagger and the Bright Young People of another generation, little knowing that it would be the final milestone event in a short but extraordinary life.

2: WAR BABY

Blond-haired and blue-eyed, Tara Browne entered the world on 4 March 1945, in a nursing home on the banks of Dublin's Grand Canal. Oonagh regarded him as her miracle baby – and not only because her doctors had tried to warn her off having any more children. Tara arrived into Oonagh's life right in the middle of a decade blighted by sadness and tragedy, a period in which she would lose her daughter, her infant son, her husband, her father and much of her fortune.

Tara's birth was a rare moment of joy in her thirties. The Second World War was in its final weeks and she could allow herself to be excited about the future. A photograph taken in front of Castle Mac Garrett on the day that Tara was christened shows Oonagh smiling while holding her new baby, surrounded by her enormous extended family. Dom is standing at the back, his face partly obscured, as if to emphasize the fissure that had already opened up in their marriage. Before Tara had even taken his first tottering steps, his father would meet the woman for whom he would eventually leave his wife.

Marriage to Dom didn't turn out to be the better life that Oonagh dreamt of. But they were happy once, before the pressures of the war years drove a wedge between them. In 1936, after a prolonged honeymoon in Scotland, they returned to Ireland with six-year-old Gay and four-year-old Tessa. For the next few years they lived between their houses in Mayo and Wicklow, as the 1930s built to a tumultuous head.

Despite her one-time ambivalence towards outdoor pursuits, the new Lady Oranmore and Browne appeared to settle happily into country life and told the *Sketch* that she no longer cared for London and the restaurants and nightclubs of which she was once so fond. And then, as if to symbolically close the door on her former life, she changed the colour of her hair, from bombshell blonde to subdued brown.

It wasn't just for Oonagh that an era was coming to a close. The great social and economic convulsions of the 1930s had forced an end to the antics of the Bright Young People. In 1931, Britain had responded to the worldwide economic crisis precipitated by the Wall Street Crash by leaving the gold standard, a considerable blow to the country's self-confidence. Suddenly, the kindergarten antics of high bohemia began to seem in bad taste to a country that had three million unemployed and the horrible probability of a war with Hitler's Germany ahead.

It was mostly from their castle retreat in the west of Ireland, surrounded by their large brood of children, that Oonagh and Dom watched the watershed moments of the 1930s unfold, from the abdication of Edward VIII – a long-time friend of Oonagh's and a spiritual bellwether for the Bright Young People – to Neville Chamberlain's return from the Munich Conference and the slow, grim realization that the world would soon be at war again.

Only occasionally were they seen in London. As a peer of the realm, Dom, together with his new wife, attended the coronation of George VI in Westminster Abbey in May 1937, both wearing ceremonial robes for the occasion. They were also at the wedding of William Somerset Maugham's daughter Elizabeth, and the reopening of the famous Ciro's Club in London. *Tatler*, noting Oonagh's presence there, compared her to Greta Garbo.

She was still incredibly glamorous. She loved clothes. And, as the society magazines spotted, she was taking her fashion cues from the new stars of Hollywood's first talking pictures. After her vanity case was stolen from Castle Mac Garrett by a party guest, she went to court in nearby Claremorris wearing a trouser suit with tapered legs, and a hat, cocked to one side, so that it covered her right eye, in the style of Carole Lombard or Loretta Young.

Her husband was similarly enamoured by clothes. 'He was a

very debonair dresser,' according to his daughter Judith, 'just like Tara and Garech really. He always got his clothes made by the best tailors in London.'

Oonagh and Dom's social life now revolved around shooting weekends and white-tie balls in castles in the west of Ireland, with their ever dwindling circle of aristocratic friends, members of the diplomatic set and foreign royals who used Ireland as a playground for their pastimes.

Thanks to Oonagh's wealth, the couple enjoyed a life of considerable comfort, with a large house staff. But much like her marriage to Philip, Oonagh's relationship with Dom was far from the happy domestic idyll. Their arguments were famous, with house guests regularly pressed into choosing sides. Marriage to Oonagh had also failed to put an end to Dom's sexual wanderlust. 'Oonagh's father,' Judith recalled, 'used to call him the Stallion.'

Their life in the west of Ireland was at least filled with one thing that Oonagh loved: children. As well as Tessa and Gay, there were Dominick, Martin, Patricia, Brigid and Judith, the five children from Dom's first marriage, who visited regularly from their new home in London.

'At first it was difficult to go back to Castle Mac Garrett,' remembered Dominick, Dom's eldest son. 'It had been our house and it was no longer our house. It was the house of Gay and Tessa. They were sleeping in our old bedrooms. That's one of the awful things about divorce. And maybe the biggest shock of all was that they had horses and ponies and Guinness money and, well, we had nothing. We were arriving back to this castle where we once lived, but we were arriving back as poor people.

'But then, after a time, we loved it. And Oonagh was a lovely person. I adored her. This is where I felt I let my mother down, because I should have hated her. But you couldn't help adoring her. She was so kind and so sweet.'

Soon, more children arrived at Castle Mac Garrett. First came Neelia and Doon Plunkett, Aileen's daughters. She had divorced their father and deposited the two girls with her sister before removing herself to America for the duration of the war. Oonagh was more than happy to become a surrogate mother to her two nieces. And by the time of their arrival in 1940, Oonagh and Dom had started a family of their own.

Their first son, Garech Domnagh Browne, was born on 25 June 1939, in Glenmaroon, the Dublin home of Oonagh's parents, close to the Guinness brewery. He was baptized in St Patrick's Cathedral in Dublin, with water from the River Jordan, surrounded by his half-brothers, sisters and cousins. Garech was delivered by caesarean section. The delivery exacted such a physical toll on Oonagh that, at twenty-nine, she was advised not to have any more children.

•

Within weeks of Garech's birth came the news that Germany had invaded Poland and the world was once again at war. Dom attempted to enlist in the British Army but, at thirty-seven, he was deemed too old for service. A recruiting officer told him that his energies would be more productively spent farming his land, since food rationing was likely to be a fact of life for as long as the war lasted.

Oonagh's ex-husband, Philip, who had since married Valsie and set up his own stockbroking firm, did succeed in enlisting. He joined the Coldstream Guards and saw action in France and in North Africa, before he was captured by the Germans. He spent almost two and a half years as a prisoner of war, first in Italy, then in Germany.

From captivity, he would direct a bitter legal battle with Oonagh over the custody of their son, Gay, which would make newspaper headlines around the world.

When their parents' marriage was dissolved, Gay and Tessa had been made wards of court. Philip acquiesced to his children spending their childhood in Ireland on the condition that, once Gay reached the age of ten, he would be sent to Colthill, a preparatory school near Abingdon, then on to Eton, just like his father. Gay spent a year at Colthill, but in the summer of 1940, the Luftwaffe was subjecting Britain's cities to the largest and most sustained aerial bombardment the world had ever seen. Oonagh and Philip both agreed that Gay would be safer in Ireland and he was enrolled in Castle Park, a Protestant boarding school with Anglocentric leanings, in Dalkey, south of Dublin.

On Christmas Day 1942, Philip was captured by the Germans near Tunis and was fortunate to escape with his life when the officer escorting him accidentally trod on a mine. The young man, Philip noted in his diary, was 'blown to bits from the waist down', while he himself was thrown clear and escaped with cuts and shock. He was sent to a Tunis hospital to recuperate, then on to the first of several prisoner-of-war camps.

In 1942, as Gay approached his thirteenth birthday, and with the skies over England largely quiet, Philip's father, Sir Robert Kindersley, demanded that the original agreement be honoured and that Gay be sent to Eton. Through the English courts, Sir Robert applied successfully for custody of his grandson. Oonagh ignored the order of the court. An application was then made to the High Court in Dublin, where Oonagh was ordered to hand over her son in time to start school at Eton in September 1942. Again, Oonagh defied the order. 'My mother's lawyers advised her that she couldn't lose,' according to Garech. 'They said an Irish court would never force a mother to hand over her child.'

On legal advice, and much to the anger of the Kindersley family, she took out Irish citizenship for both Gay and Tessa.

The fate of Oonagh and Philip's son became an international cause célèbre as the court proceedings dragged out over the seven months that followed. Oonagh held firm in her refusal to – as her counsel put it – 'take the boy from a country at peace to a country engaged in a life and death struggle, to remove him from his mother and turn him into a sort of orphan . . . supported by a well-to-do grandfather'.

In July 1943, the High Court in Dublin decided that the wishes of Gay's father must be ascertained before it ruled where the boy should be educated. The case was adjourned while efforts were made to contact Philip. He was being held in Fontanellato, a small town in the province of Parma in northern Italy, in an orphanage that had been requisitioned for use as a prisoner camp for Allied soldiers.

Gay had no doubt what his father would say if they managed to get a communication to him. Philip, he said, had a deep loathing of the Irish. For several months there was silence. As the September 1943 deadline passed, Gay was enrolled in St Columba's College in Dublin.

By that time, Oonagh, having ignored medical advice, was pregnant for the fourth time.

The stress of the custody case took a heavy toll on her. Some days she travelled to court from a Dublin nursing home, where she was forced to stay, owing to difficulties with the pregnancy.

Finally, in November 1943, Oonagh – wearing a fur coat and a black hat and veil – was in court to see her one-time father-in-law produce a telegram, received from Philip through the British Foreign Office. 'Application for release of Gay to enter Eton,' the message said, 'has my full knowledge and approval.'

In a separate letter to his father, Philip wrote: 'It is really wonderful for you to have done this for me, as I had visions of Gay being educated as a Sinn Feiner.'

The High Court upheld the order of the English court and instructed Oonagh to hand over her son to his grandfather. Oonagh appealed to the Supreme Court, which unanimously upheld the decision of the High Court, while acknowledging that Oonagh's actions were motivated by 'nothing other than a genuine love for her son and regard for his safety and welfare'. On 15 January 1944, a last appeal, based on a technical issue, failed to overturn the original order. At three o'clock that afternoon, Gay was reading a comic book in the office of the registrar of the High Court, when he was told that he was being handed over to his grandparents to be brought to England.

Oonagh wasn't in court to see the final act play out. On 28 December she had given birth to a boy. Two days later, before she even had an opportunity to name him, he died. 'He was almost stillborn,' according to Garech. 'He didn't have a hope really.'

Oonagh was too ill and riven by grief to be in court to see Gay

placed in the care of Sir Robert and his wife for the journey to
England. 'I remember Dom, my stepfather, leading me out of the
court,' recalled Gay, shortly before his death in 2011. 'A boy, rather
bewildered. I remember all these old Irish ladies lined up outside
the court, shaking their fists at my grandparents, saying, "Taking
a boy from his mother! You should be ashamed!" They followed
us out to the taxi. They banged on the windows. I was quite frightened. We went to the Gresham Hotel. We stayed the night and got
the mail boat the next morning.'

Three days later, Gay started school at Eton, while Oonagh
laid her unnamed baby to rest close to the lake at Luggala under
a stone marked with the simple inscription, 'Baby Browne'.

•

Neutral during the war, Ireland may have seemed like a peaceful
sanctuary on the periphery of a continent tearing itself apart. But
the war years brought a considerable amount of unhappiness and
tragedy to Oonagh and Dom's door. In 1941, two years before the
custody case and the death of Baby Browne, Dom had lost one of
his children. Fourteen-year-old Brigid – or Biddy, as she was
fondly known – died of pneumonia in Scotland. 'She caught it
coming home from school,' her sister, Judith, remembered. 'It was
a particularly bad winter when all the lakes froze over. My mother
always said that if penicillin had been more widely available at the
time, she wouldn't have died.'

The war itself laid waste to another generation of men in their
prime and the aristocratic classes were not spared from loss.
Oonagh's sisters, Maureen and Aileen, both lost the husbands
they'd married in the giddy, jazz-filled years that followed the First
World War. Brinny Plunkett – by then divorced from Aileen –
enlisted as a flight lieutenant in the RAF Volunteer Reserve and
was killed when he crash-landed his Spitfire in Aden in November
1941. It fell to Oonagh to break the news to Neelia and Doon,
who were living at Castle Mac Garrett, that their father was dead.

Maureen's husband, Basil, the Marquess of Dufferin and Ava,
was engaged in a propaganda operation in Burma, designed to

stop the Japanese advance on Mandalay. On 25 March 1945, he was killed in an ambush, close to the ancient capital of Ava, the town whose name he shared.

Oonagh's father, Ernest, lost his younger brother, also in the colonies. After a distinguished political career, Walter Guinness, the Lord Moyne, had been appointed British minister of state in the Middle East by Winston Churchill in January 1944. In the early afternoon of 6 November of that same year, Eliyahu Bet-Zuri and Eliyahu Hakim, two members of the militant Zionist group Lehi, shot him dead in the back of his chauffeur-driven car close to his home in Cairo.

Right in the middle of a decade that would be marked by further tragedies, Tara arrived into Oonagh's life like a blessing. The death of Baby Browne had made her even more determined to conceive again, even against medical advice. 'One of the reasons,' according to Garech, 'was of course that she'd lost a baby and she wanted another child desperately. But it was also because being a mother was something she happened to be rather wonderful at.'

Tara was delivered by caesarean section in Portobello House, a private nursing home, in Dublin. He was born healthy and with no complications for either mother or child. Oonagh, who had a deep love of Irish history, considered naming her new baby Fiach, after Fiach mac Aodha Ó Broin, a sixteenth-century Robin Hood figure whose clan controlled the mountains around Luggala and fought the Tudors during the Elizabethan conquest of Ireland. 'He was going to be Fiach,' according to Garech, 'but then everyone started saying that, if he ever left Ireland, he'd be known as Fuck or Fucker, so she decided against it.'

Instead, she chose Tara, after the historic Hill of Tara, the ancient seat of the High Kings of Ireland. On 15 April 1945, he was christened by the Archdeacon of Tuam at Crossboyne Church in County Mayo.

The war in Europe was coming to an end – Hitler's death was only two weeks away – and there was a sense of optimism about the world into which Tara was born. He could look forward to a childhood of Blytonish fun and adventure in the company of his brother, half-siblings and cousins. Dom and Oonagh and their large brood of children looked like one big, happy, extended family in photographs taken in the months after Tara's arrival. Tessa, by now a very accomplished rider, won the Children's Championship jumping competition at the Royal Dublin Horse Show that summer. The following day's newspapers carried photographs of Oonagh standing next to her thirteen-year-old daughter and her pony, Brown Jack, looking every inch the proud mother.

A sense of normality seemed to be returning to their lives. Fifteen-year-old Gay, on holiday from Eton, had just enjoyed an emotional reunion with his father, who had been liberated from Oflag 79, a prisoner-of-war camp near Braunschweig in Germany.

With her new baby boy, Oonagh was as happy as she'd been for years. But the following year, her world was once again shattered by tragedy. On the evening of Friday, 2 August 1946, Garech fell ill. At the time, there had been an outbreak of diphtheria in the west of Ireland. Fearing the worst, Oonagh summoned Dr Heneghan, the family GP, from nearby Castlebar. He arrived shortly after dinnertime. To her relief, it turned out that Garech wasn't suffering from diphtheria, but since the doctor was there, Oonagh asked that he inoculate the entire household. The doctor administered seven injections of diphtheria antitoxin, including one to Tessa.

Fifteen minutes later, Tessa, an asthmatic since childhood, ran into her mother's room, complaining of breathing difficulties. Within five minutes, she had slipped into a coma. The doctor returned to the house and administered a shot of adrenalin, but Tessa's heart began to fail. For an hour, Oonagh tried desperately to revive her by means of artificial respiration, but to no avail. Gay, who was at Castle Mac Garrett on his summer holidays, remembered his mother coming to his room along the passageway. 'She said, "I'm afraid your sister has died",' he recalled. 'I was just devastated. I went into her room. The sight of her pale face and her blonde hair, like a halo, on her pillow is something I never forgot.'

The news of his daughter's death was broken to Philip over the telephone. He arrived at Castle Mac Garrett the following day and he and Gay fell weeping into one another's arms. Gay took his father to the room where Tessa was laid out. He kissed her on the lips, before turning to comfort Oonagh, who had stayed with her daughter's body all night, knowing how much she hated the dark.

Dom, meanwhile, was in London, supposedly on Lords business, although, according to Gay, he was there to visit one of his mistresses. When Oonagh phoned her husband at the May Fair Hotel, a receptionist told her that 'Lord and Lady Oranmore' had gone out for the evening. Dom was finally located the following day and he returned home stricken with grief. For the rest of his life, it was said, he carried the burden of guilt around with him that, had he been at home, he might have questioned the doctor on the possible side effects of the injection and saved his stepdaughter's life.

Oonagh and Dom had problems in their marriage long before Tara was born. But the death of Oonagh's beloved daughter caused a fracture between them that would never heal.

A post mortem revealed that Tessa's death was due to cardiac arrest brought on by anaphylactic shock. Members of the Castle Mac Garrett house staff carried her small coffin the one and a half miles to the church at Crossboyne where Tara had been christened just sixteen months earlier. The following day, Tessa was taken to Luggala in County Wicklow and buried by the lake next to Baby Browne, the half-brother she never got to know in life.

The loss of Tessa tightened Oonagh's bond with her infant son. 'She loved all of her children,' according to Garech, 'but if there was a favourite, then it probably was Tara.'

In March 1949, just as she was emerging from the blackest period in her life, she suffered yet another blow when her father died suddenly at the age of seventy-two. Ernest had suffered a blood clot in his leg as a result of a boating accident. His doctor told him, ill-advisedly, to take a hot bath. Ernest followed his instruction and suffered a fatal heart attack.

His unexpected death would have serious financial consequences for his family. Unlike his brothers, Ernest hadn't taken the precaution of transferring the bulk of his wealth to his children to avoid Britain and Ireland's punitive post-war inheritance taxes. On his death, almost half of his fortune went to the Irish exchequer.

Tara might have grown up almost destitute had it not been for a trust fund that had been set up by his great-grandfather years earlier. Edward, the brother whose cunning had been recognized by James Joyce, had rather presciently sought to secure the livelihoods of his descendants by making them the beneficiaries of a trust. Under its terms, future Guinness sons and daughters would inherit a substantial sum upon reaching the age of twenty-five. However, they were not permitted to withdraw capital from their inheritance. Instead, they could use it to buy property or make investments, provided that the board of trustees, who managed the money, considered them prudent. This was aimed at preserving the wealth within the family and also ensuring that future Guinness scions wouldn't become wealthy idlers.

Ernest's death, coming so soon after his brother's assassination in Cairo, created a succession crisis for the Guinness business. For the first time since the family began brewing porter, there was no male heir either willing or qualified to assume control of the business. As his eldest grandchild, Ernest had once considered Gay as his most likely successor. However, at the end of the nineteenth century, in an effort to ensure a more scientific approach to the method of brewing, the company had adopted a policy whereby all senior recruits were required to have a degree in chemistry from either Oxford or Cambridge. 'It was my worst subject at Eton,' Gay recalled. 'So there was no way it was ever going to happen.'

By the time his grandfather died, Gay, who was then nineteen, was doing his military service with the Fourth Royal Tank Regiment in Yorkshire, after which he was planing to embark on a career as an amateur jockey.

Tara was born into a family that was fast losing control of the business that had made their name and their fortune. His grandfather's death set in motion a chain of events that would eventually lead to the brewery passing out of the Guinness family's hands altogether and prompt Oonagh's cousin, Benjamin, to reflect many years later: 'We could have been the British Rockefellers or Rothschilds . . . But we lost our way.'

•

While she was still coming to terms with the deaths of her daughter and father, as well as the loss of much of her inheritance, Oonagh had to face up to the fact that her second marriage was coming to an end too. Oonagh and Dom were incompatible in all the same ways that Oonagh and Philip had been. Their friends and their enthusiasms were different. Like her first husband, Dom liked country life and the company of other hunting types. Oonagh was rather more cultured and preferred the company of bohemians and intellectuals. There was also the not inconsiderable question of Dom's philandering. In the autumn of 1946, not long after Tessa's death, he had met and quickly fallen in love with a movie actress whose porcelain features and husky voice had earned her a reputation as Britain's own Marlene Dietrich. She was known as Sally Gray and she was regarded as one of the world's most beautiful film stars.

They met on the first day of November at the Empire Theatre in London's Leicester Square. Sally was one of several celebrities prevailed upon to sell programmes at a charity preview screening of the romantic fantasy movie *A Matter of Life and Death*, starring David Niven. Dom first espied her, across a smoke-filled theatre lobby, crowded with members of the royal court and movie stars in dinner jackets and ballgowns. He was immediately smitten and soon he would be openly declaring his love to his 'darling girleen'.

Sally Gray was born Constance Stevens in working-class Holloway, north London, on Valentine's Day, 1916, the daughter of a ballet dancer who was abandoned by her husband and who struggled to bring up five children on her own. Drawn to performing from an early age, Connie, as Sally was then known, began her career on the stage at the age of ten, and later, as a teenager, blacked up her face to star in a minstrel show at the Gate Theatre in London. In 1933, at the age of seventeen, she got her first major break when she appeared in Cole Porter's *Gay Divorce* at the Palace Theatre on Shaftesbury Avenue, alongside Fred Astaire, who gave her private dancing lessons during breaks in performances. Soon, she broke out of the chorus to get her name on the bill.

But it was under her assumed name of Sally Gray that she became one of the biggest names in British cinema during the mid to late 1930s. She was mentored by her married lover, Stanley Lupino, an actor, producer and writer, and a star of British cinema's golden age. It was her leading role in the 1941 movie *Dangerous Moonlight* that established her as a true star of wartime cinema. In it, she played the part of Carole Peters, an American war correspondent in love with a Polish airman and piano virtuoso, who is suffering from shellshock. Released at the height of the Blitz, British cinema audiences adored it.

In 1941, not long after the aerial bombardment of London ended, Sally and Stanley returned to the stage in *Lady Behave*, the city's first major musical since the outbreak of the war. But a month later, the show was forced to close because, by then, Stanley was seriously ill with cancer. He died in 1942, at the age of just forty-eight.

That same year, at the height of her fame, Sally suffered a nervous breakdown. It was thought to have been triggered by Stanley's death, although Charles Doble, a movie archivist familiar with her career and life, believed it was her romantic involvement with another married man, the director John Paddy Carstairs, which brought about her mental collapse. For three years Sally became a virtual recluse, but she was in the midst of a triumphant return to acting, playing mostly bad-girl roles in noir dramas, when Dom, smiling raffishly, asked her for a programme in the crowded foyer of the Empire Theatre.

Like her previous lovers, 'Dom Dom', as she came to call him, was considerably older than her; fifteen years older, in fact. Also like her previous lovers, he was tantalizingly off-limits, with a wife and two young children, including eighteen-month-old Tara.

'Sally told me years later,' said Dominick, 'that the moment she met my father, she said, "He's my man." It didn't bother her that he had a wife and children in Ireland. It didn't bother my father either. What a naughty man.'

Oonagh had many friends in London and it was only a matter of time before news of their affair reached her ears, which it did in 1949. One day, while they were at Luggala, she very calmly invited Dom to join her in a small boat kept on Lough Tay.

'They rowed out into the middle of the lake,' according to Garech, 'and that's where she confronted him. My father admitted everything. She told him that she would give him a week to finish it. He said that he needed two weeks. She said no and that was that.'

It's doubtful whether the deadline was the real issue. Oonagh could likely see what Garech can see now when he looks at old photographs of his father and Sally together: 'They were just so in love. You can tell from the way they looked at each other. So, so in love.'

Oonagh told her husband that their marriage was over. Shortly afterwards, Dom broke the news to eleven-year-old Garech and four-year-old Tara at Castle Mac Garrett, the same news he'd had to impart to the children of his first marriage.

'I remember being taken from school by my father,' Garech recalled, 'and he asked me with whom I wanted to live. He thought he was being reasonable. He was offering me a choice. But, for me, it was horrifying. Being eleven years of age, I took it that I was being asked whom did I love the most? So I said, "My mother," on the basis that I thought she would be more upset to have to say goodbye to me.'

At nineteen, Oonagh had moved from her family home into her first marriage, then, at twenty-six, straight into her second. Now, a few weeks short of her fortieth birthday, she found herself, for the first time in her life, on her own. But there was at least the sense that she was leaving an unhappy decade behind as she walked out of Castle Mac Garrett for the final time and, with Garech and Tara, retreated to the sanctuary of her Wicklow house.

3: OONAGHLAND

In February 1950, shortly after her divorce from Dom, Oonagh celebrated her fortieth birthday. It was a watershed moment in her life. With her two youngest children, four-year-old Tara and eleven-year-old Garech, she left behind her a decade filled with sorrow. Now, in her middle years, she had the opportunity to carve out a new identity for herself, not as Mrs Philip Kindersley, nor as Lady Oranmore and Browne, but as Oonagh Guinness, the chatelaine of Luggala and a hostess of great renown.

For the first time in her life, she could summon around her the kind of people whose company she enjoyed. Over the course of the six years that followed, Tara and Garech's childhood home became famous for its parties, as Oonagh entertained an ever-widening circle of interesting friends that included writers, poets, musicians and artists, as well as diplomats and the titled remnants of Ireland's old aristocracy.

It was literally at their feet, in the loquacious atmosphere of his mother's drawing room, that young Tara learned about the world. He rarely saw the inside of a classroom, his entire school career accounting for little more than two years of his childhood. But the lessons he learned from his mother's offbeat coterie of writers, intellectuals and aristocratic black sheep helped form his personality from an early age.

Even as a child, he was precocious to a degree that would leave strangers open-mouthed in shock. The late Kenneth Rose, a journalist, historian and occasional house guest, recalled his first sight of Tara in 1953. 'I remember Oonagh giving a very big dinner party one night,' he said. 'It was about nine o'clock in the evening and this little boy joined the dinner party. I'll never forget this. He climbed up onto the table, in these blue satin pyjamas, and he walked barefoot down the centre of the table, greeting everyone, saying, "Hello, I'm Tara." He must have been eight. And no one commented on it, of course. It was nothing unusual.'

It was mild compared to some of the goings-on at Luggala. Tara's childhood home had a reputation as a kind of bohemian salon, where the normal rules of Irish society did not apply. Ireland of the 1950s was a colourless, economically poor, neo-Catholic country, founded on the romantic vision of the archly conservative Eamon de Valera, the country's most dominant political figure since independence. Unemployment, poverty and emigration were a fact of life for a large percentage of the population, while the Church set the social and cultural agenda, helping to enforce, amongst other things, the most prescriptive literary censorship laws outside the Communist world.

Against this backdrop, the Guinness family remained unapologetically a law unto themselves. Luggala's location, deep in the bowels of the Wicklow Mountains, far from the censorious eyes of Catholic Ireland, encouraged guests to act in a more carefree manner than they might have elsewhere. They arrived for dinner and sometimes stayed for days. When asked to account for the time missing from their lives, they explained that they'd been 'Luggala-ed'.

In his 1956 memoir, *Living Like a Lord*, John Godley, third Baron Kilbracken, described the house as an escape from the humdrum piety of de Valera's island state. 'Whenever I pass between those gateposts,' he wrote, 'and plunge down into the valley beyond, I feel as though I have left Ireland and entered a strange, unreal, independent principality: Oonaghland.'

Oonagh's were not the kind of dinner parties where the women left the table for the men to discuss politics over brandies and cigars until the early hours. They were intellectually inclusive occasions, made all the more interesting by Oonagh's love of mixing people from disparate backgrounds.

As Claud Cockburn, the journalist and Communist, and a

frequent visitor to the house once asked, where else could you find the Duke of Brissac and Brendan Behan having a row with the Director of the Bank of England about the Grand National, only to be soothed by a man singing a poem in Gaelic?

From a very early age, Tara and Garech became accustomed to watching intellectual sparks fly. The well-born were thrown together with the artistically gifted, and little pleased Oonagh more than if her thoughtfully calibrated mix of people yielded some drama or other.

'She had a wicked sense of where to place people,' according to the Irish poet John Montague, 'either in the rooms in which they slept or at the dinner table. Ex-husbands would find themselves sitting next to ex-wives whom they detested – or sleeping in rooms next to each other. She had what I would call an Anglo-Irish wickedness. It was the kind of thing that Oscar Wilde would have taken pleasure in. I always got the sense, looking at Tara as a child, that he was bemused by it, trying to make sense of this circus.'

Dinner was served by the butler, Patrick Cummins, at a long table in the dining room. Afterwards, guests would repair to the drawing room, the soul of the house, to talk and drink and sometimes behave outrageously. Brendan Behan, who was skilled in all three areas, once wrote that Luggala was a house where you could say anything you liked, 'provided you were witty and didn't take too long about it'.

The morning after a party, a tureen of vodka and tomato juice was placed on the dining room table as a cure for those who had to leave – and, for those who were planning to stay, as a pleasant segue into another day's drinking.

Oonagh's coming-out as a hostess in her own right was the twenty-first birthday party she threw for Gay in August 1951. Six years after the war ended, Britain and Ireland were still living with the privations of food rationing and the menu for the party was considered newsworthy of itself, featuring fresh lobster, cold chicken and ham, and fruit salad with lashings of fresh cream. Two hundred party guests danced the Raspa and the Can-Can to music performed live by the birthday boy's favourite band, which in the era of the Irish showband, was Tommy Kinsman and his Orchestra.

It was a party that set a high bar for the decade to come and helped burnish the Guinness set's reputation for dissolute behaviour. The Spanish Ambassador and the United States Chargé d'Affaires were among the guests who watched a well-known writer drive his car at high speed into the packed marquee after another guest made a pass at his wife. It was, it was generally agreed, an excellent party, with squealing echoes of the pre-war days of the Bright Young People.

'When I think about Oonagh now,' said Martin Wilkinson, one of Tara's teenage friends, 'I think she was always trying to get back the life she had to put on hold during the Second World War. She was still quite young when the war broke out and I think there was a sense that her fun had been stolen from her by this dreadful war and all these tragedies that happened to her.'

At forty, she was a single woman for the first time since her days as a teenage debutante back in the 1920s. It was often said that she became more beautiful with age and she had many suitors. 'Lots of people were in love with her,' according to Tara's cousin, Desmond Guinness. 'Men couldn't resist her. She was so extraordinary.'

In 1951, just over a year after her divorce from Dom became final, she began an affair with a younger man, an RAF war hero with saturnine good looks. His name was Robert Kee and he would go on to become one of the most distinguished historians, broadcasters and documentary-makers of his generation. At thirty-two, he was ten years younger than Oonagh and, like her, recently divorced. In his twenties, he had written two highly acclaimed autobiographical novels, *A Crowd is Not Company* and *The Impossible Shore*, based on his experiences in the Second World War. Now, he was working for *Picture Post*, a photojournalistic magazine modelled on America's *Life*.

Fiercely intelligent and almost equally intense, Robert was more intellectually suited to Oonagh than either of her two husbands had been. By the end of 1951, they were deeply in love. In the days before a telephone was installed at Luggala, Robert would express his feelings for her in telegrams, sometimes several a day. These were usually delivered by Willie Gilbert, the local postman, who was required to cycle the three-mile distance to the house from Roundwood, the nearest village. Once the telegram was handed over, he would walk his bicycle back up the steep road to the top of the valley. When he returned to the post office, there was often another telegram waiting to be delivered. 'Sometimes,' recalled Garech, 'the telegram would simply say, "Goodnight, Darling".'

•

Oonaghland was a wild and exciting world for an adult. But for children, it could be a remote and lonely place. Tara enjoyed all the normal adventures of boyhood, exploring Luggala's dense and deer-filled woods in search of the best trees to climb, or venturing to the top of the Fancy, the enormous rock promontory that stares down on the house. He learned how to row a boat on Lough Tay and became acquainted with its peculiar currents and the safest spots in which to swim.

But unlike Oonagh's other children, he didn't have the company of siblings who were close in age. There were six years between Tara and Garech, who, in any case, was away at boarding school from the time Tara was eight.

Growing up, the son of Irish 'royalty', at the bottom of a valley in a deserted pocket of Wicklow, wasn't conducive to forming the ephemeral, fun-filled friendships that are a feature of more ordinary childhoods. It tightened his bond with his mother, but might also have accounted for the air of melancholia that often surrounded him as a child.

'I would say he was quite lonely,' said Rabea Redpath, his closest childhood friend. 'When I met him, he told me that Patrick the Butler was his best friend in the world.'

Even the circumstances of Tara's friendship with Rabea were unusual. She lived in London, he lived in Wicklow, separated by a veritable ocean of distance to a boy of six and a girl of seven. She was the daughter of Heywood Hill, the famous Curzon Street bookseller, and his wife, Lady Anne Hill. They met – or rather they were thrown together – in Oonagh's favourite Mayfair hotel in the summer of 1951.

'My mother knew Oonagh through the social round,' said Rabea, who was Lucy Hill until her marriage and conversion to Islam as an adult. 'One day, Oonagh rang. She was staying in Claridge's – she had a suite there – and she asked would Lucy like to come to Claridge's to play with Tara. My mother said yes. I was furious. I really didn't want to go. I cried and stamped my feet. But my mother made me go.'

In the end, she was pleased she did. Together, they enjoyed a day of raucous, no-holds-barred fun. 'We ran up and down the corridors of Claridge's banging on people's doors, roaring with laughter. And Oonagh didn't stop us at all. That was the point. She couldn't have cared less. And Tara and I got on wildly well from that point on.'

So much so that Oonagh resolved not to allow the geographic inconvenience of living in two different countries to keep the young friends apart. 'I used to get flown off at weekends to Luggala, aged seven, to play with Tara, air fare paid for,' Rabea remembered. 'I completely fell into it and enjoyed it all. We used to spend a lot of time outside. Out in the boat on the lake, climbing trees. And pillow fights, I remember. The usual stuff of childhood.'

Tara and Oonagh were devoted to each other, but it wasn't a mother-son relationship that was typical of the times. In an era when the popular wisdom held that children were better seen than heard, Tara was allowed to do pretty much as he pleased. His playground stretched from horizon to horizon and there were no adult-imposed parameters on his life. It would be difficult for any boy so raised to maintain a sense of scale.

'There was, in the background, this sadness in him,' Rabea said, 'even as a child, because his life was completely unconventional. I was used to eccentric people. My parents had very eccentric friends. As a child looking at Oonagh, what I remember is lots of make-up. I mean, she looked like a film star. But she was rather a distant figure to me. I don't remember her as a mother figure at all.'

Oonagh's indulgence of her youngest son shaped his character from an early age. His tastes were eclectic and they would remain so throughout his short life. His enthusiasms, then and later, tended to be intense but short-lived. 'He'd have bouts where he liked one particular thing, then he'd move on,' Rabea remembered. 'Once, for a while, it was Battersea Funfair. When he was in London, he'd go every night to Battersea. He'd get five pounds from his mother, which in those days was an absolute fortune.'

In one of her family albums, Oonagh kept a photograph of the three of them, taken in a photo booth at the fair during the summer of 1953. Eight-year-old Tara, in a little suit and tie, is sitting on his mother's knee, blowing her a kiss, while little Lucy looks slightly removed from the fun, staring not at the camera, but off to the side, appearing slightly lost or worried.

It may have been exhaustion. Whenever she was around Tara, they never seemed to go to sleep.

'At home, I'd been made to go to bed at seven o'clock every night,' she said. 'When I went to Ireland, I could stay up all night. It was almost complete freedom. I had my own room and a maid would come in the morning, light the little fire and give me my breakfast. And I'd be exhausted, having been up until four in the morning. I remember enjoying every moment, but at the same time feeling this exhaustion and not wanting it. You know, wanting to have some limits. I think maybe sometimes Tara felt the same.'

•

But there was no let-up in the pace of life at Luggala. The list of names in the visitors' book grew exponentially through the 1950s and Tara's childhood came to be coloured by a cast of bright, sophisticated and frequently inebriated artistic types. They included the painter Lucian Freud, whom Tara's cousin Lady Caroline Blackwood married in December 1953, against the wishes of her mother. Maureen wanted her daughter to marry into the aristocracy and Caroline was only too pleased to disappoint her.

At the time, Lucian, grandson of Sigmund Freud, was staking out his position as the greatest British portrait artist of his generation, a cold-eyed – some critics argued cruel-eyed – observer of the human form. He was immediately mesmerized by this shy, twenty-one-year-old aristocratic beauty.

At least part of the attraction for Caroline was that Lucian was all of the things she knew would horrify her mother. He was a married man, almost ten years her senior, a penniless and avowedly anti-authoritarian artist, living in a dilapidated rental house in Paddington. And he was Jewish. Many of Maureen's circle remained casually anti-Semitic even after the horrors of the Holocaust were revealed. In a letter to the writer Nancy Mitford, Evelyn Waugh wrote, 'Poor Maureen's daughter made a runaway match with a terrible Yid.'

Though ostracized by Maureen, Caroline and Lucian were always welcome at Luggala. Caroline found a kindred spirit in her Aunt Oonagh, who was more interested in art and culture than the personages that fascinated her own mother. According to Garech, 'Caroline always said she regretted that our mother wasn't her mother.'

She fantasized about this very thing in 'How You Love Our Lady', a short story in which a thinly disguised version of Oonagh features as the narrator's mother, a woman who opened up her drawing room to a cast of 'painters, poets and talkers', scornfully dismissed by the narrator's husband as 'provincial Irish bullshit artists . . . living in a crazy Irish twilight'.

The mother of Caroline's imagining never tells her daughter when to go to bed, for she hates the tyranny of the clock, even as the narrator walks to school in the morning feeling weightless from lack of sleep. For the mother in the story, the greatest sin in life is 'to allow the humdrum to see into your soul'. People who allow themselves to become trivial and mundane are like blighted elms, she believes, rotting from the inside out.

Oonagh assembled a dramatis personae of interesting characters around her as if she feared that this, indeed, might be her fate. And when brilliant people came together in the intellectual hothouse of her drawing room, there was no telling what might happen.

In 1951, Claud Cockburn, a former foreign correspondent for *The Times*, was staying at Luggala when John Huston came to visit. Cockburn had been broke since his Marxist newspaper, *The Week*, ceased publication during the war. In dire need of money, he had recently written a potboiler thriller called *Beat the Devil*.

It was published under the pseudonym of James Helvik, for fear that the author's Communist sympathies might hurt sales in the paranoid, early days of the Cold War. That weekend, he set about trying to interest the American director in the film rights to the book. In his memoir, Huston recalled that copies were placed all over the house – including one on his nightstand – in the hope that he might pick it up out of casual interest. 'He badly needed the money that a motion-picture sale would give him.'

Fortunately for Cockburn, Huston read the book and loved it. A few days later, still under Luggala's spell, he phoned Humphrey Bogart, who had a film production company, and persuaded him to write Cockburn a cheque for $10,000, which Bogart did, without ever reading a word of the book.

Two years later, Oonagh, who was thrilled to have made the match between writer and director, was invited to watch the movie being shot in Italy. She took eight-year-old Tara with her. It was filmed in Ravello, a small town south of Naples. Huston had decided that the movie – starring Bogart, Peter Lorre and Gina Lollobrigida – would be a parody of his famous noir film *The Maltese Falcon*. The plot involved four crooks who pose as vacuum cleaner salesmen to try to smuggle uranium out of East Africa and the farcical obstacles they must overcome along the way.

The problem for the director as the first day of shooting loomed was that he didn't have a single word of dialogue to give to the actors. As fortune would have it, while he was on the road to Naples, Huston and Bogart were involved in a car crash, which cost Bogart his front teeth and almost half of his tongue. During the delay in filming, the director persuaded Truman Capote, who was then living in Rome, to produce a script from Cockburn's book. Oonagh and her son spent several days on the set. Tara was mesmerized by the sight of Bogart arm-wrestling the eccentric, velvet-suit-wearing and flamboyantly homosexual Capote for money, while the dialogue was somehow conjured up during breaks in filming.

Brendan Behan joined Oonagh's County Wicklow set in 1954, when he was on the threshold of becoming an internationally successful playwright. He first arrived at the house with Lucian Freud and quickly developed a friendship with Oonagh and her sons that would endure until his death a decade later.

Brendan came with a notoriety that eclipsed even Lucian's, having served time in an English borstal for plotting to bomb the Liverpool docks at the age of just sixteen. In 1942, a year after his release and expulsion from Britain, he was sentenced to fourteen years' penal servitude by a Dublin court for attempting to murder two members of An Garda Siochána, the Irish police, during a commemoration for Wolfe Tone, the father of Irish Republicanism. He spent almost four and a half years in Mountjoy Jail and the Curragh Camp before he was released as part of a general amnesty for IRA prisoners and internees after the Second World War ended.

A house-painter by trade, Brendan had designs on becoming a writer. He insinuated himself into the hard-drinking fraternity of literary and intellectual types who frequented Dublin pubs such as McDaid's, Neary's and the Bailey – and, when they closed, the subterranean late-night wine bars around Leeson Street and Fitzwilliam Square. This loosely knotted group of frequently squabbling friends and acquaintances included the poet Paddy Kavanagh, the novelist Flann O'Brien and the artist Sean O'Sullivan, as well as young literary turks like J. P. Donleavy, John Montague and Anthony Cronin. It was Brendan, with his quick wit and bawdy humour, who emerged as the stand-out 'character' in the company, as he settled into the habit of heavy drinking that would bring about his decline.

It was in this smoke-filled netherworld that Brendan first met Lucian, who had moved to Dublin after becoming fixated with the work of the painter Jack B. Yeats. Five years later, shortly after marrying Caroline Blackwood, Lucian took Brendan along to meet Oonagh, Garech and Tara at Luggala. Brendan was in the prime of life. He was thirty-two years old and his first major play was about to be staged at the Pike Theatre in Dublin. The foul-mouthed, rough-hewn Dubliner was immediately charmed by Oonagh and her children and the feeling was mutual. Tara adored him from their very first encounter.

Oonagh attended the triumphant opening night of *The Quare Fellow* that November and loved it every bit as much as the critics. Brendan – who, in his second play, *The Hostage*, would memor-ably define an Anglo-Irishman as 'a Protestant with a horse' – became a regular presence at the Luggala table, especially at Christmas time, when Oonagh would send her chauffeur-driven Rolls Royce to collect him and his wife Beatrice. He would enliven these gath-erings with anecdotes from his IRA past, old songs culled from his Dublin tenement childhood and the occasional cry of 'Up the rebels!'

Sometimes he behaved badly, but Oonagh was a non-judgemental hostess who overlooked her guests' trespasses, especially in the case of Brendan.

•

When Tara and Garech weren't at Oonaghland, they were at Castle Mac Garrett with their father, who had married Sally Gray in secret in December 1951. Sally made her final movie the follow-ing year, a slow-paced thriller called, appropriately enough, *Escape Route*, in which she starred alongside the American actor George Raft, whom she hated intensely. Afterwards, she quit acting, turn-ing down a reported million-dollar contract offer from RKO Pictures in Hollywood, in favour of a quieter life in the west of Ireland as the third Lady Oranmore and Browne.

Dom and Sally managed to keep the news of their marriage a secret, even from Oonagh, until the day of the coronation of

Queen Elizabeth II in 1953. 'Tara and I watched the parade from a shop window,' recalled Garech. 'I think it might have been Self-ridges. And what I remember most is that it was the day that everyone first knew that our father must have married Sally, because she wouldn't have been allowed to attend if they hadn't been married.'

But Dom's third wife was an almost spectral presence at Castle Mac Garrett whenever Tara and Garech visited. In fact, she rarely ventured from her room. 'I think she felt terribly guilty about taking our father away from us,' said Garech.

She also picked up on Tara's hostility towards her. According to his half-sister Judith, he made his feelings for his stepmother plain. 'Tara hated Sally. He used to sit at the dinner table and just stare at her until she would get quite upset. And I would have to nudge him and say, "Don't start, Tara."'

Like many children with divorced parents, he became skilled in playing one off against the other. 'He would say, "Oh, my mother said I don't have to go to bed until eleven o'clock."'

By now, Tara was a bright and precocious child who loved anything that was new. 'We used to play roulette, which he liked a lot,' remembers his half-brother Dominick. 'His little face would light up when he won. I thought, at first, it was because he loved the money aspect of the thing. But it wasn't. He just had what I would call enthusiasms. Even at the age of six or seven, Tara was always excited by the latest thing.'

That included the latest swearwords. From a young age, he had a salty vocabulary. 'There was a very elderly West of Ireland lady whose job it was to bath him while he was at Castle Mac Garrett,' his wife, Nicki, recalled. 'Tara told me she could never get him into the bath without a fight. One day, while she was strug-gling to get his clothes off him, he called her a silly old cunt. She said, "Where did you hear a word like that?" And Tara said, "From my mother!"'

Without a rich wife to subsidize him, Dom was forced to econ-omize to remain in Castle Mac Garrett after his divorce from Oonagh. He sold his racehorses, reduced his house staff and worked doubly hard to try to make the estate work financially. But in the depressed economy of Ireland in the 1950s it was a difficult and ultimately doomed enterprise.

He was, nonetheless, keen for his boys to know about the land. Tara took to growing fruit and vegetables with the same enthusiasm he had for spinning the roulette wheel. 'We each had our own greenhouse at Castle Mac Garrett,' Garech remembered. 'We grew all sorts of things. Everything from castor oil plants to zucchinis. We had peach trees, which the gardeners showed us how to pollinate using a rabbit's foot on the end of a bamboo stick.'

Despite Dom's greatly diminished circumstances, he continued to entertain lavishly, especially during the various shooting seasons. 'That was when the work on the farm stopped,' his former secretary, Philomena Flatley, recalled. 'There was a pheasant shoot every November and the aristocracy from all over Europe would come and stay for a week. The dinners were extraordinary, all prepared by French chefs. Everyone dressed for dinner. There were cocktails in the drawing room. It was all very old-fashioned and aristocratic. Finger bowls. The best silver and china. I had to type up the menu every day and it would take me ages. I didn't speak French and I was scared of making a mistake. Then I'd have to type up the shooting cards. I'd get a list from the gamekeeper of who shot how many of what, whether it was pheasant, duck, grouse, woodcock or snipe. Then, when the guests had gone, his Lordship would go back to work.'

Tara and Garech's visits to Castle Mac Garrett were an established part of their childhood routine. Occasionally they visited for the day. Oonagh accompanied them, but refused to enter the house, remaining in a hotel in the nearby town of Claremorris until they were ready for the cross-country drive home in her chauffeur-driven Rolls Royce. Throughout the summer, they stayed for weeks on end. It was during these longer visits, in the mid-1950s, that Tara and Garech fell in love with traditional Irish music.

It was difficult to avoid it in Mayo. The music was in the air. Dom employed some 150 local townspeople, many of whom played button accordions, flutes, fiddles and tin whistles. 'There was always a dance in the garage at Christmas for all the workers,' remembered Garech, 'and part of the entertainment was traditional music. My father loved those parties and he used to film them. So, through the people who worked on the estate, Tara and I met all these musicians from the locality, including George, who was a slater by trade and seemed to spend his entire working life up on the roof of our house. He introduced us to all these wonderful fiddle players, whom we would go to hear play whenever we visited my father.'

On the other side of the Atlantic, the miscegenation of white country music with the black roots of gospel and blues had given birth to a new sound called rock and roll. But in 1955, while 'Rock Around the Clock' by Bill Haley & His Comets was announcing the coming wave of popular music that would change the world, sixteen-year-old Garech and ten-year-old Tara were glued to Ciarán Mac Mathúna's weekly Irish music programme, *A Job of Journeywork*, on Radio Éireann. It featured live recordings of traditional music and songs collected from around the country. 'When we were supposed to be asleep,' Garech said, 'we'd be leaping around our bedrooms to this wonderful music.'

•

While he was receiving a rich and varied social education, Tara's school career was, like his brother's, short and chequered. Several attempts were made to settle Tara and Garech in schools, usually at Dom's urging. But neither boy was temperamentally suited to the formal education system.

'The problem for us,' said Garech, 'was that these schools didn't teach any of the things that we wanted to learn. And if God had meant us to be treated like sheep, then he would have created us as sheep.'

Tara didn't see the inside of a classroom until he was seven years old, by which time his older brother's escape from the Institut Le Rosey – the prestigious boarding school in Switzerland where royal children from around the world were educated – had become the stuff of Guinness family legend. Garech sent himself a telegram that said, 'Unforeseen circumstances. Come home immediately. Your loving mother.' A flight to Ireland was duly arranged by the school. Garech never returned. He was thirteen.

Garech was then enrolled at Bryanston, another prestigious boarding school, this time in Dorset, southern England. Oonagh placed eight-year-old Tara in nearby Port Regis, a co-educational preparatory school, in the hope that having the little brother he adored so close at hand might help Garech settle in better. 'It didn't last long,' Garech recalled, 'because I ran away again.'

His departure this time was by taxi. In fact, he ended up staying the night with the driver and his wife in Salisbury, Wiltshire, before he struck out for London the following day and went into hiding.

'When I spoke to my mother on the phone, I said to her, "I've got out of that bloody place." She was perfectly sympathetic. She didn't object at all.'

Judging by his later behaviour, Tara was clearly taking notice. Garech was removed from Bryanston, Tara was taken out of Port Regis and they returned to Dublin. At the age of fifteen, Garech's school career was over, but efforts to educate Tara continued on and off. Two years later, shortly after he turned ten, he was enrolled at St Stephen's, a relatively new, English-style preparatory school in Goatstown, south Dublin. It was founded and run by the Reverend Hugh Brodie, a wartime naval chaplain, and his wife, Lettice, who spoke French fluently and had a passion for theatre. English by birth, the couple had moved to Dublin in 1945, following the Labour Party's victory in Britain's first post-war general election. Like many members of the well-to-do, ex-military classes, they regarded this as a betrayal of Winston Churchill, the prime minister who led the country to victory in the war.

The Brodies, rather perversely, chose to make their home in Eamon de Valera's Ireland, memorably characterized by the writer Seán Ó Faoláin as a 'dreary Eden', a country with a special place in its heart for Gaelic games, the Irish language and the Roman Catholic Church. It was here that the reverend and his wife established a school dedicated to the Anglican faith, where children played cricket, rugby and hockey and received a classical

English education from teachers with names like Maude Ivatt and Godfrey Proud, to prepare them for private, secondary-level boarding schools in Ireland and Britain.

'It was an extraordinary little place,' recalled Neale Webb, one of Tara's first classmates. 'It was an enclave of Britishness. A little bit of Union Jack in de Valera's Ireland. Even though most of us regarded ourselves as Irish people, de Valera wanted Ireland to be a Catholic state for a Catholic people. There was very much an Us and Them feel about the country. Protestants still accounted for a sizeable enough part of the population. And they were proud that they had stuck it out after independence in 1922. They had money and a community and they were very keen that all their children should stick together, should be educated together and retain the Protestant ethic. So we all received a frightfully British education. Anglican prayers every morning. Lots of scripture, Shakespeare and endless games of cricket.'

The vast majority of the school's 120 students were boarders. But in his first few months at the school, the summer term of 1955, Tara attended as a day pupil, arriving from Luggala every morning in a chauffeur-driven Rolls Royce. It made quite an impression on the other boys.

'There weren't terribly many cars on the road in Ireland at that point,' remembered Neale. 'There were a few parents who had Ford Anglias and that kind of thing. But then, solemnly, every morning, this incredibly expensive Rolls Royce would come up the avenue, driven by a chauffeur. And then – it was like seeing Lady Penelope arrive in *Thunderbirds* – sitting on the back seat, there was this very small boy with a big mop of blond hair and a cap that was two sizes too big for him, propped up on his ears. And when school was over, the car would be back again and he'd disappear.'

Tara had barely opened a textbook in his ten years. But he'd learned enough at Port Regis to know that he never wanted to see the inside of a classroom again. Persuading him into the car each morning usually involved some kind of fight, filled with expletives. 'He told me that he never, ever wanted to go to school,' recalled his wife, Nicki, 'and that every morning was the same. The driver at Luggala was called Hamilton. He used to throw him, kicking and swearing, into the car without his clothes on and Tara had to dress in the back of the car on the way to school.'

Not surprisingly, the little boy with the blond, Prince Valiant haircut and the air of a young royal was a figure of fascination for his fellow students. The Guinness family's wealth and louche reputation went before him.

'We knew that when he left school, it was to go back to this fairyland castle,' said Neale. 'They were living in a world divorced from everyone else. You know, you'd come around the lake and you'd look down at this house and it was like where Snow White lived. And, of course, there were the stories about what they got up to in there. The parties and all that. That was 1950s Ireland, remember. Half the stories were probably made up. But it was still another world.'

Michael Steen, another pupil who attended St Stephen's at the same time, remembered being invited to fancy-dress parties at Luggala. 'The invitation would arrive and there would be a coronet on the envelope,' he said. 'I had a sense, even at that age, that they were fancier than us. I remember I dressed up as a jockey and I felt like a fish out of water. Everyone else seemed to be in velvet. They were a curious, effete lot, really – unconventional even by bourgeois standards.

'I had my first glass of wine at Luggala at the age of maybe ten or eleven. I wasn't expecting it. I was having lunch in the dining room. The butler asked if I wanted some of this stuff out of a carafe. I thought it was raspberry juice until I had a gulp of it. It wouldn't have happened anywhere else. They just lived by different standards.'

Physically, Tara stood out, too. 'He looked like a boy soprano, or a cherub,' said Gordon Ledbetter, who was probably his closest friend during his time at St Stephen's. 'Although he didn't fight like a cherub. I remember having a wrestling match with him once – at least I remember the suffocation I almost suffered. But he was very blond. He had a very straight fringe and his hair was fairly thick at the back. I remember that Brodie, the headmaster, never approved of anyone having hair like that at the back, but he was prepared to overlook it in his case, given who he was.'

Towards the end of his first summer term at St Stephen's, Tara entered the school's annual poetry competition – the Kolkhorst Poetry Prize – with an eight-line verse called 'The Old Stage Coach', inspired by a ghost story about a headless coachman that he liked to tell Lucy Hill.

> When on the spooky stage coach road,
> The stage coach used to go.
> The bandits used to hold it up
> And blood it used to flow.
> But now the coach is very old,
> The roof has fallen in.
> The floor is beginning to mould.
> And the doors are in the bin.

The poem failed to win. But the 1955 school annual reported that it was one of two entries to receive a commendation from the competition's judge, the poet John Betjeman, who was an old friend of both Reverend Brodie, from their time at Oxford, and of Oonagh, from their days as Bright Young People on the London social scene.

Tara's unconventional background kept him at a slight remove from the rest of his classmates, according to Neale Webb. But he also had a deadpan, aristocratic wit that he'd probably picked up in his mother's drawing room. 'I remember once I told him that I'd climbed Djouce Mountain the previous weekend. I didn't realize that the Guinness family actually owned part of it. Tara was only ten but he had this wonderfully dry sense of humour. He said to me, "Trespassers will be prosecuted!"'

•

The Christmas of 1955 was a happy one for Oonagh and her family. Tara made his stage debut in the school production of *Emil and the Detectives*, playing the role of a child detective, while Robert Kee was celebrating the success of his new book, *A Sign of the Times*, a darkly comic, post-apocalyptic novel that was widely praised by the literary critics. Oonagh lovingly pasted many of his rave reviews into her photo album.

The festive season at Luggala was made even more memorable by the presence of Brendan Behan and his new wife, Beatrice, at the dinner table. The couple were enjoying their first and – as it turned out – final days of happily married life together, before Brendan became a famous celebrity in America the following year. At Luggala that Christmas, there were signs that his drinking was already out of control. One night, he was wandering around the narrow first-floor landing of the house, singing 'Adeste Fideles', when he fell head-first over a bannister and down the short curving stairwell that led to the servants' quarters. Cis Leonard and Maura Byrne, two housemaids, discovered him there, but they couldn't open the door fully because his legs were wedged against it and he was too drunk to be woken. 'We had to reach him from the other side of the house,' Maura remembered. 'It took the butler and a footman to lift him out.'

The following day, the Behans were driven back to Dublin in Oonagh's chauffeur-driven Rolls Royce. Oonagh wasn't the type to judge. But Brendan, who had badly gashed his forehead in the fall, was embarrassed by his behaviour in front of Tara and Garech, as well as Caroline, Lucian and the rest of the Luggala set. A few days later, he composed a short verse called 'Beannacht an Nua-bhlian', or 'New Year Greeting', namechecking Tara, Garech and Oonagh, which he sent to the house by way of apology.

It seemed there was rarely a dull day in the Luggala of Tara's childhood. A few weeks later, towards the end of January 1956, his half-brother, Gay Kindersley, arrived at the house one night, having eloped with his fiancée, Magsie Wakefield. The couple had met six months earlier, in the south of France, aboard the yacht of a mutual friend. At the time, Gay was making a name for himself as a horse trainer and amateur jockey, having used his

Guinness inheritance to purchase an 85-acre farm near Dorking in Surrey, as well as Priam Lodge, a training establishment not far from Epsom. He was preparing to ride his horse, Sandymount, in the 1956 Grand National at Aintree when, on a whim, he asked Magsie to marry him at Kempton Park that January.

But his family – or at least his father's side – were far from thrilled by the news. Philip disapproved of the match, as did Gay's stepmother, Valsie. Gay's fiancée was the daughter of a jobbing character actor named Hugh Wakefield and the family were – much to the horror of the Kindersleys – members of the aspirant middle class.

The trouble came to the boil a week after Gay and Magsie announced their engagement, when they invited their two sets of in-laws for Sunday lunch. 'I was discussing hunting,' Gay recalled. 'My father, with utter disdain, said, "Do you actually hunt yourself, Mr Wakefield?" It was an extraordinary thing. Embarrassing. I just wanted to squirm under the table.'

Over dessert, in front of the couple, Valsie told the Wakefields that she and her husband did not consider Magsie a suitable choice of wife for Gay. The following day, after drinking two bottles of wine with lunch at the Savoy, Gay and Magsie made up their minds to get married in defiance of Philip and Valsie's wishes. And they decided to do it in the magical surroundings of Luggala. On 24 January 1956, on a night of heavy snowfall, they flew to Ireland and into the welcoming embrace of Oonagh. She promised to help them make the wedding arrangements the following day, little knowing what the night had in store for them.

Shortly after midnight, the house caught fire. The blaze started in Garech's bedroom, probably due to faulty electrical wiring. The house staff roused Tara, Gay, Magsie, Oonagh and Robert from their beds and they managed to get outside. Very quickly, Luggala was engulfed in flames.

Members of the family and house staff attempted to bring the fire under control against the incongruous background noise of champagne corks popping due to the heat in the cellar. Tara,

Garech and Gay helped form a human chain to ferry buckets of water from a stream at the back of the house, while other servants risked their lives to carry paintings, furniture and other valuables out of the house and onto the front lawn. Patrick Cummins, the butler, braved suffocating smoke to rescue Philip de László's portrait of Oonagh from the wall of the drawing room.

Newspaper photographs showed the snow-covered lawn in front of Luggala strewn with treasures pulled from the house. 'Her Ladyship,' the *Daily Mail* reported, 'with long blonde hair in a scarf, and a mink coat over her nightdress, sat on an old oak dining chair directing operations.'

The fire brigade arrived on the scene too late to save the house. By the time the blaze was put out at ten o'clock in the morning, the main block of Luggala, containing the dining room, the drawing room and bedrooms – the very soul of Oonagh's house – was completely destroyed. Her bohemian idyll, her hideaway in the Wicklow Mountains where she had retreated with her children after the failure of her second marriage, was now a smouldering ruin.

There was still a wedding to organize. The entire party, their faces blackened with smoke, decamped to the Shelbourne Hotel in Dublin, where, after making several phone calls, Gay discovered that quickie marriages weren't possible under Irish law. Oonagh, perhaps enjoying some measure of revenge over Philip following the wartime custody case, took Gay and Magsie to Paris, where she was confident she could arrange matters quickly with the help of her friends in the British Embassy. That didn't work out either, so they flew to London, where Gay and Magsie were eventually married at Caxton Hall, on a snowy day, in the company of Oonagh and two of her friends, as well as Tara and Garech, wearing matching grey duffle coats.

The ceremony lasted eight minutes. There were no flowers, no photographs, and, according to the newspapers, no smiles. Philip knew nothing about the marriage of his eldest son until he was informed by a reporter from the *Daily Express*. 'My son went to stay with his mother in Ireland at the beginning of the week,' he told the newspaper, publicly admonishing Oonagh for her role in the intrigue. 'I didn't even know he was back in the country.'

•

It was decided that Tara should board at St Stephen's while Luggala was being rebuilt. Oonagh went to live in Paris, although she returned regularly to see how the work was progressing. In a column for *Tatler* magazine, Lord Kilbracken recalled visiting his old friend in the spring of 1956, while construction was underway. Oonagh had taken Tara out of school for the day. Patrick Cummins, still immaculately turned out in a morning suit, informed the visitor: 'They are at present taking tea in the cowshed.'

For the first seven months of 1956, a communal dormitory at St Stephen's became eleven-year-old Tara's main home. It allowed his school friends to get to know him as something other than the pampered young prince who arrived in and out of their lives each day in the back of his mother's Rolls Royce. Preternaturally precocious, with his mother's disregard for social norms and taboos, he introduced some of his classmates to the pleasures of cigarettes.

'I ended up smoking quite a lot,' said Michael Steen. 'We all did. We used to sit out on the window ledge, this line of little boys, with a twenty-foot drop to the ground below us, smoking Wills Woodbines. And it was Tara who supplied us with the cigarettes. He always seemed to have enormous amounts of money.'

He liked to be the first to own the latest toy. It would remain an aspect of his personality right into adulthood. Some of his classmates remembered the state-of-the-art cine-camera with which he recorded the nightly hijinks in the first-floor dormitory.

'Around the time that he boarded,' said Michael, 'discipline had started to break down in the school. We used to tiptoe downstairs at night – we could hear Brodie snoring – and we'd help ourselves to his food.'

For Tara, it was perfectly normal. He'd never been told what time to go to bed and he was well used to helping himself from the fridge in the middle of the night.

'He was a real ringleader,' said Neale Webb. 'You'd hear the stories about him being pretty wild – by the standards of the time, I suppose. I remember one fine moonlit night, Tara running around the school lawn in his pyjamas for a dare. He was fearless like that. Another time, he got hold of a ladder from somewhere and climbed up it and started banging on the windows of the first-floor dorms. And I remember we all had to sit through a lecture on discipline afterwards.'

One day in the final weeks of the school term, with a certain inevitability, Tara walked out of St Stephen's just as his brother had bolted from Bryanston. He made it as far as Bray, a seaside resort, some fourteen miles away, which had happy childhood associations for him. In the years before their parents divorced, it was where Dom occasionally brought Tara and Garech as a week-end treat, to enjoy McCarthy's famous ice cream. For a boy of just eleven, it was no small achievement to get so far. Garech thinks it's likely that Tara took his lead in phoning for a taxi. 'He clearly learned the trick from me,' he said, 'because I was quite a bit older than he was when I discovered that you could actually escape these prisons.'

The Gardai found Tara on the seafront and drove him back to school. But he didn't return at the start of the following term and he wasn't there in October that year, when one of his friends, Philip Brodie – the son of the headmaster – was killed while apparently playing with his father's shotgun. The Reverend Brodie never recovered from the shock of his death. Seven years later, the school closed its doors for good.

By the age of eleven, Tara was socially years ahead of his peers. Penny Cuthbertson, who would later marry Tara's cousin, Desmond Guinness, recalled meeting him for the first time in the summer of 1956. 'It was in a house called Cludy,' she said, 'which belonged to the Waddington family, on the River Boyne, just out-side Drogheda. It was a kind of teenage party and Tara was by far the youngest there. I still have this memory of him, sitting on the stairs, looking incredibly sweet and announcing that he'd given up smoking – this is at age eleven – and that he'd given up drinking as well. I mean, talk about sophisticated. And there we all were, slightly older – thirteen or fourteen, most of us were – sitting on the stairs, looking at him with our mouths agape.'

The work to rebuild Luggala continued throughout 1956 and into the spring of 1957. Once it was finished, Oonagh hired John Hill – the brother of the painter Derek Hill and the uncle of Tara's childhood friend, Lucy – to decorate it. He chose to emphasize the house's warm and romantic character, especially through the use of thick carpets and colourful wallpapers. The walls of Oonagh's famous drawing room were covered with a distinctively patterned wallpaper called Gothic Lily, which was originally designed by Augustus Pugin in the nineteenth century for the Palace of Westminster, though Oonagh chose purple rather than the original blue colour to match the heather in the valley.

The work was completed just over a year after the fire. In March 1957, around his twelfth birthday, Tara and his mother moved back into Luggala. But by then, much had changed. The house was the same, but Oonagh's life was very different. Her relationship with Robert Kee had foundered during the year she spent exiled from her home. Within twelve months of returning to Luggala, lonely and all too aware of the fact that she was now in her middle years, she attempted to fill the void in her life by marrying a man she barely knew. In fact, as it later transpired, she didn't know him at all.

For Tara, and for everybody else, the atmosphere around Oonaghland was about to change for the worse.

4: THE TROUBLE WITH MIGUEL

Tara was growing up fast – considerably faster than other children of his age. In March 1957, he turned twelve, but his exposure to the adult world had given him an emotional and intellectual maturity of a boy way beyond his years. Lucy Hill, who was still being flown from London to Ireland for weekend play dates at Luggala, recalled the precise moment when she felt their two young lives diverge: 'He said to me one day, "Oh, your hair looks really pretty," and I remember being surprised and having this sudden sense that he'd grown up and that this was something different to the innocent childhood friendship we'd had together.'

Dressed in velvet suits, he suddenly seemed like a young adult to Lucy, rather than a child who was just comfortable around grown-ups. While other boys of his age and background were poring over their textbooks and preparing for public school, Tara was chaperoning his mother around the world, moving between Wicklow, London, Paris, New York, Venice and the south of France, absorbing lessons of a different kind.

'He got a grasp on the world pretty quickly,' she remembered. 'But it caused a sadness in him, I think, not having the same boundaries that other children had. He had a sensitivity about him and what I came to recognize later as a sadness. He said to me once, while he was still quite young – I remember we were having a pillow fight at the time; it was in London – he said, "People only like me because of my money." He said that to me several times, in fact. So he grew up with this sadness which not everyone would have noticed.'

Dom still entertained the fantasy that Tara would one day

attend Eton, just as he had done. But, at twelve years old, his youngest son had made up his mind that he was finished with school. Dom insisted that if this was the case, then he should have a full-time tutor. The gaps in Tara's education would come to be filled by a young English writer with whom Oonagh formed a platonic friendship after her break-up with Robert Kee. His name was Derek Lindsay, although he was more popularly known by his undergraduate nickname of Deacon, because of the priestly solemnity of his manner.

To placate her ex-husband, Oonagh asked Deacon to prepare Tara for the Common Entrance exam, a vital step towards gaining admittance to Britain's most academically selective schools. As his tutor, Deacon played an enormous part in Tara's intellectual development, advising him what books to read and passing on his appreciation of classical music and opera, both of which Tara came to love.

'He was one of the most important adult figures in Tara's life,' according to Nicki. 'After his mother and father, I would say he was *the* most important.'

Quiet and brooding, Deacon was introduced to Oonagh by a member of her drawing-room circle, the writer and critic Cyril Connolly, who considered him an English Marcel Proust. Deacon had just finished writing *The Rack*, a semi-autobiographical novel based on his time in a sanatorium in Switzerland suffering from tuberculosis. It would be published in 1958 under the pseudonym A. E. Ellis and immediately proclaimed a modern classic.

At Oxford, Deacon had been a close friend of Kenneth Tynan, the theatre critic, who once described him as 'an expensive limited edition of a curious object'. Among his fellow undergraduates, he was famous for having a housekeeper, a sizeable and unexplained income, and a mysterious, tortured private life. Tynan's wife, Kathleen, described Deacon as 'deeply pessimistic and a recluse' in her biography of her husband, *The Life of Kenneth Tynan*. 'Lindsay's enthusiasm,' she wrote, 'did not extend to himself, nor to life in principle.'

Nonetheless, he was regarded as one of the most brilliant

young intellectuals of the post-Second World War Oxford generation. 'He was going to be the great man,' wrote another university
friend, the writer Kingsley Amis, 'greater than all of us.'

But in his early twenties, when Amis and Tynan were carving
out their literary reputations, Deacon developed tuberculosis, the
lung disease for which there was no known cure at the time. He
was sent to a specialist hospital in the Swiss Alps, where he
endured endless experimental treatments, including the removal
of a lung. So appalling was the agony he suffered that, one day,
he determined upon suicide. In his memoir, *In Love and Anger*,
Andrew Sinclair recalled his friend's darkly comic recollection of
the episode: 'He was a great raconteur of death gone wrong. He
told me a story of leaving his Swiss sanatorium to buy a revolver
and kill himself. It was hard to buy the weapon. He had to pledge
the gunsmith not to kill anyone but himself. He went back to his
hotel suite . . . He put the revolver in his mouth, was too weak to
press the trigger, hated the taste of the gun barrel and ordered
coffee and croissants instead. With his breakfast came the hotel
manager, who insisted he left the suite immediately because a dig-
nitary wanted it. To him, suicide was a form of slapstick.'

Deacon kept the gun as a morbid souvenir of the episode.
Garech remembered seeing it in a drawer in the Mayfair flat where
Deacon was known to spend months on end hibernating from the
world. The shelves of his living room were lined with leather-
bound volumes of books by Rimbaud, Verlaine, Lautréamont,
Wilde, Balzac, Dostoyevsky, Proust, Schopenhauer and Kierke-
gaard, some of which he would recommend to Tara in the course
of tutoring him, though mostly without success.

Deacon was thought to be in love with Oonagh, though she
was old enough to be his mother. His feelings were unrequited and
they would never be lovers. Instead, he became her closest confi-
dant and financial adviser, as well as a teacher to her son, as they
stravaiged around Europe. In the summer of 1957, Deacon accompanied Oonagh and Tara on a trip to Venice, where, each July,
Oonagh took a floor in the Palazzo Papadopoli or the Palazzo
Polignac. They made for an uneasy-looking threesome in Oonagh's

photographs from that summer. In one, they're sitting together in a gondola. Tara and Oonagh, in identical, horizontally striped T-shirts, are smiling, while Deacon, in a plain white shirt, looks morose, bearing out Andrew Sinclair's memory of him as a man whose weary pessimism was perfectly suited to 'the temper of the times under the mushroom cloud'.

While Deacon struggled to get Tara to take his schoolwork seriously, he did manage to open the boy's ears to classical music. He introduced him to Schubert, Tchaikovsky, Debussy, Wagner, Beethoven, Brahms, Mahler and Bach. Deacon talked him through some of the great operas, especially *Nabucco*, *Lohengrin*, *Tristan and Isolde*, *The Marriage of Figaro*, *La Bohème* and *La Traviata*. Typically, Tara became utterly consumed by it, especially after he got to shake Igor Stravinsky's hand in a restaurant in Venice that summer. Soon, he could listen to a piece of classical music and explain in a very sophisticated way what it was about it that he loved. He bought several hundred LPs that summer – symphonies, concertos, operas and ballets – which were packed into crates and shipped back to Ireland.

Lucy Hill spent two weeks of that summer in Venice with them. It was while she was there that Tara complimented her on her hair and Lucy quickly realized that her friend had outgrown her. When she returned to England, she started boarding school and they rarely saw each other after that.

As is the way with childhood, Tara quickly moved on to new friends. As Lucy Hill departed his life, Lucy Lambton entered it. This Lucy was the eldest daughter of the Conservative MP Viscount Antony Lambton, and his wife, Bindy, both of whom Oonagh knew from the social round in London. 'I met Tara for the first time in Venice,' she recalled, 'where I lived between the ages of thirteen and fifteen. My mother thought it would be nice for me to have a friend, so it was arranged that we should meet each other. My recall of him is total. And it's a montage. Him in his suits, with the water of Venice behind him. The Grand Canal. The glistening water. He was in his alternative, everyday suits, which at that time were turquoise velvet with red lapels and red velvet with turquoise lapels. In my mind, I can still feel the texture of the velvet.

'Tara was twelve. I was fourteen, almost fifteen. But he was so worldly. He was brought up entirely among adults – and very sophisticated adults. What interests me, looking back, is that a girl of my age wouldn't have known the meaning of the word sophistication, or had the thought that someone might be sophisticated. Yet, I was just aware that Tara was different to other boys of his age. There was a magic about him.'

Twelve-year-old boys, in her experience, were selfish, yet Tara had a generosity about him that seemed wildly out of character for a young boy. 'He seemed to have no end of money,' she said, 'but he would give without any thought whatsoever as to the cost. I remember I wanted a pen and he bought it for me – this incredibly expensive fountain pen, which cost, I think, a hundred and fifty pounds, which was an absolute fortune in 1957. It didn't mean anything to him to have money and to give it away like that.'

Another visitor to Venice that summer was Tara's cousin, Caroline Blackwood, who had tired of Lucian Freud's serial unfaithfulness and left him for good in 1956. For comfort, she turned to Oonagh, rather than her own mother, who Caroline knew would feel vindicated by the failure of her marriage. On the rebound, Caroline had a brief affair with Deacon, which began in London in the spring of 1957 and continued in Venice. But she was already thinking about escaping to America to make a new start and she confided in Oonagh her plan to go to New York to try her hand at acting. Oonagh was delighted to see her emerging from what had been a dark period in her life. But Caroline's decision to move to America would set in train a course of events that would have grave consequences for Oonagh's life and cast a shadow over Tara's life too.

•

In September 1957, shortly after their return from Venice, Oonagh threw a party at Grosvenor Place in London to see her favourite niece off. Caroline spent the autumn and winter of 1957 studying under legendary acting teacher Stella Adler, a proponent of the Stanislavski method, which encouraged actors to explore their own feelings and past experiences to fully realize the character they were portraying. It should have been rich ground for Caroline, but Adler considered her too shy and too stuck-up to be a successful actress. Caroline eventually abandoned her acting ambitions to become a journalist and Booker-nominated author.

In January 1958, to celebrate her upcoming forty-eighth birthday, Oonagh visited Caroline in New York, taking her usual suite at the five-star Drake Hotel on Park Avenue and 56th Street. She placed Tara with Caroline's cousin, Lady Veronica Woolfe, and her husband, Peter, in London. Deacon visited him each day to tutor him for the Common Entrance exam, which Dom insisted that he sit that summer.

Caroline was thrilled to have Oonagh in New York. Whether dining at Delmonico's, or shopping in Bergdorf Goodman for shoes for Oonagh's child-sized feet, the pair resembled two sisters rather than a middle-aged woman and her young niece.

It was during a visit to a dressmaker whom Caroline had discovered on Manhattan's Upper East Side that Oonagh met the man who would become not only her lover, but, with a haste that shocked even her louchest bohemian friends, her third husband.

He was a short, stocky, thirty-something-year-old Spanish-American, with the dark smouldering looks of a matinee idol. The *Daily Express* thought he looked like the actor Mel Ferrer; the *Daily Mail* thought Mike Todd. He called himself Miguel Ferreras, though his name, like much of his back story, was a fiction.

According to his own account of his life, he was born in Cuba in 1928, and brought to Spain at the age of three months by his mother and father, both of whom later died. Orphaned at the age of thirteen, he was then raised by his mother's brother, who was Franco's military attaché in Berlin. It meant that as a child he travelled extensively through Nazi Germany and Fascist Italy during the years of the Second World War. Two years after the war – again, according to the account he constructed for himself – he applied for a student visa to study fashion design in New York. There, he was apprenticed to Charles James, the brilliant, temperamental, English-born atelier. He eventually set up his own shop on Manhattan's East 56th Street, where he was working on the day that Oonagh walked through the door and into his life.

Miguel had originally propositioned Caroline while he was fitting her for a dress, telling her quite openly that he was looking for a rich wife to bankroll his ambitions to become an international couturier. Caroline offered to introduce him to her rich aunt, who had told her in Venice that she intended to marry the very next man who proposed to her.

'Years later,' according to Garech, 'I asked Caroline, "What were you thinking?" And she said, "I never thought she'd marry him." Because Caroline knew him and she thought he was a joke figure. If my mother really did say she was going to marry the very next man who asked her, all she meant was that she wasn't going to be all that choosy.

'If Caroline had known that my mother was going to suddenly marry this clown, she would never have taken her there. She was very vulnerable at that point of her life. She was lonely and, yes, I would say rather afraid of getting old.'

Oonagh was physically attracted to him. In 1997, two years before his death, Miguel told *Harpers & Queen*, with a lack of chivalry that was his apparent trademark, that Oonagh married him for sex, which they engaged in the third time they met each other. 'Oonagh told me her first two husbands did not give her any pleasure,' he told the magazine's reporter, Nicholas Farrell. 'She wanted to have the youth which she never had.'

Yet Oonagh truly believed she was in love, according to Garech. 'I think she was trying to wish this image of him as a dashing, Spanish bullfighter figure into reality,' he said. 'But he wasn't anything like that. He was just a fool. And I never heard him praise anyone or anything unless it was to his own advantage.'

Whatever the source of the attraction, within weeks of their first meeting, Oonagh agreed to become his wife. Laughing at the crazy impulsiveness of it all, Miguel told the *Sunday Express*: 'I fell in love at once. Oonagh was a little doubtful for the first three hours.'

They tied the knot only six weeks after they met. It was just enough time for Miguel to obtain a divorce from his existing wife, Margaret Clarke, with whom he had two daughters, but who, he told reporters, had grown 'rather bored with me'. The marriage was dissolved in Alabama. Two days later, on 25 February 1958, Oonagh and Miguel were married. The ceremony was conducted by a Presbyterian minister in her suite at the Drake Hotel, one block away from the salon where Caroline introduced them as a joke the previous month.

The bride wore black, the *New York Herald Tribune* reported, while the suite was decorated with blue flowers – 'the groom's favourite colour,' said one syndicated story, its author clearly tickled by this detail. Caroline acted as Oonagh's bridesmaid, while Joaquin Ferreras – whom Miguel claimed was his brother – performed the role of best man. The newlyweds spent a week at the Drake Hotel, then departed for Cuba, which Miguel claimed was the country of his birth.

While she was honeymooning with her young lover, Oonagh became a grandmother for the second time, when Gay's wife, Magsie, gave birth to Catheryn, a sister for eighteen-month-old Robin. Oonagh, who adored babies, couldn't wait to return home to meet the latest addition to her son's family. She was also excited about introducing Tara and Garech to her new husband, a man about whom she knew almost nothing. She wouldn't even know his real name until six years later, when, in an effort to show that the marriage was invalid, her legal team began exhuming the secrets of his past.

According to documents uncovered by White & Case, Oonagh's international lawyers, the man she married was in fact born José Maria Ozores Laredo; not in Havana, as he claimed, but in Madrid; and not in 1928, as he always insisted, but in 1922. This made him six years older than his stated age of thirty, and, significantly, an adult rather than a child during the years of the Second World War.

His childhood was one of poverty and abandonment. He entered the world in the Calle del Mesón de Paredes Maternity Hospital in Madrid and was placed by his mother in a foundling house, or orphanage. In 1934, at the age of twelve, he went to live with his mother's brother in Ribadeo, in the north-west of Spain. Poor and uneducated, he spent his teenage years living between there and Madrid, working odd jobs and supplementing his earnings through looting and petty crime during the years of the Spanish Civil War.

On 22 July 1941, at the age of nineteen, he was convicted of theft in the Spanish capital. He was spared jail, but a few weeks later, perhaps realizing that he might not always be so lucky, he took the route of redemption offered to many wayward youths by joining the army. He volunteered for the Blue Division, a unit of Spanish soldiers that served alongside the Nazis on the Eastern Front during the Second World War. Enlistees were required to swear an oath of personal allegiance to Adolf Hitler, before spending five weeks at a training camp in Grafenwöhr, Bavaria, where they were incorporated into the Wehrmacht. His unit was part of the general German force advancing on foot towards Moscow from Poland, although he enjoyed a far from distinguished military career.

Before he and his Blue Division comrades reached the Russian capital, they were re-routed north to help out in the Siege of Leningrad, the battle that would see some of the fiercest fighting and heaviest casualties of the war. In November 1941, just weeks after it began, he was arrested outside Leningrad while attempting to desert. He was imprisoned for a month, then sent back to Spain. However, in 1943, with the casualties mounting on the Eastern Front, he was allowed to re-enlist and he returned to Russia. Again, he didn't last long in battle. In December 1943, according to official records, he was part of a convoy that returned home wounded – possibly suffering the effects of frostbite, which was a common hazard.

He was discharged from the army and lived for a short time in Vigo, on Spain's Atlantic coast, before returning to Madrid and his former life of petty crime. On 24 January 1944, he was arrested by police at the North Station in the Spanish capital for stealing a suitcase. Four weeks later, on 27 February, he was arrested again, this time on suspicion of stealing clothes to the value of 1,200 pesetas.

Three weeks later, perhaps to escape trial, or possibly out of a genuine commitment to the cause of the Third Reich, which was then losing the war, he volunteered to join Hitler's beloved Waffen SS. In March 1944, he was awarded the rank of second lieutenant. As the Germans were squeezed from all sides in the final stages of the war in Europe, he saw action in Romania, Russia, Hungary, Germany and Yugoslavia. He was eventually captured by the Allies in Italy in the final months of the war and spent what remained of it detained in a camp just outside Naples.

In December 1945, seven months after the German surrender, he was repatriated to Spain. But shortly afterwards, with the several warrants out for his arrest, he decided to get out of the country. It seems that this was the moment when José Maria Ozores Laredo became Miguel Ferreras.

Miguel denied all of this in his interview with *Harpers & Queen* in 1997. But the story of his rebirth through the theft of another man's identity was later confirmed to Oonagh's lawyers by Joaquin Ferreras, Miguel's 'brother', and the best man at their wedding in the Drake Hotel. Joaquin, who was born in Havana, and who soldiered alongside his friend on the Russian Front, did in fact have a brother named Miguel Ferreras. He happened to have the man's Cuban birth certificate amongst his own papers when Miguel made up his mind to get out of Spain. In a sworn affidavit obtained by Oonagh's lawyers, Joaquin said: 'When I told Ozores that I was going to return to Cuba, he asked if he could pose as my brother, Miguel Ferreras, and obtain with me, from the Cuban consul, a visa to Cuba. I agreed as, at the time, I was friendly with him and conditions in Spain were very bad.'

In March 1946, Joaquin, and the man now posing as his younger brother, crossed the border illegally into Portugal and were arrested by the Portuguese police. The pair claimed to be Cuban nationals and demanded to see the Cuban consul in Lisbon. He approved their application to be repatriated back to the country of their birth and they left for Havana, where they lived for a time with relatives of Joaquin. Miguel found work as a gardener.

On 14 March 1949, the real Miguel Ferreras died of tuberculosis in a sanatorium in Ourense in Galicia, northern Spain. According to Civil Registry records, his body was never claimed, but his death represented the removal of a potential complication for the man who had stolen his identity.

By then, the new Miguel was living in New York, having used his falsified documents to obtain a student visa to study fashion design. His apprenticeship under Charles James is one of few details in his own account of his life that holds up to scrutiny. James clearly formed an impression of Miguel, although it didn't match Miguel's impression of himself as the heir apparent to Christian Dior. In 1961, in an interview with the *New York Times*, James would dismiss his former protégé's ambitions as a couturier, describing him as having 'great mechanical competence, great bluster, which, as Barnum & Bailey showed us, is so necessary, and what would pass for taste in the provinces'.

Miguel obtained citizenship of the United States through his first marriage. He opened his own salon on the Upper East Side, but it haemorrhaged money. As his former mentor suggested, however, he was more than capable of talking himself up. He bragged, for instance, that he had designed a maternity dress for Elizabeth Taylor. A story in *Life* magazine, which featured his work alongside that of two other Cuban designers, mentioned that he had studied architecture and had previously worked for a Paris couturier. With Miguel – as Oonagh and her children would come to discover – it wasn't always easy to separate the fact from the fiction.

Miguel had a modest output of about sixty designs per year,

according to the same article, with each piece selling for between $325 and $1,200. In September 1957, it was reported that an outfit he designed for singer Lena Horne for the Broadway opening of the musical *Jamaica* left her unable to move, let alone dance, and had to be remade entirely. The publicity had the potential to be catastrophic for Miguel's business at a time when he was struggling to pay the rent in one of New York's most expensive neighbourhoods. There couldn't have been a more opportune time for him to meet a rich woman like Oonagh.

Miguel seemed to have little doubt about the future trajectory of his life now that he was married into the Guinness family. And he had few qualms about discussing it publicly. After the wedding, he told the New York press that he and his wife would live between London and Paris, where he would be setting up his own couture house.

Back home, the marriage caused shock and consternation among Oonagh's social set. When her friends eventually met him, their worst prejudices were confirmed. To them, he was uncouth, boorish and very evidently on the make. 'An absolute swine who was quite clearly out to milk her,' was Kenneth Rose's memory of him. 'He was a real bad hat – loathsome, absolutely awful, to anyone who had any experience of the world. I'd been in the army, which I regarded as the best grounds for experience of all, and he stuck out to me straight away as a self-seeking shit.'

Deacon considered him unworthy of Oonagh and nicknamed him 'as-a-such' because of his habit of finishing sentences with that idiomatic flourish. After meeting him for the first time, Oonagh's first husband, Philip, told Gay that his mother ought to keep her new man 'chained to the bedpost'.

After a long Caribbean honeymoon, Oonagh returned to Luggala with Miguel in May 1958 to a traditional Irish welcome. To celebrate their mother's homecoming, Garech and Tara arranged a hooley in her honour in a cottage in the grounds of the house. All of the invited guests, many of them house staff, estate workers and local villagers, dressed up in nineteenth-century Irish dress for the occasion. In knee-high britches and tam-o-shanters, red petticoats and Munster and Kerry cloaks, the men and women danced until dawn to fiddle and pipe music. A banquet of pigs' trotters, baked potatoes, boiled nettles, fried kippers, roast goose and apple cake was laid out. It was devoured without the aid of cutlery and washed down with mugs of porter and whiskey.

It was a memorable night and was covered by a number of newspapers. 'The lad who appeared to eat most,' the *Daily Mail* reported, 'and to dance most, was thirteen-year-old Tara Browne, wearing a heavy white homespun suit with a red jumper, clay pipe and clogs.'

While they were happy to have their mother home, Tara and Garech hated her new husband on sight and would never come to accept him as their stepfather. 'Our mother had lovers from time to time,' Garech said. 'There's nothing wrong with that. The only one we took an instant dislike to was this creep and we hoped she would drop him very quickly.'

Quite what Miguel made of his first glimpse of his adoptive country is uncertain. A photograph from the party, taken by Tara, shows him looking almost comically ill at ease in an Aran sweater and flat cap, while, beside him, Oonagh appears brimming with happiness in her black hooded Munster cloak.

The press were keen to get the measure of the new master of the house. And the story of Miguel's life seemed to improve with every telling. Now, according to the newspapers, he was 'one of America's leading dress designers', had a salon on Fifth Avenue, New York's most prestigious shopping street, and specialized in designing dresses 'for many of America's star actresses'. But if Miguel was full of bluster, he was also full of plans. He said he wanted to bring Irish materials to the international market and planned to do a show in New York that autumn featuring his own designs in Irish cloth. 'I think Donegal tweed, in particular, should be better known around the world,' he said.

He was effusive in his praise for his new Irish home. 'This is a heavenly place,' he said. 'We are in a completely different world from my offices in Fifth Avenue, New York. There is certainly peace and quietness here. The tempo of life is so restful.'

With Miguel around, it wouldn't remain that way for long.

•

Dom's domestic arrangements were about to change, too. By now, he was struggling with the job of making the Castle Mac Garrett estate pay for itself. Ireland was in the midst of an economic depression. In the unemployment- and emigration-hit west of the country, there was no longer a market for his produce – at least not one sufficient to maintain a large house and its staff.

By the mid to late 1950s, Castle Mac Garrett was a quieter place. The gaps between the shooting parties grew. And Sally was deeply unhappy. In 1958, she gave an interview to the *Daily Mail* in which she spoke candidly about the loneliness of living in an empty castle in the wilds of County Mayo.

'We live mostly to ourselves,' she said. 'We never go to any parties. We do very little entertaining . . . I've longed just to have a television here so that I could at least see some of my old friends of film and the stage on screen. It would help to cover up some of the loneliness. But even that is impossible. My husband tried with a set, but it was hopeless. We cannot get any reception here.'

Dom and Sally began talking about selling up and moving to London. 'She was no more a country girl than I was a Norwegian,' according to Dom's daughter, Judith. 'She learned to garden and she became a very good gardener. But it was an alien life for this very glamorous London actress to find herself suddenly living in the bogs of Ireland. They were miles from anyone. There was one phone in the house and it was in a poky room at the back of the house. If my father wanted to use it, it was brought to his study and plugged into the wall. But if Sally wanted to talk to someone – which she didn't seem to very often – she had to sit in this tiny, dark room. It was unimaginably lonely for her. And of course she suffered a breakdown. But it would have been enough to give anyone a breakdown if you weren't used to it.'

According to Dom's eldest son, Dominick, Sally attempted

suicide on at least one occasion by jumping out of a window. 'My father sent her to London,' he said, 'to have electro-shock treatment, which they didn't know a lot about. But it was a horrible treatment that took away part of your memory. She was never the same after that.'

Tara and Garech still visited regularly and had become more and more immersed in the local music scene. Other boys of their age were having their young minds blown by Elvis Presley, Eddie Cochran, Bo Diddley, Little Richard, Gene Vincent, Buddy Holly, Chuck Berry and the other early exponents of rock and roll coming at them through long-wave radio. But Tara and Garech's biggest musical heroes were Irish: people like Leo Rowsome, who played the uileann pipes, a bellows-blown bagpipe that evolved from ancient Irish war pipes; and Margaret Barry, the so-called Singing Gypsy, whose unique vocal style and zither banjo-playing made her a star of London's Irish community and influenced a generation of ballad singers, including Luke Kelly.

In the mid to late 1950s, Ireland's native music, much like its language, was considered an anachronism. 'Even the town of Claremorris, close to where we lived in Mayo, thought traditional music was terribly old-fashioned,' Garech remembered. 'It wasn't that it was dead. It was very much alive. It was just that it was unfashionable. People were shocked that anyone wanted to listen to these old musicians.'

Not least the privileged sons of a peer of the realm. But Garech and Tara had developed an educated ear for native Irish music. Each summer, they had ventured further and further afield in search of good traditional musicians and singers. Tousle-haired Garech, who had taken to dressing in traditional Irish dress, and his cherub-faced little brother, had become regular fixtures at various *fleadhanna cheoil*, or traditional music festivals.

'They were an unusual sight,' according to Brid Ni Dhonnchadha, who remembers them from that time. 'I first met them at a *fleadhanna ceoil* in Longford. They both had this long blond hair, which was a very strange thing to see on a boy at that time. And then the way they spoke was different. There was nobody like them on the scene at the time. But they loved the music.'

In 1956, at a music session in Tulla, County Clare, Garech and Tara had met Paddy Moloney, the future founder and driving force behind what would eventually become the internationally famous Chieftains. The son of an army sergeant, Paddy worked for a builders' providers by day and played the tin whistle, button accordion and uileann pipes in the evenings and at weekends. He also played the washboard in various groups during the skiffle craze, which also inspired the young Beatles. At the age of seventeen, Garech had returned to Ireland after studying French at the Alliance Française in Paris and moved into a rented mews in Quinn's Lane in Dublin. Paddy took to dropping in and the pair became firm friends, acquiring the nickname Ballcock and Browne, a pun on Paddy's day job and the name of the first aviators to cross the Atlantic. Like their near-namesakes, Ballcock and Browne would become pioneers in their own right, spearheading the revival of traditional Irish music in a country in which it had ceased to exist as a form of popular entertainment.

Tara accompanied Garech and Paddy as they travelled to traditional music festivals all over Ireland and his adolescence was coloured by the characters they met during those long, music-filled summer nights – *sean nos* singers, storytellers and itinerant pipers.

In the summer of 1958, while Miguel was getting his feet under the table at Luggala, Tara and Garech spent six weeks travelling around Ireland with a state-of-the-art, two-reel Grundig tape machine, recording traditional music, folk songs and stories. They filled hundreds of hours of tape, not just at festivals, but in isolated rural cottages, where they found extraordinary musicians and storytellers who had never been heard by a wide audience.

'Tara helped me with the buttons,' Garech remembered, 'because I discovered that I couldn't listen and work the reels at the same time. It was a wonderful summer. We travelled around and we slept in bed and breakfasts, or above pubs, or on somebody's floor. We stayed with the great concertina player Mrs Crotty, who ran a pub with her husband in Kilrush, County Clare, which stayed open until five o'clock in the morning. We stayed with Lord Kilbracken in Killishandra, County Cavan, and were driven around by Dr Galligan, who was the chairman of Comhaltas Ceoltóiri Éireann [an organization dedicated to the promotion of traditional music, song and dance in Ireland] and who also happened to be the local GP.'

The recordings they made were the stem cells of Claddagh Records, a label founded by Garech the following year, with his friend, a psychiatrist called Dr Ivor Browne. Fourteen-year-old Tara was a shareholder of the company. Claddagh would go on to play a major role in the revival of traditional Irish music, both at home and internationally, beginning in 1959 with Leo Rowsome's *King of the Pipers*. Like all of Claddagh's subsequent albums, it would have a contemporary sleeve design, subverting the age-old wisdom that Irish records had to have shamrocks and rainbows on their covers to be commercially successful. In the decade to come, the label would give traditional Irish music an air of Sixties cool.

The arrival of Claddagh was, in its own modest way, part of a watershed year for music. While Garech was pressing his first LP, a Detroit factory worker called Berry Gordy borrowed $800 from his family's loan fund to set up the record label that would eventually come to be known as Motown. At around the same time, a young Memphis record store owner named Jim Stewart was making the first recordings for what would soon become Stax Records. And in Liverpool, three teenagers called John Lennon, Paul McCartney and George Harrison were finding their feet in a rock and roll cover band billing itself as Johnny and the Moondogs.

•

The marriage between Oonagh and Miguel was in trouble right from the beginning. The 'heavenly place' that Miguel spoke of in reference to Luggala was in fact his idea of hell. He missed the fast pace of life in Manhattan and he was insecure around Oonagh's intellectual friends, most of whom considered him embarrassingly gauche. He compensated for his lack of social confidence by being rude to everyone who visited the house. He failed to understand, too, why his marriage to a woman with the title of Lady did not accord him a title. 'He thought he should have been Lord Somebody,' according to Garech. 'He used to say, "Why I not? I marry a Lady. I should be a Lord – as a such."'

It must have been plain to Miguel, too, that Oonagh's children despised him. In the weeks before Garech and Tara set off around Ireland with the Grundig tape machine, he had been making awkward efforts to exert some form of parental control over them. Even at thirteen, Tara was too independent of mind and too wise to the ways of the world to accept this boorish stranger as some kind of authority figure. Like Garech, he simply disregarded him. Miguel's response was to raise the decibel level of his voice. 'I don't recall us ever once calling him our stepfather,' said Garech. 'We called Sally our stepmother. But Miguel? Never. We really thought of him as an intruder.'

It's not difficult to imagine why Miguel, an abandoned child who endured a desperately deprived upbringing, was so jealous of Oonagh's children and the privileged life they enjoyed. But in attempting to show Tara some tough parental love, Miguel overplayed his hand. Before the summer of 1958 was finished, with the marriage less than six months old, he was gone. Oonagh was tired of the shouting matches and the general disharmony he brought to the house. She went to Dublin one morning for an appointment at the hairdresser's and didn't come home. Miguel took the hint and moved out, returning to New York. Oonagh instructed her solicitors to initiate divorce proceedings. In an interview with the *Sunday Express*, she was very forthcoming about her reasons.

'The marriage failed,' she said, 'because of my husband's attitude towards my children and my friends. My children are very intelligent and sensitive, and, when Miguel shouted orders and criticisms at them, it made everyone unhappy. It made me absolutely miserable. I began to feel, too, that I couldn't have any of my friends in the house – he was so rude to them. When we were at Luggala, my place in Ireland, he was always running down the Irish, offending both my friends and my servants.'

The issue for Miguel, it was clear, was his failure to supplant Oonagh's children, especially her youngest, as the centre of her world. In an interview with the *Daily Sketch*, he revealed his resentment at how Tara travelled everywhere in a chauffeur-driven Rolls Royce and was given obscene amounts of pocket money by his mother. 'He was spending $2,000 each month,' Miguel told the newspaper. 'I thought it was ridiculous that a schoolboy should be spending so recklessly. I told my wife about this. But I am afraid we didn't agree on the matter . . . I certainly wouldn't bring up a boy like that.'

Assuming the figure was correct, it was an astonishing allowance for a boy of thirteen, the equivalent of £720 per month, at a time when the average industrial wage for a man was £546 per year. Tara – dubbed by one newspaper as 'society's reputed freest teenage spender' – splurged his pocket money on everything, from toy soldiers to opera and classical albums, which would arrive from America by the crate-load. His interests were varied and ephemeral. He bought camera equipment, budgerigars, books, train sets, comics and modern record players. He enjoyed anything that was new and novel. He had a red bow tie that lit up when he pressed a button on a battery pack concealed in his pocket. Brendan Behan loved it so much, he wrote about it in the *Irish Press*. And he was becoming obsessed with cars. He had one of the very first Scalextric sets, not long after it was introduced at the Harrogate Toy Fair in 1957.

Like his mother, Tara was of the view that money was for spending. The real concern for Miguel wasn't how much money Oonagh was lavishing on Tara, but rather how little she was spending on him. In time, she would discover, to her considerable cost, just how profligate Miguel could be with money. But for the moment, much to the relief of Tara and Garech, he was gone from their lives.

Knowing the depth of his mother's loneliness, and hoping to forestall a possible reconciliation, Gay tried to set her up with Kenneth Rose, his former history tutor at Eton, who was then working as a columnist with the *Daily Telegraph*. In late August, in an effort to put Miguel out of her mind, Oonagh had decided to take Tara on a fortnight-long Italian cruise. Gay offered to join them and persuaded his old teacher to come along in the hope that, adrift together under a Mediterranean sky, something might develop between them. 'I remember feeling that there was something indecent about being the lover of your friend's mother,' Kenneth recalled. 'Oonagh was a whole generation older than I was. But she was very attractive.'

If her real intention was to make her estranged husband jealous, then she couldn't have chosen a better sailing companion. 'Miguel hated me,' Kenneth recalled. 'But he hated me because I hated him. I could see he had no honourable place in that set-up. I had one tremendous row with him, over what I can't remember now, but I'm not sure I didn't threaten to hit him.'

The party set off for Italy, where they chartered a 50-foot vessel called the *Jastlone II*. The boat set sail with Oonagh, Tara, Gay, Kenneth and a small crew on board. Garech was planning to meet them later on the island of Corsica. 'Tara took an enormous amount of baggage with him,' Kenneth recalled. 'What it consisted of was six enormous suitcases filled with books. Whether he read them, I don't know. But he certainly took them with him. He was a very bright little boy, very amusing and good-natured. And totally spoiled, of course. If we were in port, he'd only have to say to his mother, "I'd like an ice cream," and a sailor was dispatched to go and get one for him.'

But the cruise didn't work out quite the way Gay envisaged. There was no love spark. 'The boat was a great disappointment,' Kenneth remembered. 'We all expected it to be huge. But, as always, Oonagh had been swindled and it was not much more than a little trawler. I slept in a cupboard full of fish hooks.'

On the way to Corsica, they were caught in a violent storm. 'We came very close to capsizing. We were drifting towards some rocks. The engine had cut out and it wouldn't start. We were drifting closer and closer. And I remember looking at Oonagh and Tara and Gay and thinking, "What an interesting bunch of obituaries we are going to make." Then someone got the engine started just in time.'

They were forced to take refuge in the Italian port of Livorno. Garech arrived in Corsica to discover there was no boat waiting for him.

Kenneth spent a day on the phone trying to sort out the mess. The conditions were not conducive to new romance flowering. 'She went back to Miguel shortly after that,' he said. 'He bounced back into her life in some kind of way.'

They returned home in early September, just before the start of the new school year. To Dom's great delight, Tara had passed the Common Entrance exam and been accepted by Eton. But he had a rude awakening in store. Tara returned from Italy and announced that he wasn't going. Dom was livid.

The *Sunday Dispatch* considered Tara's eschewal of Eton worthy of half a broadsheet page. While students were flocking back to school for the start of the winter term, it was reported, Tara was feeding his budgerigars in the Mayfair home of Lady Veronica Woolfe, where Oonagh had deposited him once again while she went to New York to try to patch things up with Miguel. 'I didn't want to go to Eton,' Tara told a reporter. 'I wanted to go to school somewhere in London. And now Father has agreed.'

In fact, Tara had made up his mind that he was never going to school again. 'Tara doesn't want to conform to pattern,' Lady Veronica's husband, Peter, told the newspaper. 'Somehow I don't think he'll go to any public school. I'm not saying it might not do him a lot of good . . . But Tara's like that, an individualist.'

In the great Guinness tradition, Oonagh had raised her boys not to care a jot what anyone thought of them. Shortly afterwards, Garech was creating newspaper headlines of his own, having reportedly 'run away' with one of his mother's parlour maids. Since May, he had been having a relationship with Margaret McCabe, the pretty, raven-haired daughter of a forest worker from the nearby village of Roundwood, who was employed as the second housemaid at Luggala. The news of the affair broke that winter. For weeks, the British and Irish press pursued the story of the teenage brewery heir and the local Cinderella, who earned £2.10 a week sweeping his mother's floors and lived with her family in a two-room cottage with no electricity or indoor toilet.

The newspapers eventually tracked Garech down to his mews in Dublin. He spoke about how he'd first fallen for Margaret on the night of the hooley to celebrate his mother's return to Ireland with Miguel. 'Since then,' he told the *Sunday Pictorial*, 'we have been going really steady.'

Asked what their respective families thought of the affair, Garech said, 'They don't come into it. My mother has no objections to my going out with Margaret. Nor have her parents objected to me. We are not engaged. But anything is possible when you are in love.'

Tara spent the next few weeks lodging with Lady Veronica and her husband in London and resisting Dom's efforts to try to get him to change his mind about Eton.

On 2 October, Brendan Behan's new play, *The Hostage*, opened at the Theatre Royal in Stratford, in the working-class heart of the city's East End. Tara and Garech were his guests for the evening, along with their mother, who was home from New York, her reconciliation talks with Miguel stalled. Brendan insisted on introducing Oonagh and her boys to everyone at the after-show party. He reached his career summit that winter. *The Hostage* received rave notices and would eventually transfer to the West End and to Broadway.

Less than three weeks after the show's successful premiere, the work he most cared about was published, his memoir of his teenage years in an English borstal. It was immediately acclaimed as a modern masterpiece. Tara and Garech were both at the launch party for *Borstal Boy* in London. While Brendan entertained the literati crowd with a rendition of 'The Bold Fenian Men', the *Daily Express* reported that 'two teenage boys entered the room. Without pausing for breath, [Brendan] took two strong drinks from a passing waiter and handed them to both boys, Garech and Tara Browne. They accepted them without the slightest hesitation. Several respectable British middle-class ladies could not conceal their horror.'

It was hardly surprising. Tara was still only thirteen.

Oonagh was a notable absentee from the launch of *Borstal Boy*. She was back in New York, finally, with a weary inevitability, reconciling with her husband. 'I think she was very much in love with Miguel in the physical sense,' Kenneth Rose remembered. 'He exerted a strong, erotic influence over her.'

The couple were spotted toasting their reunion at the fashionable Colony restaurant off Madison Avenue. A reporter from the *Daily Express* phoned Oonagh's suite at the Drake Hotel and enjoyed a brief exchange of words with Miguel. 'We are living together again,' he confirmed. 'The marriage is good again.'

Miguel denied reports that Oonagh had offered to buy him the haute couture design house of the late Jacques Fath. 'Absolutely untrue,' he said.

What was true – and it might well have accounted for Miguel's good mood when the *Express* phoned – was that Oonagh was about to start bankrolling his ambitions to become a rival to fashion giants like Christian Dior and Pierre Balmain. It was an act of folly that Oonagh would find herself paying for until the end of her days.

•

Miguel's return to Ireland with Oonagh that winter cast a pall over life at Luggala. The battle for primacy between Oonagh's husband and her teenage children continued. The conflict came to a head in the days before Christmas – Miguel's first at Luggala. Tara and Garech were enjoying a party in Tara's room with a group of friends that included Nicholas Gormanston, the young Irish peer, and Min Hogg, the future founding editor of the celebrated *World of Interiors* magazine.

'It was well after midnight,' Garech remembered. 'Miguel came in and started shouting. He said we were making noise. And, of course, we were. You put twelve or fifteen people in a small room and that's what happens. And, equally, it was Christmas. So Miguel was shouting and I was drinking port in a little Waterford Crystal glass. I finished the drink and I threw the empty glass on the floor, smashing it at his feet, and I said, I think, "Fuck you!"

'So Tara and I left with the entire party – this was at three o'clock in the morning – and we went to Dublin and we all slept on the floor of my mews in Quinn's Lane. And Miguel had to get up the following morning and explain to my mother why, two days before Christmas, there were suddenly no guests in the house. We went to Jammet's restaurant in Dublin for lunch. My mother begged us to come back, but we insisted that Miguel apologize first.'

Tara and Garech returned home for what proved to be a typically spark-filled Luggala Christmas. Miguel, who had been forced into a humiliating apology, kept a low profile at the dinner table while other guests provided the entertainment. Lady Veronica Woolfe had recently read Deacon's book, *The Rack*, and was so depressed by its bleak descriptions of sanatorium life that she had returned to drinking after a long period on the wagon. When she discovered that the author was sitting opposite her, she flew into a drunken rage. Other guests pitched in to defend the book. The debate escalated until her husband attempted to stab Deacon with a butter knife. It was the kind of evening that Oonagh loved. The seating arrangements were likely orchestrated to achieve such an end.

'Lady Veronica had brought along a friend of hers,' Garech remembered, 'who was called Waverly Provatorov. They were both of the Unionist persuasion and I suspect my mother sat them either side of Brendan Behan to see what would happen. Waverly became quite emotional as well. There was all this shouting – her on one side and Lady Veronica on the other. So Brendan leaned backwards in his chair, took their two heads and banged them together.'

It settled the argument over Deacon's book. But it also became abundantly clear that Christmas that there was something seriously wrong with Brendan. The man whom Tara and Garech regarded like a favourite uncle had ceased to be the 'formidable little bull', as his old friend the poet John Montague remembered him, 'crackling with energy and affection for the world'.

He was seriously ill. A GP had recently told him to give up alcohol, an injunction he chose to ignore. During the months that followed, the period of his greatest success, his life continued to spiral out of control.

In the spring of 1959, *The Hostage* moved from Stratford to London's West End, again enjoying rave critical notices. Brendan was at home in Dublin and missed the triumphant opening night at Wyndham's Theatre. But shortly afterwards, he decided that he should go to London to savour the adulation. Beatrice, who was finding it increasingly difficult to manage him, thought it a bad idea. Brendan travelled alone. It was during this trip that he began the habit of interrupting performances of his plays, engaging the actors in banter and occasionally scrambling up onto the stage to sing a song or perform a step dance known as the Blackbird.

Tara saw him at his worst in London that spring. Brendan had arrived at the theatre one night in such an inebriated condition that a doorman turned him away. The following morning, still drunk, he showed up at Oonagh's house in Shepherd Market, where Tara was staying with Frances Redmond, the Irish house-keeper. 'Tara was delighted to see him,' said Garech, 'as he always was, because he adored Brendan, just as Brendan adored him. But Brendan wanted a drink and he began hammering on Frances's bedroom door. Frances said, "I can't come out, Mr Behan, I'm naked." She was a big woman. And Brendan roared, "I want to see you naked!"'

Tara, who was then only fourteen, tried to persuade Brendan to have some breakfast, but Brendan quickly passed out. Fearing he was dead, Tara phoned Beatrice in Dublin and told her that he was unable to wake her husband. Beatrice contacted his London publisher, Rae Jeffs, who arrived at the house, then sent for a doctor. Once he was awoken, Brendan left the house in search of another drink, insulting both the doctor and his publisher on the way out. Within an hour, he was arrested. It was his first arrest in England for public drunkenness. He appeared at Bow Street Police

Court the following day, where he pleaded guilty to being drunk in a public street and was fined. He returned home to Beatrice. Thirty carloads of reporters followed him to the airport, where he sang a rendition of 'The Red Flag' before boarding a plane to Dublin.

Miguel despised him and the feeling was mutual. There had already been tension between the pair on the two or three occasions they had met. Brendan – who, at the age of fourteen, had set off on his bicycle for Belfast to enlist with the Irish Republicans who were planning to join in the fight against Franco – had taken an instinctive dislike to this new member of the household, who always seemed to be sunk in an armchair with a sullen expression on his face. One night in the summer of 1959, knowing the depth of Tara and Garech's hatred for their mother's new husband, and probably thinking he was doing Oonagh a favour in the long run, he threatened Miguel with the IRA.

'Brendan came to dinner,' Garech recalled of the night, 'and he told Miguel that he was not welcome in Ireland, and that, if he was not out of the country within three days, he would "fucking get rid of him". And that was because he knew how much Tara and I hated him. He told him that the IRA would kill him.'

As far as the other dinner guests were concerned, it was more than idle drunk talk. Although Brendan was no longer active in the organization, he and Cathal Goulding, the IRA's Quartermaster General and future Chief of Staff, were old friends, having served their time together as apprentice housepainters. 'Brendan didn't mean it as an idle threat,' said Garech, 'and Miguel certainly didn't take it as one.'

For once, Oonagh decided that it would be sensible to get Brendan out of the house. Another dinner guest that night was her friend Erskine Childers, the government minister and future President of Ireland. Oonagh asked him to take Brendan back to Dublin in his state car. 'Brendan said something to Erskine as they were helping him into the car,' Garech recalled, 'and the Garda sergeant who was driving remarked that this was no way to speak to a minister. And Brendan said, "The minister is not a member of any fucking church I know of!'"

It was an amusing punchline to what had otherwise been a horribly fraught evening. Miguel would bide his time before exacting a brutal revenge on the writer the following Christmas.

•

While Brendan was set on a downward course, Miguel was convinced that his own life was headed in the opposite direction. With Tara ensconced in London and Garech living in Dublin, he had Oonagh to himself and he spent much of the early part of 1959 figuring out how to use her fortune to gain entry to the exclusive world of haute couture.

Oonagh still hoped to assimilate him into her world by building him a studio in the grounds of Luggala. She asked Alan Hope, the architect who oversaw the rebuilding of the house after the fire, to draw up plans for an elegant pavilion, where Miguel could work on his designs for at least part of the year. But the plan never made it off the drawing board. Miguel wanted to live in Paris. And, very soon, the antipathy of her friends towards him persuaded Oonagh that their future was indeed abroad.

In September 1959, shortly after Brendan Behan threatened his life, Miguel got his way. Tara returned to Ireland, packed his belongings into more than a dozen large crates and set off for a new home in Paris, with his mother and the man he would never bring himself to call his stepfather.

5: *LA VIE EST BELLE*

They cut quite a dash in Paris, driving up and down the Champs-Elysées in a white open-top Lincoln Continental: the classically handsome Spanish gigolo, his attractive, middle-aged Irish wife, and her baby-faced teenage son, usually dressed in velvet, with a menthol cigarette burning between his fingers. Everywhere they went, they turned heads. And, for Miguel, that was the whole point of being there.

They arrived in the autumn of 1959 at a time of high tension in the city. France was going through the painful paroxysms of letting go of its pre-war imperial past. The country teetered on the brink of civil war over its disengagement from Algeria, an issue that had already brought bloodshed to the streets of Paris.

Oonagh rented a flat for them at 135 rue de l'Université, on the left bank of the Seine. And while she and Miguel plotted their entry into the world of Paris fashion, Tara familiarized himself with the city, spending hours each day exploring its tree-lined boulevards and narrow cobbled streets on foot.

He also reconnected with Lucy Lambton, his old friend from Venice. She was in Paris to attend a finishing school, one of the private colleges where the British upper classes sent their daughters in the interval between leaving second-level education and entering society. The schools tended to be run by formidable female principals, fixated on preserving the virginity of the girls in their care. Lucy was attending one of the non-residential schools, boarding with a family in the suburb of Neuilly-sur-Seine and taking the Métro into the city each morning to learn about such matters as social skills, speech and deportment and how to look like a lady. There were lessons in French, musical appreciation, cookery and ballroom dancing, and regular visits to the Louvre, where the girls would listen to interminable lectures about art. Once Lucy re-established her friendship with Tara, however, she stopped going to school altogether.

'I spent a year in Paris,' she remembered, 'and when I left I had no idea what Paris was like. I never saw it. Every single day, I would just go to Tara's mother's apartment and hang out with Tara.'

The Sixties were just over the horizon and the world was changing, not least for the daughters of Britain's upper classes. Lucy was part of the first wave of aristocratic English girls to rebel against the convention of the Parisienne hothouse turning out suitable young wives for the debutante circuit. Quite a number of the girls who followed her would also find their way to 135 rue de l'Université, where the relaxed atmosphere – the day beginning shortly before noon with vodka and tomato juice – was in contrast to the restrictive world of the finishing school.

While Oonagh's main focus that autumn was her husband's career ambitions, Lucy ensured that Tara never wanted for company. She introduced him to a whole new circle of friends, mostly English girls and boys, who were attending either finishing schools or French language courses. All were instantly enchanted by Lucy's tiny, besuited friend.

'The first time I ever heard of Tara Browne,' said Michael Boyle, who was studying at the Sorbonne, 'was when Lucy told me about this Little Lord Fauntleroy character whom she'd first met in Venice. I think she said they had palazzos opposite each other. He was this little guy who wore velvet suits and they used to wave to each other from the balconies of their palazzos. Anyway, they'd become friends and he was now in Paris and she said he wants us to go around to his flat for dinner.

'So we went and I discovered that Lucy hadn't exaggerated him at all. He looked like a small boy. I suppose he was still a small boy. But he was someone who liked the company of adults terrifically. He had no interest in friends of his own age. He'd outgrown them. He was fourteen and we were sixteen or maybe seventeen.

But there was never any question of you thinking of him as a child. You immediately saw him as an equal.'

The months that Michael spent discovering Paris in the company of Tara, his mother and her mercurial Spanish lover were like something that F. Scott Fitzgerald might have conjured up, with Oonagh as the Gatsby figure at the centre of it all. 'It was, "Come to dinner", then it was, "Come to lunch", a constant flow of invitations,' he said. 'I mean, you'd be walking up the Champs-Elysées, going nowhere in particular, then you'd look behind you and there would be this white Lincoln Continental, with Miguel at the wheel, Oonagh in the front passenger seat and Tara in the back. It'd be, "What are you doing, Michael?" and my answer was usually, "Nothing", because I was supposed to be at the Sorbonne, but I think I only went once. Then they'd say, "Well, come with us!" and you'd climb in and off you'd go.'

Often, they headed to Le Drugstore, a forerunner to the modern-day shopping mall, a maze of trendy boutiques and chic cafes on the Boulevard Saint-Germain, where they drank seemingly endless cups of café crème. Or they pointed the car in the direction of the United States Embassy on the Place de la Concorde, where the canteen sold milkshakes that were so thick that it hurt their cheeks to suck them up the straw.

Soon, more friends joined in the fun. One day, early in 1960, Lucy brought Judith Keppel, a finishing-school classmate with aristocratic ties and a navy lieutenant-commander father, to the rue de l'Université. Judith – who, forty years later, would become the first jackpot winner of the British TV quiz *Who Wants to Be a Millionaire?* – was rendered silent by the worldliness of this little boy, who was three years younger than her but seemed somehow, almost impossibly, older.

'I remember talking to him once,' she said, 'it might have been that first time I met him – and he dropped into the conversation the fact that he'd been in Venice and he was talking to Igor Stravinsky, you know, at age fourteen or something. Tara was not only young, he was also very young-looking. He was quite small and he had lovely, sort of golden hair. So when you heard these things coming out of his mouth, it was really unbelievable.'

The word spread about this extraordinary little character who looked like a boy but talked like a man. His new friends began to bring their own friends to the rue de l'Université to meet him. Judith took Lady Frances Eliot, the daughter of the ninth Earl of St Germans. They immediately hit it off. Michael Boyle took his school friend Hugo Williams, and he too joined their little coterie. Hugo, who was later an award-winning poet, remembered being in awe of this little Billy Budd character who was unlike any fourteen-year-old he had ever met. 'At a time when I was learning about life for the first time, he was very, very influential on my development,' he said. 'He allowed me to flower a bit. I was extremely backward socially and so uptight around women. At seventeen or eighteen, I had no idea how to talk to them. And Tara talked me through it all. "Oh," he said, "you just make jokes all the time. That's what they want. They want to laugh." Because they were so quiet, the girls in those days. They all had long hair and big eyes and they sighed a lot. The sigh was their weapon of choice if you were failing to impress them. Tara taught us how to make them laugh. He'd say, "If you can't think of anything funny to say, just tickle them or something."'

Hugo was in Paris to study French at the Alliance Française. He switched to the Sorbonne because Michael was there, and attended one lecture about French culture, which passed completely over his head. Then, like Lucy, he stopped going to school altogether, choosing to spend his time in Paris hanging out with this little Irish boy, who introduced him to the idea of total freedom.

Hugo was writing occasional articles for the *Brighton and Hove Gazette*, but had no idea what he wanted to do with his life. Michael had been thrown out of Oxford after twice failing his Preliminary exams. The range of options open to aristocratic girls like Lucy, Frances and Judith, meanwhile, was narrow. The conventional wisdom was that educating a daughter to the same level as a son was unnecessary and might even render her undesirable to potential husbands. 'Most girls in those days were told that they might as well get a little job until they got married,' said Judith, who had just completed her A-levels and would be returning to England the following spring to take up the classic stopgap option of a secretarial course.

Hugo, Michael, Lucy, Frances and Judith resolved to simply enjoy themselves for as long as they were in Paris. 'It was a wonderful moment in our lives between school and reality,' Hugo remembered. 'We all knew there was a ghastly future waiting for us when we went home, one in which we'd all have to grow up and become adults.'

Very quickly, they all assimilated to the rhythm of Tara's world: the long, lazy days in the flat, doing nothing at all; the afternoons in Le Drugstore drinking milky coffees and listening to Edith Piaf's 'Milord' on the radio; then the late nights, with Tara, Oonagh and Miguel, in fine restaurants and smoke-filled clubs.

When the heat of the city became oppressive, they went to the Eden Roc swimming baths in the Île-de-France, Tara and his friends wedged together on the back seat of the Lincoln Continental, their teenage eyes being opened to a world on the threshold of a social and sexual revolution. 'Eden Roc was an extremely glamorous place,' said Hugo, recalling one formative visit there. 'I saw Jean-Paul Belmondo [the French actor] stroking a girl's tits in public through her bathing costume. It made an impression on me, I can tell you. That was a typical sort of jaunt, where we all set off in this beautiful car, battling through the Paris traffic, in search of pleasure somewhere.'

Nights out with Tara were full of excitement. He and his friends went to L'Eléphant Blanc or to the Club Saint-Germain, two of the most fashionable jazz clubs in the city. Tara drank Coca-Cola, smoked Gauloises menthols and engaged in conversation with the grown-ups, always on equal terms. Usually, Oonagh and Miguel were with them, but occasionally it was just Tara. On these nights, it may have appeared that they were chaperoning him, but it was, in fact, the other way round.

'He sort of led us in a way because he knew so much more

about the world than we did,' remembered Judith. 'We'd all just left school and we'd never been allowed out on our own before, so you can imagine what a fabulous thing it was for us to be going to nightclubs. My parents would have been horrified had they known. French nightclubs in those days were much racier than English ones, although I was terribly short-sighted and refused to wear my glasses, so I suspect I missed an awful lot of things!'

Tara, who had acquired his mother and father's love of clothes, was always stylishly turned out. 'He had a very developed aesthetic sense,' said Hugo. 'He was years ahead of everyone in the way he dressed. Black drainpipe trousers, mauve shirts, green suede jackets. Brocade ties. He liked turquoise a lot. He used to write me letters in turquoise ink. Looking back, he had incredible social poise. He must have had that as a child. You don't suddenly get it at fourteen. I think it was a personal characteristic as much as anything.'

As his childhood friend Lucy Hill had correctly divined, he was very interested in girls. He enjoyed female company enormously and the feeling was mutual. 'He wasn't at all macho,' Hugo remembered. 'He was rather unthreatening to girls, I would think, because he was quite short and a little bit androgynous with these waves of blond hair. He didn't make any attempt to be manly. But he didn't need to. He was just so comfortable in his own skin.'

He had a large collection of stock lines that would elicit a smile from even the most socially awkward pre-debutante. 'He would look at you very seriously,' Michael remembered, 'and he would say something like, "Can you keep a secret?" And you'd say, "Yes, of course I can keep a secret." And he'd say, "Well, there's no point in telling you anything then, is there?"'

He had also, it seems, picked up some of his father's legendary raffishness. 'There was something about him being not quite a gentleman,' remembered Hugo, 'which was part of his fascination. By "not quite a gentleman", I mean he wasn't like the uptight public schoolboys that these girls would have been used to meeting. Here was this little chap who was completely liberated at fourteen or fifteen. He was what we called international. But that was combined with these Irish characteristics of being extremely sociable and amusing, which I presume he got from his father. I don't know if Tara had any liaisons as such at that age, but he was rather keen on girls and girls seemed to like him a lot. A good time for him was putting on a nice record and having a dance and getting all the girls around him.'

Music began to matter to Tara more than almost anything else. At some point in 1959 he discovered the pop music that was coming to Europe from across the Atlantic. He bought a portable, battery-operated record player that played 45s. 'At the time, nobody knew they existed,' said Peregrine Eliot, Frances Eliot's brother and the tenth Earl of St Germans, 'let alone owned one.'

Tara started spending much of his still considerable weekly allowance buying records by mail order from America. Boxloads of vinyl – all the latest singles from the Billboard Hot 100 – would arrive at the rue de l'Université flat each week. Most of these records Tara bought without ever hearing them before. There was a great thrill of discovery for him in placing the needle into the first groove of each disc, never knowing what he was going to hear.

There were songs of young love and teenage longing. Boy meets girl, girl meets boy, then boy or girl meets someone else. There was 'Dream Lover' by Bobby Darin, 'Smoke Gets in Your Eyes' by The Platters, 'Lipstick on Your Collar' by Connie Francis and 'Bye Bye Love' by The Everly Brothers. Then there were songs with insidious beats and infectious hooks that you could dance to: 'At the Hop' by Danny & the Juniors and 'Splish Splash' by Bobby Darin.

Tara and his friends took the portable record player out into the city's grand squares and listened to the music with the volume up high. 'He took it everywhere,' said Peregrine, whose sister reminisced about those days right up until the time of her death in 2004. 'They would all jive in the park, on river cruises and anywhere they damn well liked – to the astonishment of bystanders.'

They listened to 'Donna' by Ritchie Valens, 'Poison Ivy' by The Coasters and 'A Teenager in Love' by Dion and the Belmonts. These songs would forever remain the soundtrack of their memories of Paris. Some records they played over and over again, including 'Cut Across Shorty' by Eddie Cochran, in which a country boy named Shorty and a city boy named Dan have a race to win the hand of a girl named Lucy. Not surprisingly, it was Lucy Lambton's favourite.

Sometimes, late at night, Hugo remembered, when Oonagh and Miguel were otherwise engaged, they headed for the Aérogare des Invalides, where they put the record player down on the deserted floor and kept the party going, dancing with the cleaners and the jaded airline staff, drinking coffee from the vending machine and creating souvenirs of the night's fun in the airport's black-and-white photo booth.

'I thought of him as one of my best friends,' said Michael Boyle. 'Even though I was coming up to nineteen and he was essentially still a child, I thought of him as an absolute equal. He wasn't spoiled at all. Well, of course, he was spoiled in one way, in that he seemed to get everything he desired. But he also wanted to share it with you. He never said, "This is mine."

'I remember the rest of us began to say, amongst ourselves, you know, we can't keep taking money off this young boy. So we started saying, "Come on, Tara, enough now – you paid yesterday. It's time to go home." And then there'd be this scream from Lucy. She'd say, "Look what I found!" And Tara would have left a *dix-milles* note down on the pavement on the Champs-Elysées for one of us to find. So suddenly it was *our* money and there was no need for us to be embarrassed. That's what he was like. He didn't give a hoot about money. He wanted to spend it on his friends and to see them enjoying themselves.'

•

All of this fun took place against a backdrop of political tension and social unrest in France. For years, the country had been engaged in a brutal war in Algeria, which had seen elements of the army revolt. This crisis triggered the collapse of the Fourth Republic, which had overseen the rebuilding of France since its liberation.

In 1958, former president Charles de Gaulle had agreed to come out of retirement and was invested as prime minister by the National Assembly with full power to rule by decree for six months and to draw up a new constitution for France. In 1959, de Gaulle became the President of the Fifth Republic. The return of the statesman who led the Free French Forces during the Second World War was greeted with jubilation by French Algerians, who were convinced that he would stand unwaveringly behind the cause of retaining its north African colony.

However, shortly afterwards, at just about the time that Oonagh, Miguel and Tara were making their home in the city, de Gaulle offered Algeria and its Muslim majority the chance to decide its own fate. It was seen by many as a betrayal of France, would lead to another abortive army coup and eventually to riots on the streets of Paris, which Tara watched one night from his bedroom window overlooking the rue de l'Université.

Miguel, who now had access to Oonagh's money, lustily embraced the playboy lifestyle. Drunk or sober, he tooled around Paris in the big American automobiles that she bought him, forever seeking pleasure and regularly finding trouble. He went through a lot of cars – two Lincoln Continentals, a Rolls Royce Corniche, two Chevrolet Corvettes – often abandoning them where he crashed them.

'He was always on the wrong side of the road,' said Garech, who shared a car with him many times, 'passing something out on a bend in the road at about ninety miles per hour. He was always lucky that nothing was ever coming the other way.'

He drank his way into bar fights and he satisfied his wandering sexual appetite in the gay bars of Paris. Oonagh professed to know nothing about Miguel's interest in men, although among Tara's friends it was an open secret. Once, he even made a clumsy pass at Hugo. 'He tried it on with me,' he remembered. 'I stayed the night in the flat when I was on my way somewhere and he was there. I was eighteen at the time. He came into my room and sat on the bed and put his hand on my knee. I remember telling Tara about it but in a kind of jokey way.'

Those who observed Oonagh and Miguel together were fascinated by the odd symbiosis they shared. 'Miguel was just a
nightmare person,' Lucy Lambton remembered. 'He oozed slime.
But there wasn't the bad atmosphere between them that one would
perhaps expect. He never seemed to be nasty to her, even though
he was opulently repellent to everyone else.

'She was very coquettish around him. I can remember her
looking at him, fluttering her eyes, with her lips pursed. I always
remember that look. She was in love with him. That was clear. I
mean, none of us took him seriously. But she did. There was an
element of her leaning on him because she needed a man of the
house.'

The dynamic between Tara and Miguel was equally compelling. After Miguel's failed stand on the issue of his pocket money,
Tara understood that his mother would always choose him over
Miguel. It gave him a certain self-assurance around him. 'Tara
would have been completely uninterested in what was going on
with Miguel,' according to Michael Boyle, 'because he knew he
always had the ace, which was that his mother absolutely adored
him. Miguel wouldn't have dared lay a finger on him because he
would have been decapitated and torn apart in a second by
Oonagh. When it came to Tara, she would have been a tigress of
the first order. So Tara could afford to be completely unfazed by
Miguel.'

A close acquaintance of Miguel's during this period was the
grandiloquently titled Prince Stanislaus Klossowski de Rola,
Baron de Watteville, a young playboy aristocrat, who, like Tara,
would go on to become a face on the Sixties London scene and
a close friend of Brian Jones and the other Rolling Stones. Stash,
as he was popularly known, was born in 1942, in Berne, Switzerland, the son of Balthus, the Polish-French modern artist who
was regarded as one of the greatest painters of the twentieth
century, and Antoinette Von Watteville, a member of one of
Switzerland's most venerable aristocratic families. In 1960, Stash
was eighteen, living in Paris and leading the life of a rich,
pleasure-seeking sybarite. It was perhaps inevitable that at some

point in their night-time ramblings he and Miguel would cross paths.

'Miguel was unavoidable really,' he remembered. 'He got himself into insane situations. Oonagh was extremely tolerant of him. How she put up with him and his goings-on, I'll never know. He was always blind drunk and behaving scandalously, either fighting or crashing cars. He was very prodigal. Bisexual, of course. And very disreputable.

'At the same time, I liked him. He had a flamboyance about him. He would distribute wads of banknotes to people. He was an extraordinary character. Probably unsavoury on some levels. He had a *Scarface* side to him. You know, he was a Cuban gangster type. I think we all had a grudging respect for his antics. He was very successful at his trade. I mean, he was no mere ordinary confidence trickster. Conmen play it very safe. He didn't play it safe at all. He was larger than life. And he was always ready to fight.'

Brendan Behan discovered that to his cost on Christmas Eve 1959, when Miguel finally exacted his bloody revenge for threatening him with the IRA. According to at least two eye-witness accounts, Brendan was wandering drunkenly around the snow-covered, cobbled courtyard at Luggala, singing his favourite Christmas hymn, 'Adeste Fideles', when Miguel suddenly emerged from the house and felled him with a punch to the head. 'He got him down quite easily,' according to John Montague, who watched the incident with Garech from an upstairs window. 'Then he started kicking him mercilessly while Brendan lay on the ground.'

John ran downstairs and stepped in to save him from any serious and lasting injury. Oonagh, who had heard the commotion from the courtyard, came outside and covered Brendan with a blanket. 'She viewed the entire thing, as she did most things, with a certain detachment,' John recalled. 'And I don't mean that in a critical way. She had that Anglo-Irish way of observing the world as a series of antics, rather like a character from an Evelyn Waugh novel.'

Miguel claimed that Brendan had been 'interfering with children', implying that he had made sexual advances towards Tara. It was commonly known that Brendan had homosexual leanings from his time in a young offenders' institution and occasionally he talked to friends about what he referred to as his 'Herod Complex'.

According to Ulick O'Connor's 1970 biography of his life, the type of boy or man he admired sexually was the type he had met in borstal – 'clean-skinned fresh lads'. Tara evidently fitted the profile. However, no one, including Oonagh, believed Miguel's claim.

'Brendan never made any kind of pass at Tara,' according to Garech. 'If he had, Tara would have told me. He certainly wouldn't have confided it in Miguel. The story about Brendan interfering with children was something that Miguel came up with the following morning to try to justify his behaviour. The real reason he beat Brendan up was that Brendan had told him to get out of Ireland.'

A crucial line was crossed at Luggala when Miguel violently assaulted such a beloved member of the household in full view of the other guests. In many ways, Oonagh's bohemian idyll, the happy intellectual crossroads where writers and painters and the pleasure-seeking remnants of Ireland's old aristocracy met to drink and talk and be enriched by each other's company, died that night.

In January 1960, Tara returned to Paris with his mother and her increasingly unpopular husband. There was work to do. Miguel may have been a gigolo, but he was a far from idle one. While he continued to enjoy the life of a libertine in Paris, he was also busy planning his entrée into the Paris fashion world. With his wife's capital behind him, he set his sights high. In early 1960, not long after they returned to Paris, he tried to persuade his wife to buy him the House of Dior.

The internationally famous fashion house had been in chaos since the death of its founder, Christian Dior, in 1957. But the name remained a synonym for luxury and style. Dior had founded his business in 1946, at a time when Paris had ceased to be the style capital of the world. After years of fabric shortages, when drably coloured, defeminizing clothes became a fashion of necessity, Dior invented the 'New Look' that helped make Paris the most import-ant city in the world again when it came to women's clothes. His designs were 'ultra-feminine' with rounded shoulders, cinched waists and full skirts that accentuated busts and hips. He revolu-tionized the way women dressed all over the world. By 1949, Dior's international empire was so big that it accounted for 5 per cent of France's total export revenue.

Dior had an international client list that couturiers like Miguel could only fantasize about, including Hollywood celebrities and members of the British royal family. But by the spring of 1960 the business was in trouble.

Christian Dior had died of a heart attack three years earlier, at the age of fifty-two, creating a leadership vacuum in the com-pany. It was initially filled by Dior's young Algerian-born assistant, Yves Saint-Laurent, who was promoted to the role of artistic director at just twenty-one. His debut collection was hailed as a triumph. Emboldened by his success, however, he began to take risks, resulting in the 1960s bohemian 'Beat Look', which drew its inspiration from the existentialists who frequented the cafes and jazz clubs of Saint-Germain des Prés. The archly conservative French fashion world was aghast. When Saint-Laurent was called up for his National Service shortly afterwards, no one in the com-pany objected to him going.

Miguel was convinced that he himself was the strong and visionary leader the company needed to steer it into the coming decade. But the Paris fashion world was notoriously unwelcoming of outsiders. 'He saw himself as the head of a major fashion house,' recalled Tara's cousin, Desmond Guinness. 'But companies like Dior were whales. Miguel was a minnow. And minnows cannot swim with whales.'

Miguel's interest in the business was very swiftly rebuffed. If his pride was hurt, his confidence remained undiminished. With his rich wife's backing, he decided, he would simply establish his

own label. If he couldn't own the House of Dior, he would give
the world the House of Ferreras.

•

The question of Tara's schooling, or rather the absence of it,
became an issue again during that first winter they spent in Paris.
Although he was now approaching his fifteenth birthday, his
father hadn't quite let go of the idea of him going to Eton. At
Dom's urging, Oonagh hired a full-time tutor to prepare him to sit
his O-level examinations. Dom's hope was that, if he passed them,
then the school might allow him to enrol for the more academically rigorous A-levels.

Deacon was temporarily off the scene. 'He tended to steer
clear whenever Miguel was around,' according to Garech. In his
place, Oonagh hired Godfrey Carey, who had been a classmate of
both Hugo Williams and Michael Boyle at Eton, and who would
go on to become a QC.

'Oonagh was a patient of my father,' he recalled, 'who had a
practice in Connaught Square. Anyway, during a consultation one
day, she was sort of musing with him and she said, "Do you know
of anybody who might be a tutor for my son?" And he said, "Well,
I've got a son – he might do." So that was how I was engaged to
try to get Tara through his O-levels. Because there was a feeling,
even late in the day, that he might still go to Eton for the very last
years.

'I did a certain amount of research into the syllabus. Then I
had a very erratic job interview, for which I was flown over to Paris
to meet Miguel in a very good French restaurant called La Médi-
terranée. And then, having decided that I should have the job, he
made a silly move, which was to take me to a club for a nightcap.
I noticed the sort of club it was straight away – it was a homosexual club, not a woman in sight – and I made an excuse that
my landlady insisted I was home by midnight. And from that
moment on, even though Oonagh had already made the decision
to hire me, Miguel was determined to make life difficult for me.'

As it happened, so was Tara. In the five months that Godfrey spent visiting their flat on the rue de l'Université on a daily basis, Tara rarely opened a book. 'I had agreed a plan with Oonagh,' Godfrey recalled, 'even before my supposed interview with Miguel, which was that I would arrive at their place first thing in the morning and that from 9 a.m. until midday, I would lecture him – and they would be hard lectures. Then he would go to the Berlitz school, which was nearby, to learn French for one hour. Then he was allowed to go to meet his friends for lunch. He had another appointment with me between 2.30 p.m. and 4.30 p.m., a break for half an hour, then we would work again between 5 p.m. and 6 p.m. The evening was his own.'

The schedule went out the window immediately. 'I cannot remember any day in Paris when the programme was carried out,' he said, still amused, more than fifty years later, by the memory of Tara emerging from his bedroom, rheumy-eyed, in the middle of the day. 'I was quite a punctual chap and I would arrive at a quarter to nine every morning, when I'd be given my second café-croissant of the day by the maid. And I'd sit there waiting for Tara to get out of bed. He'd eventually show his face and he'd be full of apologies. He had this way of saying sorry. It was like a drawl. It was, "Surrraaay!" He was invariably polite and, in his own funny way, terribly considerate. He just wasn't always considerate about the things that I, as his tutor, wanted him to be considerate about!'

Tara was having far too much fun with his new friends and his record player to give even a passing thought to his schoolwork. And soon, another young English aristo friend would join his Paris circle. Nineteen-year-old Mark Palmer moved into the rue de l'Université flat in early 1960. Mark was, in fact, 'Sir' Mark and had been from the moment he was delivered into the world by his war-widowed mother. His father, Major Sir Anthony Frederick Palmer, had been a member of the Special Operations Executive, a highly secret government agency that conducted espionage and acts of sabotage behind enemy lines. In May 1941 he was killed off the coast of Syria and Mark entered the world with the title of fifth Baronet Palmer, of Grinkle Park, Co. York and Newcastle-upon-Tyne. He had been First Page of Honour to Queen Eliza-beth II. He attended Eton and was following the usual upper-class trajectory towards either Oxford or Cambridge when he had a difference of opinion with his stepfather, who was of the view that a couple of years in the Rhodesian police force might toughen him up. Mark pretended to go along with the idea, then did a runner to France. He remembered living rough for a while in Paris, in shop doorways and on people's floors.

He eventually got some money together and enrolled in a French-language course at the Sorbonne, where he reconnected with Michael Boyle, an old classmate from Eton. Michael took Mark around to introduce him to Tara one evening. At the time, Mark was living with cousins in Paris, but he wasn't happy. Tara suggested he move in with them. Mark couldn't believe his confidence, how nothing appeared to faze him. Oonagh wanted Tara to have a mate, so she told Mark to go and fetch his bags, then make himself at home.

And just like that, Mark became a kind of surrogate older sibling to him. There was no chance of getting Tara to do any schoolwork now.

The only book that any of his friends remember him opening in Paris was *Angelique*, the first in a series of historical adventure stories by Anne and Serge Golon, which would have been consid-ered racy for boys of his age. The heroine of the series was a French noblewoman described as being 'half-angel, half-devil, and wholly woman'. He was also a fan of the syndicated American cartoon strip *Peanuts*, featuring Snoopy and Charlie Brown. But he rarely, if ever, cracked the spine of a school book.

Eventually, feeling hopelessly redundant, Godfrey Carey quit as his tutor. In March 1960, he told Oonagh that he was going home. 'I went to her and I said, quite honestly, "You're wasting your money. I'm thoroughly enjoying being in Paris, because I'm a Francophile, but I'm being given quite a large salary and I'm not earning it."'

Oonagh asked him to reconsider. At Easter, she reminded him, his friends would be returning to England. And soon after that, she and Miguel would be taking Tara to New York, where she was planning to throw the first of a series of parties to announce Miguel's 'coming out' as a couturier. There, removed from the distraction of his friends, she assured him that her son would settle down to work. Godfrey agreed to accompany them on the trip.

One by one that spring, Mark, Hugo, Michael, Lucy, Frances and Judith left Paris, each of them with the sad sense that a gilded chapter in their lives was coming to an end. Tearfully, they said goodbye and promised to remain in touch.

After a farewell party at Claridge's in London, Oonagh, Miguel, Tara and Godfrey flew to New York. 'The new plan was that we were to take up residence in two adjoining suites in the Drake Hotel,' said Godfrey, 'which of course seems totally appropriate to work! I said to Tara, "Look, we've got to please your mother, so when we get to America, let's have the regime we were meant to have in Paris. There won't be the same interruptions, because you won't have the Berlitz school around the corner. You won't have all your friends. You'll only have me."

'On the first day, I woke up – he and I were sharing a room – and he was sitting on the floor at the end of his bed at six o'clock in the morning, having discovered that television channels in America didn't shut down in the evening. He'd been up all night. So I could see that this plan was going to go marvellously!

'I reported this to Oonagh and she said to him, "Oh, darling, you really must do your work." But all he would ever say when she tried to remonstrate with him was, "Oh, Mummy, Daaarliiing!" Anyway, not long after we arrived in New York, he said to his mother, "Mummy, Daaarliiing, don't you think I should be in London for Lucy Lambton's coming-out party?" And Oonagh just gave in. So Tara flew back to London, never again to return to the Drake Hotel.'

Tara made the cross-Atlantic trip alone, while Miguel and Oonagh remained in New York, along with Godfrey, who was under the mistaken impression that he was going to return. 'I stayed, enjoying the New York social scene for two weeks, still thinking that he was coming back. I don't think I ever saw him again after that. And my involvement with the family came to an end shortly afterwards when Miguel accused me, aged eighteen, of having an affair with Oonagh, aged fifty, and I thought, okay, this is more than I can stomach. So I left.'

•

Christopher Gibbs, the well-known London antiques dealer, aristocratic dandy and friend of the Stones, remembered catching his first sight of Tara at Lucy Lambton's coming-out party in June 1960. 'He was this charming, very young-looking, rather frail-looking child,' he recalled. 'Very blond, with big eyes and I think clad in something that put me in mind of Little Lord Fauntleroy. And he was dancing in a very wild and deranged fashion. I'd never clapped eyes on him before and I thought, "Who is this strange flower that's suddenly sprouted in the garden?"'

With Oonagh and Miguel still in New York, Tara was staying with Deacon in his Mayfair flat. He was fifteen, as free as the wind and London was his playground. Everywhere he went that summer, he seemed to be surrounded by a flock of privileged girls with cut-glass accents and perfect bone structure, usually the teenage daughters of artists, ambassadors and aristocrats whom Oonagh knew from the social round.

He became especially close to Charmian Scott, the nineteen-year-old daughter of the portrait painter Molly Bishop and the granddaughter of Lord George Montagu Douglas Scott, once Scotland's largest landowner. A society beauty, Charmian shared some of Tara's worldliness, having spent two years in Florence studying art and several months learning drawing at the Chelsea School of Art. That summer, she was trying her hand at modelling.

Another older teenage girl who entered his life in the summer of 1960 was Candida Betjeman. Oonagh knew her father, John Betjeman, from their days as Bright Young People and, later, from his time as the press attaché at the British Embassy in Dublin during the Second World War, when the IRA had seriously considered murdering him for being a spy.

'Tara and I immediately clicked,' Candida remembered, 'even

though he was almost three years younger than me. He was, I don't want to use the word iconic, but he was, even at that age, this totally peculiar, young man about town. Blond, very petite, almost pocket-sized. And his style beggared belief. He was a hugely influential figure in my life in terms of how I dressed, what music I listened to, what I thought about people, what I thought about the world. I listened to him. And there he was, what, three years younger than me? How could that have happened? And at an age when a three-year age gap is huge. I mean, what other fourteen-year-old boy could influence people like that?'

Theirs was an innocent, familial love. 'I don't remember him having any what we called liaisons around that time. He got on incredibly well with women, not in a gay way, but just as a terrific friend, chatting on the telephone and things.

'And he made very elegant passes. He said he owned my breasts, I remember, and he was going to mortgage them. I don't think either of us knew what the word mortgage meant, but that's what he used to say. Later, I went to Paris and we slept on the same bed, but he never actually tried anything.

'We cuddled and laughed a lot. He was a terrific giggler. He used to call rhododendrons "Rosiedandrums". I remember that about him. I really, really loved that boy. I mean, I *really* loved him. We had what I would call a brother-sister relationship. He was genuinely kind. There was absolutely not a glimmer of cruelty about him, which I think there could be in Oonagh.'

That summer, Candida invited Tara, along with Charmian Scott's boyfriend, Hercules Belville, to stay at the Betjeman home in Wantage, Berkshire, where the two young friends were introduced, bemusedly, to the idea of manual labour. 'My mother used to embarrass me incredibly,' she said. 'She wouldn't have people to stay unless they did chores. She thought it would be fun for them to make bonfires and things, which is what she made them do. And I remember Tara being absolutely amazed at being asked to do things. And so was Hercy, actually, because he wasn't used to it either. "A good bit of manual labour," she told them. "That's what you need." I think Tara was quite amused by it all.'

Her parents were rather less than amused by the phone bill that he managed to run up while staying in the house. One of the things that Tara had in common with Oonagh was his love of the telephone. Every day, and sometimes several times a day, he enjoyed long, sprawling transatlantic conversations with his mother at daytime rates. John Betjeman, who would become Britain's poet laureate in 1972, was lost for words when the bill arrived.

The London that Tara tripped insouciantly around in the summer of 1960 was still a far cry from the city that would become the capital of Sixties cool. It was still a grey, buttoned-up, battle-scarred city. But socially, and culturally, Britain was changing, especially for Tara's aristocratic girlfriends. The so-called Season – the round of balls and dances at which the sons of the ruling elite would choose suitable life partners, thus preserving the social stratification of the classes – was enjoying its last hurrah.

In 1958, the Lord Chamberlain had announced an end to the 200-year-old practice of presenting the daughters of Britain's well-bred families to the reigning monarch. The spectacle of well-spoken teenage girls in expensive dresses and white gloves, forming a queue along the railings in front of Buckingham Palace, with their top-hatted fathers and mink-wrapped mothers, was consigned to the past. It was a moment of profound historical and sociological importance for a class of people already coming to terms with the end of the empire.

The Season would limp on for a few years yet. But rich girls who came of age in the 1960s were no longer interested in a stuffy coupling ritual in which marriages – often unhappy ones, as Oonagh and her sisters could testify – were made on the grounds of intangibles such as pedigree and prospects.

Britain was on the cusp of an age of rebellion against old social codes and norms.

In February 1960, Princess Margaret married Anthony Armstrong-Jones, a former fashion photographer, who, despite the hyphenated surname and the Eton and Cambridge schooling, was regarded by those who keep score in these matters as a 'commoner'. The idea of the Queen's younger sister stooping to conquer was cited as evidence that Britain was becoming a more socially democratic country, where the children of the entrenched upper classes would have opportunities to form friendships and even marriages outside the claustrophobic confines of their own social circle.

In London in the coming years Tara and his friends would form close relationships with a new kind of aristocracy: the stars of rock and roll. His friend Lucy Lambton, in fact, got the ball rolling that summer when she fired a gun over the heads of The Everly Brothers.

One night, not long after her coming-out party, she was at King's Cross station, preparing to board the Flying Scotsman to Edinburgh, when she noticed an unruly scrum of people on the platform ahead of her. She asked someone what was happening and she was told that Don and Phil Everly – huge favourites of both Lucy and Tara – were attempting to get onto the train, along with the members of the late Buddy Holly's band, The Crickets.

'They were being mobbed by fans,' she recalled, 'and I thought, "How am I going to attract their attention?" My mother had given me a little gun to shy off would-be attackers. It was made in Paris, only a few inches long and light as a feather. But it made a terrific noise. So when the Everlys and The Crickets were standing on the platform, I fired this thing over their heads. They got a real shock. Everyone was terrified. So I just said, "I'm honouring the great songsters who have given so much joy and so much pleasure to the people of England! Don and Phil Everly, welcome to The Flying Scotsman, one of Britain's greatest trains!" So one thing led to another and I ended up sitting in their first-class sleeper with them and The Crickets, singing songs right the way through the night, all the way to Edinburgh. That was really my coming-out.'

•

In July 1960, Tara returned to Dublin, briefly, to celebrate Garech's twenty-first birthday. There was a party in Jammet's, at the time Ireland's most famous restaurant. The evening was really a double celebration. His record label, Claddagh, had issued its first LP –

Leo Rowsome's *King of the Pipers* – and it would very shortly be sold out. After the party, Garech set off on a three-month trip to the Far East, his birthday present from his mother, who wanted her son to enjoy some of the experiences she had when she sailed around the world with her father and sisters as a thirteen-year-old girl.

Dom and Sally were also at the party. They were marking a significant event of their own. Two days earlier, they had left Castle Mac Garrett for good and were on their way to London and a new life in the more modest surrounds of a flat in Belgravia. Almost all of the furniture and works of art from Tara and Garech's childhood home were sold off during the course of a four-day auction. Shortly, the house would become a nursing home for the elderly.

For Dom, the final straw had been money. 'He got a nail on the door – a writ to pay a bill,' said Garech. 'And he had to face up to the fact that it just wasn't possible to run a big farm in the west of Ireland in those years. There were no grants. He tried everything. He bred horses, but the west of Ireland was too far from the Kildare racing circuit. All the things he tried to do were too innovative or they were in the wrong place. But it's also true that he couldn't afford the upkeep because he was no longer with our mother. Her trustees were very careful to make sure he didn't get hold of much after the divorce. Her input into the home would have been very valuable. My mother helped make the castle luxurious.'

Her second husband may have been denied her money, but her third was cheerfully working his way through it. In July, Oonagh and Miguel were back in Paris, where they hosted a cocktail party at Chez Laurent, an exclusive restaurant on the rue du Faubourg Saint-Honoré, to once again announce Miguel's coming-out as a couturier. On arrival, each guest was handed a magnifying glass, with which to view a collection of microscopically small paintings by the German artist Max Ernst, which Oonagh had purchased for twelve million francs. Asked about the connection between Ernst's work and his own, Miguel said that, like great paintings, clothes, too, were art. He also told the press that he planned to open a *maison de couture* in the centre of Paris in September.

Among the three hundred guests was Oonagh's friend Jacqueline, Comtesse de Ribes, the French aristocrat, socialite and fashion icon, whose imprimatur Miguel was desperately seeking to try to establish his name in Paris.

'The de Ribes is one of those slinky, sloe-eyed, beautifully-boned types who is forever in a Dior,' the *New York Mirror* said in its report of the party. 'Miguel is hoping she'll be forever in a Ferreras from now on and it surely won't hurt. Jacqueline is among the ten best-dressed women in the world. When one of those starts tripping into your salon, you have more or less got it made.'

In August, they were back in Ireland for the Dublin Horse Show, one of the highlights of the Irish social calendar. The British upper classes had always regarded it as an extension – a kind of 'away day' – to the London social season. Its week-long round of cocktail parties, hunt balls and all-night house parties were a meeting point for Anglo-Irish landowners, the racing and horsey set and young debutante girls who were brave enough to make the trip across the Irish Sea for what the social commentator Nigel Dempster called 'a wild, Rabelaisian week of total drunkenness'.

Traditionally, the Guinnesses had the biggest and most talked-about parties of the week. In 1958, Oonagh's sister Aileen had thrown a party at Luttrelstown Castle that cost a reported £10,000, or £200,000 in today's money. Desmond Guinness and his then German princess wife, Mariga, regularly threw open the doors of their home, Leixlip Castle, to more than one hundred guests. The carryings-on at these parties was reported, usually in breathless gasps, by the British and Irish newspapers.

Returning from her year abroad, Oonagh was determined that her party would be one to remember and was reportedly on the phone three times a day from France arranging the alcohol, music, menus and invitations for the week-long event. 'My guests can come and go as they wish,' Oonagh told the *Daily Mail*. 'All I want is to ensure they enjoy themselves, dance, drink, eat, sing and be merry.'

Tara invited all of his Paris and London friends. Judith Keppel, Michael Boyle, Frances Eliot, Charmian Scott and Candida Betjeman all visited Luggala for the first time, improvising beds on floors or wherever they could find them.

Candida remembered the air of quiet foreboding in the Betjeman kitchen as her mother read the invitation. 'From the moment she heard that I'd become friends with Tara,' she said, 'I think my mum was suddenly terribly worried about me falling in with a bad lot. She warned me about Luggala. I was seventeen and a half or eighteen at that stage. She said it's very loose there. That was the word she used. She said you've got to keep your wits about you. She would have spoken to Judith Keppel's mother, who was just as worried about her daughter going.

'Although I was brought up in a bohemian household, with artists and writers and the odd smart aristocrat thrown in, the Guinnesses were something else altogether. For instance, there weren't any divorced people in my parents' immediate circle. So divorced people, you know, I used to stare at them, because they were so rare. I think by that time Oonagh had been thrice married, was it? And so had Maureen, I think.'

The guests included Brendan Behan, who appeared in Oonagh's photographs smoking a large cigar, with a pink carnation in his button hole. It was the first time that he had come face to face with Miguel since the beating he received the previous Christmas. Brendan was temporarily on the wagon, having determined to stay sober ahead of the opening of *The Hostage* in New York later in the year. 'We all sat on the floor of the drawing room listening to him telling stories and singing songs,' remembered Judith. 'A friend of his came for dinner one night – we all had to dress for dinner – and everybody said he was in the IRA. So that was atmosphere.'

The day after Oonagh's party, hung-over and weary, Tara and his friends, along with Oonagh and Miguel, drove to Russborough House, the spectacular Palladian home of the former Conservative

MP Sir Alfred Beit, nearby in County Wicklow. Sir Alfred had one of Europe's finest private art collections, which included paintings by Goya, Vermeer, Rubens and Gainsborough. Miguel had difficulty believing that the works of such masters could be found in a rural backwater such as County Wicklow. 'He kept walking around,' remembered Desmond Guinness, who was also on the trip, 'examining the signatures on each painting, then saying, "No, not real. Is copy."'

Everyone, not least his wife, found it deeply amusing.

Afterwards, Tara went to Marbella, where his father and Sally were holidaying. There, he met up with Hugo Williams, whose father, the actor Hugh Williams, had a villa nearby. 'I remember one day,' he recalled, 'my father said, "Would you like a Coke or something?" And Tara, who was fifteen years old, said, "I'd like a Bloody Mary, if you don't mind." My father was obviously a bit taken aback. He started making it for him, but not to the standard that Tara was used to. Tara watched him rather sceptically in fact, then he said, "Would you mind if I made it myself?"'

When the summer ended, Oonagh, Miguel and Tara were back in Paris, driving up and down the Champs-Elysées in Miguel's white Lincoln Continental. Tara had said goodbye to one group of friends, but soon he would say hello to another. It was in their company that this little man-child who seemed determined to live his life as if aware of how short his time would be, completed his entry to the adult world, discovering what would become three of his greatest loves – fast cars, modern jazz and recreational drugs.

6: ALL THAT JAZZ

Tara was at last beginning to look like a teenager, even though he'd been one, it seemed, for most of his life. His physical appearance changed quite significantly during the course of his second winter in Paris. Puberty sheared the puppy fat from his features and left him with a thin, languid face that carried the same note of knowing mischievousness as that of his father. He grew several inches, while his voice dropped by an octave or two and he allowed his long pudding-bowl hair to grow into a more adult style.

John Montague, who moved to Paris in 1960, remembers him strolling, arm-in-arm with his mother, through the streets of the city that autumn. 'I was with them and we were walking down the rue Saint-Dominique. They spotted a house that sold caviar. Tara went in and bought a tin and he walked along eating it with his finger. He was fifteen and I'll never forget that image of him, the very picture of a young fop, walking along, licking this caviar off his finger.'

Paris became an even more exhilarating place for Tara in the company of Glen Kidston, a young, engine-obsessed English mod, under whose wing he would complete the transition from precocious mummy's boy to one of the hippest cats in Swinging London. Cool was the great adulatory phrase of the day and it fitted Glen like it was custom-made. Mark Palmer remembered Glen as being withdrawn, saying very little, but with a strong aesthetic sense. He always dressed in black.

Mark was back living with Tara, Oonagh and Miguel in their rue de l'Université flat and pretending to go to the Sorbonne. One weekend, he invited Serena Gillilan, a childhood friend from England, to come and visit him in Paris. She brought Glen, her boyfriend, who was the Eton-educated scion of a wealthy British shipbuilding and banking family whose name was famous in motor racing circles. His uncle was one of the legendary Bentley Boys from the 1930s.

Glen's first impression of Tara was that 'he looked like something that had fallen from the ceiling of the Sistine Chapel'. He was nine years older than Tara but the pair hit it off instantly, so much so that Tara took him out that evening to Le Petit Bedon, where Tara scarfed down a plate of raw beef that he ordered in perfectly accented French. 'He was like a king in his own terrain,' Glen remembered. 'He was miles ahead of his years. I'd never met anyone like him. He was completely unique.'

Tara, similarly, was convinced that he'd made a rare connection. Glen was by far the most interesting person that he had ever met. He dressed in black, said only as much as the polite exigencies of conversation required and wore dark sunglasses that kept the world and its woes at one remove.

Glen was one of the first wave of mods, or modernists: savants of cool jazz, who read Camus and Sartre, frequented Italian coffee bars, enjoyed movies with subtitles and were fastidious about their clothes and hair. They wore winklepicker shoes, narrow ties, drainpipe trousers and bumfreezer jackets, so called because they were cut above the derriere, and they hung out in Soho, where the music of modern jazz greats like Thelonious Monk, Miles Davis and Chet Baker could be heard in cellar bars.

'Glen was the essence of cool,' said Hugo Williams, who remembered him at school. 'He had this phrase that he used to say all the time: "That's the way it goes."' At Eton, he was nicknamed Bugsy, after Bugsy Siegel, the charismatic, Probihition-era mobster, whose pictures dominated his dorm wall. Much like his boyhood hero, a great many legends built up around 'Bugsy' Kidston. One was that he improvised a new way of clearing the high-jump bar almost ten years before Dick Fosbury made the back-first technique his own.

'He always slouched around school, with this very long hair, combed straight back,' remembered the future Mayfair tailor Rupert Lycett Green, a classmate who claimed to have witnessed Glen make sporting history. 'This particular day, he was passing the athletics field, sort of sloping along, and he noticed all these people scissor-jumping over the high-jump bar, which Glen – despite having not the slightest interest in sports – could see was the least efficient method of getting your body over the thing. So he ran up to the bar, still in his ordinary clothes, and he threw himself backwards over it, clearing a height that no one else could reach. It was his version of the Fosbury Flop, which is what everyone does now, but it wasn't legal then. And of course the athletics coach looked upon this as heresy and Glen wasn't allowed to win the event. But he didn't care. After reinventing the high jump, a lot of kids would have stuck around and tried it a few more times, basking in the glory of the thing. But that wasn't his style. He did it once, then he just walked away. That was Glen. He was just effortlessly cool.'

A jazz lover from childhood, Glen was a regular visitor to Paris and he was well acquainted with the city's dark and interesting side. He became an instant guru figure to Tara, opening his ears to a different kind of music to the bubblegum pop records he'd been buying from America.

Jazz was a freer form of music, in which the performer became the composer, and it reflected perfectly the skittish mood of a Europe freed from the terror of the Nazis. Most of the great black jazz artists of the 1950s, from Charlie Parker to Dizzy Gillespie to Louis Armstrong, spent time in Europe. Many set up home in London or Paris to escape racial discrimination in America. 'They could be freer here,' Glen remembered. 'People like the great Dexter Gordon spent years in Europe. And in London and Paris there were all these great clubs where you could listen to them perform this fantastic music live.'

By 1960, modern jazz had been eclipsed commercially by rock and roll, the sound that a young Lennon and McCartney had just started beating out in the clubs of Hamburg, or its close cousin, rhythm and blues, the music that was inspiring the career ambitions of the teenage Jagger, Jones and Richards. Yet jazz remained infinitely cooler, especially in Paris, where it had been elevated to the level of serious art.

The neighbourhood of Saint-Germain des Prés became synonymous with bebop – a style of playing that flourished during the first years of the Nazi occupation and that was characterized by its quick tempo and complex harmony, a happy counterpoint to the sound of German jackboots. It also chimed with the mood of existentialism in the city in the years that followed the liberation. Clubs sprouted up everywhere, sometimes in dingy basements that had held a sinister purpose during the war years. They were dark, smoke-filled places, their condensation-soaked walls covered with framed photographs of the greats who had played there. You could order the house special of chilli con carne on a baguette, with a rum and Coca-Cola, and listen to the brilliant improvisations of some of the American expat jazzmen who had chosen to exile themselves in the city.

'I saw Lionel Hampton's Big Band at the Olympia in Paris,' Glen remembered. 'He was a hero of mine from the 1940s, because he did boogie-woogie jazz, which, when you're a kid, just bowls you over. The flashier, the better. The louder, the better. But for me, the best place was the Club Saint-Germain. You were paying more to get in there but you knew you were going to see five or six real giants of jazz in one night. It would be Lee Morgan and Benny Golson, with Art Blakey on drums and then on piano Bobby Timmons, who was the man for the soul stuff. These people were my heroes and I could just go along and see them.'

His obsession with the music was quickly shared by Tara. 'Glen became a kind of guru to him,' Serena Gillilan recalled. 'He took him to all these fabulous modern jazz places – dives, basically – where all these black musicians used to come from America to play. If you were interested in jazz at all, these people were legends to you.'

Even for someone who had seen and done a lot more than the average young man of fifteen, the new world that suddenly opened up to Tara must have been beyond exciting. Glen, Tara and Mark's faces became known in famous venues such as La Bohème, Le Chat qui Peche and the Blue Note, where they first saw Bud Powell, one of the founding fathers of modern jazz and perhaps the greatest bebop pianist of them all. Powell, a tortured veteran of New York's Birdland, had just arrived in Paris. The old virtuosity had left him by then, a result of drug, alcohol and psychiatric problems, but his name was still revered.

Tara started to add the latest jazz records to his orders from America. 'He started off with Dave Brubeck,' Glen recalled. 'He was really just putting his toe in the water. Serious jazz people looked down their noses at Brubeck because he was pop and he didn't pretend to be avant-garde, but he was good. And Tara was a kid who knew his own taste.'

Soon, a new musical sound began to emerge from his bedroom in the rue de l'Université. The saccharine harmonies of 'Lipstick on Your Collar' and 'A Teenager in Love' were replaced by the melodic soloings of Miles Davis's *Kind of Blue* and the sunny, lyrical sound of *Clifford Brown with Strings*.

They'd sit in his room, Glen teaching his young friend how to play chess, or maybe telling him about cars, while Tara ate thick slices of French bread, generously smeared with GYE, or Guinness Yeast Extract, an Irish version of Marmite, and listened to the syncopated rhythm played out on the trumpet, the piano and the sax.

•

Tara found a girlfriend that autumn. His first girlfriend. Her name was Melissa North, and she was an English country girl attending Mademoiselle Anita's, a language school that was run out of a convent in Paris. She was first attracted to Mark, a posh boy with a studied coolness: red velvet suit, long hair and untalkative in a way that added to his allure. Saying very little – or, better still, nothing at all – was an irresistible quality for teenage girls who'd grown up worshipping the sulking images of Marlon Brando and James Dean. Mark and Melissa became friends, then one day he brought her to the rue de l'Université.

'It was the most exotic thing I'd ever seen in my life,' she recalled. 'First of all, there was Oonagh, this tiny, ravishing, blonde woman who had shoes to match every dress, whether it was by Givenchy or Balenciaga. My own mother was a sort of gardener who wore my father's shirts all the time. So Oonagh was unlike anyone I'd ever met. And she was married to this man who I'd heard was a dress designer and who liked to be bought very, very shiny sports cars, which he then immediately crashed. He was sort of boyish and petulant and they made a very exotic couple.

'And then the other person who lived in the house was Tara, who was fifteen. The first two things that stood out about him for me were his voice and his laugh. He had this divine laugh and this rather sort of husky, rather sort of sophisticated, slightly drawly voice, so that everything he said seemed to be terribly witty. That was his style. And I fell madly in love with him.'

At sixteen years old, her only romantic reference points came from pop music and films. Their love was the stuff of old Everlys 45s: full of yearning, but innocent and unconsummated. It didn't progress beyond holding hands and kissing. 'He never proposed having sex with me. There was a lot of lying on the bed, but there was no taking our clothes off.'

They also listened to a lot of music at a very high volume. Like many others, he discovered the crossover between modern jazz and blues via Ray Charles. 'He liked a lot of black musicians that I didn't know,' said Melissa. 'John Lee Hooker. Howlin' Wolf. And I remember Sam Cooke. "Only Sixteen". "Chain Gang". All this music was very new. He would receive packages that were obviously being sent from America. We'd sit in Tara's room and listen to them until four o'clock in the morning, whacking up the sound.

'And Oonagh never had any complaints. None at all. Tara was a mummy's boy, but a mummy's boy who told mummy what to do. Oonagh would come into the room at three in the morning. Tara smoked Salem cigarettes. Menthol. Oonagh would saunter in, clouds of smoke everywhere, very, very loud Howlin' Wolf or whatever it was, and Tara would say, "Not now, Mum!" and she'd leave the room! In the Buckinghamshire countryside where I grew up, fifteen-year-old boys were like children. And they did what they were told. I was just amazed at this.'

Like Tara's other Paris friends, Melissa became quickly acculturated into the way things were done at the rue de l'Université. These new people she'd met seemed to exist in their own time zone. Soon, she was eating dinner around midnight with Tara, Miguel and Oonagh, in restaurants that were so exclusive their numbers were ex-directory. Or she was exploring the below-stairs Parisian jazz scene in the company of Tara, Mark and – whenever he happened to be in town – Glen, watching these impossibly cool musicians do their thing, then catching a taxi to Madame Buttercup's Chicken Shack in Montparnasse, where Bud Powell was the house pianist and where customers could eat fried chicken and pork ribs while silently checking each other out.

The place was a particular favourite of Tara's. The proprietor, Buttercup herself, was an obese black woman called Altevia Edwards, who was Powell's business manager and common-law wife, and who reputedly took all of his money and kept him locked up in a drugged-out state of dependence in the home they'd made for themselves in the Hotel La Louisiane. The nightly crowd would sit transfixed by the spontaneous brilliance of Powell's playing, then, abruptly, mid-improvisation, the music would stop, and Powell was fast asleep at the piano, an apparent consequence of his washing down the tranquillizers he took for his depression with his beloved vin rouge. 'He'd be playing the most wonderful piano any of us had ever heard,' said Melissa, 'then suddenly he'd go plonk and have a little snooze at the piano. Then he'd wake up again and go back to playing this fantastic jazz.'

It wasn't long before Mademoiselle Anita came to hear about Melissa's nocturnal life. One night, one of the nuns from the convent was detailed to follow her. Melissa was observed ducking into one particularly disreputable dive in the company of two long-haired boys in velvet suits. She was summoned by the Mademoiselle, who told her that the boys with whom she was spending her time were *mal élevé*, or badly brought up. To which she replied: 'One is a baronet and page to the Queen and the other is the son of a member of the House of Lords. How can they be described as *mal élevé?*'

Even the threat of expulsion didn't dissuade her from returning every day to the rue de l'Université flat, then out to wherever the night took them. She was having too much fun. 'Oonagh would take us out for dinner at the George V,' she recalled. 'She'd be wearing one of her Balenciaga dresses with the tiny, matching shoes. Tara would wear his green velvet suit. Mark would wear his red velvet suit. And I was the dowdy one in the company of these terribly glamorous people.

'Miguel was like the fourth child at the table. I was amazed that a grown man would make a scene in a restaurant like he always did in the George V. He'd get up and he'd throw his chair on the floor and it'd be, "This is disgusting" or, "The service here is a disgrace!" and Oonagh would just giggle. She thought it was funny – the car crashes, the dramas, the sort of strutting, the silliness. He was like her pet. The more silly and dramatic and spoiled he was, the more she just laughed it off.

'I don't think he was very bright, but he was rather gorgeous, I remember, and he was spoilt rotten. He was always showing off his new clothes, or his new, shiny cars, which lasted all of twelve days, then they were smashed, and then Oonagh would buy him another one.'

Tara, she remembered, viewed Miguel's behaviour with an attitude of bemused detachment. 'In his own way, he thought it was funny, too. Miguel's fits and Miguel's clothes and Miguel's car crashes. Clearly, he didn't like him, but he was also this incredibly non-judgemental person. In a very laconic way, he would say, "Oh, yes, Miguel's car – this one's gone now." Or it was, "Miguel's six new suits are very nice," but not in a jealous way. It was never, "I can't believe my mother keeps buying cars for this ridiculous, spoiled, South American gigolo." It was always ironical and then with that great laugh.'

Though she was still only sixteen and not yet wise to the ways of the world, she formed the impression very quickly that her boyfriend's stepfather was gay. 'One just felt that because you had to spend hours admiring his clothes. And he was always saying things like, "You must wear the emerald green tonight, Oonagh." He'd sort of choose what she wore. And she loved that.'

In fact, Miguel had a seamstress's dummy made to his wife's precise measurements, so he could work on clothes for her whenever business took him away from Paris. 'He takes my body with him everywhere he goes,' Oonagh told the *Daily Mirror* in 1960. 'When he has an odd moment or two, he works on one of his creations. He designs everything I wear.'

Melissa found the dynamic between them compelling to watch. 'I couldn't say whether she was in love with him,' she said. 'I was a sixteen-year-old girl with no experience. But she certainly adored him, because she never refused him anything. He would come to her and he would say, "I want to go gambling. Give me some money," or something like that. And she'd just open her wallet and give him some money and then he'd disappear into the night, probably to look for boys.'

·

In October 1960, during a visit to New York with his wife, Miguel outlined his ambitious plans to *Women's Wear Daily*, the international fashion bible. He was planning to go into business with Jacqueline, Comtesse de Ribes, who had acquired a three-storey building at 55 avenue George V to house his Maison Ferreras. At around the same time, he told the *Sunday Express* that his wife was 'not involved in the new venture, either financially or in any other way'. It was yet another of Miguel's outrageous fictions. Maison Ferreras was established through the medium of a Canadian company in which his wife had a five-million-dollar holding. Oonagh wasn't just involved in Maison Ferreras – as would become clear in time, Oonagh *was* Maison Ferreras.

On a visit to New York that autumn, she was content to play the part of the supportive, older wife on the arm of the hot-tempered, young dress designer, whose genius would soon be apparent to the world. She stood beside him, beaming proudly, while he announced to the American press that Maison Ferreras would present its first collection in the spring of 1961.

While in New York, Oonagh got to visit Caroline Blackwood, who had married the composer Israel Citkowitz and had just given birth to her first child, a daughter named Natalya. Oonagh also attended the triumphant opening night of Brendan Behan's *The Hostage* at the Cort Theatre on Broadway, with Garech, who flew to New York for the occasion.

Tara remained in Paris, in the care of Deacon, who had returned to Paris as his tutor and was preparing him for his O-levels. Dom had elicited a promise from his son that he would sit his exams the following June, though Tara continued to keep essentially nocturnal hours, rarely going to bed before five o'clock in the morning and never surfacing before one o'clock in the afternoon.

Inevitably, given how pervasive drugs were in the jazz clubs, it wasn't long before Tara discovered for the first time the pleasures of getting high. Pills and dope were part of the modern jazz scene in Paris. For the equivalent of fifteen bob, or 75p, you could buy a *mille*, a matchbook filled with some illicit delight that could be put into a cigarette. Tara smoked his first joint in Paris. Later still, he discovered poppers, or amyl nitrate, which were enormously popular in the clubs of Paris. They always sent Tara into convulsions of laughter.

In December 1960, he returned to Ireland with Oonagh and Miguel for Christmas. Brendan Behan was back in the house as the toast of the Great White Way. He had fallen off the wagon in spectacular fashion in New York, but he was back on the dry again for now. It would be his final sober Christmas.

One thing that was clear to everyone at Luggala that Christmas was the extent to which Tara and Garech's lives had diverged. Tara adored his older brother and the feeling was mutual, but their lifestyles couldn't have been more different.

'There were six years between them, but they could have been from different generations,' said Nicholas Gormanston, who was invited to Luggala as Garech's friend but soon discovered he had far more in common with his jazz- and blues-loving little brother.

'At Luggala, you had a very straightforward formal dinner with his mother and everybody sitting down in dinner jackets. And Tara usually had some pretty girls over from England. And then, after dinner was finished, Tara and Garech would go their separate ways. Garech got into his Aran sweater and his Donegal tweed trousers and he went, with his little crowd, to a cottage in the grounds, which was designed like a Famine-era peasant's cottage, with a cauldron over a fire, and people listened to traditional Irish music and danced. Tara got into his Levi's and he went into his own private sitting room, which had an old-fashioned gramophone in it, and he'd listen to jazz and blues and drink Cuba Libre, which was white rum and Coca-Cola – absolutely disgusting – and smoke the most wonderful dope.

'Even though I was the same age as Garech, I was far more interested in music from America and that's what Tara had. I liked black blues music because I was brought up in the States. Then, in art school, I got into jazz. I said to Tara that I liked John Coltrane. He said, "No, no – you've *got* to listen to Ray Charles!" And, of course, he was right!'

By the age of fifteen, Tara had learned a great many things, one of which was how to roll a good joint. 'He introduced me to Durban Poison, which was grass that was imported in sherry bottles. It smelled of sherry. We smoked it that Christmas at Luggala. After Oonagh's gracious dinner, we got stoned on it in Tara's room, listening to rhythm and blues.

'He was terrific company. He swore like a Glasgow docker as well. There was a famous story about him in Claridge's as a child when he caused a scene by shouting, "I asked for cold vichyssoise, not hot, you cunt!" People dropped their spoons. And of course when they looked around, there was this kid who looked like something from the Westminster Choir. I don't know where he picked it up from. I expect it was Brendan Behan.'

Because he came across as so worldly wise, there was a tendency to forget sometimes that Tara was still essentially a child. When they returned to Paris in January, he badgered his mother to take him to see Alfred Hitchcock's *Psycho*, a movie so terrifying that there were reports of people fainting while watching the iconic shower scene. Because it carried an adult rating, Oonagh had to smuggle Tara into the cinema under her coat. 'The movie started and very quickly he discovered that he didn't like it very much,' according to Tara's son, Dorian, who heard the story from his grandmother. 'He said, "Mummy, I think I'd like to go," so they stood up to leave. But on the way out, there was all this booing and hissing from the other cinemagoers, who didn't approve of my grandmother bringing a child in to see it.'

Naturally, Oonagh thought it hilarious.

Oonagh's main focus in the early months of 1961 was helping Miguel to get Maison Ferreras up and running. Jacqueline de Ribes dropped out of the picture for reasons that were never clear and Miguel failed to present a spring collection as promised. Instead, he and Oonagh spent the early months of 1961 searching for premises with a prestigious address that matched his view of himself as the next Christian Dior. The search was suspended for a week in February, when Oonagh rushed back to England to visit Gay, who had fractured his spine for the second time in his career when he was thrown from a horse at Hurst Park. At the age of thirty-one, Oonagh's eldest son, who was preparing to ride in the 1961 Grand National, was told by doctors never to race again – advice he would ignore for another four years.

While Oonagh and Miguel were busy with the fashion business, Tara was left mostly to his own devices and he continued his rounds of the city's jazz dives, though this time without his girlfriend. Melissa ignored Mademoiselle Anita's injunction to stay away from her *mal élevé* English friends and she was expelled.

'It was referred to as being sacked,' she recalled. 'I was sacked from Mademoiselle Anita's. I was coming home at four o'clock in the morning and probably not being very attentive in school. And because I was sacked from Mademoiselle Anita's, the admiral's widow with whom I was staying as a paying guest, sacked me as well. So I was sent back to England in disgrace. And I'll never forget the sadness I felt being parted from Tara and from Mark.

'When you're young, and you've grown up, first in the countryside, then at a posh boarding school with lots of other people from exactly the same background as you, well, your life has been rather sheltered. So when, at the age of sixteen, you meet extraordinary people, you think that there are probably hundreds of people in the world just like that, because you don't have a context. Tara and Mark were the most glamorous and extraordinary pair of boys I'd ever met. And I thought, oh, this must be what it's like to be a grown-up. Then you go out into the world and you realize that people like Tara and Mark were so extraordinarily rare that you were probably never going to meet anyone like them again. And I never did.'

•

The peer's son who refused to go to Eton remained a source of fascination for the British and Irish press. At sixteen, Tara was a media celebrity in his own right and newspapers carried occasional updates on his father's efforts to get him to sit his exams. In the summer of 1961, it was reported that he had taken his O-levels. Whether this was true or not remains a subject of conjecture. None of his family or friends can recall him ever sitting exams or receiving results. But Tara told a journalist that he did, while describing how difficult the experience had been for him.

'It's been pretty awful,' he told the *Dublin Evening Mail*. 'I've had to be in bed by nine o'clock most nights and ten at the very latest. I've hardly been at a party for weeks, but now, thank goodness, I can relax and enjoy myself for a while.'

Asked about the prospect of going to university one day, the old-headed sixteen-year-old added, without any hint of irony: 'I've lived long enough to know that in this life nothing is certain.'

It was a subject upon which his stepfather Miguel could expound at length. But, for the moment, things appeared to be going well for Paris fashion's newest arriviste. By the summer of 1961, he had found the premises from which he would launch his couture empire, at 11 rue du Faubourg Saint-Honoré. The location was a statement of Miguel's ambition. Virtually every major global fashion house in the world had a presence on the street.

Miguel's first Paris salon was situated directly opposite Lanvin-Castillo and a catwalk's length away from the offices of French *Vogue*. If he was going to fail as a couturier, it wasn't going to be for the want of being noticed.

Oonagh paid to have the retail unit fitted out in a style that was in character with the address, decorated in lush caramel and white silk and lit by an exquisite crystal chandelier, her gift to her husband to congratulate him on his arrival as a member of the Chambre Syndicale de la Haute Couture. At the back of the salon, she installed an indoor tropical garden, behind whose fronds – according to a *New York Times* article – 'women sew to music'.

The outlay didn't stop there. Next, Oonagh hired Denise Hivet, the former private secretary to the Duchess of Windsor, to help publicize the new salon. The media were invited to view the place at the beginning of Paris Fashion Week. A photographer from the weekly magazine *Paris Match* captured several images of Tara, dressed all in black – a sign of Glen's growing influence over him – with calf-high cowboy boots and a cigarette glowing between his fingers, while his friend, Charmian Scott, modelled a number of Maison Ferreras designs in the light of the magnificent chandelier.

In case any of the reporters present missed the great historical significance of the moment, Miguel was on hand to remind them that he was the first American couturier to open a design house in the French capital since Main Rousseau Bocher in 1929. Then he proceeded to describe the way American women dressed as *démodé*, or out of fashion. 'Society women who spend several hundred dollars on a ready-made dress have no imagination,' he was quoted as saying in the *New York Times*. 'They are lazy.'

His clothes, he told reporters, would be an emphatic rejection of what he called the new fashion. He spoke often about his loathing for the androgyny that was creeping into women's and men's clothing at the beginning of the 1960s. A girl should not expect a boy to court her when she's wearing blue jeans, he liked to say. For a young designer, on the threshold of a decade that would revolutionize the way both sexes dressed, his instincts seemed woefully out of step with the times.

On 28 July 1961, with the last coat of paint barely dry on the salon, Miguel presented his first Paris collection. He was true to his promise that his clothes would represent a return to old-fashioned values, with a heavy emphasis on plastron fronts, architectural seaming, tunic overskirts, slightly raised waistlines and sleeves puffed to the elbow. The collection reflected his love, too, for full-length evening dresses, which, he said, made women feel more feminine and men feel more masculine. One of the few genuine innovations was a round-toe women's shoe with a medium Cuban heel, a nod to his claimed heritage, while Irish tweed was also a theme, a gesture to the woman who was, after all, paying for all of this.

That night, he, along with Oonagh, Garech and Tara, celebrated with a champagne reception for 350 guests aboard a Bâteau Mouche on the River Seine. The invitees included Jeannette Edris, the American socialite who was married to the politician and philanthropist Winthrop Rockefeller, and the Marchioness of Queensbury. Fireworks spelled out Miguel's name in the night sky over Paris. Garech would remember the event primarily for its vulgarity. 'In those days, the general opinion was that the Bâteaux Mouches destroyed the Seine,' he said. 'It demonstrates Miguel's bad taste in some sense that he chose to have his party on one of them.'

The reaction to his collection was mixed. In some newspapers, he was hailed as the new Balenciaga; in others, he was dismissed as a simple and unimaginative fabric cutter using his rich wife's money to indulge his dreams.

The most important question was contained in the subtext of most of the coverage: what was all of this costing Oonagh?

'A vast amount of money,' according to Garech. Some reports suggested that it may have been as much as £6 million by the time the shutters were finally pulled down on the place. 'For which she got no benefit or pleasure,' he added.

•

Tara had started driving Miguel's cars. No lessons. No driving licence. No insurance. It may have been a small act of rebellion against the man he refused to regard as his stepfather. More likely, the intention was to impress Glen, who knew everything there was to know about cars, except how to drive one. It started that summer, in Sainte-Maxime, on the French Riviera, where Tara was holidaying with Oonagh and Miguel – a few weeks after the launch of Maison Ferreras. He invited Glen and Serena to come and stay.

'The thing about Tara was that you never thought about how old he was,' Glen remembered, 'so it never crossed your mind that he was only sixteen and shouldn't have been behind the wheel of a car. The first night I got there, I remember he was showing me around his mother's place. We were looking in the garage and there was an Aurelia Spyder B24 in there and also a Chevy Corvette, which was Miguel's. The keys were in it, so we just jumped in and off we went. It was automatic, very squishy, great engine, though not state of the art steering-wise. But Tara could handle it, even at that age. He was what I would call a natural driver.

'He'd take the Lincoln Continentals out, too. Bear in mind, they were very large cars: you're talking about the kind of car that Kennedy was shot in. They were easy enough to drive if you were in Paris, where it was all wide boulevards and straight lines. But in the south of France, it was all twists and turns. But even going downhill, at eighty miles per hour, Tara could handle those big cars.'

He had the same fearlessness as his half-brother, Gay, who by that time was riding horses again in defiance of doctors' orders. Serena remembered Tara driving a speedboat on adrenalin-fuelled trips to Saint-Raphaël, fourteen miles up the Mediterranean coast, thrilled by the danger of it. 'He used to cross the bay in the dark,' she recalled, 'which was such a dangerous thing to do. I've always been scared of water, so I'd go in the car and I'd arrange to meet him in Saint-Raphaël. Tara was like one of those fearless toddlers. He was completely unafraid of anything.'

Several of his friends visited him in France that summer,

including Nicholas Gormanston. They went to the Antibes Jazz Festival. 'We saw Ray Charles play,' Nicholas remembered. 'The man was strung out on heroin. He had to be carried onto the stage by two minders and placed in a sitting position at the piano. Then he started moving: you know, he did that nautical roll thing. Then he started to play. It was extraordinary to watch.'

Tara returned to Ireland for the Dublin Horse Show in August 1961. The social diarists couldn't help but comment on the world of difference that had opened up between Tara and his brother. On the night the festival started, Garech was at a *fleadh ceoil* in Miltown Malbay, County Clare, according to the *Dublin Evening Mail*, and dancing the Walls of Limerick. Meanwhile, Tara – 'resplendent in tight trousers, an electric-blue shirt and a maroon tie' – spent the night touring the round of parties and embassy balls with his date, Camilla Wigan, an English aristocrat and debutante.

The new decade was two years old, yet the Fifties were only just beginning to cede to what would be remembered as the Sixties. Fashions were changing, the traditional giving way to the new. The conflict between conservative and modern values was neatly encapsulated in the moment when Tara's date was refused entry to the Kildare Hunt Cotton Dance in Dublin's Shelbourne Hotel. She and her friend, Camilla Rumbold, were deemed to be improperly dressed. 'I'm not particularly worried,' Tara told London's *Evening Standard*, before the three headed off into the night. 'But it seems the people on the door did not like my friends wearing slacks.'

David Mlinaric, future friend of the Stones and interior decorator to the stars, sampled the hospitality at Luggala for the first time that week at the invitation of his friend, Garech.

'It was always this mix of people,' he said, 'which is what made those parties so interesting. Oonagh understood that. And she had this thing about not being boring. In London, if you went to dinner in Eaton Square or something, I just remember walking around the square a couple of times to get my courage up before ringing the bell, because it was so dry and boring and the people were sort of formal and tense all the time.

'English life at that point was very hierarchic. And very, very grey. And I was very shy of it. I think most people who'd been to boarding school came out pretty shy on the whole. I mean, we were extremely well educated, but there wasn't much in the way of knowing how the world worked or how social life worked. There were all sorts of restrictions or things to make you feel inhibited. But there was none of that at Luggala.'

Candida Betjeman was back for more that August in spite of her mother's continuing misgivings about the Guinnesses and their reputedly loose ways. She could see how much Tara had grown up in the previous twelve months: from giggling boy to switched-on teenager. 'We smoked a joint,' she remembered. 'I'm sure it was the first joint I ever smoked. It was with Tara and it was on that louche weekend at Luggala. So it turned out that my mum was quite right!'

•

Miguel was undeterred by the modest notices his first collection received and was soon talking about opening a second salon in England. In September 1961, Oonagh, Miguel and Tara were back in London, toasting the success of Maison Ferreras with a party in Claridge's. The suite that Oonagh booked for the event was so full, the newspapers reported, that guests had to shout to be heard. They included Caroline and Israel, as well as Oonagh's cousin, Lady Jeanne Campbell, who was there with her future husband, Norman Mailer. Also there was Talitha Pol, an attractive, Indonesian-born socialite, who, like Tara, would go on to become one of the 'faces' of Swinging London, a friend of Mick Jagger and the wife of John Paul Getty Jr, heir to what was believed to be the biggest privately held fortune in the world.

A journalist from the *Evening News* likened Miguel to the Communist revolutionary who, two years earlier, had seized control of what Miguel still claimed was the country of his birth. 'When I told my Cuban host,' the newspaper's social diarist reported, 'that he has been described as the Castro of *haute couture*, he laughed and replied, "Castro is top man at the moment!"'

Miguel must have felt that he was, too.

When the summer of 1961 ended, Tara returned to Paris for what would be his final months at the rue de l'Université. Mark Palmer had left to go to Oxford, but September brought a new wave of upper-class English girls to the city's finishing schools. At sixteen, he was now a year closer in age to the students at Mademoiselle Anita's and Madame Fleurie's. Totally at ease around women, he toured the various schools visiting girls he'd met that summer on the London social circuit.

It was at Madame Fleurie's that he became friends with Jacquetta Lampson, the daughter of Sir Miles Lampson, the former British Ambassador to Egypt who had overseen the abdication of King Farouk. Jacquetta, a society beauty who would become a muse for Lucian Freud, had been at boarding school with Tara's old girlfriend, Melissa. 'He came around one day to see someone else,' Jacquetta remembered. 'I think it was Sophie Litchfield, whom he was friends with in London. Anyway, he swooped us up and we went out that evening and it was the beginning of the whole fun time we had in Paris.'

They followed the tramlines around the city that Tara had laid down with his other friends. As much as he loved blues and modern jazz, he remained partial to pop music. He still had his boxes of 45s and his portable record player.

Noticing how enamoured she was by it, Tara told her to keep it. 'He just said, "Oh, you like it? You can have it," and he just gave it to me, which was very much Tara. People looking at him from the outside might have thought he was spoiled because he had absolutely everything. But he wasn't corrupted by it. He'd give everything away.'

He took her to the Blue Note and they tried to affect the cool poses of the jazz players.

On those nights when Jacquetta and her friends couldn't escape from the finishing school, they crept downstairs, slipped the catch on the door and smuggled Tara into their dorm room. 'Which was absolutely not allowed, but Madame Fleurie would be sleeping. We did things like the Ouija board, which Tara also introduced us to. We would get terribly spooked as the glass started moving. We never knew who was doing it. I suspect it was Tara. But as the glass whizzed across the table, we were absolutely excited by it but also scared out of our wits.

'Then one of us would sneak down to the fridge, where we'd hidden some beers, and we would make a night of it. It was terribly naughty. And poor Madame Fleurie. She must have had a terribly difficult job, because she was taking all of this money from our parents and, once Tara entered our lives, we were just living it up in the most spectacular way. And shortly after we left Paris, the school actually finished up. So Tara played probably a significant part in bringing Madame Fleurie's to a close!'

By the autumn of 1961, his mother's marriage was once again in trouble. It's conceivable that Tara spent so much time at Madame Fleurie's to avoid going back to the flat and witnessing another of Oonagh and Miguel's scenes. 'They would have these tremendously passionate rows,' Jacquetta remembered, 'where shoes were flying across this wonderfully ornate, rather marvellous drawing room. And Tara would just be there, smoking, saying, "Oh, don't worry. A shoe or two, that's fine."'

At that time, Oonagh was drinking heavily. 'A bottle of Haig Dimple whisky a day,' according to John Montague, who saw her regularly in Paris during that period. 'It was on the table in the morning.'

Her drinking reflected her increasing unhappiness. The business was haemorrhaging money. According to Garech, she had also found out about Miguel's secret sexual life, but she was by now massively invested in him, if not emotionally, then financially.

'There was also the problem that she couldn't prove adultery,' Garech said, 'because he only ever went to bed with men. If she could catch him in a hotel room with a woman, then it was an open and shut case. But if he was in a hotel room with a man, he could argue that they were sharing the cost of a room. It wasn't considered irrefutable evidence that they were having a sexual affair, which it would have been if she'd caught him in a room with a woman. That was the law.'

1. Castle Mac Garrett, two miles south of Claremorris, County Mayo, where Tara spent his early childhood.

2. Luggala, the 'fairytale' house at the bottom of a Wicklow valley, a wedding gift to Tara's mother, Oonagh, from her father, Ernest Guinness, in 1936.

3. Tara's mother, then Oonagh Kindersley, painted by the royal portrait artist Philip de László. The portrait was commissioned by her first husband, stockbroker Philip Kindersley, to celebrate her twenty-first birthday.

4. Tara's father, Dominick, Lord Oranmore and Browne, at the Coronation of George VI at Westminster Abbey, 1936.

5 & 6. Oonagh was considered one of the most beautiful young women in England. She appeared regularly on the cover of *The Tatler* and *The Bystander*.

7. Oonagh with Gay and Tessa Kindersley, her son and daughter from her first marriage. Tessa was one of her three children to die young and in tragic circumstances.

8. Oonagh holding Tara at Castle Mac Garrett on the day of his christening in 1945. Dom is third from the left, his face partly obscured.

9. Garech Browne, holding Tara, the baby brother he adored.

10. Gay, Tessa, Tara and Garech at Castle Mac Garrett, County Mayo, 1945.

11. After the end of her second marriage, Oonagh retreated to Luggala, where her drawing room became a kind of literary salon in the 1950s. Brendan Behan and his wife Beatrice were among the regular guests.

12. Oonagh with Miguel Ferreras, the couturier with the shadowy Nazi past, whom she married in New York in February 1958, just weeks after they first met.

13. Oonagh and Tara in Ravello, Italy, with Oonagh's friend, the movie director John Huston. At the time, he was making *Beat the Devil*, starring Humphrey Bogart, Peter Lorre and Gina Lollobrigida.

14. Tara in Venice in 1953, aged eight. 'He looked like something from the Westminster Choir,' said his friend Nicholas Gormanston.

15. *Below, left.* Tara, aged thirteen, in the courtyard at Luggala, taken by Lucy Lambton from a guest-room window.

16. *Below, right.* Twelve-year-old Tara in Venice, where his mother took a palazzo for a month every summer.

Lucy Lambton
and
Tara Browne
135 Rue de l'université
Paris VII

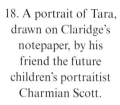

17. Tara and his friend Lucy Lambton in Paris. 'Tara was different to other boys of his age,' she said. 'There was a magic about him.'

CLARIDGE'S

TELEGRAMS Claridge's London   TELEPHONE Mayfair 8860

18. A portrait of Tara, drawn on Claridge's notepaper, by his friend the future children's portraitist Charmian Scott.

19. Oonagh and a teenage Tara at the opening of Maison Ferreras on the rue du Fauborg Saint-Honoré, Paris, 1961.

20. Tara in Maison Ferreras, Paris, in July 1961. He had started to dress all in black, influenced by his new mod friend, Glen Kidston.

Jacquetta sensed a loneliness in Tara that autumn, as his mother's time was increasingly taken up with her foundering marriage and business. 'Oonagh clearly adored Tara,' she said, 'as he adored her, but in those days people didn't have the same obsession with their children as we do now. Oonagh would lay on everything for us. I remember she used to say, "You *must* have a nice time," and that was always the priority. At the same time, Tara was ignored at times. Oonagh and Miguel were very much getting on with their lives.'

Then an incident happened, which, according to Tara's wife, Nicki, caused a fracture in his relationship with his mother. On 17 October 1961, Paris exploded in violence, after the French police opened fire on a demonstration of 30,000 Algerians who were marching for independence. At least forty demonstrators were killed and the riots that resulted continued for days. Oonagh and Miguel were temporarily out of town and they left Tara in the care of Deacon, who had popped out just before the rioting started and was unable to get back to the flat. Tara lay in his bed, according to Nicki, listening to the sound of bomb blasts and gunfire outside. 'It was in cloud cuckoo land they lived,' she said

When they returned to Ireland at the end of 1961 for the traditional Christmas at Luggala, Tara had made up his mind that he wasn't going back to Paris. He didn't wish to be a witness to the slow unravelling of his mother's third marriage. He preferred to be in London around Glen, Mark and the rest of his friends. Uncannily intuitive, perhaps he sensed, too, something in the air over Albion. It may not have been obvious to many people at the start of January 1962, but the city was about to become the cultural focus of the world again, the capital of cool. And Tara was about to become one of its best-known faces.

7: VENUS IN BLUE JEANS

London had no idea what was about to hit it. The decade may have been two years old, but the revolution in music, fashion, attitudes and behaviour that would come to be defined as the Sixties was not much in evidence in January 1962, when Tara moved into the flat his father shared with Sally in Eaton Square, Belgravia.

London in the 1950s was a bleak and sunless place; in 1953, a full eight years after the defeat of the Nazis, the population were still eating rationed food, relieving themselves in outdoor loos and negotiating their way around the bomb craters left by the Luftwaffe.

'You'd see houses that were blown wide open,' remembered David Mlinaric, who was at art college at the time. 'The top or the side of the building would be missing. You could see a fireplace up there with a little armchair next to it and the rest of the house was gone. Those kind of things were a feature of London until well into the 1950s.'

Contributing to the general mood of greyness, a thick fog – the infamous 'pea soup' – regularly enveloped the city, even bringing the traffic to a standstill. 'I remember buses being abandoned on Oxford Street because the driver couldn't see the road six feet in front of him,' recalled Michael Rainey, a fashion designer who would help define the Sixties look. 'You'd have to get off and somehow feel your way home.'

In a philosophical sense, the people of the city were similarly uncertain of their bearings. In the days when Britain's empire had covered one quarter of the planet, London could lay claim to being the capital of the world. In the wake of the Second World War, the country was broke; worse, it had lost its relevance in the wider

world. Eclipsed by the United States in respect of its global influence, economically frozen out of the Europe it helped to liberate,
and with its colonies falling away one by one, Britannia – and its
bomb-scarred capital – was coming to terms with the sad reality
that it no longer ruled the waves. 'It was the whole end of empire
thing,' said David Mlinaric. 'India went and that was the big one.
And then after Suez, you knew that the entire political landscape
had changed. I think people's confidence was pretty bashed up.'

But that was about to be swept away by the coming youth
quake. By the time Tara came to live with Dom and Sally, the city
was on the cusp of a cultural and social renaissance that would
make it once again the focus of the world.

The economic roots of Swinging London were in the late-
1950s financial boom that moved Prime Minister Harold
Macmillan to inform the people of Britain that they'd never had
it so good. From the debris of the past, a new London began to
emerge that was different to the one that *Time* magazine once
described as a 'horizontal city with a skyline dominated by Mary
Poppins chimney pots'. Shining steel and glass structures ascended
from amongst the charred remnants of Britain's war with Germany as retail and services began to supersede manufacturing as
the main source of employment in the city. And as the topography
of the city changed, so too did the lifestyles of its citizenry. The
office replaced the factory as the main place of work for a new and
aspirant middle class who had money in their pockets and no war
to fight.

As Britain dared to dream of a happier and more prosperous
future, there was suddenly a new focus on youth. The babies of the
Blitz era had become teenagers: a phrase not even recognized a
generation earlier, when adolescence was a sort of social purgatory
to be endured between childhood and adulthood. Now, they were
the architects of the country's future. Compulsory military service
was abolished at the end of 1960, an enormously significant
moment in the making of the Sixties. For young men of Tara's age,
it was as if some hideous grey rock face had fallen away, offering
them a clearer sight of their life ahead. They no longer had to

follow in the footsteps of their fathers; they had the chance to define themselves on their own terms. The young ones – as Cliff Richard sang in his January 1962 paean to youth – didn't need to be afraid. Unlike their parents, they could afford to have educational and career aspirations – and they had money.

'At the start of the Sixties, London had this cloak of dullness about it,' recalled Michael Rainey. 'If you were rich, you went to the 400 Club or you had dinner at the Dorchester. But there wasn't a whole lot going on for anyone else, especially if you were young. Then the Sixties came along. There were suddenly a lot more young people and they were employed. They could buy records. They could buy clothes. Young people started to think and act independently. There was a huge energy released.'

In the mid to late 1950s, young London trendies with money in their pockets had gravitated towards Soho, to the Italian-style coffee bars that were suddenly springing up like mushrooms overnight. There, teenagers, who were still too young for the pub, could drink tarmacadam-thick espressos, listen to live jazz and show off their new clothes with the studied coolness of Fellini characters. The new vogue for coffee bars and the *la dolce vita* trend for kicking back and watching the world go by was an important trigger for the lifestyle changes that were coming in the 1960s. And, like so many of the elements that made London suddenly interesting again, its roots were in immigration.

After the war, the Italian government allowed young men to defer their military service until the age of thirty-six, on condition that they could find work abroad. The United States had imposed restrictions on immigration, so London became the destination for a generation of young Italians who didn't want to put on a uniform and play at being soldiers. They brought with them many of the tastes that became staples of life for London's youth – pasta, an interest in men's fashion, and those dainty little cups of steamed coffee that seemed to be so conducive to sitting around and shooting the breeze. In 1953, the first Gaggia espresso machine was imported into London. By the early 1960s, coffee bars were huge business – and even the landed gentry were trying to grab a piece of the action. With money from the Guinness family trust, two of Tara's half-brothers, Gay and Dominick, opened one in Paddington called the Two Bare Feet. The name came from a line in 'Star of the County Down', an Irish ballad that Gay loved. 'We hired a pastry chef,' remembered Dominick, 'and a black singer named Mundo. It was fine until Lucian Freud started to turn up with all of his criminal friends at eleven o'clock at night. They used to start terrible fights. In the end, we had to close it down.'

•

After arriving in London, Tara quickly picked up his friendship with Glen Kidston and joined the scene around Soho, which had become a hub for young, fashion-conscious mods.

The imperative for them was looking sharp – working hard all week to buy nice threads, then spending Saturday afternoon posing in the window of the latest, coolest coffee shop. Glen and his crowd weren't much into alcohol. They despised the drinkers, Mark Palmer remembered, considering them old hat.

As far as their personal tastes went, they enjoyed rhythm and blues as well as modern jazz, they buzzed around on scooters and they bought their garb from John Stephen on Carnaby Street, once a little-known throughway, which had become a cultish place to shop among the new breed of straight young men who cared about how they looked.

Carnaby Street was an unlikely birthplace for the look that defined the Swinging London man about town. Before the 1960s, the street was a forgettable succession of trade premises, workrooms, a tobacconist and a pub called the Shakespeare. It was situated within easy walking distance of Mayfair, Piccadilly and Soho, close to the London Palladium and the shops of Regent Street and Oxford Street, yet the vast majority of Londoners couldn't have picked it off a map.

That it became the epicentre of an explosion in men's fashion that reverberated around the world was down to one man: John Stephen, a gay, former welder's apprentice from Glasgow, who had arrived in London in 1952 with a James Dean quiff, £13, and a head full of ideas for revolutionizing the way men dressed. He worked in various clothes shops around Soho that specialized in the Continental – meaning Italian – look, and catered to a largely 'theatrical', or gay, clientele. With his partner, Bill Franks, he saved up enough money to open his own workshop at 19 Beak Street, at the southern end of Carnaby Street, recognizing the commercial potential in straight, young mods who wanted to wear the kind of clobber their fathers wouldn't have been seen dead in.

His plan was to become a supplier to several of the shops where he'd worked, but one day in 1957, while he was out at lunch, an electric heater set fire to some curtains and his workroom was destroyed. The landlord offered him alternative premises at number 5 Carnaby Street, a ground-floor unit with the advantage of having a giant window in which to display his wares and the opportunity to retail them himself. The only drawback was that few people ever walked past. That didn't remain a problem for long. Very quickly, all of London's young Vespa-riding dudes were seeking out his shop, His Clothes.

Stephen's outré fashion sense and his impeccable eye for cut and detail made his jackets, shirts and trousers must-have items among the wannabe 'faces' of late 1950s and early 1960s London. He and Franks used the money they made to lease even more unit space on the street, using the windows to showcase the new styles they turned out on a weekly, even daily, basis. Shirts in pink and lilac. Moccasin shoes. Brightly coloured denim hipsters. Reefer jackets. Yachting caps. Towelling shirts. Roll-neck sweaters. Sky-blue Italian jeans. Horizontally striped matelot T-shirts. Elephant-cord trousers. Mohair sweaters, fashioned from a rug – when they sold one to Cliff Richard, they couldn't deal with the sudden demand.

Meanwhile, further west in what was once regarded as the sleepy, riverside village of Chelsea, something very similar was happening in women's fashion. The bellwether for this revolution was John Stephen's friend Mary Quant, the daughter of two schoolteachers, who invented a way of dressing that defined what it was to be a cool and carefree young woman at the dawn of the beat boom.

Quant was married to Alexander Plunkett-Greene, a blue-blooded, pyjamas-in-public-wearing eccentric, whom she met while they were studying at Goldsmith's College of Art in southeast London. The couple became part of a circle of rich and restless creative types living out an extended art school adolescence in and around the King's Road. The so-called Chelsea Set was a down-the-generations echo of the Bright Young People: artistic, bohemian rich kids who were just as determinedly silly as their forebears and similarly inclined towards outrageous, headline-grabbing stunts.

The window of Bazaar, Quant's Chelsea boutique, became a sort of exhibition space for her latest twist on fashion, with rubberneckers gathering three deep on the pavement outside for the opportunity to be shocked. She did things that were truly subversive, refashioning children's clothes, even men's underwear, into clothes for women that were interesting to look at and easy to wear.

Before long, she was flogging her designs as quickly as she could run them up. In early 1962 she received her first order from J. C. Penney, the US retail behemoth. At twenty-eight, the career and reputation of the woman who would go on to create the most iconic fashion symbol of the decade – the miniskirt – was about to go global.

London hadn't yet started to swing, but a revolution in taste and style was being cooked up in quiet corners of the city in those early months of 1962. Musically, Londoners were still moving to an American beat. The British pop charts were still dominated by acts like Elvis Presley, Bobby Darin, Neil Sedaka and Frankie Valli & The Four Seasons, or English knock-offs, like Cliff Richard, Billy Fury and Adam Faith. Musically, it still felt like the 1950s. But that was about to change. While Quant and Stephen were busy setting what would become the aesthetic template for the Sixties, Mick Jagger, Keith Richards and Dick Taylor, three members of a teenage garage band that played American rhythm and blues covers, crossed the city from Dartford to take in a gig at the Ealing Jazz Club. While they were there, they watched a young man from Cheltenham who called himself Elmo Lewis play slide guitar. Blown away by his version of Elmore James's 'Dust My Broom', they stuck around afterwards to say hello. Elmo's real name, it turned out, was Brian Jones and he had plans to form his own band. He said he would consider letting them join.

Around the same time, two hundred miles up the M6, the four members of the rock and roll and skiffle band formerly known as The Quarrymen were about to receive some bad news. Following an audition in West Hampstead on New Year's Day, Decca Records had decided to pass on The Beatles. 'Guitar groups are on the way out,' Dick Rowe, the head of A&R at the label, reportedly told Brian Epstein, the twenty-seven-year-old record-shop manager who was stewarding their career. Shattered, Epstein left Rowe's office in London for the return train to Lime Street station, to consider his next move for John, Paul, George and the soon-to-depart Pete.

Meanwhile, James Bond, a fictional secret-service agent created by Ian Fleming, the foreign editor of the *Sunday Times*, was about to enjoy his big-screen debut in *Dr No*, the first of a series of movies that would establish a new ideal of heroism for Britons still coming to terms with their place on the margins of the new geopolitical order.

It wouldn't have been evident, even to the most intuitive social observer, but all of the elements of Swinging London were about to come together, with music, fashion and 007 – no scruff himself – setting the new cultural agenda.

•

While young mods weren't big drinkers, their poison, other than espresso, was speed, usually in the form of Purple Hearts or Black Bombers, which were not only legal but unavoidable once you graduated from the coffee shops to the nightclub scene on Wardour Street. Soho's clubs, which had once hosted live jazz acts and even swing bands, were suddenly vibrating to the new American R&B sound that allowed smartly dressed young dudes like Tara to get their groove on without the hindrance of a dance partner.

Wardour Street had the Flamingo and La Discotheque. In Ham Yard, there was Scene, which was run by Ronan O'Rahilly, the young Irish music entrepreneur, who was in the process of setting up the offshore pirate station Radio Caroline. But most famous of all was the Marquee, a giant, cavernous space below a cinema on Oxford Street, which would help make the careers of some of the best-known bands of the era.

Dance floors began to feature mirrored glass, so that all the wired-up, smartly dressed peacocks could check themselves out while they performed the Shake, the Block and the Mashed Potato, not to mention the dance that was sending Britain's vicars into a tizzy in the spring of 1962. They called it the Twist.

The music newspaper *Melody Maker* had carried a feature about the new American dance at the end of 1961, describing, in dry language, its sexually suggestive component parts of rotating hips and pelvic thrusts. The article was headlined 'The Most Vulgar Dance Invented', and it wasn't long before it was being denounced from church pulpits as an affront to common decency, a righteousness that seems almost comical now in view of what the rest of the decade had in store.

As with most things that were new and carried a whiff of danger, Tara got there way ahead of the crowd. He'd discovered Chubby Checker in Paris almost two years earlier, when 'The Twist' was among a box of new releases he'd ordered from America. Now, as the nightclub scene took off, there were umpteen songs inspired by the new dance craze. Sam Cooke was twisting the night away, The Isley Brothers were twisting and shouting and Chubby Checker was twisting again like he did last summer.

When he returned to Ireland for Easter week in 1962, Tara's mother had a surprise for him. 'She flew this chap over from New York,' remembered Nicholas Gormanston, who had joined Tara's Soho circle. 'He may have been involved with Chubby Checker's band, actually. There was certainly some connection between them. And he was hired to teach Tara the Twist.'

The instructor outstayed his welcome at Luggala, however, breaking the house rule that guests must never be boring. 'He was a frightful man,' Nicholas recalled. 'A bunch of us went for a climb to the top of the Fancy, which is the steep mountain that overlooks the lake at Luggala. He tagged along with us. We were coming down the rocky way and the chap said, "I can't go down that way. If I broke my ankle, I'd be out of business." In other words, no more twisting. Tara, who'd probably learned everything he needed from him at that stage, said, "Sorry, old chap," and he left him there! He had a wicked sense of humour, like his mother. The poor man's probably still up there to this day!'

Miguel was about to present his second Maison Ferreras collection to a largely uninterested fashion world. The business was losing money at a rapid rate and his marriage to Oonagh was becoming even more tempestuous. Oonagh wanted Tara to come back to Paris with them, but he was happy living with his father – for all he and Dom saw of each other.

Tara, still only sixteen, had thrown himself into London life like a sailor on furlough. The city suddenly seemed more vibrant and 'happening' than existentialist Paris.

In the 1950s and early 1960s, London had seen a mass wave of immigration from the English-speaking Caribbean, especially Jamaica, as the country struggled with a labour shortage in its effort to rebuild its bomb-damaged cities. These new immigrants drove buses. They helped build the new lines on the London Underground. And they brought their music with them.

'There was a club called the Roaring Twenties,' Nicholas remembered, 'where Tara and I heard Jamaican music for the first time – not Reggae, which hadn't even been invented yet. This was Ska. It was in a huge basement in Carnaby Street. The DJ was called Count Suckle, a great big black guy.'

This wasn't the London that Tara discovered in the company of his mother: shopping in Harrods of Knightsbridge, watching the coronation of a young queen from the window of Selfridges, or taking tea at Claridge's with one of Oonagh's titled friends and perhaps a debutante daughter or two. He was now at the centre of a new and exciting adult world.

It was Glen who introduced him to Michael Beeby, a popular 'face' around both Chelsea and Soho, known for his sense of style, wideboy charm and Sam Weller repartee. Enlivening and entertaining company, Michael was also impossibly cool, impeccably dressed and was driving around London in a red Mini long before it became part of the popular iconography of the times. 'He was a mix of French and American cool in the way he dressed and presented himself,' remembered Nicholas Gormanston. 'There were a lot of people like him around at that time: they took most of their imagery from films.'

Michael became Tara's newest best friend.

•

Like many teenagers in Britain, Tara was enjoying every minute of his new-found independence. And he was navigating his way around London in his very first motor car. On 4 March 1962, the day he turned seventeen, he had his own set of wheels: a red, two-door Alfa Romeo Giuletta Sprint, a birthday present from his mother. He collected it from a garage near the Cumberland Hotel. Oonagh, who was in London for a week, took a photograph of him sitting proudly on the bonnet, in a grey duffle coat, smoking a cigarette, in the bitter cold of the garage courtyard. Glen, who was with them when they picked it up, said Oonagh had no idea of the power of the car she'd placed in the hands of her teenage son.

'She took one look at it,' he remembered, 'and thought it was a nice little car for him to run around in. What she didn't know, of course, was that it was a racing car. It was 1290cc, four cylinder – it was exquisite.'

It was even more so when Tara, who was surprisingly knowledgeable about engines, got under the bonnet and made some adjustments to make it go faster. He hadn't yet passed his driving test, but he had an Irish provisional licence, which could

be obtained without having to demonstrate any kind of profi-
ciency behind the wheel. From the moment he sat in the car, it was
clear that what excited him most was its speed.

'The first night he got it,' Glen remembered, 'we took it down
to Beaconsfield. It was in the days before they built the motorway.
There was a whole series of roundabouts from Blackbushe
onwards and he liked to drive around them at speed and make a
bit of a show for his own amusement. It was a challenge for him.
It was his first car and it was the first time he'd driven it. It wasn't
like the Lotuses we drove later on. Lotuses tended to go wherever
you pointed them. You had to control this car. It was work. But
he still pushed the boat out. We were sideways, left, right, on the
road. The final roundabout was at Uxbridge. It was somewhere
around there that we pulled into a garage to get petrol. The fellow
who served us said to me, "If he carries on driving like that, he'll
kill himself." And that was the first night he got the car.'

For Tara, it was hugely liberating to at last have his own trans-
port. London, a city in the throes of becoming the definition of
coolness itself, was suddenly his playground. He especially loved
doing the Chelsea Cruise, driving the stretch of the King's Road
between Sloane Square and World's End that was turning into a
catwalk for the young and the with-it. With another portable,
battery-powered record player resting on the door of the open
glovebox, he coasted up and down the road, listening to Gene
Chandler's 'Duke of Earl', 'Twistin' the Night Away' by Sam
Cooke, or, if the mood took him, something more raw – maybe a
little 'Smokestack Lightnin'' by Howlin' Wolf – the stylus bouncing
across the grooves whenever he was forced to step on the brake.

Having his own set of wheels allowed Tara to get around to see
his finishing-school friends from his Paris days. 'He came around
to our house in Montpelier Square to meet my parents,' Jacquetta
Lampson said of a warm, ambrosial evening she had reason to
remember – it was one of the last times she ever saw him. 'I
remember sitting on the roof with him. It was a kind of forbidden
hideaway. You had to climb out of this tiny upstairs window and
crawl along this sort of perch, then you could sit on this flat roof.

We played records there until it was morning. I remember *Blue Moon* by the Marcels and *Runaway* by Del Shannon. And then I remember the birds singing in the square in front of the house and it was the following day.'

A change had come over him since they'd been friends in Paris, she noticed. There was an air of sorrow about him, like something was weighing on his mind. 'At one point, he grew quite melancholy,' she recalled, 'then he said, "People only like me for my money – but at least they like me."'

What Jacquetta didn't know was that Tara was now moving with a faster crowd. And he'd met someone – a girl. As a matter of fact, he thought he might be in love with her.

•

Unlike most of the girls who made up his social circle, Noreen MacSherry had no entry in the pages of *Burke's Peerage*. She was the runaway daughter of an Irish-born postman. Slim and pretty, with dyed blonde hair, cut in the geometric fashion of the time, she was a well-known face around Soho, where she worked cloakrooms, sold amphetamines and was frequently mistaken for the American actress Jean Seberg. Nicki, as she'd decided to be known, was the essential Sixties butterfly child.

'She had a kind of slightly androgynous quality,' Christopher Gibbs remembered. 'And she always appeared to have no fixed abode – you were always unsure of where she'd slept the night before, or what she was going to do tonight. She was very winsome and charming. And she certainly had some kind of survivor genes, which were apparent from very early on. And she was wild – she was very, very wild.'

She was friends with Ronan O'Rahilly, who was thought by some to be in love with her, although Nicki's regular boyfriend was a painter named Graham Rogers, whose surname she somehow managed to acquire. To one and all, she was Nicki Rogers.

Adding to her allure was the fact that no one seemed to know who she was or where she'd come from. Big cities allow people to hide in plain view and Nicki Rogers was certainly doing that. She was born in Yeovil, Somerset, and spent her childhood in Tulse Hill, south London, except a period during the war when she was sent to live with her grandparents in Northern Ireland. She was the eldest of three children born to Séan MacSherry, or Shane, a London postman, originally from Newry, County Down, and his wife, Anne, who came from Carrickmacross, County Monaghan.

She was, by her own admission, rather wild in her youth. In 1960, when she was seventeen, there was a row in the house and she ran away to Birmingham to live with her mother's friend, whom she knew as Auntie Eva. What caused the trouble is unclear, though later in life she confided in friends that she'd had a baby, which she'd given up for adoption.

After several months in Birmingham, she returned to London, where she got a job as a clerk with the Bank of England, earning £4.10 a week. She was not a success. After a few weeks, she thought about quitting to enrol in art college.

'The bank thought that was a very good idea,' she said shortly before her death in 2012, 'and they very much encouraged me to pursue it! The only problem was that I had no art to show. My boyfriend at the time was a painter called Graham Rogers, so I decided, okay, I'll move in with him.'

She never made it to art college. Instead, at night, in form-hugging, ice-blue denims, she worked as a coat check girl, first in the Marquee, then in several clubs around Wardour Street, where she sold amphetamines to the clientele and fell in with a number of Soho faces, including Ronan O'Rahilly and – as fate would have it – Tara's new friend, Michael Beeby.

She met Tara for the first time in the middle of March 1962, one week after he turned seventeen and not long after her relationship with her artist boyfriend had fizzled out. She was sharing a flat in Cromwell Gardens, Kensington, with a girl whom Michael was dating. 'This flatmate of mine said Michael was calling around and he was going to have this seventeen-year-old Irish kid with him,' Nicki recalled, 'and would I come with them on a double-date? I said, "Seventeen? I'm sorry, I don't do babysitting."

'I was actually trying to get out of the house when Michael

pulled up in his red Mini. I stood at the door and I watched this tall fellow get out, which was Michael, then his passenger – Tara – who was wearing a crash helmet, for reasons I never discovered. Perhaps it was a joke about Michael's driving. I just thought, "What a twit!" but it was too late for me to sneak out the door.

'So we all went to Battersea Funfair, which was Tara's idea. He'd loved it since he was a boy. He was *still* a boy, really. He had this blond hair and this beige skin – he was quite tanned – and these green eyes. I can't say that I was attracted to him for the first, I don't know, two and a half hours. But it was his manners that drew me to him. He had the most beautiful manners and the most beautiful nature. He was incredibly polite without ever seeming smarmy. I can't think where he got that from, because his mother wasn't like that at all. It was probably his father.

'And, very unexpectedly, I ended up having a wonderful day, playing on the waterslide and everything else. His mother had bought him an Alfa Romeo for his birthday. He'd only had the thing a week, but his hands were already covered in calluses and blisters from tinkering with the engine to try to make it go faster. We went to see a fortune-teller at the fair. This gypsy woman looked at his hands and said, "I think you do some kind of manual labour for a living," which of course he found absolutely hilarious.'

Tara, inexperienced in sexual matters, was immediately smitten. In fact, the following morning, he was back at the door of Cromwell Gardens, this time alone, with the Alfa Romeo parked outside on the road, the engine idling. He drove Nicki to Devon to see *Fantôme*, a three-masted luxury yacht that his grandfather, Ernest, bought forty years earlier to take his daughters on a year-long cruise. It was moored in the Exeter Ship Canal. 'He wanted to show me the boat on which his mother had sailed around the world as a little girl,' she said. 'And after that, for the next few weeks, we barely left each other's side.'

The relationship was intensely physical from the beginning. They spent days in bed together, grateful for that other vital ingredient in the social metamorphosis that Britain underwent in the

1960s: the oral contraceptive. The Pill had gone on general sale for the first time the previous year and would change the sexual mores of an entire generation.

'Tara was very sweet,' said Nicki. 'He told me that the only woman he ever loved before he met me was an American woman he saw demonstrating the hula hoop in Harrods when he was thirteen years old. It was all very intense. But then he had to go away to Switzerland for three weeks that April. He was going skiing. He loved skiing, but he hated being away from me, because being in a relationship – being in love – was all very new to him.'

There was something else, which he referred to in an oblique way during the night he spent listening to music on the roof with Jacquetta. He had a suspicion that his new friends only liked him because he was rich. What if this girl was only after his money, too? He was sufficiently confused about his feelings for Nicki to keep the relationship a secret from his mother.

'He knew she wouldn't approve,' Nicki said. 'Charmian Scott or Candida Betjeman: that's who Oonagh saw as an ideal partner for Tara. In fact, he was a little bit besotted with Charmian when he met me, although I'm not sure that she thought of him in that way. She was going out with Hercules Belville, a dear friend of Tara's. But I think Oonagh would have been pleased if he'd ended up with her and I expect he knew that. So before he went to Switzerland, I told him to decide if he liked her or if he liked me. But she wasn't having sex with him and I was. I think that's what swung it in my favour.'

After three weeks, Tara returned from his skiing trip, having made up his mind that he wanted Nicki to be his girlfriend. 'From that point on,' she said, 'we were inseparable.'

As Tara's relationship with Nicki intensified, some of his older friendships began to slide. Hugo Williams met Tara once or twice in London, but was scared off by the company that his young friend was keeping. 'He outgrew us really,' he remembered. 'We weren't fast enough for him. He was moving on up, to the Chelsea set, then on to the rock and roll set. And life is dangerous in such company. If you didn't have money, you couldn't keep up. I was working on a literary magazine and my life was so humble compared to the kind of life Tara was leading. It was just too much for me.'

According to Michael Boyle, Tara had a very clear understanding that at least some of his new Wardour Street friends were using him for his money. He may have even suspected it of Nicki. But he was too in love with her to do anything about it. 'He used to say to me, "I know they're hustlers. I don't mind. I'm a hustlee."'

According to Nicki, however, there wasn't any money to hustle. The Guinness trustees were keeping a tight grip on the purse strings, presumably alarmed at the pace at which Miguel was bleeding Oonagh dry. Tara was living on an allowance of £7.10 a week, although several of his friends remember him carrying a chequebook, which was virtually unheard of for a boy of seventeen.

Several other friends picked up on the same melancholia that Jacquetta noticed in Tara that summer. He was in love, but there were too many complications with the relationship for him to properly enjoy it. Nicki wasn't like the demure, well-born girls of his experience. She was wild. Tara wasn't in control.

One day that summer, he called to see Lucy Hill, his childhood friend with whom he'd reconnected since he moved to London. She was living in Little Venice when Tara showed up in his car, close to tears. 'He was with Nicki at the time and I think things were already difficult,' she remembered. 'He opened up to me a bit. He was almost weeping and he said the same thing he'd said to me when we were children: "I know people only like me for my money."'

His favourite song that summer was 'But I Was Cool' by Oscar Brown Jr, the jazz and soul artist, who sings about his golden rule: always have nerves of steel and never show folks how you really feel. Tara would quote lines from the song like they were a spell that could ward off bad karma.

'He got his motto from that record,' Williams remembered. 'He used to say, "Be cool, act cool, stay cool, keep cool." So this became a deliberate act for him – not showing things, especially what he was feeling. But I would have thought his defences were skin-deep.'

•

That summer, Tara and Nicki went on their first holiday together. They took the Alpha Romeo and a stack of 45s onto the Channel ferry, then drove down through France to Saint Tropez. 'His father had told him there was no way he was taking the car,' Nicki remembered, since the legal driving age in France was eighteen. 'He was much more in awe of his father than his mother, because his father used to say no to him, whereas Oonagh let him do whatever he wanted. But in this case, Tara decided that he was going to take it anyway.'

He was tearing along the road when, just outside Antibes, the police attempted to pull him over.

'We heard a siren,' Nicki said. 'And they were behind us, ordering us to stop. I remember Tara and I exchanged this look, like he was trying to make up his mind what to do. And then he just put his foot down. He outdid the police car and he did it on roads that he didn't know terribly well. They didn't catch us – he was thrilled by that. And looking back I think that was the start of his obsession with motor racing.'

They spent three weeks together in Saint Tropez, along with some of Tara's Paris friends, including Mark, Jacquetta and Michael Boyle, as well as Melissa North, who was still carrying a torch for her former boyfriend. Yet theirs had been an innocent, unconsummated love; very quickly, she divined that what Tara had with Nicki was something altogether different.

'I think Tara and Nicki were the first couple I ever understood to be incredibly sexually in love,' Melissa said. 'One felt immediately that they must have had incredible sex together. I had never noticed that before in people. It was chemistry. Nicki would always be sitting on top of him or leaning on him and they would always be close. And he was always tactile around her. She was a sex goddess to me.

'The first time I saw her, like everyone else, I thought I was looking at Jean Seberg. She was this very narrow person. Stick thin. She only wore Levi's. And she had very, very short hair, dyed peroxide blonde. And lots of eye make-up. She was just so unlike any of us ex-debbie girls and exactly what I would have expected Tara's girlfriend to be. Gorgeous, exotic, glamorous, with amazing style.

'And a fantastic dancer. We would go out to these clubs in the south of France and Nicki was like a magnet for people. People couldn't take their eyes off her. Everyone wanted to be around her.

'She seemed so much older and more worldly than any of us and she had confidence, no matter what situation she found herself in. And of course there was this story doing the rounds that she had been a gangster's girlfriend in Wardour Street, which wasn't true, but it made her even more glamorous in our eyes, this rumour that she came from the world of criminals.

'I remember being very impressed that they were in the south of France with absolutely no interest in doing anything. The house was full of all these posh people. It was Lord this and Lord that. And it was: "Ra, ra, ra – let's go to the beach!" and off everyone would go in their cars. But Tara and Nicki didn't want to go anywhere. Nicki was white as a sheet. As it happened, I got terribly badly sunburned on the first day we arrived, so I had to stay home as well. Tara, Nicki and I had the house to ourselves. We'd spend the days reading and playing records and chatting – it was heavenly – before everybody would come back and it'd be, "Ra, ra, ra – let's all go go-karting!"'

After three weeks, they returned to England, managing to avoid any further police chases on the road to Cherbourg. But two days after arriving back in London, Tara managed to rear-end another car on Kensington High Street: the first of many crashes to come.

•

In August, the couple were parted for a week when Tara returned to Dublin for the Horse Show. He threw himself headlong into a week of parties, including a debutante ball in Castletown House,

County Kildare, for Sarah Catherine Connolly-Carew, the youngest daughter of William, the sixth Baron Carew. It was one of the last formal coming-out balls ever held in Ireland. And, as if to mark the passing of one era to the next, the *Daily Express* carried a photograph of Tara on the dance floor, in a navy corduroy suit, performing the scandalous Twist.

While he was in Ireland, he told his mother about his new girlfriend. Oonagh's response to the news is not recorded but it can't have been good. While she despised her sister Maureen's kind of snobbery, she clearly had something different in mind for her darling baby boy than a postman's daughter who worked in nightclub cloakrooms.

He listened to his mother's concerns, but he didn't care what she, or anyone else, thought. It was, after all, how Oonagh had raised him. He decided that summer that he and Nicki were going to live together, whatever it took. Quite a number of his friends believed, mistakenly, that he was cut off because of his love for a commoner. Tara and Nicki may have contributed to this impression themselves by spending the autumn and winter of 1962 squatting with friends, or living in grotty and numbingly cold bedsits. Ferdinand Mount, the future policy adviser to Margaret Thatcher and editor of the *Times Literary Supplement*, remembered sharing a mews off the Fulham Road with the couple that winter: 21 Bury Walk. It was owned by two sisters, Guinevere and Jacintha Buddicorn, who had an interest in the occult.

Tara and Nicki occupied a small room with twin bunk beds in it – 'suitable only for children' – but they were so enthralled with each other that they didn't seem to mind either the witchy decor or the cramped conditions. 'In the morning, towards eleven,' he wrote in his autobiography, *Cold Cream*, 'they would tumble out of bed in their rompers, looking like illustrations to Wee Willie Winkie as they foraged for cornflakes.'

Soon afterwards, they found more habitable lodgings. Melissa North invited them to come and live with her. She was sharing the top two floors of 33 Thurloe Street, a Georgian house opposite South Kensington tube station, with Jacquetta, another friend, named Theodora Brinckman, and Camilla Wigan, Tara's date for the Dublin Horse Show from the previous summer.

'I was still in love with Tara,' Melissa remembered. 'That was the main reason I wanted him to come and stay. I went to the other girls and said, "Tara's living in his car," probably exaggerating, "and I want to offer him and his girlfriend my room, which means I'll be sleeping in the sitting room from now on," and everyone said, "That's cool." I was just so enchanted to have him near me. As long as he was staying there as my guest, then he was kind of my protégé.'

It didn't take long for Nicki to unpack her belongings. All she owned of any real value, she remembered, were two pairs of blue jeans, two pairs of flat shoes and a white coat that looked like mink but was actually nylon.

'She seemed so much older than us,' Melissa said, 'even though there couldn't have been more than a year or two between us. But she was a very sophisticated girl. And then she just blew you away with her style, which had a sort of careless quality to it. She didn't seem to have to make much effort. She didn't seem to own very much. But she had a real look. She was an original.

'And I could see how absolutely and utterly in love they were with each other. They always seemed to be in bed having sex. Then they'd get up at eight o'clock at night – they'd emerge from my room, maybe to get something to eat.'

By the time they moved into Thurloe Street, Nicki had had an uneasy first meeting with her future mother-in-law, who had made her feelings about the relationship clear. 'Oh, I was a gold digger,' Nicki said. 'That's what Oonagh thought. I was after Tara's money. Which was a joke. There wasn't any money. Tara was seventeen. He wasn't due to inherit anything until he was twenty-five, which was eight years away when I met him. The reason we were squatting with Tara's friends was because we didn't have a bean. If he wanted money, he had to go to the Guinness trustees and beg. Half of them were family members who weren't on speaking terms with Oonagh, including Maureen, her sister, who absolutely hated her.

'They gave him a weekly allowance, almost all of which went on petrol for the car. No one gave a thought as to what he was supposed to eat. We had one and ninepence to spend a day on food. He'd phone them up and ask for more and the answer would be no. There was a cafe in South Kensington station called the SKR, which served this awful soup and that's what Tara and I lived on. Sometimes, if we were lucky, it was two bowls a day – one in the morning and one in the evening.'

Nicki took a job as a waitress at an all-night coffee bar near Piccadilly Circus, where her shift ended after the Tube had stopped running. Tara insisted she take a taxi home, which accounted for most of her wages, so she decided she was better off not working. At least they could be together all the time. They spent most of the bitterly cold winter of 1962 living like vagrants under the bedcovers, watching their breath fog in front of them. The soup diet helped them maintain their slender figures, but they were constantly cold.

'We were never happier than we were at that time,' Nicki said, 'when we had absolutely nothing. The flat was a wonderful mess. Theodora's dad was called Napoleon. I remember when he came to visit, the shout would go out, "Napoleon's coming!" and suddenly Theodora was busy sweeping the stairs.

'There was an excitement about London at that time. Rudolf Nureyev had just defected from the Soviet Union and he was performing somewhere nearby. He used to walk by our house at two o'clock every morning. He had the most extraordinary bottom any of us had ever seen. We'd hang out the window, lusting after him. It was such a fun time for us. We just laughed all the time in that house.'

An occasional visitor to 33 Thurloe Street, Nicki remembered, was a thin and slightly gawky teenager from Dartford who was going out with Camilla's friend, Chrissie Shrimpton. Mick Jagger was living in a filthy, mould-infested flat in Edith Grove, at the less salubrious end of King's Road, with Keith Richards and Brian Jones. They were in an R&B and Chicago blues band called The Rollin' Stones and had a regular set, performing mostly Muddy

Waters, Chuck Berry and Bo Diddley covers in the Wetherby Arms on the King's Road. He told Tara and Nicki that they should come and see them some time.

It might not have been evident to Tara as he careened around the West End in his Alfa Romeo that winter, but Britain was on the verge of a social and cultural revolution. In October, The Beatles, having signed to EMI, released 'Love Me Do', a stop-start, harmonica-led pop song with cloyingly simplistic lyrics. It did slow business, peaking at number 17 in the UK singles chart.

According to Nicki, 'Tara absolutely hated it.'

8: ONE PLUS ONE MAKES THREE

It was the year the revolution began. The year when London became the coolest point on the planet. And it kicked off with one of the coldest winters on record. It had snowed on Boxing Day 1962, just enough to add a touch of romantic sparkle to the Christmas season. But three days later, a bitter easterly wind dumped seven inches of the stuff onto the city. New Year's Eve had an eerie, almost post-apocalyptic quality to it, with no one prepared to brave the drifts – two feet deep in places – to reach Trafalgar Square.

Then, like some hellish Christmas guest, it outstayed its welcome by about ten weeks. Roads, railway stations and airports were shut. Rubbish piled up, uncollected and stinking. Power cuts became the norm. Even the Thames froze over. You could drive up it. And people did. There was even a car rally on it.

For Londoners, it was the longest, strangest winter in living memory. In January and February 1963, the city was mostly bathed in sunshine, yet the temperature barely got above zero. Tara and Nicki spent most of January sharing each other's body warmth under a mountain of bed sheets in Thurloe Street, their teeth chattering during the regular electricity outages. Once or twice a day, swaddled in layers of clothing, they ventured across the road to the restaurant in the tube station for a bowl of soup, making it last, so they could remain indoors for as long as possible.

Oonagh was unhappy to see her son so besotted with a girl whom she was convinced was on the make. But Tara shared her stubborn streak. She knew that the harder she pushed, the more he would resist. And who was she to give out relationship advice anyway? Three times married and with her latest consort working his way through her money like some dilettante Saudi prince. It was likely just a phase. Hadn't Garech once eloped with one of her staff? And hadn't that run its course, as teen romances tended to do?

But his father wasn't prepared to wait for him to come to his senses. When Dom heard about Tara's living arrangements, he decided that enough was enough. The boy had been running wild since he arrived in London a year earlier: tearing around the West End in a sports car, hanging out with all sorts in the disreputable clubs of Soho and now shacked up with a postman's daughter under someone else's roof. And still only seventeen!

Men of Dom's stripe had warned that this would happen when the government did away with National Service: young people free to run amok. Dom may have blamed Oonagh for not taking a firmer hand in their son's upbringing, but surely when he looked at Tara he could see something of his louche, younger self reflected back at him. Either way, he knew just the thing to stop the boy's gallop: school.

With an optimism that seemed endearingly misplaced, Dom put Tara's name down for Millfield, a private, co-educational boarding school in Somerset, where he could sit his A-levels that summer. But Dom's plan to bring his son to heel by institutional-izing him was doomed.

'Tara could hardly write,' according to Nicki. 'Which isn't to say that he was illiterate. Not by any means. He read a lot. But he'd forgotten how to write because he never really needed to write. It didn't really come up much in the course of his life. Whenever he did put something down on paper, you just couldn't read it.'

And anyway, Tara had news for his father. He wasn't going anywhere if it meant being separated from Nicki even for one night. 'He said I'm not going unless I can bring my girlfriend with me,' she remembered. 'I think Tara wanted me to enrol in Mill-field, too. Well, obviously, Oonagh and Dom said no to that one.'

Tara dug his heels in and eventually they arrived at a compro-mise. He would move into a rented house in Somerset, where a tutor would home-school him to sit his A-levels at Millfield that summer. If he wanted to bring Nicki along, they were happy to turn a blind eye to it. They may have figured that, torn from the excitement of the London scene, Tara and Nicki would tire of each other and the relationship would burn itself out. If that was the case, they had a shock in store.

Much as she loved London, Nicki was keen to escape the city for a while. It seemed that Tara wasn't her only admirer. 'The clubs in Wardour Street tended to be full of gangsters,' she recalled, 'or at least very unsavoury types. There was some fellow who really was not a nice person but he was interested in me and wouldn't take no for an answer. I'd met him through Ronan O'Rahilly and he had this gang and, well, I got rather scared of him and I wanted out of London altogether.'

So Tara and Nicki decamped to Somerset at the beginning of February, while a blanket of snow still covered the country. Their dramatic disappearance from London gave rise to the rumour that the pair had been bumped off in an act of mob retribution. The two weeks they spent in the south-west of England were an extension of what their life in London had been. Snowed-in indoors, they stayed in bed, enjoying lots of sex and eating very little.

The tutor never materialized and the only book Tara opened was *Angelique in Love*. Once Dom's anger had cooled – and presumably the ardour of Nicki's gangland suitor – they quietly returned to Thurloe Street towards the end of February, just as 'Please Please Me', the second single by The Beatles, was shooting up the charts and ringing the bell for the start of Beatlemania. The screaming had begun in earnest and so had the era of Swinging London.

While John, Paul, George and new boy Ringo were having their hearing assailed by the advance guard of hysterical teenage fandom, Camilla Wigan's friend Mick and his band were doing rather well for themselves, too. The Rollin' Stones (still no 'g') had played their first major billed gig at the Marquee on Oxford Street on the bitterly cold night of 3 January 1963 and they'd hardly had a night off since then, touring suburban pubs and West End jazz clubs, many of which were transitioning into rhythm and blues venues. The Red Lion in Sutton, Sandover Hall in Richmond, the Flamingo Jazz Club in Soho, the Ealing Jazz Club, then back to the Marquee again: they had plenty of change to feed the electricity meter at Edith Grove that winter. Mick's shtick of yowling out Muddy Waters, Howlin' Wolf, Little Richard and Fats Domino covers in a black American accent was generating something of a cult following. When the band played the Crawdaddy Club at the Station Hotel in Richmond at the beginning of March, even Liverpool's newest hit makers had to put their heads around the door to see what all the fuss was about.

But Tara had things on his mind other than music that spring. At the end of March – just a few weeks after he turned eighteen – his girlfriend told him she was pregnant.

It was a genuine accident, according to Nicki. 'There was a time that winter when I was very pale,' she said. 'I was a really, really pale shade of white, because it was a freezing cold winter and we were living on soup. Tara said, "You should take some vitamin pills." So I did. And whatever effect they had, as soon as I started taking them, I got pregnant.'

It was plausible. Certain vitamin supplements can render the contraceptive pill ineffective. But however it happened, the immediate question for Tara and Nicki was what they were going to do about it. 'We discussed a termination,' she said. 'We went to see a doctor – it was somewhere in Park Lane – to talk about our options. He neither talked me into it nor talked me out of it. He just talked through the issues involved and in the end I said no, I wasn't going to murder this little child.'

Once she'd decided to keep the baby, Tara was thrilled. 'Except he said, "We've got a problem here."'

Which obviously meant Oonagh. They resolved to keep the news from her – at least for the time being.

*

The thaw eventually arrived. So keen was Britain to see the back of the winter that Cliff Richard's 'Summer Holiday' went to the top of the singles chart in March while a sheet of snow still covered everything. It was the beginning of the end of Cliff's reign as the nation's favourite teenage heartthrob. The future belonged, not to the country's Elvis Presley and Buddy Holly impersonators, but to bands: particularly one, who produced a sound that became very identifiably British, though it was, in truth, a blend of rock and roll, skiffle, R&B and doo-wop, with a driving four-on-the-floor beat that originated in the clubs of Hamburg. It was known as Beat Music, or, if you wanted to be geographically pedantic about it, Merseybeat.

The Beatles spent the first six months of 1963 touring the country, performing and doing hundreds of TV, radio and newspaper interviews. And somewhere on the road, John Lennon and Paul McCartney came up with a bit of stage business that would become their trademark, standing cheek to cheek in front of the same microphone, shaking their mop hair and going 'Wooo!' It sent teenage girls up and down Britain into paroxysms of high-decibel delirium. Within a year, they'd be doing the same in America.

Brian Epstein didn't have just one hit band on his hands. He had also taken over the career of Gerry and The Pacemakers, their local Liverpool rivals and fellow veterans of the Hamburg circuit, who were similarly suited and booted to resemble a variety club act. They scored number one hits with their first three singles, the first of which, 'How Do You Do It?', had been passed over by The Beatles. It spent three weeks at the top of the charts in April 1963 before it was knocked from its perch by 'From Me to You', the third single by The Beatles. As a manager, Brian Epstein couldn't lose – for a while, he only had himself for competition.

The record companies were quick to see that there was a popular wave to be ridden and they grabbed a piece of any band that could play its instruments and had the look. And, if they happened to be from the one-time cultural dust bowl of the north, then better still. They were signed up, dispatched to the tailors, then to the recording studio to get something down on vinyl. There was an explosion of new acts of varying musical ability: The Searchers, The Hollies, The Fourmost, Freddie and The Dreamers, Herman's Hermits, The Merseybeats, The Swinging Bluejeans, The Dave Clark Five. Some lasted, some were flashes in the pan. Most people thought the whole Beat thing would be over in a year.

By the end of the summer, in addition to a highly excitable teenage fan base, The Beatles would have a second number one single, 'She Loves You', and a number one album, *Please Please Me,* more than half of whose tracks were original Lennon–McCartney compositions rather than covers of American standards. Anticipating the so-called British Invasion by a good eight months, *Melody Maker* pronounced in June 1963: 'The inferiority complex that British popstars have had about American music is already starting to disappear. Because the new wave have shown that they can beat America at its own national music game.'

The sense that, culturally at least, the country was no longer America's milksop kid brother had a powerful visual metaphor to go with it that same month – the sight of Henry Cooper, a greengrocer from Lambeth, flooring a young American braggart named Cassius Clay at Wembley.

John Stephen and Mary Quant had been marching to their own beat since the 1950s, refusing to slavishly follow American trends, as Britain had done for generations, and setting their own template as to what was cool. By the spring and summertime of 1963, Carnaby Street was in full swing. Like London, it was suddenly a riot of colour. Clothes had once been a largely female or a gay preoccupation; now, thousands of straight, image-conscious young men made shops with esoteric names like Adonis, Mates and Gear their Saturday afternoon mecca, including Tara, who was by now a well-known face in all of John Stephen's shops.

Similarly, further west, on the other side of Buckingham Palace Garden, Bazaar had become a compulsory destination for young women who wanted what was quickly being defined as the Swinging London look. Dropped-waist 'sack' dresses. Polo-neck sweaters. Knee-high cowboy boots with short skirts. High-waisted tunic suits with tweed knickerbockers. Pinafore dresses with plunging V necks. And, of course, those ever-northward-inclining hemlines.

Mary Quant's mini harmonized perfectly with the spirit of the times – a skirt for the girl who was liberated, fun-loving and on the Pill. All of this was seditious stuff, even in the early 1960s. Victoria Ormsby-Gore, a friend of Tara's, who spent most of her childhood in America, returned to London as a teenager and discovered that there were firm generational battle lines on the question of what was and wasn't 'proper' to wear.

'I remember being hit over the head with umbrellas,' she said, 'by men in suits with bowler hats. "Disgusting! How can you go out like that?" I remember being brought to a restaurant by my father and the maître d's hand shot out and he said, "I'm sorry, you can't come in." My father said, "I've booked. What do you mean, we can't come in?" And the maître d' said, "Madam's dress does not comply." So then there was a major scene. I was obviously devastated, but for my father, who had a very libertarian view, it became a point of principle. You can't discriminate against people based on race, or colour, or religious belief, or what they looked like, or what they wore – that was absolutely fundamental to him. So he stood there, not backing down, and eventually we were shown to a table behind a plant!'

Like the front-of-house staff in upmarket restaurants, the mainstream fashion industry initially scoffed at the new clothes. But eventually they had no choice but to copy what was happening on Carnaby Street and the King's Road.

By the summer of 1963, all of the ingredients that went into making London the hip capital of the world were in the pot and coming to a furious boil: music, clothes, contraception and a thousand or so Beautiful People who were determined to enjoy every minute of their freedom.

And against this backdrop, Tara, who had just turned eighteen, a baby by the standard of the times, was coming to terms with the fact that he would soon have a baby of his own.

•

Whenever the prospect of being a father became too much for him, he could at least escape in the car. Behind the wheel of his Alfa Romeo, he could banish his fears about the future and focus instead on the speedometer and the road ahead. There was only one way he liked to drive and that was fast. 'He used to drive through Piccadilly,' according to Melissa North, who shared the car with him many times, 'and he'd see if he could get the car up to one hundred and ten miles per hour.'

He especially loved the drive west through Hammersmith to London Airport, now Heathrow, one of the few places where you could order a cooked breakfast – or roast beef and Brussels sprouts, if you were in the mood – in the early hours after the Soho clubs had closed. He timed his journey there and he timed his journey back, a Chuck Berry record on the turntable, maybe a little John Lee Hooker, perhaps a joint burning between his fingers as he steered, running red lights and laughing excitedly if he managed to set a new personal best time.

He and Glen had become good friends with Camilla Wigan's boyfriend, another cool customer named Martin Wilkinson, who shared their interest in fast cars, rhythm and blues music and smart clothes. When Martin started dating Tara's housemate, their lives sort of bled into each other. 'Tara appeared in my life fully formed,' he remembered, 'as if from an egg. I mean, obviously, he had to have evolved, because he must have been a child once. But he had this quality about him – it was as if he'd already lived several lives before he got to you. He had the kind of self-confidence that derives from a lifetime of experience. And he obviously got that from all of the adventures he had travelling the world with his mother, the range of things he must have seen, the very sophisticated people he must have met.

'At the same time he was totally unselfconscious. He dressed in a way that was very different. I remember we were trying to be like that – me and about five or six of my friends. We were trying to find a style and he was there already.

'And Glen, his friend, was a singular and extraordinary man. In a way, he was the perfect older companion for a teenager like Tara. He probably modelled himself a bit on James Dean or one of the characters he played. Very shy – he always spoke into his chest – but very cool. And he always wore black. He was what we would have called a Beat really.'

Tara, Glen and Martin were on the same wavelength when it came to all of the things that mattered to them: clothes, music, and especially cars. Martin was something of an adrenalin junkie himself, having struck out for Spain as a teenager to try to become a bullfighter. They sharpened their driving skills at Brands Hatch, the racing circuit in Kent that would host its first British Grand Prix in 1964. For a fee, you could drive the track in your own car, hitting speeds and performing manoeuvres that would have got you arrested on a public road.

They went to the motor shows at Earls Court, to admire the latest, state-of-the-art automobiles on revolving platforms: the Vauxhall Viva, the Hillman Imp, the Mercedes 600, the S-Type Jaguar, the Aston Martin, the BMW Grand Tourer, the Rover 2000, the Austin 1800 and the NSU Spider, with its revolutionary rotary engine.

'I wanted to be a racing driver from very early on,' Martin remembered, 'and it was the same for Tara. The difference was that he had access to all this money to indulge it. Glen and I were looking at these cars and, you know, sort of dreaming. Tara could write a cheque and drive any one of them away. Tara had the Alfa Romeo, I had a Mini Cooper and Glen had a particular make of Lancia that was very rare at the time. We used to go for long drives and there was a sort of *lingua franca* that developed between the three of us, just from admiring the way one or other of us was driving, maybe even criticizing how you took a particular line.

'We'd go out to Gerrards Cross, before the motorway was built. We'd go out past London Airport and we'd do a big circle about fifteen miles wide, pretty much smoking dope all the way. And every corner, it was like, "I'm going to take it like this" – you know, we were like wine buffs discussing a good vintage. It was about the way the car moved, the line you took, the sound of the engine. And, of course, the speed.'

Breaking the speed limit gave vent to feelings of aggression for which young males of their generation had few other outlets. 'Unlike our parents and our grandparents, we had no war to fight. You simply cannot overstate the significance of that. We never took much account, if any, of consequences.

'To us, taking a Mini Cooper around Belgrave Square, through the rush-hour traffic on Hyde Park Corner and Piccadilly to Soho, at eighty or ninety miles per hour, without touching anything or anyone, was a poetic gesture, rather than a lunatic speed-addict's unconscious attempt to kill himself.'

Yet, as the petrol station attendant had warned Glen a year earlier, there were consequences to tearing around the roads at high speed, even if they chose not to consider them. They'd all suffered bumps and knocks, some even worse. Michael Beeby had started going out with Tara's cousin, Lady Henrietta Guinness, and the couple were lucky to escape unhurt early that summer when Michael rolled her powder-blue Mini Cooper onto its roof in Putney. The next time they had a crash, they wouldn't be so fortunate.

'Mike was the most dangerous driver I met,' according to Glen Kidston. 'He had no fear. But then we didn't really either, even though everybody I watched racing cars while I was growing up was killed. One by one, they all died.'

But for a young man like Tara, facing the very sobering prospect of becoming a father later in the year, the notion of the road, even with all of its attendant dangers, was very liberating. When he felt the weight of his impending responsibility pressing down on him, he could do something impulsive, like jump into the car and hop across to France on a Channel ferry. One night, Melissa's boyfriend, a young architect named Tchaik Chassay, was in the house in Thurloe Street, extolling the wonders of the 700-year-old

Chartres Cathedral, one of the finest examples of Gothic architecture in Europe.

'We decided that we were going to go to see it,' Tchaik remembered. 'We might have been smoking something.'

Early the following morning, when the dope fog had cleared,
Tara was waiting outside, warming the engine for the drive. 'We
had breakfast in the SKR with the car ticking over outside. By the
time we'd finished our breakfast, it was ready to drive.

'We got to France, we went to his mother's place in the rue de
l'Université. Oonagh had bought Miguel this incredible new car,
which was white, and Miguel told Tara he could borrow it. We
jumped in, top down, and drove to Chartres. I remember people
just staring at us in this car in absolute amazement. We felt like
film stars.

'When we arrived in Chartres, there was suddenly a smell of
burning and we didn't know what it was. It turned out that there
was no oil in the car and we'd burned the engine out.'

Tara couldn't keep the smile from his face as he dropped the
keys into Miguel's hand.

•

By the June of 1963, Nicki had started to show and they realized
that it wouldn't be possible to conceal her pregnancy for very
much longer. They made up their minds to tell Oonagh in July
while they were visiting her in her holiday home in Sainte-Maxime.
Nicki braced herself for her reaction.

The summer of 1963 was, fittingly enough, a season for scandal. In the first week of June, John Profumo, Britain's Secretary of
State for War, admitted that he had lied to the House of Commons
about his relationship with Christine Keeler, a West End call girl
whose affections he happened to be sharing with a Soviet spy
named Yevgeny Ivanov. At around the same time, back in Ireland,
Tara's brother Garech was embroiled in a tabloid intrigue of his
own. At a traditional music festival in County Mayo, he had
enjoyed a brief dalliance with a married mother of three. Now, her
solicitor husband was suing him for criminal conversation, an

ancient common law action that allowed cuckolded husbands to sue adulterers for damages. Oonagh was sufficiently tickled by the story to stick the newspaper clipping about it into the family album. Her reaction to Tara's news was rather different.

As Nicki anticipated, Oonagh was convinced that she had become pregnant deliberately to ensnare her son and get her hands on a chunk of Guinness money. She urged them to consider their options again. Tara was too young to be a father, she argued.

'What she wanted me to do,' Nicki claimed, 'was to have an abortion. We were in the south of France and she had this doctor who was coming to give me an injection that was going to terminate the pregnancy. I was lucky that he was a French Catholic, because there I am sitting in the south of France, faced with this injection, and I said to him, "I don't want this," and he said I didn't have to have it.'

Nicki told Oonagh that she was keeping the baby; in which case, Tara announced, he wanted to marry her. Because he was still under the age of twenty-one, he required the permission of both of his parents to get married. One night, he tearfully poured out his feelings to his mother. 'He told her he loved me,' according to Nicki. 'And he said if you don't let me marry her, I'll never speak to you again for the rest of my life.'

Oonagh gave in, certain, as she was, that the relationship wouldn't last the course. The scandal of a divorce was far less great than the scandal of a baby born out of wedlock. 'All she wanted was to legitimize the child,' Nicki said. 'She thought, "We'll get the baby legitimized and then I'll break them up."'

Oonagh sent a telegram to Tara's father in London, telling him that Tara and Nicki wanted to get married. Dom, who'd finally given up his dream of his son one day attending Oxford, replied that they had his blessing. And so Tara and Nicki found themselves engaged to be wed.

'I didn't give a damn if I was married or not,' Nicki remembered. 'It wasn't going to change the way I felt about him. I loved him.'

When they returned to London, they set about arranging a quickie wedding. Oonagh knew just the venue: St Ethelburga's, a small medieval church in Bishopsgate, very discreet, close to Liverpool Street station. Tara and Nicki made an appointment to see the rector. 'When we met him,' Nicki said, 'he told us we couldn't do it there because we weren't resident nearby, although I suspect the real reason was that I was very obviously, heavily pregnant.'

Nicki had experienced a difficult second trimester and was in no condition to stand through a lengthy ceremony anyway. So they decided to simply sign the necessary documentation at Islington Register Office. They made an appointment for 31 August 1963. But while they counted off the days until they were husband and wife, some terrible news reached them from the south of France. Michael and Henrietta had been involved in another car accident – and this time it was serious.

On a Sunday afternoon, the couple had driven from Paris to Saintes-Maries-de-la-Mer to see a bullfight along with Glen and his girlfriend, Serena. They were on the way home. Michael was at the wheel of Henrietta's brand-new bottle-green Aston Martin, testing the limits of the engine. Meanwhile, Glen and Serena, following behind in another car, were admiring the unexpected sight of hundreds of flamingos wading in the shallow waters of the Camargue, an area of wetland half an hour south of Arles.

At some point, Glen noticed that the Aston Martin was no longer on the road in front of them. Michael was a fast driver, but not so fast that he could have been out of sight. Fearing the worst, he pulled in, turned the car around and went back to investigate. A short distance down the road, he and Serena heard the sound of a car alarm coming from the bottom of a steep ravine.

Glen got out to investigate and spotted the Aston Martin in the water below him, its windscreen smashed and its front misshapen. He made his way down to the water and switched off the engine. Henrietta, wearing a fashionable jockey hat, was still in the car. Glen thought she was dead. He looked for Michael, but he couldn't see him. Then he heard groans coming from a short distance away. He spotted what he thought was a newspaper, but it turned out to be a shirt. Michael was lying face down in the water, drowning. Glen managed to pull him to the safety of the riverbank while Serena tried to flag down passing cars to raise the alarm.

Michael had a fractured skull and was taken by ambulance to Montpellier. Henrietta had, amongst other serious injuries, a broken back. She was given the last rites on arrival at the hospital in Arles. When her mother, Elizabeth, arrived in France to see her daughter, Glen had to explain to her that Michael was her daughter's boyfriend. Henrietta had never mentioned him.

The couple eventually recovered from their physical injuries, though it was said that neither was ever the same again, especially Henrietta, who was left mentally damaged by the accident. Forbidden from ever seeing her again, Michael slipped from the London scene for a quieter life in Bath. Fifteen years later, after turning her back on her society life and moving to Italy, Henrietta committed suicide by jumping off an aqueduct in the town of Spoleto.

The crash should have served as a warning to Tara and other teenage leadfoots that they weren't invincible, however much they felt it. Some heeded the lesson and eased off the accelerator. Tara wasn't one of them.

Still estranged from her family, Nicki told her parents nothing about the impending wedding. 'They didn't know she was married,' according to a friend of Nicki's mother, Nan, 'until they saw it in the paper.'

On the final day of the summer, the deed was done.

It was a far cry from the society event that Oonagh must have envisioned for her darling son. A shotgun affair. A pregnant bride. A child-faced groom with the air of a little boy lost.

No Saint Margaret's, Westminster. No crowds of smiling people waiting in the sun for a look at the dress. No pretty daughter of some noble family being escorted up the aisle in a breathtaking white creation. No Garech. No Glen, Mark or Martin. Just Oonagh, and her friend Deacon Lindsay there to witness it.

'We had a lovely day,' according to Nicki, 'and once it was over, Oonagh decided, "Now I'll get rid of this woman!"'

•

There was no honeymoon for the newlyweds. 'We didn't need one,' said Nicki. 'We were on honeymoon the entire time we were together.'

She couldn't have faced one anyway. She was too sick. The doctors told her she needed to put some more meat on her bones. It was unnatural to be so thin. The third trimester was even harder than the second. September dragged. October felt like it would never end. Tara suspected the baby was going to be a girl. Nicki was convinced it was going to be a boy. They passed the time considering names for either eventuality. They couldn't agree on one.

Finally, in the second week of November, Nicki went into labour. On 13 November 1963, she gave birth to a baby boy, weighing eight pounds and three ounces. 'It was such a long labour,' she remembered. 'The best words I ever heard in my life were when I woke up afterwards and Tara said, "We have a son." And then he went out and got completely pissed with Glen Kidston.' The following day, they returned to the job of choosing a name for their baby. 'We considered family names,' Nicki said. 'The Brownes just seemed to rotate the same names down through the ages. It was Dominick, Geoffrey, Dominick, Geoffrey – generation after generation. We wanted something different. So we thought, okay, what goes with Browne? We couldn't think of anything we both liked. So then we thought what other surnames are colours? Black. Grey. And I thought of *The Picture of Dorian Gray* by Oscar Wilde, a book I loved. So I said, "What about Dorian Browne?" and we both liked it.

'Then we needed to come up with a middle name. Tara really loved modern jazz, before all the rockers came into our lives. And there was a trumpet player, who was his favourite musician, called Clifford Brown. So he said, "Can I put Clifford in there somewhere?" So we called him Dorian Clifford Browne.'

They went to Ireland for a couple of weeks, to allow Nicki to recover her strength. One night, Tara and Garech were in Galway, wetting the baby's head in Fox's Bar in Eyre Square, when they noticed that the landlady and several customers were openly weeping. They asked what was wrong and were told that John F. Kennedy had been assassinated in Dallas. Garech said they couldn't understand why Irish people could be so upset about a dead American president.

As Swinging London's coming-out year wound down, a second-generation Irish girl with a blonde bouffant and a figure like a jewellery box ballerina, born plain old Mary O'Brien, but calling herself Dusty Springfield, appeared on television for the first time, clicking her fingers, swishing her mini dress and singing 'I Only Want to Be With You'. The song became a hit, in Britain and America, even though the sentiment it expressed was out of step with the spirit of the times. Monogamy was out. Young people were having fun, sleeping around and avowedly not settling down.

And, while his friends were enjoying their freedom and promising not to make the same mistakes their parents had made, Tara found himself, like his mother, married in his teens to someone he didn't know terribly well.

•

Nicki was making a poor fist of gaining her mother-in-law's approval. That summer, when they went to France to break the news of her pregnancy to Oonagh, Tara had taken her to a popular local strip club called Chez Ghislaine. She got talking to one of the male strippers, a Moroccan named Daud Monseur, who was rather sweet on her. Some people, including Tara, wondered if the feeling was mutual. That autumn at Luggala, whether as an ill-judged joke, or the result of too much alcohol, Nicki made the mistake of telling Oonagh that Daud had asked her to run away with him.

'They were standing in the drawing room,' Garech remembered, 'when she told my mother that she'd had a choice between marrying, on the one hand, this incredibly good-looking stripper who used to put fresh cream on his nipples as part of his act but who didn't have any money, and, on the other hand, Tara, with his soppy, wet face – that was the expression she used – who just so happened to be very rich. And she'd decided to stay with Tara. My mother never forgave her for saying that. I know she disapproved at the beginning, but she knew that Tara loved Nicki and she'd accepted her into the family. But from the moment Nicki said that to her, my mother was finished with her.'

They can't have been aware of the hazards waiting on the road ahead. But as London began to move into full swing, Tara and Nicki were suddenly faced with the imperative of growing up fast while everyone around them was determined not to grow up at all.

9: SPEED

Newly married and now with a seven-week-old baby to care for, Tara and Nicki had two priorities as Christmas approached and the decade gathered momentum. The first was to find somewhere to live; the second to find a nanny to look after little Dorian.

Tara was now an adult, with a wife and child to support. The Guinness trustees loosened the purse strings, allowing Tara and Nicki to give up their life of squatting with friends and living off the soup in the SKR.

They had already identified a smart little mews that was available to rent, at the end of a quiet cul-de-sac, amid the white-stucco Georgian terraces of Belgravia. Just before Christmas, the Guinness trustees approved the rent and Tara collected the keys.

Then, during Christmas at Luggala, they spoke to Mary Fanning, a sixteen-year-old girl from the nearby village of Roundwood who occasionally worked in the kitchen of the house. They offered her a job in London as Dorian's nanny and she accepted. Tara filled the mews with furniture: beds, a table and chairs, a sofa, a cot, and a large Magnavox black-and-white television set for the living room. If he happened to be watching it on the evening of 1 January 1964, he may have seen the very first episode of *Top of the Pops* – the BBC's answer to ITV's own *Ready Steady Go!* – featuring, live in studio, The Dave Clark Five performing 'Glad All Over'. There was also a video for The Rolling Stones' first top-twenty single, 'I Wanna Be Your Man', a gift from The Beatles, whose own celebrity was about to go stratospheric.

The British Beat sound, once written off as a musical flash in the pan, would soon become a certified cultural phenomenon. In the first week of February 1964, 'I Wanna Hold Your Hand' reached number one in the American charts. One week later, a record television audience of 73 million Americans – two-fifths of the population – watched The Beatles perform on the *Ed Sullivan Show*, the horn blow that announced the British Invasion. Their sharp suits, moptop haircuts and smiling vivacity sent the audience into a screaming frenzy – and with it, it seemed, an entire nation, who could at last give up mourning their murdered president. In the first six months of 1964, Beatlemania covered America like a contagion. One week, in April 1964, they held the top five positions in the US chart. Their success opened the country to other Beat acts, including Dusty Springfield, Gerry and The Pacemakers, Peter and Gordon, The Animals, Billy J. Kramer, Manfred Mann, Petula Clark, Freddie and The Dreamers, Herman's Hermits, The Dave Clark Five, The Troggs and, eventually, The Rolling Stones.

When The Beatles returned home on 22 February 1964, an estimated ten thousand fans were waiting at London Airport to claim them back. Truly, it was the return of England as the most hip and happening place in the world. For decades, the exchange of new cultural ideas between the United States and Britain had run one way only. Now, the current had been reversed by a generation of young musicians who were doing something so revolutionary they could hardly believe it themselves: repackaging rock and roll and selling it back to the country that invented it.

Suddenly, everything that was British, from its music to its cars, and from its clothes to its stars of stage and screen, became the epitome of cool. And so much of what was exciting about Britain was emanating from the same corner of its capital city, where The Beatles had chosen to make their home: Paul McCartney in the attic of his girlfriend Jane Asher's family home on Wimpole Street, Marylebone; John Lennon, his wife Cynthia and baby son Julian in a flat in Emperor's Gate, Kensington; and George Harrison and Ringo Starr, the band's two singletons, in a bachelor pad in William Mews, near Knightsbridge.

There may never have been a more exciting time to be young

in London and Tara and Nicki weren't about to settle into a life of quiet domesticity. While Mary Fanning stayed at home minding the baby, they slipped back into their old routine of partying and clubbing that had been interrupted by Nicki's pregnancy. 'I barely saw them,' Mary remembered. 'I was just looking after the baby. I didn't go outdoors much in London. But they knew how to enjoy themselves. There was plenty of life in them.'

And life, or at least the social aspect of it, began to revolve around a nightclub called the Ad Lib, the hippest of London hotspots, four storeys above the Prince Charles Cinema, close to Leicester Square. It was opened in December 1963 by two brothers, Al and Bob Burnett, and was enjoying its moment as an exciting social crossroads where members of the old aristocracy, like Tara, could rub elbows with the new nobility of pop stars, actors, fashion designers, photographers, models, artists, hairdressers and anyone who was anyone in this vibrant new city that suddenly seemed to belong to its youth.

The decor was tasteful – oak-panelled and fur-lined walls, coloured lights set into the ceiling, crystal chandeliers, low stools and tables and floor-to-ceiling windows that stared out across Piccadilly, Soho and Mayfair. The music wasn't British Invasion pop, but something more grown-up: black American R&B and soul, either Motown or its Memphis rival, Stax: The Supremes, Marvin Gaye, Otis Redding, Booker T and The MGs. Friday and Saturday nights at the Ad Lib were a snapshot of a city that had changed beyond recognition: it was hip, youthful, meritocratic, classless London under one roof, with flashing lights and The Four Tops singing, 'Baby I Need Your Loving'.

If you could wheedle your way past the door staff, you were shown to a tiny lift, which took you to the fourth floor then opened to reveal the swingingest of Swinging London scenes. On any given night, you might see Terence Stamp catching up with his old housemate, Michael Caine; David Bailey and Jean Shrimpton twisting on the envelope-sized dance floor; Julie Christie admiring Mary Quant's new bob cut; or John Lennon and Paul McCartney, like a pair of latter-day Francis Drakes, home from conquering new worlds, and sharing their experiences with Mick Jagger and Keith Richards, who would soon be making the same crossing to America.

Tara and Nicki always seemed to be at the centre of the coolest crowd in the Ad Lib, Tara in one of John Stephen's tailored suits with a brocade tie and cufflinks in aquamarine, his signature colour, and Nicki in a jersey dress and knee-high boots. 'I wouldn't say it was a mutual, made-in-heaven arrangement,' Michael Rainey remembered of them, 'but they complemented each other very well in a social sense. Couples are a very strong element in society and it's not very often you get a good couple, who just fitted together in terms of their looks and their dress and their style.'

Swinging London was, if nothing else, a spontaneous outbreak of good feeling among the city's youth and Tara found himself in the right place to become an icon of his time, a man of taste, style and sensitivity. 'He didn't court attention,' Martin Wilkinson remembered. 'People were just attracted to him and I put that down to the wonderful certainty he had about himself. He had that elusive quality of complete and utter self-possession and people are drawn to that. But he didn't show off. He was very cool. He had a sort of smile. He could be very, very charming. And he was exceptionally kind. People just loved being around him.'

The Ad Lib was where you could watch Britain's once-sacred class structure being shaken like a snow globe: Chelsea bohemians, dolly birds, musicians, models, chinless aristos, actors, criminals, photographers, the occasional Kennedy, and sometimes – it was rumoured – even Princess Margaret, all caught in the same happy, social maelstrom. People from vastly different backgrounds, who would have found nothing in common to talk about a generation earlier, were meeting on equal terms: high life, low life and everything in between. Quite often, it was Tara making the introductions.

'He was absolutely central to it,' remembered Jane Ormsby-Gore, the eldest daughter of the family that always seemed to be at the heart of everything that was happening in Swinging

London. 'We were meeting people from different walks of life, but we needed somebody in the middle saying, "Oh, so-and-so, have you met such-and-such?" And that was what Tara did – much like his mother, who was also involved in breaking down social barriers, because she was more interested in what people did and what they had to say than who their parents were or where they came from.

'And that was what Tara brought to the scene. He had this very light way of being interested and curious, but at the same time remaining cool. He spent his whole life around highly educated, clever people, so nobody ever fazed him.'

It was probably inevitable that, in the great social switchyard of the Ad Lib, Tara Browne and Paul McCartney would meet. One had a ravenous curiosity about the world; the other, the assured air of a man who had seen and done it all. 'Paul McCartney liked being around people he thought he could learn something from,' said Nicholas Gormanston. 'I think he would have been absolutely fascinated by Tara's accent and his appearance, whereas John Lennon, who moved in different social circles to Paul, was a much more contrary creature – he either liked you or he didn't. I don't know if Tara was John's cup of tea. But in those days, the early days of The Beatles, Paul was living with Jane Asher and he was always looking to find things that he could adopt. And someone like Tara – and Nicki as well – would have interested him. They were a very good-looking couple, very approachable, laughed a lot and seemed totally open to every new experience. And I suspect he thought that some of this might rub off on him.'

Tara first met Paul's younger brother, Mike, a member of an aspiring comedy musical hall act called The Scaffold. They fell into conversation as two strangers admiring one another's clothes. 'I first knew him as just a guy on the scene,' Mike remembered. 'A young, good-looking guy. Long, blond hair. Thin. Velvet suits. Very Sixties. Very fashion-conscious. Sort of a Roddy Llewellyn type character. Posh, but then not at all pretentious. We hit it off straight away. People like Tara were different to the usual aristocratic types, because they were Irish money, like Oscar Wilde, which is a whole different world. There wasn't the same snobbery that came with it. Ireland was cooler.'

Mike, who used the stage name McGear, introduced him to Paul and they found no end of things to talk about: clothes, cars, music, girls. From that moment on, whenever they were in the Ad Lib, they looked for each other. Tara took Paul and Mike into his circle of high-born friends. For two young brothers raised in Liverpool, all this running with the Debrett's set was truly revolutionary stuff.

'Before the 1960s,' said Mike, 'if you were from anywhere north of London, there was a certain class of person who instantly looked down on you. It was, "Oh, he's just from Liverpool," or, "He's just from Glasgow," or, "He's just from Newcastle." You'd be in company and they'd hear your accent and it wasn't hatred, it was worse than hatred. It was like you suddenly weren't there. They would just smile politely and let you finish your conversation – because they were raised as gentlemen – and then it'd be, "Jolly good!" and, "Off you go!" You were no use to them. You were nothing.

'In the Sixties, that all changed, mainly because of The Beatles. We're suddenly at these posh parties in London, where people would welcome you by saying, "Hello, I'm Peregrine. How lovely to meet you. Jolly good! Come and meet Siegfried!" It was suddenly a different world. They'd ask where you were from and you'd say, "Liverpool!" and they'd try to pronounce it in a Liverpool accent, but they always sounded like Brummies. That's how alien we were to them. But being working class and from the north became not only cool, it was practically imperative. Because we were suddenly the power and the glory. We had all the money. We had all the birds around us.'

Tara and Nicki's house in Eaton Row became the centre of an after-hours scene. When the Ad Lib stopped serving and disgorged its regulars into the London night, those in the know would hail a black cab and tell the driver to take them to Tara and Nicki's place, where they could drink rum and Coca-Cola, maybe smoke some grass, and listen to Bob Dylan's 'The Times They Are A-Changin'' until morning broke over Belgravia.

Tara had bought a state-of-the-art music system that was powerful enough to wake the neighbourhood and often did. 'Quad 303 amplification,' Glen Kidston remembered. 'It was absolutely cutting edge. No one else had anything like it in their house.'

You never knew who you'd see back in the house, thumbing through Tara's vinyl collection, flaked out on a bean bag under a cloud of exotic-smelling smoke, or scarfing down a bowl of cornflakes or a plate of scrambled eggs, the only food anyone ever remembered seeing in Eaton Row. The house became a regular part of the scene. There were rich young men with trust funds, titles and hyphenated surnames, and musicians who were suddenly earning more in a year than their parents had earned in a lifetime. Young Lords and Ladies. An Ormsby-Gore or two. Paul McCartney and Jane Asher. Sir Mark Palmer and Viscount Gormanston. And Patrick Kerr, the former cruise ship dance instructor, who demonstrated the latest moves for viewers of *Ready Steady Go!*.

Tara had his mother's gift for hospitality. He topped up glasses, passed around cigarettes and made sure everyone had a good time – friends, casual acquaintances and hangers-on alike. People drifted in and out of Tara's life, but the McCartneys were always around whenever they happened to be in London. They'd never met anyone like him before – this strange and well-spoken man-child, who was innocent in some ways, yet impossibly sophisticated for someone who had just turned nineteen.

One night, in March 1964, Tara took Mike to a French restaurant in Little Venice, which was so upmarket that the menu didn't carry prices. Tara had just heard some sad news from home. Brendan Behan, who had enlivened so many of his childhood Christmases, had died in Dublin's Meath Hospital as a result of his chronic drinking and neglect of his diabetes. He was only forty-one. Tara was deeply saddened by his death. Over dinner, he told Mike some of his Brendan stories, then at the end decided to see him off with a toast.

'He ordered a brandy,' Mike remembered. 'He said, "Michael, will you have a brandy?" He always called me Michael – in his posh voice. I said, "Brandy? I don't fucking drink brandy, you soft sod," because, you know, I'm Liverpool working class. So his brandy arrives and he starts swilling it around in the glass. I said, "What the fuck are you doing? Just drink the thing!" and he said, "I'm releasing the flavour, Michael. This is what we do – we've been doing it for centuries." Then, eventually, he stops swilling it and he says, "Michael, you must taste this brandy!" and I said, "Okay, only for you, you smooth-talking bastard." So I took a sip – my first ever sip of brandy – and he was right. It was one of the nicest drinks I'd ever tasted. I suppose that's what the friendship was about.'

It was about discovery.

●

Tara's reputation as a daredevil driver had spread far and wide. Back home, in the hills of County Wicklow, his death-or-glory antics behind the wheel had turned him into a kind of famous outlaw figure, according to Monsignor Tom Stack, who was then the parish priest in the nearby village of Glendalough. 'People used to say, "Be careful driving over the bridge to Annamoe. Tara Browne might be coming over it!"'

Around April 1964, Tara began to harbour serious ambitions of becoming a full-time racing car driver. He and Nicki had recently driven a Mini across the continent to Sicily, where Nicholas Gormanston was studying art and was hosting an exhibition of his work. While he was there, Tara drove the route of the famous Targa Florio, the oldest car race in the world, which was held every year on the notoriously unsafe mountain roads near Palermo. The course, comprising more than ninety miles of needle-sharp corners on roads that were often slicked with hoarfrost, held no fear for him.

'He drove it,' Nicholas remembered, 'with me in the passenger seat next to him, absolutely terrified. There were sharp bends and then sheer drops to the sides and donkeys walked across the road in front of us. I really didn't think we were going to survive it. But he had a driver's instincts. He was extraordinary behind the wheel of a car.'

He also pushed his luck to the limit and beyond. Once, Nicki remembered, while they were in Ireland for the weekend, he knocked a policeman off his bike. 'We were going to Bray,' she said, 'and he skidded coming up to a red light, trying to stop in time, and he hit this Garda, who then fell off his bike. Tara said, "I'm awfully sorry," and the Garda, who was incredibly polite, just said, "Not to worry – my fault entirely," and let him go on his way – no licence or anything.'

He went through cars at a quicker rate than even Miguel. 'Oonagh was worried about the way he drove,' Nicki remembered. 'She'd say to me, "Nicki, you must tell him to slow down." Then she'd go out and buy him a Porsche or something.'

He was looking for a car that suited him. Once, Glen Kidston remembered, he was considering buying a Ferrari from Sir William Pigott-Brown, the kaftan-wearing champion amateur jockey and heir to a banking fortune. 'Tara took it out for a test drive,' he said, 'but it was making all sorts of strange noises. He had a look underneath the car and the whole undercarriage was torn away. I think Sir William had been using it to drive across the fields to his horses – a Ferrari!'

Shortly afterwards, at Brands Hatch, Tara got to meet Jim Clark, who had just won the Formula One World Championship in the revolutionarily designed, slim and low-to-the-ground Lotus 25. 'Clark was a humble fellow,' said Glen, who was with him that day, 'rather like Tara in that way. He wasn't flash. He was a farmer from the Borders. We watched him drive the circuit in a Lotus Cortina, taking the corners with three wheels on the track and one up in the air. We didn't even know a Cortina could do such a thing.'

From that moment onwards, Tara was a Lotus man. In April 1964, he became one of the first people in Britain to own an Elan, a two-seater sports car with a lightweight fibreglass body that was built for speed. It was a lethal combination of fast and fragile.

'I drove it one night,' remembered Hugo Williams. 'We were on Finchley Road and Tara said, "Do you want to have a go?" I got behind the steering wheel. The place was stuffed with traffic and I was terrified. Tara said, "Come on, Hugo, put your foot down!" so I did, and the thing just took off like a bullet.'

The early models were available in kit form, to be assembled by the customer, as a way of avoiding purchase tax. 'They arrived in pieces in a series of crates on the back of a lorry,' said Nicholas, who bought one shortly after Tara. 'You assembled it – or you got a mechanic to assemble it for you – then you had to take it to the Lotus factory somewhere in Hertfordshire so they could check that you'd put it together properly. I was coming back from the factory, having got mine passed. I was stopped at a traffic light and a cement mixer ran into the back of me and I realized what kind of protection a fibreglass car offered you. It just buckled. It looked like Shredded Wheat afterwards.'

Tara's first Elan was put together by a mechanic in Notting Hill named Norman Webster. But having seen it done once, he assembled every model he bought subsequently himself, including the one he bought for his wife as a present for her twenty-second birthday.

As Tara's fascination with racing cars grew, Nicki said, he started to take an interest in the story of Sir Algernon Lee Guinness and his younger brother, Kenelm, cousins of his grandfather who were famously fearless drivers from the early days of motor racing.

Algernon – or 'Algy' as he was known – had specialized in straight-line speed trials and record attempts in his boxy two-seater Darracq. He would tow the car, with its naked chassis and bicycle-like wheels, to Blackbushe Airfield in Hampshire, where Kenelm would mark Start and Finish lines on the runway one kilometre apart using flour, then clock his brother's speed, before the police were, inevitably, summoned from Camberley. According to the legend, Algy always sent the law packing, with rude hand gestures and an earful of colourful abuse. He competed in a number of British and international circuit races and set a World Land Speed record in 1908, before he succeeded to the baronetcy and left the field open to his younger brother.

Kenelm was a member of the Bright Young People set and the very astute Guinness director who persuaded Oonagh's father to advertise the black stuff. He also invented – and lent his initials to – the KLG spark plug, although it was his feats behind the wheel of a car that defined him and eventually cost him his life. He won a number of major international races and, in 1922, set a new World Land Speed record of his own in a Sunbeam 350HP. But two years later, he was involved in a horrific crash at the San Sebastian Grand Prix, which caused him serious head injuries and killed his mechanic, who had been sitting alongside him in the passenger seat. He quit racing. The accident was said to have changed him. He suffered from debilitating headaches and, in later years, delusions that he was being pursued by American gangsters. He gassed himself at his home in Kingston upon Thames in 1937 at the age of forty-nine. Algy told the subsequent inquest that his brother had, to all intents and purposes, been a madman for a number of years.

According to Nicki, Tara wondered whether his own obsession with speed was in some way inherited. In pursuing a racing career, however, he saw himself following not so much in the steps of Algy and Kenelm, but rather those of his own half-brother, Gay – a gentleman of means who raced horses for the thrill of it rather than for the money.

'I think he was going to do Formula Three first,' Martin Wilkinson recalled, 'and try to get into Formula One that way. And he quite likely would have been killed along the way, because motor racing in those days had a very Battle of Britain atmosphere around it. You knew that if you raced, you were very likely to die in a crash, as Jim Clark and lots of others eventually did.'

There was no question that Tara possessed the skills and fast instincts required to handle a race car. 'I remember one time we were going to Ireland,' Glen said, 'and I was driving a two-litre Spyder. It was a left-hand drive. Tara was in the front passenger seat. We were driving through Wales, on the way to Holyhead, flying along the road, when the front end of the car started creeping and I wasn't in control anymore. I really thought we were going to have a horrible smash. Tara saw I was in trouble, and, straight away, he said, "Put your foot on the throttle." As soon as I did, the tail came around. He had a racing driver's instincts.'

In May 1964, Tara decided to put those instincts to the test for the first time when he returned to Ireland for the Mercantile Credit Trophy, a road race organized by the Motor Enthusiasts Club in Rathdrum, County Wicklow. It was a handicap time trial, which took place over three laps of a triangular course, less than a mile in length and full of tight bends and hairpin turns. In his first ever road race, he would be up against an experienced field, which included, most tantalizingly of all, Rosemary Smith, the twenty-seven-year-old Dublin-born beauty, who was competing at the highest level in the male-dominated world of rally driving.

Because he'd never raced competitively before, the organizers advised Tara to go to see Larry Mooney, an experienced driver who was also in the field and who could talk him through the course and its dangers. The day before the race, Tara showed up at the head office of Volkswagen on Dublin's Long Mile Road, where Larry worked as a service manager.

'I was aware that two grand-uncles of his had raced in the 1920s,' Larry remembered. 'They were exceptionally good racing drivers, even though most people would never have heard of them. So I was looking forward to meeting him, to find out what kind of driver he was. So in he came. He was very young, quite reserved, not at all flamboyant like I expected him to be.

'I gave him some general advice about driving and racing, talked him through the hairpins, how to drive into them as deeply as you can and don't overheat the brakes – that kind of thing. I gave him as much knowledge as I could. He nodded very politely and said thank you very much, even though I'm not sure he needed my advice at all.'

The following day, Saturday, 30 May 1964, a day so hot that the sun melted the tar on the road, Tara arrived at the Rathdrum circuit in his Lotus Elan. The other cars entered for the race came in all shapes and sizes: Volkswagens, Alfa Romeos, Morris Coopers, Ford Cortinas, MGs. Tara was given a handicap of 47 seconds, based on the speed of his car and his experience as a driver. 'The handicaps were worked out very scientifically,' according to Larry. 'They tended to be correct to within a fraction of a second.'

But when the race officials inspected Tara's car just before the start, they discovered a problem with his windscreen. It wasn't laminated, which meant the car was in breach of the rules. Tara was told he couldn't race, until he suggested a clever solution. He would drive Formula One style – that is without any windscreen at all.

'I took it out for him,' remembered Larry. 'As it happened, it was the kind of glass that breaks into tiny pieces, so I had to be very careful taking it out. And then, because of the wind factor, he put his leather jacket on backwards and got into the driver's seat.'

In his very first competitive race, Tara blew away a highly experienced field with a display of precision driving, finishing three seconds ahead of his nearest rival, Freddie Smith. 'The Honourable Tara Browne,' *Autosport* magazine reported, 'was literally the sensation of the meeting,' while the *Irish Times* reported that he had driven 'faultlessly'.

Rosemary Smith wasn't among the five fastest finishers. 'I was in quite a slow car,' she recalled of the race. 'Larry's was slow as well. And Tara had this Lotus Elan, which had a wow factor in those days. You could keep up with it on the bends – the Rathdrum circuit was one of those squirt-and-brake, squirt-and-brake, squirt-and-brake circuits – but on the straight it just went *vroom* and it was gone. I would say that, as a driver, Tara probably had no fear whatsoever, otherwise he wouldn't have been cut out to be a racing driver, which, on the basis of the way he drove that day, he clearly was.'

Larry was equally impressed. 'It was pretty clear to everyone that he had a gift,' he said. 'He was a natural. There's one thing that competitive motorsport drivers are all good at apart from driving and that's dancing. Because when you're a motor racing driver, the dexterity of your feet is far more crucial than anything you do with your hands. I did competition céili dancing, for instance. Petter Solberg, who is one of the top five rally drivers in the world, was a Swedish disco dancing champion. It came as no surprise to me to find out subsequently that Tara liked dancing.'

After collecting the trophy, Tara invited everyone in the field back to Luggala, where they had tea in Oonagh's drawing room. 'It was a fabulous place,' Rosemary remembered. 'We weren't used to fine china and silver teapots. We were worried about even sitting down, because we had our dirty overalls on. So I sat on the edge of the seat, china cup rattling away on the saucer, terrified. It was a different world.'

She resolved to look out for Tara's name in the future, since it was clear to her that he had a great racing career ahead of him if he wanted it. But Tara never raced again. His victory in Rathdrum that day was the only time he ever drove competitively. No one really knew why, except that life just got in the way.

•

The mews needed doing up. All those late-night parties back at Eaton Row – the cigarette smoke, the knocked-over drinks, the four-inch pencil heels tramping back and forth across the threshold – had left the place a bit of a mess. Tara decided to redecorate. Nicki chose pearl and lavender as the colour theme and a brand-new carpet of deep maroon. They found an Irish decorator and set him to work at the beginning of June. But Oonagh told them that they couldn't expose Dorian to paint fumes, so they all decamped to the Ritz, then became so comfortable there that they didn't want to leave. They kept finding fault with the decorator's work so they wouldn't have to.

'Every week or so,' Nicki remembered, 'we'd go and inspect how it was all going and Tara would say, "Oh, look, there's brush hairs stuck in the paint. You can't have brush hairs stuck in the paint. I'm terribly sorry – you'll have to do it again."'

Mary Fanning reckoned they spent about six weeks living in the hotel. 'A sixteen-year-old girl from a tiny village in County Wicklow,' she said, 'and I was living in the most famous hotel in the world. It was an unbelievable time.'

But then it was an unbelievable time for a lot of people. It was the summer that Beatlemania went global. The band went to Hong Kong, Australia, New Zealand, then back to the United States for a month-long tour that incorporated thirty concerts in twenty-three states. The screaming had reached such a high pitch that the music was barely audible.

It was also the summer when mods and rockers went at it with chains and open razors at seaside resorts up and down Britain. It had all kicked off at Clacton-on-Sea in March and it continued through the summer of 1964 in Margate, Brighton, Bournemouth and Southend. The grandchildren of the generation that fought Nazism on the beaches of Normandy were locked in pitched battles on the beaches of Britain; on one side, young men in suits who liked rhythm and blues music, on the other, young men in leather jackets who preferred rock and roll. It's not difficult to imagine Dom having a thing or two to say about juvenile delinquents having far too much time on their hands.

Tara and Nicki spent their summer holidays in the more genteel seaside climes of Sainte-Maxime on the Côte d'Azur. Oonagh was staying there for three months, her marriage to Miguel having recently entered the final stages of collapse.

Tara and Nicki's photographs from that summer suggested a young, happily married couple having the time of their lives: Nicki, her hair dyed strawberry blonde, at the wheel of a rented speedboat, while Tara water-skied behind; the pair of them sitting in the last car that Oonagh bought for Miguel, a white, soft-top Corvette. Tara had discovered the southern California sound of The Beach Boys and their new album, *All Summer Long*, with its sweet-as-honey harmonies on the themes of surfing, cars and young love, became the soundtrack of their holiday.

But their marriage, too, was showing signs of strain. On the London scene, they were one of those couples whose identities were so intertwined that their names were indivisible. No one talked about 'Tara' or 'Nicki'. They were 'Tara and Nicki' to one and all. But though they clearly loved each other, they had started to discover their essential incompatibility as husband and wife.

At least some of the trouble could be put down to their age and some of it to the times. All around them, young people were breaking out and enjoying the freedom that came with the general loosening up of sexual mores. No one was getting hitched in their teens or early twenties, as they had done. People were having fun, sleeping around. Tara and Nicki had very different expectations of what married life would be like. Nicki was far less prepared for a lifetime of stay-at-home fidelity than Tara. She strayed. He knew it. She didn't regard it as cheating. It was the Sixties. But Tara, who wasn't one for chasing skirt, struggled with it. Fast cars he could control, but a fast wife was a different proposition altogether.

Tara would have liked a more settled domestic life, according to Garech. But Nicki wasn't ready to conform to the outdated role of the traditional wife and homemaker. For starters, she couldn't cook – and neither could Tara. 'He once made me beans on toast,' said the artist Douglas Binder, who got to know him later on, 'and he managed to burn the beans.'

So while Dorian was watched over by Mary Fanning and a succession of other nannies, Tara and Nicki ate out every night, often in the Hungry Horse on the Fulham Road, a favourite of Tara's, which served traditional English fare like fish pie and kedgeree at a time when every second restaurant in London seemed to be Italian.

Oonagh was less concerned about Nicki's shortcomings as a wife than her failings as a mother. Most of the Guinness and Browne children had nannies, but it seemed to her that she didn't want to spend time with Dorian at all. Nicki resisted Oonagh's interference. She put it down to a mother-in-law's refusal to sever her umbilical tie to her son. 'She had lost her baby to me,' she said, 'and it shook her rigid.'

There were some terrible rows. Caught in the middle, Tara's

impulse was to side with Nicki rather than Oonagh, but the arguments just added to his general feelings of unhappiness with the marriage. And there was an added complication, something Tara thought it best to keep from his mother for the moment. Nicki was pregnant again.

Joe Hollander, a local American journalist who was friendly with Oonagh, visited the villa that July, and chatted to Tara and Nicki, who, he reported in his syndicated column, were wearing matching velvet drainpipe slacks 'in defiance of the St Tropez fashion'. They told him about the work they were having done to their Belgravia home and dropped a hint that there might one day be an addition to their number.

'I don't really want a large family,' Tara told him, 'but I think Dorian should have a playmate.'

The responsibility of having a second child on the way may have explained Tara's response when asked about his plans for the future. He grinned and said, 'I think it's about time I found something to do.'

Nicki qualified this statement by adding, 'He only thinks!'

Oonagh had other matters on her mind that summer than her daughter-in-law's perceived failings as a wife and mother. At the age of fifty-four, she was about to be the mother of twins. Oonagh adored babies and had been looking to adopt one for almost two years – 'a reaction to her loss of control over Tara,' according to Nicki. Another factor may have been the knowledge that her marriage to Miguel was coming to an end and she would soon be on her own again, this time, in all probability, for good.

It seems reasonable to speculate that Oonagh tolerated Miguel's behaviour, at least in their final year together, because she needed a husband if she was going to adopt. Even countries with soft adoption laws might have baulked at the idea of handing an infant over to an unmarried woman in her mid-fifties. Similarly, Miguel still needed Oonagh's money to keep Maison Ferreras open. So they remained together, grating on each other's nerves, long after the marriage was, to all intents and purposes, over. Oonagh was known to enjoy a scene, especially at the dinner table, but Miguel's behaviour was beginning to challenge even her famously high embarrassment threshold. Michael Rainey, who, along with his then girlfriend, Jane Ormsby-Gore, was part of Tara's London circle, remembered visiting Luggala around Easter of that year and witnessing one of Miguel's outrageous tantrums in the dining room.

'There was another fellow who came to dinner,' he remembered, 'called Lord Windlesham. He had a sort of travelling companion with him who organized his flights and things like that. Kind of like a valet – like Lord Byron would have had. Anyway, when Miguel found out who he was, he exploded. He said, "If he is going to have his servant at the table, then I am going to have mine!" So he started bringing all the kitchen staff in and telling them to sit around the table.'

With or without a husband, adopting a newborn baby had proved far from straightforward. Oonagh was too old to adopt in either Britain or Ireland and was forced to cast her net further afield in search of a country with a more liberalized adoption regime. She tried to adopt in Greece but was turned down on account of her age. 'She also went to Denmark,' according to Nicki, 'because she wanted a child who looked like her own bunch: blond. They refused her as well. Too old.'

Oonagh had all but given up when, late in 1963, she received a telegram from her old friend, the movie director John Huston. The previous year, he had invited her and Miguel to Mexico, where he was filming *The Night of the Iguana*, starring Richard Burton and Ava Gardner. Over dinner one evening, she confided in him her desire for another child. John had investigated the possibility of her adopting in Mexico, where he kept a home in the remote fishing village of Puerto Vallarta. In December 1963, he phoned her to tell her about a set of newborn twins – a boy and a girl – who were born into extreme poverty in a nearby town and were in need of an adoptive family.

Oonagh filled in the necessary paperwork and waited. In the first week of July 1964, shortly after Tara and Nicki returned to

London, she travelled to Paris to collect the babies from a Mexican social worker at Orly Airport. They were small and sickly, having weighed just two pounds each at birth and had spent the first few weeks of their lives in an incubator.

Oonagh decided to name them Manuela Marienne and Desmond Alejandro. She took them back to Sainte-Maxime, again leaving Miguel in Paris, where he was reportedly finalizing his Autumn/Winter collection. Oonagh was the happiest she had been for years. She showed off the twins to the newspapers, explaining in tender terms how she mashed up carrots for Desmond, because he suffered from colic. 'In a few months,' she told the *Irish Independent*, 'when the twins have settled down, I shall adopt another baby. There is so much misery in the world.'

Within days, she had done something about her own misery. She banished Miguel from her life for good. By then, according to Garech, she had finally faced up to the truth about her husband's sexual wanderings. She discovered he had recently spent a night with another man in the Carlton Hotel in Cannes and charged the suite to Oonagh.

Now that she had the babies she'd been longing for, she didn't need him in her life anymore. At that point, Miguel was more than happy to move on anyway. It wasn't true that all of his affairs were with people of the same sex. Miguel went to bed with at least one other woman while he was still married to Oonagh – a woman who happened to be in a far better position to bankroll his foundering career as a couturier.

Flor Trujillo was the daughter of the former dictator of the Dominican Republic, Rafael Trujillo, who was assassinated after robbing the tiny Caribbean country blind for years. Miguel met Flor early in 1964 in the Drake Hotel in New York, where he and Oonagh were staying in their usual suite. According to Oonagh's version of events, her husband told her that he had to return to Paris on urgent business, packed his suitcase, then decamped to Flor's more impressive suite on a higher floor.

'He told Oonagh, "I have to go back to France to get my

collection together," then he went to [the room of] this other mil-
lionairess,' remembered Nicki. 'Except this woman was filthy,
filthy, filthy rich – she had the kind of money that Oonagh could
only dream about. You couldn't help but laugh at the cheek of the
man.'

In August 1964, within days of the arrival of the twins,
Oonagh instructed her American solicitors, Whyte & Case, to initiate divorce proceedings and extricate her from the expensive
mess of her husband's business affairs. It was only when they
began investigating Miguel's background that they managed to
excavate the secret of his previous life as a former Nazi soldier
who had stolen his alias from a dead man to escape Franco's
Spain. Joaquin, his best man, whom Miguel claimed was his
brother, signed an affidavit, admitting the subterfuge. A solicitor
even found the real Miguel's mother, selling newspapers in Madrid.
She confirmed that the man whom Oonagh married wasn't her son
at all.

Initially, Oonagh tried to get the marriage annulled on the
grounds that she couldn't have legally married a man who was
dead. 'Under English, Irish and French law,' said Garech, 'there
was no marriage, because he wasn't Miguel Ferreras. You can't
marry a man who's dead. But it was quicker to just go to America
and get divorced than to go through the process of trying to prove
that the marriage was null and void. The advice she got was just
to get rid of it, so that's what she did.'

Hugo Williams received a call from Tara shortly afterwards,
when the divorce business turned ugly. 'He remembered what I had
told him years earlier about Miguel sitting on my bed and putting
his hand on my knee,' he said. 'Tara called me up on the phone – I
was sitting in my office – and he asked me would I go into court
and say that Miguel had done this? And I just couldn't be
bothered. I thought it would be embarrassing and boring and I
said no, I didn't want to do it. And I never heard from Tara again,
which makes me incredibly sad that that was the last conversation
I ever had with him.'

It's difficult to place an exact figure on what her five and a half years with Miguel cost Oonagh in financial terms. Garech agreed that the figure of £6 million sounded about right. It was certainly enough to force Oonagh to live out her final years in considerably reduced circumstances in Guernsey.

Unsurprisingly, Nicki, who would one day be corresponding with Oonagh's solicitors herself, had sympathy for the way Miguel was summarily dispatched. 'I know he wasn't God's gift to humanity,' she said, 'but he was just another one from the wrong side of the tracks who they eventually did down. The story was that he'd spent all her money – millions and millions of pounds, they said. But he didn't steal it from her. She gave it to him. And she didn't mind dragging him around New York, Paris, London, Venice and the south of France either, with him on her arm. I knew Miguel was gay. Tara knew Miguel was gay. Oonagh knew he was gay, too. Of course she did. Miguel was treated like dirt. A king for a day and then he was beheaded. No compassion whatsoever.'

Compassion was the last thing Miguel needed. While his wife reverted to her former name of Oonagh, Lady Oranmore and Browne, Miguel fell out of one rich heiress's bed and straight into another. Within weeks, the *New York World-Telegram* reported that he was planning to marry Flor. Unfortunately for Miguel, access to her money was rather less straightforward than it had been with Oonagh and her trustees. Rafael Trujillo – the self-styled Great Benefactor – had sired a lot of progeny with his three wives and many mistresses. Flor was locked in a legal battle with eight siblings and half-siblings for her cut of his estimated billion dollars in stashed loot.

While Oonagh announced that she planned to continue running Maison Ferreras herself, Miguel told the *New York Daily Mirror* that he would continue 'dressing the very rich' and hoped to open a salon soon in Manhattan using capital from Switzerland. He was presumably referring to some of the $100 million that Flor's father was reported to have hidden there and elsewhere in Europe.

The following summer, Suzy Knickerbocker – the nom de

plume of *New York Daily Mirror* gossip columnist, Aileen Mehle – reported that Miguel and Flor had been spotted in Maxim's, one of Oonagh's favourite restaurants in Paris. They were discussing, with their American lawyer, how to get their hands on Flor's share of the money that her father had salted away in various European countries. Their dinner date, an eavesdropper reported, was hoping to use his influence to persuade President Franco to allow Flor to sue her brother Radhames for her share of a reported $58 million on deposit held in Spain. According to the report, Miguel and Flor's lawyer was on good terms with the Generalissimo, having helped negotiate the country's entry into the United Nations back in 1955.

The man couldn't have come cheap. It was Richard Nixon.

•

In September, Tara saw The Rolling Stones play for the first time in the Astoria Theatre, Finsbury Park. Shortly afterwards, he was introduced to Brian Jones. The band had recently fallen in with some of Tara's upper-class dandy friends who frequented the clubs of Soho, including antiques dealer Christopher Gibbs, Mayfair art dealer Robert Fraser, and Julian, the eldest of the Ormsby-Gore children. It should have been no real surprise that the band, who were fast earning a reputation as dangerous delinquents, should have hit it off so famously with Tara's circle of switched-on, Chelsea decadent friends. After all, the hedonistic lifestyle that the Stones had so lustily embraced was how Britain's upper classes had lived for generations. 'The thing that people often forget about the Sixties,' said Marianne Faithfull, 'is that the permissiveness that was supposedly new was there all along. The only thing that happened in the Sixties was that it suddenly went public. It hit the masses.'

It was Mick and Brian who made most of the early running in the relationship, realizing that these party-loving bluebloods had something to offer them. More than any of the Stones, Mick had the social-climber's desire to be taken to the bosom of the aristocracy. Marianne, his future girlfriend, once characterized him as someone who would 'attend dinners given by any silly thing with a title and a castle'. For Brian, the 'posh' Stone, it was about curiosity, according to Anita Pallenberg, who entered his life to following year. 'He wanted to know everything,' she said, 'which is why he wanted to meet people who were different from him. He was always investigating the truth about things.'

The relationship wasn't all one way. People like Tara, Christopher Gibbs and Robert Fraser were as flattered by the Stones' passing attention as the Stones were by theirs. They were at the centre of the action. They had all the girls.

'A lot of these aristocratic kids had a lot going on in their heads,' Marianne said. 'People tended to think of them as being the idle rich – privileged, but with nothing to say. But Tara and Christopher Gibbs and Mark Palmer, they were all incredibly bright people. And they were meeting these musicians on equal terms, because they had all the same things in common – they were all young, good-looking and rich.'

Tara and Brian hit it off instantly. With their Carnaby Street threads and their identical pudding-bowl haircuts, they looked like twins. In the dark recesses of the Ad Lib, they were often mistaken for each other.

'Excuse me,' a stranger would say, interrupting Tara, mid-conversation, 'aren't you that chap from—?'

'Sorry,' Tara would answer, cutting them off, 'I'm actually the chap's younger brother.'

'They were very alike because they were both small, blond and pretty,' remembered Jane Ormsby-Gore, who was soon to become the voice of modern youth at *Vogue*. 'But they were different in that Tara was quite shy. He didn't come into a room and make a big noise. He was a ray of sunlight rather than a blast. Brian was more of a blast. He'd come in and the room would move a bit. Whereas Tara would slip in unnoticed and work his magic in a totally different way.'

They had a lot of common interests, especially rhythm and

blues music and fast cars. Like Tara, Brian was a fearless driver. He'd recently taken delivery of a sleek E-type Jaguar, which he'd managed to roll over onto its roof and was fortunate to escape with his life.

Brian became a regular visitor to Eaton Row whenever the Ad Lib closed. He and Tara would drink the finest Hine cognac, listen to Bob Dylan and The Beach Boys and play with Tara's latest Scalextric set, shoving all of the furniture against the wall to lay down a track on the new carpet.

'I don't know if you believe in astrology,' said Nicki, who remembered being kept awake many nights by their pot-fuelled giggles, 'but their birthdays were within three or four days of each other. They were both Pisces. Free-spirited. Very moral in their ways, without ever being sanctimonious. They were like brothers to each other.'

However, Anita thought the friendship was based on the differences in their nature. Tara was the rock that Brian needed as the Stones became phenomenally big and he began to show signs of unravelling.

'Tara was such a mellow kind of person,' she remembered. 'Brian never had that. He was tortured. Very paranoid. Very sensitive. But he would have loved to have had the peace of mind that Tara had. That's why he wanted to always spend time with him. Brian didn't have many friends. And the friends he had, he didn't keep them for very long, because he was too messed up.'

Even by Tara's standards, Brian had lived a full and interesting life. He grew up in Cheltenham, Gloucestershire, the son of an aeronautical engineer father and a mother who worked as a piano teacher. From early childhood, he showed signs of being musically gifted. Highly intelligent but complicated, he rebelled against his middle-class upbringing and by the age of twenty-two he had fathered four children by four women, with a fifth on the way.

He got his first guitar for his seventeenth birthday and began to think that music might be his escape from uptight, buttoned-down Cheltenham. Eventually, after a series of dead-end jobs, he moved to London, reimagining himself as slide guitar player Elmo Lewis in the anonymity of the big, fog-filled city.

'Brian was the grown-up one,' Anita said. 'Mick and Keith were still kind of schoolboys. Brian had all these illegitimate children and he was already driving a car and dressing in suits. He was way ahead of his time, which is why Mick and Keith were very jealous of him. They were still tinkering away on their guitars. Mick still wanted to be an accountant or something, so there was a big gap in wisdom and knowledge and lifestyle between Brian and the others.'

But that night when they first saw him play slide guitar in Ealing was two years earlier – and two years must have seemed like a terribly long time ago as The Rolling Stones started to become huge and Brian felt the band's creative centre of gravity slip away from him. It had been a breakthrough year for the band. Their New Year's Day appearance on the first ever *Top of the Pops* was the start of a hectic six-month period in which they scored their first top-ten hit with a cover of Buddy Holly's 'Not Fade Away', then, in June, their first number one, with their twist on The Valentinos' hit 'It's All Over Now'. Their debut album, consisting mostly of R&B covers, went straight to the top of the charts on the back of 100,000 advance orders and they even made inroads into America with a two-week tour at the start of the summer that took in seven states.

But for the Stones, the most significant day of 1964 had come in early January, when their manager, Andrew Oldham, locked Mick Jagger and Keith Richards into a kitchen (metaphorically, according to Jagger; literally, according to Richards) and demanded they start producing more songs of their own, as John Lennon and Paul McCartney were doing. The result of this unusual, gun-to-the-head commission was a melodic ballad called 'As Time Goes By' that sounded so far removed from a Stones song they decided not to record it. Instead, Oldham changed the title to 'As Tears Go By' to avoid confusion with the song from *Casablanca* and gave it to Marianne Faithfull, then a pretty, seventeen-year-old, former convent schoolgirl and Ad Lib regular, whom he was convinced he could turn into a recording star.

It became a top-ten hit for her in August 1964. By then, Mick and Keith were starting to find their stroke as songwriters, although it would be a whole year before they wrote a song they considered a worthy single for a band that took its musical cues from Jimmy Reed, Muddy Waters and Howlin' Wolf.

Their emergence as songwriters changed the internal dynamics of the band. Over the next two years, the Stones would become less and less centred on the savant musical genius of its founding member, Brian, who didn't write songs, and more on the creative abilities of Mick and Keith, who were starting to show that they could. In addition, while Brian had always been the most popular Stone with the female fans, Mick's growing confidence meant that he was becoming the group's main aesthetic reference point.

The more successful the Stones became, the more Brian would feel estranged from the band he created. Over the next two years, he would come to lean more and more on his new friend, a young man who was cool and self-contained and utterly at ease with himself; all of the things, in fact, that Brian wished he could be.

'Tara wasn't trying to get on any trip,' remembered Michael Rainey, who spent many nights with him in the Ad Lib. 'That's why people like Brian and Paul McCartney weren't frightened of him. He wasn't trying to ride their glory. He already had his social position. He was financially secure, which I think gives a man a relaxed air. He was an extremely good-looking young man. He had all those things in his favour. He was like a young prince really. So they saw him as a complete equal.'

•

In October 1964, young, hip and happening Britain had a new prime minister when Labour squeaked home in the General Election, bringing to an end thirteen years of Conservative rule under a succession of patrician elders. At forty-eight, Harold Wilson was ancient by the standards of the young Londoners keeping the tills ringing in Carnaby Street and the King's Road, but a mere child compared to Britain's last four prime ministers. Better still, while he was a Yorkshireman, he was from 'up the same way' as The Beatles – an MP for Huyton in Merseyside, who went to Wirral Grammar School, just six miles from the centre of Liverpool. He even managed to capture something of the wisecracking, irreverent tone of the times when he stepped through the front door of 10 Downing Street for the first time and proclaimed, 'Nice place we've got here!'

The new PM had already made his views on Britain's old class system clear. 'Everybody should have an equal chance,' he said, 'but they shouldn't have a flying start.'

That same autumn, as if heedful of the changing political wind, Tara – the son of a peer and heir to a million-pound fortune – applied for a job as an apprentice mechanic. He hadn't been joking that summer when he said he wanted to find something to do. The prospect of having not just a wife and son but a family had given him an urgent sense of purpose. He applied for a job with Rootes Motors Limited, a car manufacturing plant in the West Midlands. He was still keen on becoming a full-time racing car driver and he thought it would help if he learned everything he could about cars and how they worked.

'He was obsessed with engines,' Nicki said. 'Our brand-new pearl and lavender colour theme didn't last very long. He'd bring these engines home and dismantle them in the middle of the living room. Puddles of oil all over the beautiful new carpet. We had this ghastly German woman who used to come in and clean and she'd get so angry with the mess. Tara would just laugh and say, "Oh, put a bean bag over it!"'

At the beginning of October, he drove to Coventry to sit an interview, then he waited for word. Shortly afterwards, he and Nicki returned to Dublin for the christening of Desmond and Manuela at St Patrick's Cathedral. All of Oonagh's children – Gay, Garech and Tara – had agreed to act as godparents to their new, adopted siblings.

By then, the secret of Nicki's pregnancy was out. She couldn't hide it any longer, even in the loose-fitting short coat she wore on the day. Oonagh was furious. 'She thought she'd get me married to Tara to legitimize Dorian,' Nicki said, 'then set about breaking us up. What she didn't bargain for was me getting pregnant again.'

All of the main national newspapers covered the christening of Oonagh's adopted twin. Even in the new era of pop superstardom, the lives of the Guinness family remained the subject of media fascination, the twists and turns in their lives reported as though they were bona fide celebrities. Tara chatted to a reporter from the *Daily Express* about their own forthcoming arrival and also about his recent interview in Coventry. 'It will be my first job if I get it,' he said. 'I expect my wife and I will rent a flat there.'

When he returned to London, a letter had arrived at Eaton Row to say that the job was his. He and Nicki found a cottage in the West Midlands countryside, then they turned their backs on Swinging London, the Ad Lib and the all-night parties with their pop star friends. From the time of his childhood, Tara had always been a nocturnal animal. Now, he was giving up the late nights for a 7 a.m. alarm call, eight- to ten-hour shifts on a factory floor and evenings poring over engineering books and car manuals.

'People in London thought he was mad,' Nicholas Gormanston remembered. 'This aristocrat, walking around with dirt under his fingernails. They just couldn't understand the fascination.'

But the job didn't last long. According to Nicki, it was less than two weeks. 'The plan was to start at the bottom,' she remembered, 'which was always the Guinness way, even with the bosses – they all had to do menial work on their way up. Well, starting at the bottom in this case meant cleaning out these whopping great vats of God knows what. I just remember it was horrible work and Tara didn't like it at all, especially the fact that he was meant to start at eight o'clock every morning.

'We had this crappy, rundown, rented bungalow that we had to live in. The heating wouldn't work. It was a ghastly place. We had Dorian living with us and I was pregnant at the time and I said to Tara, "I don't think this is very nice, do you?" And he said, "I couldn't agree more." So he quit after, I think, ten days and we went back to London.'

Tara began to consider an alternative route into the motor industry, looking around for a garage to buy. And the parties resumed at Eaton Row. Peter Sellers and his wife, Britt Ekland, who were living around the corner at 25 Eaton Place, popped in from time to time. Roman Polanski, who was in London to shoot his first English language feature, *Repulsion*, was another regular caller.

Every Friday morning, Nicki bought five dozen eggs to make breakfast for whichever guests had improvised beds for themselves on the living room floor. 'The house was always strewn with bodies,' she remembered. 'You never knew who was a Beatle, who was an Animal, who was a Trogg and who was a Pretty Thing.'

Life was chaotic – too much so for her disapproving mother-in-law. Oonagh believed Tara and Nicki were making a bad job of parenthood and now they were about to bring a second baby into the world. She then did something that, in hindsight, was only going to make a difficult relationship even worse. She bought a mews across the road.

'Her intention', said Garech, 'was to keep an eye on things whenever she happened to be in London and to make sure the children were okay.'

Not surprisingly, Nicki saw things rather differently.

10: FULL SWING

Nicki thought her second pregnancy was going to go on forever. The baby was more than a month overdue. Tara took her across London in his Lotus Elan to Cable Street in the East End – the scene of a famous battle between Oswald Mosley's Blackshirts and anti-Fascist protesters back in 1936 – and they drove up and down the cobbled road. 'Someone told us that you could induce labour that way,' she remembered, 'driving over cobbles in a low suspension car. Of course, it didn't work.'

In the end, the baby was delivered by caesarean section on 1 March 1965, three days before Tara's twentieth birthday. It was a boy. They named him Julian Dominick: Julian after Tara's friend, Julian Ormsby-Gore, and Dominick after Dom, the baby's grandfather.

They went to Ireland to allow Nicki to recuperate at Luggala. Tara had some business to attend to in London and he arrived a day or two later. Nicki was waiting for him in the arrivals hall of the then tiny Dublin Airport when she fell into conversation with an American teenager, who was waiting for his French girlfriend to arrive on a flight from Barcelona. He told her that his name was Rock Brynner.

'Nothing to do with Yul Brynner?' Nicki wondered.

Rock laughed in an embarrassed way. 'Actually, yeah,' he said, 'he's my dad.'

Growing up, Rock had become fixated with Ireland. He loved the plays of Samuel Beckett and, at the age of sixteen, knew his way around James Joyce's *Ulysses*. So he enrolled in Trinity College in Dublin and moved into a flat in Rathgar, south of the city, just a couple of miles from the nursing home where Tara first entered the world.

'I had this wonderful French girlfriend,' he remembered, 'who was extraordinarily beautiful, who lived with her parents on the Costa Brava and who used to commute backwards and forwards to Dublin to see me. And this particular evening, I was waiting at Dublin Airport for her to arrive when I got chatting to this girl, Nicki, who was waiting for her husband, Tara.

'Nicki was from – I think – an Irish farming background, but she didn't sound like a girl from an Irish farming background. She sounded like she was English upper class – like a young, crazy aristocrat. And I suppose that's part of what made London so exciting in the 1960s. You could reinvent yourself like that. You know, men could wear furs and doormen didn't blink an eye!'

Tara eventually arrived. Nicki made the introductions and Tara invited Rock and his girlfriend to come with them to Luggala. Over the course of the weekend, Tara introduced him to hashish, and, as they bonded over a joint, they discovered how much they had in common. 'We came from different social backgrounds,' Rock remembered, 'but our place in those societies was much the same. Tara, like myself, was often the only child in a room full of remarkable adults – adults who didn't usually tolerate the presence of a child. Because of who my father was, I'd spent a lot of time with some of the most interesting people in the world. I looked after Salvador Dali's ocelot. Jean Cocteau was my godfather. My babysitter was Marlene Dietrich. At eleven years old, I was bartender for the Rat Pack. So that had been my life. And Tara had had a very similar upbringing, always around very, very smart, sophisticated people. And in his case, it rubbed off. To me, he was the Prince of Ireland. That's how I looked on him. And I was the Prince of God knows what kingdom Yul Brynner was the king of.'

It was, he remembered, a magical weekend, at the end of which they all vowed to remain in touch. What Rock probably couldn't see, amidst the haze of hashish smoke in the breathtakingly picturesque Wicklow valley, was that Tara and Nicki's marriage was coming apart at the seams.

A few weeks later, when Julian was christened at St Patrick's Cathedral in Dublin, Nicki was absent. She was described as 'indisposed' by the *Daily Mail*, though the truth was that she and Tara had had another of their now increasingly frequent rows over her mother-in-law's interference in their marriage. It was Oonagh who held Julian at the font and who posed for newspaper photographs with Tara and the baby after the ceremony. In hindsight, there was something very ominous about her playing the role of surrogate mother for the day.

Oonagh was a busy woman in the spring of 1965. She had two young babies of her own, not to mention a couture house to run. She was determined to make a success of Maison Ferreras, if just to prove a point to the man whose name remained over the door. 'I have never worked before,' she had recently told Hebe Dorsey, the celebrated fashion writer for the *International Herald Tribune*. 'I'm looking forward to it. I'm sure it will be great fun.'

She had appointed Jacques Fougeriol, a thirty-four-year-old former assistant to Miguel, to the position of Creator-in-Chief and he had put together a collection for Spring/Summer. But it would be the last collection ever presented by Maison Ferreras. In the summer of 1965, the Guinness trustees – but mostly Oonagh's sister, Maureen – decided that they'd been flogging the dead horse of Miguel's couturier business for too long and they cut off the money.

Tara went into business himself that spring, shortly after Julian's arrival, making good on his promise to do something useful with his life. Although he wasn't due his £1 million Guinness inheritance until the age of twenty-five, he was allowed to borrow money from the Trust to buy a share in a garage in Bayswater, which was owned by a man he knew from the motor trade.

Len Street was a former mechanic with the Lotus Formula One team. Tall and gregarious, with blond hair swept back from his forehead, Len was on friendly terms with Lotus founder Colin Chapman and Jim Clark, who was then the world's leading racing car driver. For six years, he worked as a foreman at the Lotus factory in Cheshunt, Hertfordshire, overseeing the production of the company's ultra-light, two-seater road cars, first the Elite and later the Elan. In 1964, he quit the factory to set up Len Street Engineering, a garage and Lotus dealership, along with his half-brother, an amateur boxer with the gift of the gab named Alan Oliver.

The business operated out of a mews garage in Bayswater. Len serviced cars and Alan sold them. They were the official Lotus dealers in London, so young swingers who wanted one of the sleek little two-seaters driven by Emma Peel in *The Avengers* invariably ended up at Len Street Engineering. Tara was a regular caller. Then one day in the spring of 1965, he arrived with a proposal for Len and Alan. He wanted a piece of the company.

Buying into a garage business meant Tara could serve his apprenticeship as a mechanic on his own terms. There would be no early mornings, no menial work, such as cleaning up oil spills, and – most importantly of all – no books. The perfect employment conditions, in fact, for a rich young gadabout who liked to stay out late, then sleep in the following morning, and who couldn't have faced the classroom element involved in a formal apprenticeship.

The injection of Guinness money meant that Len Street Engineering could move to a mews garage in the more upmarket area of Drayton Gardens, between the Fulham Road and the Old Brompton Road in Chelsea. Tara paid himself a lackey's wage of £9 a week (about £150 in today's money), pulled on a set of overalls and set about learning the business of car mechanics from Len and his team. He was far from work-shy. Sometimes he went in seven days a week. Engines fascinated him. 'Everyone in London wondered,' said Nicholas Gormanston, 'why on earth Tara wanted to get his hands dirty by, you know, actually working for a living. Everyone else was flouncing around in lace and satin and there was Tara, in the garage overalls, under the bonnet of a car, tinkering with the engine.'

The year that Tara bought into Len Street Engineering was the heyday for a certain kind of criminal celebrity in London. The Krays and the Richardsons ruled over vast criminal empires and flaunted their wealth in the same extravagant manner as the pop stars of the age. In the new, non-judgemental milieu, in which the lines between the social classes became blurred, a host of under-world figures – arsonists, armed robbers and racketeers – blended in with the London 'in crowd', old money, new money and dirty money happily wadded together. So incestuous was the relation-ship that when Reggie Kray married Frances McShea in April in Bethnal Green, it was David Bailey – the most famous photog-rapher in Britain – who took the official pictures. 'I know people will hate me for this,' Bailey said at the time, 'but I like him. I suppose that's like saying I like Hitler.'

He was far from alone in feeling an affinity for old-fashioned London gangsters. In July, Ronnie Biggs, one of the Great Train Robbers, used a rope ladder to break out of Wandsworth Prison. Millions of ordinary, law-abiding Britons revelled in the daring nature of the escape, as Biggs underwent plastic surgery to alter his appearance and slipped out of the country for a destination as yet unknown.

As it turned out, the garage that Tara bought into started to attract a rather interesting clientele. Dubious characters would show up in their motors from time to time: stereotypical east London geezers with fingers full of sovereign rings, who were known to have done a bit of bird. They would have unusual and very specific instructions for the work they wanted done.

'They wanted their cars turned into getaway cars,' according to Nicki, 'which was something Tara happened to have a gift for. He could tinker with the engine of an old Anglia to allow it to do one hundred and twenty miles per hour, then conk out after twenty minutes when you didn't need it anymore. He used to come home with these stories of all these villains who came in, wanting their cars done up for bank robberies and whatever else.'

•

Winston Churchill had died in January following a stroke at the age of ninety. If there was a single moment that marked the pass-ing of the London of air raids and smog to the London of miniskirts and Beat music, then it was the death of Britain's war-time leader. Hundreds of thousands of ordinary Britons filed past his coffin in Westminster Hall at the heart of Parliament. As flags were lowered to half-mast across London, there was a resurgence in pride for the Union Jack, which suddenly became co-opted into the iconography of the swinging city.

The death of Churchill was another indicator that Britain was now in the hands of a new generation. But not everyone was pleased with what they were choosing to do with the freedom he had helped secure for them. In March 1965, on their way back from a gig in Essex, Brian Jones, Mick Jagger and Bill Wyman got themselves in trouble for urinating in a petrol station forecourt in East Ham. Mick reportedly informed the attendant, 'We will piss anywhere, man!' The three were later found guilty of public inde-cency and insulting behaviour, fined £5 each and issued with a schoolmasterly rebuke by the magistrate: 'Just because you have reached an exalted height in your profession, it does not mean you can behave in this manner.'

Andrew Oldham milked what was really a minor public order offence for all the publicity value he could. It was just the kind of notoriety he was looking for in his efforts to turn his band into the anti-Beatles, happily colluding in the media's presentation of the Stones as a threat to public morals, common decency and the happy feeling engendered by the chirpy Beat bands.

The Beatles were the exemplars of the new, re-emergent Britain that was happy, confident and forward-thinking. While The Rolling Stones were being upbraided by a magistrate, The Beatles were receiving the ultimate pat on the head from the Establishment. In June 1965 they were informed that they were each to receive an MBE, an honour that was originally awarded for meritorious ser-vice in war. After twenty years of peace, Britain was finding new heroes to pin medals on, prompting a number of previous recipients – members of the old order – to return their honours in disgust.

For The Beatles, it was just one more date in the diary of yet another phenomenal year. They had recently been in Austria and the Bahamas, making a film called *Help!*, an absurdist comedy that was intended to cash in on the commercial success of their first movie, *A Hard Day's Night*. It premiered on 29 July at the London Pavilion in Piccadilly Circus, causing the usual crowd chaos outside. Two weeks later, on 15 August, they produced another watershed moment in musical history when they played the first ever stadium pop concert. The scenes at New York's Shea Stadium were almost beyond belief – 56,000 people crammed into every available seat, not to watch a ballgame, but to listen to music, or rather not listen to it, since even The Beatles themselves couldn't hear their instruments over the din of screaming teenyboppers.

'At Shea Stadium,' John Lennon reportedly said, 'I saw the top of the mountain,' which wasn't to say that he enjoyed the view. In fact, in the blue light of that Queens evening, he confessed his misery at what his life had become when he sang 'Help!', the *cri de coeur* of a man who wanted to get off the carousel of touring and produce something more interesting and enduring.

Similarly, the Stones were also coming to the end of their own musical adolescence. The breakthrough moment for the Jagger and Richards songwriting partnership came when they reworked an old gospel standard and called it 'The Last Time'. It was released in March and it provided the band with their first number one in Britain and their first top-ten hit in the United States. Their confidence sky high, they put their heads together and came up with '(I Can't Get No) Satisfaction', with its irresistible, three-note opening guitar riff. It spent four weeks at the top of the US charts in July and would become the band's musical calling card for all eternity. More significantly, in the popular mind, it marked the moment when Mick Jagger replaced Brian Jones as the leader of The Rolling Stones.

By the summer of 1965, the British Invasion was slowing down and popular music was about to completely reimagine itself. In April, Bob Dylan had released 'Subterranean Homesick Blues', an angry protest song loaded with political references. It marked Dylan's shift from folk to rock and it blew the minds of the listening Beatles. On 9 May, they sat starry-eyed in a box when he played the Royal Albert Hall. It was one of those game-changing moments, when all four Beatles – and John Lennon especially – glimpsed the potentiality of music, of what a song could sound like, of what an album could be.

At the end of April, speaking at a music industry event in London, Goddard Lieberson, the Columbia Records president who was credited with inventing the LP, said something that would prove extraordinarily prescient. 'There will be a growth in album sales,' he predicted, 'such as you've never seen before.'

Singles were still the bread and butter for most pop acts. Traditionally, albums contained two or three retrospective hits and a lot of inferior-quality filler. But music was about to witness the birth of a new era in which artists cut every track on an album as though it was going to be a single in its own right. It would change the way music was recorded and the way people thought about records. And for bands like The Beatles and the Stones, it would create great testaments to their music that would last for fifty years and more.

Brian Wilson had already gone through the same feelings that John Lennon was experiencing in the summer of 1965. On a flight to Houston the previous December, he collapsed, sobbing in the aisle, at the thought of embarking on yet another Beach Boys tour. He told his band mates that he was finished with live performing and he retired to the studio in search of a new sound for the band. In November 1965, The Beach Boys would start recording *Pet Sounds*, an album that would set the bar at a new height for The Beatles and for everyone else.

•

The Ad Lib's time had come and gone. By the summer of 1965 it was no longer the place where the hippest of the hip went to get their groove on. Tara and the rest of the in-crowd had migrated to the Scotch of St James in Mason's Yard, near Piccadilly, which opened its doors for the first time on 14 July. The Scotch was decked out in the Caledonian style, all tartan lampshades, bagpipes and stag's heads on the wall, resembling, in David Hockney's memorable phrase, 'a rhythm and blues Angus Steakhouse'.

The Ad Lib would limp on for another year or so, but in Swinging London, fashions changed quickly, and the Scotch was suddenly the place where The Beatles, The Rolling Stones, The Who and The Animals all went to let their hair down. An officious door policy gave the place an air of exclusivity that its habitués loved. Inside, it was necessary to maintain a dispassionate, even unimpressed, air around the celebrity clientele. Do something as uncool as asking Keith Richards or Ringo Starr for an autograph and you could find yourself being escorted to the door by one of the club's tartan-waistcoated lounge staff. If you were absent for even one night from the Scotch, you knew you had likely missed something vital. The answer was to make sure you were there every night. And Tara did.

It was in the Scotch one night in the summer of 1965 that he first met Gerard Campbell, a public relations executive with the advertising firm Hobbs and Bates, who was to become one of his closest friends. 'He made me laugh,' Gerard recalled of their first meeting. 'There was a song out at the time by Otis Redding called "I've Been Loving You Too Long (To Stop Now)" and Tara, with that sly smile of his, told me it was about the difficulty of performing coitus interruptus. That was Tara. He'd say things like that. He was just a lot of fun.'

•

By the mid-summer of 1965, Britain was revelling in the outbreak of positive feeling and the explosion of style and colour that was the Swinging Sixties. The miniskirts and bob haircuts, the Chelsea boots and the suits with tapered waists, the Mini Coopers in Union Jack colours, the cinema crowds flocking to see Sean Connery in *Thunderball* and Michael Caine in *The Ipcress File*, the use of contraception as a lifestyle choice, the teenage girls pursuing the malnourished look of Twiggy, the model of the moment – all of these things were common features of life up and down the land.

But against this happy, optimistic backdrop, Tara and Nicki's marital difficulties were becoming worse. A second child had only increased the strain on them. Tara still loved Nicki, but he was beginning to question his haste in marrying her and his mother's contributions on the subject didn't help ease his mind. He began to spend more and more time at the garage, according to Nicki, with his head under the bonnet of a car, or drinking in the Scotch with Brian Jones or whoever happened to be in town.

'You could see it was going wrong,' remembered Martin Wilkinson. 'I think it was the pressure of living in a small house and having two children and being so young themselves.'

But Tara bore his troubles far more ably than Brian, who had recently given an indication as to the lie of his mental landscape when he told Peter Jones, a writer with *Record Mirror*: 'No one would choose to live the life I live.'

In May, Brian was served with affiliation papers by the mothers of two of his children, who were seeking to establish proof of paternity and a right to child support. During the band's tour of America that summer, he shambled baggy-eyed around the stage, under the influence of drink and drugs, his increasing use of which only heightened his paranoia that he was being manoeuvred out of the band.

But his love life, at least, was about to take a happy turn. On 14 September he met Anita Pallenberg backstage at a Stones concert in Munich. Anita was a model with a toothsome smile and a worldliness that seemed almost impossible in a girl of just nineteen. She was born in Rome in 1944 while her father – a travel agent, but really a frustrated composer – was away fighting in the war. As a teenager, she was sent to boarding school in Germany, but was expelled at sixteeen. By the time she appeared in the lives of the Stones, she'd already tasted life with the *La Dolce Vita* crowd in Rome and with Andy Warhol's Factory circle in New York and knew her way around Swinging London, too. Brian and Anita had already met each other, briefly, in Paris. They had mutual friends in Robert Fraser, Christopher Gibbs and the socially omnipotent Ormsby-Gores, with whom she'd stayed during an earlier visit to London.

Anita was initially drawn to him, not because she found him more attractive than the other Stones, but because he spoke German.

'That was the first thing that struck me about him,' she remembered, 'after his hair, of course. And also that he was very well-spoken – more so than the others. He wasn't like, "Innit." He didn't have a London accent like Mick and Keith. He wasn't a Dartford lad or whatnot. He spoke very well and he chose his words very carefully.'

After the concert, he took her back to his hotel. 'The first night I was with him, he cried all night about Mick and Keith and what they were doing to him. At that point, there was a lot of competition. There was Mick and Keith and Brian and Andrew and the four of them never got on together at the same time. Sometimes three of them would get on, but one was always excluded and usually it was Brian.'

When the Stones returned to London a few days later to start a three-week tour of England, Anita had become a permanent part of the band's comet tail. Brian seemed happier than he had been in years. 'Anita was this sophisticated, exotic, international creature,' said Stash de Rola, who saw the change in his friend that autumn. 'She demanded intellectual stimulation. They were the kind of relationships Brian was looking for. He was a very gentle person who enjoyed conversation and his mind was avid for an esoteric kind of love. In Anita, I would say he found a lot of the same things he found in Tara – someone who was intelligent and well-read, with a high degree of refinement and sophistication.'

She moved into his rented house in Elm Park Mews, just off the Fulham Road in Chelsea, with its gold wallpaper and its radiogram, a state-of-the-art record player and radio that was designed to resemble a piece of furniture. Occasionally, Tara and Nicki called round. One night that October, Nicki remembered, Brian played Tara a record he loved called 'Do You Believe in Magic?', by the American folk rock band The Lovin' Spoonful. Then Tara handed everyone a small thin square made out of gelatin and they all went on a trip together.

Anita Pallenberg wasn't the only exotic thing to land in London in 1965. LSD arrived, too.

11: LONDON TAKES A TRIP

By October 1965, Tara, along with every other young Londoner in the know, had caught wind of what was happening in a basement flat in Pont Street, a short distance away from his mews in Belgravia. The flat was the home of Michael Hollingshead, a British-born researcher in psychedelic drugs and hallucinogens at Harvard University, who had recently arrived in London with a plan to turn the country's youth on to the consciousness-altering effects of lysergic acid diethylamide, or LSD, a then perfectly legal drug that had been used in the treatment of psychiatric patients.

Hollingshead was an apostle of Timothy Leary, a lecturer in clinical psychology at Harvard, who, through a number of experiments, had become an advocate of the drug's value in changing people's perception of the world around them. Leary, who coined phrases such as 'turn on, tune in, drop out' and 'think for yourself and question authority', would later be described by Richard Nixon as 'the most dangerous man in America'.

Hollingshead travelled to London to prepare the ground for Leary, who was planning to arrive in January 1966, renting out the Albert Hall for a psychedelic jamboree at which, he hoped, either The Beatles or The Rolling Stones would perform. At the climax of the evening, Leary would be introduced to the crowd as the High Priest of the psychedelic movement.

Armed with quite probably the largest quantity of LSD in private hands in the world, Hollingshead's mission was to educate young people in London about the spiritual benefits of the psychedelic experience.

Leary gave Hollingshead a set of marching orders, which included setting up a centre where people could take LSD in a quasi-liturgical setting, involving, among other things, acid-laced grapes; music by Ravi Shanker, Debussy and Bach; readings from various mystical texts; and slides projected onto the ceiling of Tantric yantras and Tibetan mandalas.

He rented a large flat at 25 Pont Street, where he opened the World Psychedelic Centre, along with two old Etonians, Desmond O'Brien – London's self-proclaimed 'Mr LSD' – and Joey Mellen, a proponent of trepanation, a medieval surgical procedure that involved drilling a hole in the human skull as a means of relieving pressure and inducing a permanent high.

Always ahead of the curve when it came to the latest thing, it wasn't long before Tara found his way to Hollingshead's door. 'Hollingshead was the only source of LSD in London at the time,' remembered Martin Wilkinson, who accompanied Tara the first time he went around there. 'Pont Street was basically an acid factory and it was pretty saturated with people. Hollingshead used to put acid on the door handles – very, very strong acid on the door handles, then you touched it and you went and stood in front of a thing that was called a scroll. It was about twelve feet high. It started off with a whole skull down the bottom, then gradually worked up to a skull at the top with rays coming out of it, which meant total consciousness.'

Tara wasn't much interested in the mystical dimension to Pont Street, but he did rather like LSD, which was available to buy in the form of Windowpanes, coloured gelatin squares that contained enough acid to induce a consciousness-altering experience lasting up to eight hours.

Hollingshead believed that his aristocrat regulars like Tara, Nicholas Gormanston, Julian Ormsby-Gore and Christopher Gibbs could become important proselytizers in the mission to spread Leary's psychedelic gospel. His initial impression of them was that they were self-regarding and shallow, being only interested in grooving, getting high and making the scene. But he changed his mind, describing them in his autobiography, *The Man Who Turned on the World*, as 'intelligent' and 'profound'.

'It was a period when people paid attention to dress,' he wrote, 'and clothes were no less essential than their bodies – it was a means of expression, and their dressed condition mirrored in their consciousness the outer expression of themselves. "By changing his clothes, he changes the man within." The mode of dress assisted in expressing certain traits of his being. In this way, the process of dressing-up can not only heighten or lessen the individual's power of expression: it can indeed bring about self-realization.'

Soon, anyone who was anyone was calling around to Pont Street in search of self-realization. Very quickly, London became saturated with acid. Gerard Campbell remembered a night in late 1965 when Tara turned him on to it. 'One evening, I was with Martin Wilkinson and Tara had managed to get his hands on some LSD, which I'd only heard of before. These little bits of blotting paper – where he got them from, I don't know.

'Everyone else was seeing all these wonderful colours. Nothing happened for me, so I took another one and I ended up nearly overdosing. I had all these visions – things moving on the walls. Then we went, all of us, to Bob Fraser's flat – Groovy Bob, as he was known. He had that art gallery and he had this machine in there that reacted to the beat of the music and shot lights on the walls. It was kind of frightening but very exciting, too.'

Acid would change the landscape of Swinging London utterly. 'You took acid and you actually thought you were very close to God,' said Jane Ormsby-Gore, an early visitor to Pont Street. 'You *saw* God, practically. And suddenly everyone realized something that I think Tara was probably aware of all along – that you didn't have to live your life in a regimented way. You didn't have to live your life in a box. You took psychedelics and you could see how your skin was made. You could see pieces of the atmosphere. You could see how we're all part of each other. There's no separation. It was the great social leveller.'

Acid blew away what remained of outmoded social concerns such as status, tradition, ambition – and the notion of an aristocratic class. 'This rather strange, cosmic explosion,' said Christopher Gibbs, 'blew away the flimsy structures that separated us all in a way that drink never would have. They made a lot of

social niceties seem as absurd as they were. We suddenly understood, you know, why on earth am I thinking that this matters and
that matters when obviously they don't? A lot of young people
became suddenly aware of the fact that, like A. J. Balfour said,
"Nothing matters very much and few things matter at all." And
life becomes so much more interesting and exciting with the freedom of knowing that.'

•

Nicki was fed up with spending her holidays in the south of
France in the company of her disapproving mother-in-law. For
almost two years now, she and Tara had been searching for a holiday home of their own somewhere on the continent. They had
seen a villa they loved in the French hilltop village of Ramatuelle,
but in the end Nicki decided it was still close enough for Oonagh
to make her influence felt.

Another time, while they were in Sicily, Tara found what he
thought was the perfect holiday home for them – a medieval tower,
halfway down a steep hill that plunged towards the Mediterranean
below. He and Nicki climbed down the hillside to reach it and
discovered it was empty. Captivated by the view, they decided that
this was where they wanted to spend their summers together.
Nicholas Gormanston, who knew the island well, offered to make
some enquiries locally as to who owned the place. The answer
came back quickly. It belonged to Joseph Bonnano, the boss of
one of the New York Mafia's Five Families. Tara and Nicki
decided not to make an offer on the place after all.

In the autumn of 1965, Nicki was tired of the constant rows
with Oonagh, who was now at a loose end after the closure of
Miguel's couture business and was in a position to judge her
efforts at being a mother from the house across the road. Oonagh
could see everything, including how often Nicki went out, what
time she came home and how little time she was spending with
Dorian and Julian. 'She was living right on top of us,' Nicki
remembered. 'Literally ten feet away.'

Dorian and Julian began to spend more and more time at their grandmother's place. Tara and Nicki didn't have a garden in which they could play, whereas Oonagh, conveniently, did. They also had the company of Oonagh's adopted twins, Desmond and Manuela. There were occasional rows over Oonagh's choice of nannies, but the arrangement suited Nicki, who could come and go as she pleased. What Nicki didn't know was that Oonagh was taking notes.

'She had already made up her mind what she was going to do,' she said, 'which was to break up my marriage and to take my children for herself.'

'She led an absolute campaign against Nicki,' remembered Rock Brynner, 'and she drove them apart by just weirding the situation out. Telling Tara constantly that he was with the wrong woman. Look, were they one hundred per cent faithful to each other? No, they probably weren't. It was the Sixties. Infidelity was not unusual at the time. But Oonagh used it to damage not only their connubial relationship but also their friendship.'

Nicki tried to persuade Tara that they should make a permanent home for themselves and the children abroad.

'By then, I was sick of London,' she said. 'I was tired of waking up every morning and finding all these people I didn't know sleeping on our living room floor. One day, I took away all the drink. I hid it. And I said to Tara, "Let's see how long everyone stays when there's nothing here for them." A crowd arrived from the Scotch. When they realized there was no booze, they left after ten minutes and it was just Tara and me looking at each other. I said, "This is nice, isn't it?" I put the drink back in the sideboard and the next night the house was full again.'

She had become enamoured with the Costa del Sol, a region in southern Spain that was becoming popular with young Britons as an alternative to the old English seaside holiday standbys of Margate, Southend and Clacton-on-Sea. She was interested in opening a small boutique, cheap and cheerful – nothing on the scale of Maison Ferreras – in Marbella, which was then just a village. But Tara wasn't ready to move abroad. In his mind, Spain was where old people went to retire. London, on the other hand, was a city pulsing with excitement. All of his friends were there. The garage was there.

And there was something else that was becoming obvious to Nicki in the latter half of 1965. Tara was disengaging from the relationship. Stories of his wife's unfaithfulness had reached his ears. LSD – Hollingshead's prescription for self-realization – may even have helped him see the truth more clearly, that, while he still loved Nicki, their marriage wasn't working. And a change of scenery wasn't going to save it.

But Nicki persisted and persuaded him to at least consider the idea. At the beginning of November they headed for Spain, Tara for some winter sun and Nicki to investigate local properties. They rented a house in Marbella and, as if to emphasize the space that had opened up between them, Tara invited his friends Gerard Campbell and Theodora Brinckman, as well as Mark Palmer, to go with them. They all had a thoroughly miserable time. 'When we got there,' Gerard remembered, 'it was cold and wet and raining and the house didn't have any heating.'

They spent their days in the local bistros and tapas bars. Tara, who had a sweet tooth, had never much liked the taste of wine, but Gerard, who was something of a connoisseur, did his best to educate him about such matters as balance, depth, complexity and finish, while they sat indoors and waited for the sun to reveal itself. It never did.

The tension between Tara and Nicki made the week even more unbearable. 'It was no secret that his family weren't keen on her,' Gerard said. 'That song by Sonny and Cher was out at the time: "I've Got You, Babe". And they both liked that song, I remember, because it was like their reply to the world.

'Anyway, while we were there, they had a terrific fight – as they did from time to time – and they decided they were going home. Theodora and I went to Seville. We were quite happy to get out of there because the tension was awful.'

This row, however, was more serious than one of their usual run of the mill disagreements over Oonagh's interference or Nicki's occasional affairs. Tara had fallen for somebody else.

A few months earlier, one afternoon in June, Tara arrived home and told Nicki that he'd just seen the most beautiful woman in the world. She was having lunch in a restaurant on the King's Road with April Ashley, a transsexual who had once been George Jamieson, a merchant seaman from Liverpool and one of the first people in Britain to have sex reassignment surgery. April was a familiar figure on the London scene, but Tara had never seen her friend before. He described her to Nicki as being about six feet tall, with long blonde hair and slightly Oriental features. 'I was jealous,' said Nicki. 'Of course I was, I was his wife. But I tried not to let it show. We were able to say things like that to each other. We were best buddies.'

Two days later, Nicki was reading a copy of the *Daily Express*, featuring a picture of a woman who worked as a striptease under the name Peki D'Oslo in Raymond Revuebar in Soho. She was photographed leaving court after giving evidence against two men accused of stealing the mink stole she used in her act, as well as jewellery, cash and a flick knife.

'I think she was French-Vietnamese,' Nicki said, 'with this long, blonde hair. I had to admit she was a very beautiful creature. Tara saw the picture over my shoulder and he said, "That's her! That's the girl!" and from that moment on he was totally infatuated with her.'

The girl for whom Tara had fallen was Amanda Lear, model and, later, a muse to the artist Salvador Dali. One of the most fascinating figures to emerge from the Sixties, she revelled in the aura of mystery and sexual ambiguity that she created for herself. Even her memoir, *My Life With Dali*, begins when she's twenty-five, with no reference whatsoever to her childhood, her parents, or even where she was born. During the course of her life, it has been variously reported that her mother was French, Vietnamese, French-Vietnamese, Chinese and English, and that her father was French, Indonesian, English and Russian. Her place of birth has been variously given as Hanoi, Hong Kong, Paris and Saigon.

However, by far the greatest matter of conjecture surrounding Amanda was whether she was born a boy or a girl. One popular account of her life had it that she had sex reassignment surgery in the early 1960s. Amanda always denied it, but for a time was happy to trade on the infamy that the story generated. 'Dali and I built the Amanda Lear persona,' she once said, 'into something very intriguing and very ambiguous and it worked.'

It wasn't that Amanda moved through life without leaving any footprints; it was just that she had a tendency to deny that the footprints belonged to her. April Ashley has claimed that she worked with Amanda in the 1950s at Le Carrousel, as part of a transvestite revue in Paris. In her book *April Ashley's Odyssey*, she claimed that Amanda was originally a man named Alain Tapp, who, like her, had had sex reassignment surgery, then stripped under the name Peki D'Oslo – a reference, it was said, to her half Chinese, half Scandinavian heritage – before she reimagined herself as Amanda Lear.

However, Amanda later denied that she was ever a man, or that she ever stripped, or that she was ever Peki D'Oslo. 'I was going to sue,' she later told an interviewer, 'but I thought, what is the point? People don't want normality. They want people from Mars.'

What is known for certain is that she first fetched up in London in the mid-1960s, where she studied fine art, rented a small flat in Sloane Avenue and fell in with Chelsea's hip crowd, the kind of people who, according to the writer Jonathan Meades, 'once shared a line with someone who shared a line with a Rolling Stone'.

According to April Ashley, her ambition was to be a respectable English lady with a British passport. As fate would have it, the woman for whom Tara had fallen in a King's Road restaurant in June happened to be in Spain that November.

There was a scene developing in Marbella. It was where regular King's Road habitués, such as Michael Rainey and Jane Ormsby-Gore, went to get away from it all. April Ashley had a bar there and Amanda was an occasional visitor.

On the beach one afternoon, Nicki saw her emerging from the water. 'She caught me staring at her as she came out of the sea,'

Nicki remembered. 'She said, "I'm Venus – who are you?" I had to admire her. Of course, the story was that she'd been born a boy. I thought, "Well, she looks good for a girl!" Tara's birthday was coming up. I thought to myself, "What do you get a twenty-one-year-old who has everything for his birthday?" And I said to her, "You are going to be my husband's twenty-first birthday present." And of course it all backfired on me because he went and fell in love with her.'

Amanda remembered events very differently. She had an affair with Tara, she said, which started that week in Spain, but it wasn't as a birthday gift and it didn't happen at his wife's instigation.

'One evening,' she recalled, 'I was in the Marbella Club and this beautiful girl offered me a drink. She was very friendly – and that was Nicki Browne. We became good friends, Nicki and I, and then her husband, Tara, whom she introduced me to that night. Mark Palmer was staying with them in the house. We spent a few days together and we got to know each other very well. We had a good time, smoking joints together and just having fun.

'First, I think, I was fascinated by Tara. He had such a charming smile. He had such good manners. He was really sweet. There was a feminine side to him. He was very soft and very well-spoken and he had very long hair. He was slim and good-looking and a typical Pisces – a bit of a dreamer. And what happened was that very quickly I fell in love with him. We started having an affair behind Nicki's back, which was not nice, of course, but I could not help it.'

Amanda denied that Nicki had any knowledge of the affair, though friends assumed it was the souce of the row between Tara and Nicki in Marbella. Whatever the truth of the matter, one thing was clear: Amanda and Tara were besotted with each other. 'I said to Tara that I should leave,' Amanda remembered, 'because the situation was getting out of hand. Years later, Nicki told me that Tara was completely infatuated with me. She said, "He lost his head for you, Amanda." But then who knows with men?'

Amanda left Marbella with Mark. They went to Paris then on

to Portugal, while Gerard and Theodora headed for Seville, relieved to escape the fractious atmosphere in the house.

Nicki remained in Marbella while Tara returned to London alone. It's quite likely that the newspapers had heard the rumours that the marriage between one of London's hippest young couples was in trouble. A day or two after Tara walked out on her, Nicki announced her plans to open a boutique in Marbella the following spring. She told the *Daily Express* she had also identified a home where she hoped to live and was involved in negotiations with the owners. 'It is a delightful, old house,' she said, 'and the Spanish family are really delighted to be moving into something more modern.'

All of which came as news to Tara, back home in London. He, too, had a visit from the *Daily Express*, who ran a story, headlined 'Young Mr Browne – he's a Guinness heir – plays nannie (sic),' alongside a photograph of Tara, looking more than a little miffed, as he watches over Julian and Dorian in their playpen. He was reported to be bathing the children himself and pushing them around Hyde Park in their pram. 'My wife, Nicki, is in Spain looking for premises where we might open a shop in Marbella,' he told the reporter, presumably through gritted teeth. He added that, whatever happened, he wouldn't be giving up the garage.

While Nicki remained in Spain, Tara bought himself an early Christmas present – an AC Cobra, a British-manufactured sports car with a 4.7-litre, V8 engine. It was green in colour and even more powerful than the Lotus Elan. Mike McCartney was with him when it was delivered on 11 November.

'Tara said to me, "You have to have a go of it, Michael. It's fantastic." So I got behind the wheel. He said, "Just press on the accelerator, like it's an ordinary car." So I put it into first gear, put my foot down and – whoa! – talk about power. The whole front of the car lifted up. I just got out and said, "Sorry, that's too much car for me."'

Tara's heart was still set on becoming a full-time racing car driver, using his inheritance to finance his career, just as Gay did to train and ride racehorses. On his visits home to Luggala he had become friendly with Gore Taylor, the local postman, who was an expert on car mechanics. In December, Tara wrote to him, offering him a full-time job as his manager and mechanic when he eventually made the leap into Formula Three. In the end, it came to nothing. While he knew how to handle a car, Glen Kidston wondered if Tara had the discipline to give up the late nights at the Scotch and the regular trips to Pont Street.

'He would have had to modify his lifestyle if he was going to do it,' he said. 'There were a lot of gentlemen drivers, it's true. He could have done that, but you can't take liberties with, let's just say, your intakes and stay on the road. Once you're racing, you've signed on the line and agreed to leave all that stuff to one side. Tara had bottle. But if you have bottle, you also need luck. And you won't have luck if you weigh the odds against yourself.'

Tara was undoubtedly searching for a new focus as he felt his marriage listing. Nicki arrived home from Spain a week later. Even those who weren't privy to his holiday fling with Amanda could see that Tara and Nicki were on the rocks.

'As an alliance between two people,' said Christopher Gibbs, 'it bore no relation to any marriage I'd ever encountered, so I guess I'd never really taken it particularly seriously. It was two waifs in a storm hanging on to each other, whose union had been blessed – in inverted commas – with two nippers. And I can't remember the nippers being paraded around in the arms of either parent, because the parents were too busy having a good time – as you are when you're twenty.'

•

On a rainy Saturday lunchtime that December, a group of Chelsea football fans on their way to a match were stopped dead in their tracks by the sight of three outlandishly dressed individuals putting a sign up over a retail outlet in World's End, at the unfashionable end of the King's Road. The sign, written in red art deco script, said, 'Granny Takes a Trip'.

'Weirdos!' was among the cleanest comments shouted.

If only the fans had looked inside. The shop was fitted out to resemble a New Orleans bordello as seen through the eyes of someone who had just had something off the menu at the World Psychedelic Centre. The decor was grotesque, opulent, erotic; the marble-effect walls adorned with Aubrey Beardsley illustrations, saucy, French postcards of girls with long eyelashes in silk stockings, and a sign that borrowed from Oscar Wilde: 'One should either be a work of art or wear a work of art.'

'There was a lot of yahoo, yobbo kind of catcalls,' remembered Nigel Waymouth, one of the shop's owners, 'but I knew from the reaction, as we were putting up the sign, that they were also slightly confused, or bemused, but certainly fascinated – and that was the whole idea.'

Waymouth was a former grammar school boy and economics and history graduate who worked for a year and a half as a freelance journalist, 'writing in-depth features about tramps, homeless people, junkies, schizophrenics, people living in Glasgow doss houses, my George Orwell years – *Down and Out in Paris and London* kind of thing.'

He set up the shop along with his girlfriend, Sheila Cohen, a collector of vintage clothes, and John Pearse, a mod, who came out of the Soho coffee bar milieu and had served an apprenticeship as a Savile Row tailor. Granny's, as it became known, was one of two London boutiques that opened at the end of 1965 that would have an enormous influence on the way young people dressed, and would persuade Tara himself to go into the rag trade.

Granny's actually started off as a jumble sale. The first clothes they sold were items from Sheila's own wardrobe, which she'd resolved to declutter. 'They were piling up everywhere in the flat where we lived, just off Baker Street,' Nigel remembered. 'And it was getting slightly out of hand, so we thought we'd open an outlet to sell them.'

Sheila's clothes were mostly vintage items from the 1920s and 1930s, which John went at with scissors and a needle and thread to give them a modern twist. 'We were really making it up as we went along. This wasn't the world of Stella McCartney. This was street design.'

World's End couldn't have been more off the beaten track. It was far from the West End and from the heart of the King's Road, the latter the base of operations for Mary Quant, whose companies were now grossing millions of pounds annually. But, as John Stephen showed on Carnaby Street, if you piqued people's interest, they would find you.

The name of the shop captured the whole point of the enterprise, which was taking clothes that their grandparents might have worn and giving them a more modern look. But it was also a cheeky wink to the still relatively small constituency of people, like Tara, who were in the know as to the effects of psychoactive drugs. Granny's was the first indicator that Carnaby Street's day as the arbiter of what was hip was coming to an end. By the end of 1965 it was choked with tourists and weekend mods. The real groovers, their heads suddenly filled with surrealistic shapes and fantastical colours – phosphine and paisley patterns, spirals and concentric circles, blindingly bright purples, reds and yellows – would soon be migrating west in search of something to wear that matched the new visual aesthetic.

Mod snazziness and the beatnik look were on the way out, replaced by a new fixation with Victorian frills, Edwardian velvet and satin, and ethnic materials and designs, all infused with a pop-art sensibility. Very quickly, Granny's became an essential destination.

When Sheila's wardrobe was empty, they started acquiring clothes, including men's clothes, from other sources: colourful floral shirts; white flared trousers made of Venetian cloth; flapper dresses; jackets in trademark William Morris prints; tight velvet trousers; Chicago gangster suits; fezzes and turbans; Victorian bustles; satin blouses with frills – for women *and* men. That was what was truly revolutionary about the new look that began to emerge, post-Carnaby Street – the homogenization of fashion. Jackets, trousers and, yes, even blouses were no longer for women *or* men.

'Then we started designing our own stuff. Sourcing vintage

stuff – you can't keep doing it. Beautiful, haute-couture clothes were becoming more and more rare. We had to start making our own. Sheila was keen to do dresses and things for girls and John had a lot of ideas for men. I did most of the drawing. I remember we got this outrageous floral material and we asked this woman named Mrs Trot in New Cross to turn it into shirts. They flew off the shelves at five guineas each – outrageous, half a week's wages, you know. It was extraordinary.'

They changed the front of the shop regularly, sometimes to attract passing trade, but occasionally just to amuse themselves. One day, a giant smiling sun shone out from the boards that covered the front window. Another day, it was a pop-art image of Jean Harlow. Another, the front half of John's broken-down 48 Dodge which they'd sawn in two and fixed to the outer wall to make it look like it was crashing out of the shop.

One day, early in 1966, John Lennon and Paul McCartney wandered in. They left with a couple of signature Granny's shirts, slim-fitting, loudly coloured and ornately patterned with long rounded collars, which made the Carnaby Street look seem positively old-fashioned almost overnight.

Tara loved the sheer oddness of Granny's and became a regular visitor. He considered opening a shop just like it. 'Tara had an extraordinary visual sense,' said Martin Wilkinson. 'He went to huge lengths to get an old Hungarian guy to make special shirts with frills for him. He'd visit tailors with instructions. The impulse behind all of these new shops that were suddenly opening up was a return to eighteenth-century dandyism. It was more than just a dress code. It was, "I've just had a very large joint and I'm going to take tremendous enjoyment from the fact that I'm wearing a blue silk shirt with frills on it and it's really pissing off the guy in the bank."'

A mile away from Granny's, on Cale Street, just off the King's Road, a friend of Tara's who was also clued in to what was happening in Pont Street was making waves with his own visual style. In December 1965, Michael Rainey, who was sometimes described as the best-dressed man in London, opened a shop called Hung

On You, named after the B-side to the Righteous Brothers hit 'Unchained Melody'.

'I had no background in the rag trade,' he remembered. 'Like Nigel and the crowd at Granny's, I really wasn't thinking, "How do I make money out of this?" Make enough to pay the rent and go to a nightclub every night – that was what I wanted to do.'

Hung On You had its own signature style that would set a new benchmark for cool. Like his new rivals at the other end of Chelsea, Michael Rainey also dealt in vintage, military and ethnic clothes, intended to be worn in a subversive or satirical way: tapered guardsmen's trousers with red stripes down the sides; mandarin-collar shirts; dragoon coats; military bandsmen's uniforms; kipper ties; floral chiffon shirts; and the soon-to-be-famous high-buttoned Mao jackets, favoured by Brian Jones, the 'dancing child in his Chinese suit' in Bob Dylan's 1966 song 'I Want You'.

The shop had something of a wild reputation, which Tara loved. Michael would thrash around on a drum kit in the basement, while Jay and Bo, the shop's two most famous assistants, would sit on a chaise longue in the window, between customers, smoking joints.

'I suppose it had an energy about it,' Michael said. 'The energy of the times. We were learning every day, through acid, smoking dope, going to Glastonbury. We were all full of interests. Open to being influenced. We found this young Irish girl who hand-painted these beautiful ties with designs inspired by the whole Arthurian thing and Gustav Klimt. It was such an exciting time.'

•

Paul McCartney was the only member of The Beatles who hadn't taken LSD by late 1965. John Lennon and George Harrison had first sampled its sensory enhancing effects back in April, when George's dentist, John Riley, slipped it into their coffee at a dinner party in Bayswater.

Despite their initial fear and their anger with the dentist, John and George didn't find the drug's effects altogether disagreeable. John may even have slipped a reference to the experience into the

21. Tara and his wife, Nicki, whom he married at eighteen while she was pregnant with the first of their two sons. The photograph was taken for *Vogue* by Michael Cooper, who also took the photograph for the cover of *Sergeant Pepper's Lonely Hearts Club Band*.

22. Tara wins the Mercantile Trophy in his Lotus Elan in Rathdrum, County Wicklow, May 1964. It was the first and only time he ever raced.

23. Dandie Fashions, Tara's clothes shop on the King's Road, which opened shortly before Christmas, 1966.

24. Douglas Binder, David Vaughan and Dudley Edwards, members of a pop art collective who painted Tara's AC Cobra. On the right is their assistant, Gary White.

25. Tara was immensely proud of his 'acid' car. In September 1966, it was exhibited in the trendy Fraser Gallery on Duke Street in London.

26. Brian Jones (left), Nicki Browne (second left) and Anita Pallenberg (second from right) and other guests take in the view on the way to Tara's twenty-first-birthday party at Luggala, April 1966.

27. Brian, Anita and Nicki. 'We had a lot of affinity together,' said Anita, 'but the main one was acid.'

28. Oonagh, Derek Hart of the BBC and Tara at the party in Luggala.

29. Tara with Amanda Lear, muse of Salvador Dali, in Paris. Their affair hastened the end of his marriage to Nicki.

30. Mick Jagger was among the guests entertained by The Lovin' Spoonful at what would be Tara's last birthday party.

31. Five aristocratic dandies photographed for *Gentleman's Quarterly* in the summer of 1966. From left to right, Christopher Gibbs, Mark Palmer, Tara Browne, Nicholas Gormanston and Julian Ormsby-Gore.

32. Oonagh and Tara at the christening of Julian at St Patrick's Cathedral, Dublin, in 1965. Nicki was described as 'indisposed'.

33. Tara with his friend Brian Jones and his son Dorian at Luggala, November 1966. Just weeks later, Tara was dead.

34. Suki Potier, Tara's date, who survived the car crash that killed him. On the left is Brian Jones, whom she dated after Tara's death. Suki was to die in another car accident sixteen years later.

35. The aftermath of the crash in Redcliffe Gardens, South Kensington, in the early hours of 18 December 1966.

36. Tara was buried close to the shore of Lough Tay, County Wicklow, under a stone containing the two dates bearing out the tragedy of a life cut short.

37. A view of Tara's boyhood playground. With its dark water and white beach, visitors often comment on Lough Tay's similarity to the porter that made the Guinness name famous.

lyrics of 'Help!', when he sang about opening up the doors, after Aldous Huxley's acid-inspired *Doors of Perception*. They were intrigued enough to at least give it another try. On 24 August, just over a week after they played Shea Stadium, John, George and Ringo had taken it in a rented house in Los Angeles, along with Roger McGuinn and David Crosby of The Byrds and the actor Peter Fonda, who kept creeping everyone out by whispering, 'I know what it's like to be dead.'

Paul sat out the trip. 'Paul felt very out of it,' John recalled in 'Lennon Remembers', his seminal interview with *Rolling Stone* magazine, 'because we were all a bit slightly cruel, sort of, "We're taking it, and you're not."'

The prospect of taking LSD terrified Paul. 'I'd not wanted to do it,' he told Barry Miles, his friend and the author of the authorized biography, *Many Years From Now*. However, he knew he would have to succumb to the peer pressure in time. He wanted to do it in an environment where he felt safe and an opportunity presented itself one night back in Tara's mews. A number of accounts had it happening early in 1966, although Nicki was certain that it was in late November 1965, shortly after her return from Marbella and before the release of *Rubber Soul*, which The Beatles had recorded earlier that autumn.

Paul was the only Beatle who showed up regularly at Tara and Nicki's place. John moved in different circles, although Nicki remembered him being there once, drunk, with Peter Sellers. Tara gave John a copy of *Pygmalion*, George Bernard Shaw's 1913 play lampooning, of all things, Britain's rigid class system. But John was still too class-conscious to ever warm to Tara, or even to let his guard down around him, according to Nicki. 'I think he really sneered at people from Tara's background,' she said.

Martin Wilkinson had observed the same standoffishness in him in clubs like the Scotch and the Ad Lib. 'John didn't say much. He was quite aggressive. He was bloody angry. I don't think he would have allowed himself to be impressed by someone like Tara, but Paul was far more open to people from different backgrounds.'

One night, after closing time, Paul was back at Eaton Row

with a party that included Sir Mark Palmer; Patrick Kerr, the dancer from *Ready Steady Go!*; and Viv Prince, the drummer with The Pretty Things; as well as a bunch of girls who had become attached to them in the Scotch.

Tara was taking acid on blotting paper in the toilet, McCartney remembered in *Many Years From Now*, and offered him some. McCartney was unsure, but he accepted. According to Nicki, Tara didn't actually take it that night. 'Because it was Paul's first time,' she said, 'he felt it was important for him to stay lucid just in case Paul had a bad trip. And what Paul did was he spent his whole trip looking at this art book of mine called *Private View*. He wasn't interested in any of the females there. He wasn't interested in listening to music either. He was just staring at this art book. I wish it had been more fun for him.'

Paul stayed up all night having what he described as a 'spacy' experience. He told Barry Miles that he saw paisley shapes and was super-sensitive to the fact that his shirtsleeves were dirty. He had an engagement the following day, but he couldn't get it together. When Brian Epstein's secretary tracked him down to Tara and Nicki's mews, he told her he had flu and asked her to cancel his commitments for the day.

John later said he thought Paul regretted taking it. Paul said it was something that he wouldn't want to have missed but he would always have mixed feelings about what happened in Tara's house that night. For all his ambivalence about taking acid, it would have a profound effect on him.

On 3 December, *Rubber Soul* was released. It was the first Beatles album that Tara really loved. Musically, it was a bolt out of the blue. There had been hints in *Help!* of a growing maturity in the band's creativity. *Rubber Soul* marked the dramatic transition of The Beatles from a boy band, knocking out songs to order on the theme of boy-wants-girl, boy-loves-girl, boy-loses-girl, to a group of musicians who were setting a new template for how a rock and roll album should sound.

It contained no filler. Every song was a potential single, even the ones that went places where no pop song had dared to venture before, from the trippy seduction scene of 'Norwegian Wood' to the existential musings of 'Nowhere Man', the first song John Lennon wrote on anything other than the theme of love.

Musically, they were exploring too, bringing new instruments, like George's sitar, into the studio. They speeded up a recording of a piano solo to create a baroque sound and experimented with fuzz bass. And, most seditiously of all, the song 'Girl' featured an inhalation of breath that sounded suspiciously like four newly made Officers of the Most Excellent Order of the British Empire toking on a joint.

Rubber Soul was the sound of The Beatles deciding they'd seen enough hotel rooms, concert halls and airport lounges. With one or two exceptions, the songs on the album – thoughtful, auto-biographical and musically sophisticated – weren't the kind that drove teenage girls to hysterics in American ballparks. On 10 December, Tara and Nicki saw them play at the Hammer-smith Odeon in London, part of what would be the band's final tour of Britain.

Nicki's relationship with her mother-in-law had reached such a low point that she decided she wasn't going to Ireland for the traditional Christmas at Luggala. Tara didn't go either. They spent Christmas Day in London, then, on Boxing Day, they took up Paul and Mike McCartney's invitation to visit them in Liverpool.

They left Dorian and Julian with a nanny, jumped into the AC Cobra and – in defiance of the 70mph motorway speed limit that had come into effect a week earlier – tore up the M6 to the mock-Tudor house that Paul had recently bought for his father and stepmother in the Wirral.

Paul had rented a couple of mopeds. That night, after smoking a few joints, Paul suggested that he and Tara use them to visit his cousin Bett, who lived in nearby Bevington. 'I'd spent some of my allowance on a very nice red and white scarf,' Nicki recalled of the evening. 'It was knitted, very long, a bit like a football scarf. They were all the mode at the time. It cost a fortune. Eight pounds or something like that. So they were going off to see Paul's (cousin) and it was chilly. Paul said he was cold, so I said, "Take my scarf." He took it.'

A few hours later, they returned. Paul's face was all swollen and stitched up and Nicki's scarf was saturated with blood. 'He looked like he'd been in a boxing match with Sonny Liston,' Mike remembered. 'I said, "Oh my God!" and he said, "No, it's fine." They'd been taking some sort of substances and he was still high. He said, "You must take a picture! You've got to! Michael," he kept saying, "this is the truth. This is life. This is reality." It was mind-expanding drugs is what it was.'

Paul had gone over the handlebars of his bike, breaking a front tooth and splitting his lip. The spill would later become the source of an outlandish, but no less enduring, Paul is Dead conspiracy theory.

Paul recounted what really happened in *The Beatles Anthology*. They were riding along and he was pointing out various local landmarks to Tara. Paul's attention was snagged by the sight of what appeared to be an especially huge full moon. Suddenly, his front wheel hit the kerb and he found himself falling face-first to the pavement.

Tara helped him to his feet. Paul had chipped his front tooth and split his upper lip badly, but they got back on their mopeds and continued on their journey. His cousin Bett phoned a doctor friend, who came round and stitched up his busted lip.

When they got back to his father's house later that evening, Paul insisted that Mike go and get his brand new Nikon camera to take photographs of his damaged face. Nicki, meanwhile, was looking at her very expensive scarf, ruined. 'His stepmother took it,' she remembered, 'and said, "I'll wash it," and I said, "Well, I really think it ought to be dry-cleaned," because it was wool and I knew it was going to come out of the washing machine looking like a tie. I said, "Please don't put it in the washing machine," and she said, "I have to wash it because it's got Paul McCartney's blood on it and you could sell it." So she did wash it – and, yes, she ruined it.'

The day after the accident, Tara and Nicki sat in the Cobra, discussing Paul's lucky escape, as they headed back to London, a city in its colourful, optimistic prime. Neither of them dared to imagine that they'd just spent their last Christmas together.

12: A DAY FOR A DAYDREAM

Brian Jones and Anita Pallenberg moved out of Elm Park Mews due to the attentions of the local police and an army of groupies. They set up home in a mansion flat at 1 Courtfield Road in Kensington, a soon-to-be legendary rock pad where they entertained friends, fellow musicians and hangers-on when the Stones weren't touring or recording. Tara and Nicki became regular members of their court.

'We had this crazy apartment,' Anita remembered, 'which was on three floors, like a house, flat, whatever. There were all these secret hatches, one of which went up to a secret room at the top of the house that we used to call the flying saucer. We'd pull down the metal staircase and we'd all climb up there and take LSD and pretend we were in a flying saucer.'

At that point, the early months of 1966, Tara was about as close to Brian as anyone was allowed to get, according to Anita. Tara would call round after a day at the garage and they'd smoke pot, listen to The Lovin' Spoonful and talk about life. Or they'd stay up all night at Eaton Row, drinking brandy and watching Tara's Scalextric cars describe circles and figure eights on the maroon carpet.

'Brian loved model trains when he was a boy,' said Anita. 'And Tara loved these little racing cars. They played with them all night, all the time laughing, like two little boys.'

Anita and Nicki became close, too. The two couples even looked similar: four smartly dressed blonds with his-and-her, Sassoon-style bobs. From fifty feet away, it was impossible to tell them apart.

They went out on long middle-of-the-night jaunts to nowhere

in particular, Tara and Nicki in the Cobra and Brian and Anita in Brian's black Rolls Royce with its infamous number plate, DD 666 – all of them tripping. 'We had loads of affinity together,' Anita said, 'but the main one was acid.'

'We'd get in our cars and drive to Staffordshire to look for UFOs. All of us, just lying on a hillside, looking up at the sky. We'd stay up all night, then we'd drive back to London. I remember once, we were all in the same car, which Tara was driving up the King's Road, towards Sloane Square . . . For some reason we all decided to get out. We were tripping all night and we had a sugar lack or something, so Tara stopped and we opened the doors and just left the car standing in the middle of the King's Road with the motor running and the doors open while we went to this cafe and had a piece of toast with some marmalade on it. Tara would do things like that. He'd be up for it. He wouldn't say, "Oh, I have to find somewhere to park." He just left it. That was how he lived his life.'

Brian and the other Stones had recently returned from California, where they recorded *Aftermath*, their fourth studio album and as seminal a moment in the career of The Rolling Stones as *Rubber Soul* had been for The Beatles. *Aftermath* would be their first 'real' album, not a ragbag of blues covers rendered in Mick Jagger's Mississippi Delta via the River Darent accent, with the occasional Jagger-Richards composition thrown in as grouting, but a thoroughly original collection of songs, comprising several very different musical styles, melded together in a way that suggested a coherent vision at work.

Every song on the album was written by Mick and Keith, though many of *Aftermath*'s best moments were pure Brian. Frozen out of the songwriting process, he went searching for ways to add new textures to the band's music, as The Beatles had done. He played more than a dozen instruments on the record, including many never before associated with Chicago electric blues: the Appalachian dulcimer, the marimbas, the Japanese koto, the harpsichord and a child's plastic banjo, as well as the more familiar props of guitar, keyboard and harmonica.

The *Aftermath* sessions also threw up 'Paint It Black', a single in which Brian played the sitar in the manner of a lead guitar, to produce an apocalyptic Eastern sound. He was on top of his game, and, professionally at least, something close to being happy. But his private life was as chaotic as it had ever been. At the start of 1966 he was faced with another paternity case brought by his ex-girlfriend Pat. He failed to appear in court and was ordered to pay costs of £2 10s per week. Shortly after that, Dawn Malloy, a girl with whom he enjoyed a brief fling, brought his fifth child into the world, a boy, and immediately sought a paternity settlement. Brian left it to the band's management to pay her off: £700 in full and final settlement, the money to be deducted from his future earnings.

It's perhaps not surprising that he failed to find the inner peace that he admired so much in Tara.

The drugs only made things worse. While Tara's experiences with LSD were mostly positive, Brian's were destructive. 'Brian was a tortured soul,' Anita said. 'I discovered that when we used to take acid. I never got a bad trip, but he would go completely mental, get paranoid, all of that. He would get it right away. He had horrible trips. He would go into the cupboards. He thought there was something outside. I don't know if it had something to do with his mental illness, but that's when I realized there was something wrong. We used to take acid to have a laugh, but then it wasn't a laugh anymore.

'We had a massive row everywhere we went. Caused by jealousy, possessiveness from his side, insecurity from his side. I was more, like, mellow. I'd been to America and I'd been travelling and I was streetwise, so to speak. He wasn't. So there was a lot of problems. He used to throw me out. He used to get so violent and then he just put me outside the door and I didn't know where to go and I used to run over to Nicki and Tara to lick my wounds. I spent many nights there. Then, the next morning, I would go back home.

'Once, I went over to Nicki one night after we had this massive row. Tara was out. I don't know where he was, but I said to Nicki,

"Brian threw me out, he's gone mad – blah, blah, blah." So Nicki said, "Let's make a doll of him." She was talking about voodoo. I said, "No, no, no." She said, "Come on, let's do it." So we made a doll of Brian and she said, "Stick a pin in his stomach," and I did. I felt better. The next day, when I went back home, I saw this Pepto-Bismol by the bedside and all of that. I said, "Brian, were you sick in the stomach?" He said, "Oh, yeah, I was really sick." And so I really freaked out. This thing works! I never did anything like that again. It really scared the shit out of me.'

Marianne Faithfull joined Brian and Anita's bohemian ménage in the spring of 1966. It had been eighteen eventful months since she scored a top-ten hit with 'As Tears Go By'. There were more hit singles, but Marianne was mostly known as a girl with a knack for being in the right place at the right time, turning up looking fabulous, in a far-out kind of way, at every important 'happening'.

At eighteen, she married John Dunbar, the co-founder of the Indica Gallery, London's first conceptual art space, in Mason's Yard, a few doors down from the Scotch. In November 1965 she gave birth to their son, Nicholas. But by early 1966 she had grown disenchanted with the settled life and fell in with Anita, having determined upon snagging herself a Stone. Brian was already taken, of course, by her new best friend, but the word was that there might soon be a vacancy with Mick, whose three-year relationship with Chrissie Shrimpton was known to be on the skids.

Marianne became part of the regular crowd at Courtfield Road.

'That's when I met Tara for the first time,' she remembered, 'around at Brian and Anita's place. He was right in the middle of that same group of musicians that I was; always flashing around in cars, which were very low and very cool and very fast. He and Brian were quite close at that time. I suppose what they had in common was they were both young, good-looking and rich. And very worldly. It's hard to remember Brian now, but I think of him as this worldly, intelligent man, but fucked up in a way that Tara wasn't.

'We all hung out together. I don't know if you could describe a lot of these relationships as friendships, because it all happened in such a short space of time. Friendship comes later, down the line, over the course of years. But things were happening so fast in London in the Sixties that you didn't stop to define what your relationship with anyone else really was.'

Looking at Tara and Nicki, however, it wasn't difficult to divine that they'd made the same mistake as she had in marrying too young. 'He'd married a village girl while they were both still kids and they'd had these children. And now he was changing and becoming something else, which was putting a strain on them. I think they liked each other very much, but it was clear they didn't have anything in common.'

They did have psychedelic drugs – and perhaps the consciousness-altering fun of tripping helped forestall the inevitable for at least a few months longer.

The possession of LSD was still legal at that point and the subject of curiosity in official circles. In April, in what was intended as a serious scientific enquiry, the BBC threw a party in Christopher Gibbs's house in Cheyne Walk, Chelsea, at which they distributed free LSD to invited guests, with the intention of filming the results.

The footage can't have made for a compelling viewing experience. Unlike alcohol, marijuana or pills, acid wasn't a social enabler. Melissa North, Tara's girlfriend from his days in Paris, remembered the change in the energy around at Eaton Row when LSD replaced drink and pot as the main item on the menu after hours.

'All of a sudden, it was a very, very non-talking environment,' she remembered. 'Lots of very glamorous people like Chrissy Gibbs, maybe Brian Jones, lying around, smoking enormous amounts of dope and taking LSD. There'd just be the occasional remark. Someone would put on a record and someone else might say, "Cool!" or something like that. It was all very monosyllabic. And very cliquey – especially if you weren't taking LSD. Nobody ever told you anybody else's name. And Nicki was suddenly very

– not frosty, but uninterested. We never got the line, "Lovely to see you," or anything like that. So in the end, we stopped calling around.'

The BBC weren't the first media outlet to become interested in the new youth obsession with exploring inner space. In March, *London Life* magazine had blown the whistle on what was going on around at Michael Hollingshead's Pont Street flat with an exclusive story advertised as: LSD – THE DRUG THAT COULD THREATEN LONDON. The story revealed that 'some famous artists, pop stars and debs' were risking psychotic illness by tripping on 'the most powerful and dangerous drugs known to man'.

The police decided to put an end to the fun and games at Pont Street. They raided the World Psychedelic Centre, arresting Hollingshead and Joey Mellen, amongst others. Because LSD wasn't a controlled drug, all of the charges subsequently brought related to cannabis possession and, in Hollingshead's case, permitting his flat to be used for the smoking of cannabis.

'The cops were pretty corrupt,' said Martin Wilkinson, who stood bail for Hollingshead, 'and they didn't have a clue about drugs at all, except they knew what dope was.'

On both sides of the Atlantic, the authorities had decided to call time on the psychedelic era. Timothy Leary had already been busted before he got a chance to stage his acid jamboree at the Royal Albert Hall. He was arrested for bringing a small amount of marijuana into America after a holiday in Mexico and was sentenced to thirty years in prison, fined $30,000 and ordered to undergo psychiatric treatment. In April 1966, four weeks after Leary was sent down, the Sandoz Corporation in Switzerland, which manufactured LSD, announced that it was suspending distribution of the drug.

In May, Hollingshead, who attempted to conduct his own defence while tripping on LSD, was sentenced to twenty-one months in prison.

'Being busted is like going bald,' Hollingshead later wrote. 'By the time you realize it's happening, it's too late to do anything about it.'

But it was also too late to do anything about LSD. It was already shaping the music of the day. And once that happened, there was no rebottling the genie.

•

'It seemed to happen so quickly,' Michael Rainey said of London in the early months of 1966. 'One day it wasn't there, the next day it was everywhere. Fashion. Robert Fraser's gallery. Indica Books. Granny Takes a Trip. Hung On You. All these places that were suddenly part of a movement, they all came up like mushrooms. It was in the air. Things were happening. People like me, who remembered that dull post-war London of their childhood, where you had to change your shirt if you went into the city for the day, because it smelled of smoke, we were suddenly living in this bright, colourful city and realizing what an exciting time it was to be alive.

'It seems silly now, but LSD made you think that anything was possible. You could spend seven or eight hours staring at a buttercup, convinced that it was talking to you. I remember there was a thing at St Pancras station. All these people got together, held hands and tried to make the station levitate. I mean, they really believed it was going to. That's how strong good acid was.'

This new London may have seemed to happen overnight, but it had been building for the best part of a decade. The King's Road, a short walk away from Michael's shop, had become a catwalk for the most outré fashions. And it wasn't just women in miniskirts with knee-high Biba boots and their hair stacked high. It was men in brilliantly coloured Victorian frock coats with ruffles, fluttering from shop to shop, with Union Jack bags from shops like Granny Takes a Trip and Lord Kitchener's Valet, picking up some eye-catching clobber to wear that night, something that might have got a man beaten up in the street two or three years earlier.

In the wonderfully satiric mood of the day, they were even sent up in a song by The Kinks that reached the top ten in April 1966. In 'Dedicated Follower of Fashion', Ray Davies mocked the 'Carnabetian army' who were one day in polka dots and the next day in stripes. And, though there was a sharp edge to the song – Davies was frustrated at how once spontaneous fashions were becoming just another uniform – it was embraced as an anthem by the very people that it ridiculed.

It wasn't a time for taking offence. The year 1966 was the apogee of London's happy, optimistic, golden age. England, the home of football, was about to host the World Cup and the team's manager, Alf Ramsey, predicted that his Wingless Wonders would win it. Michael Caine was starring as *Alfie*, a Cockney womanizer who would soon be seducing American cinema audiences on his way to a string of Oscar nominations. *Aftermath* was being played at full volume everywhere you went.

Formal, international recognition that London was now the spigot of everything that was cool in the world of music, art, fashion and cinema came in April, when America's *Time* magazine made 'the Swinging City' the subject of an era-defining cover story.

Piri Halasz's article was originally conceived as a travel feature, but was pushed to the front of the magazine when her editor saw it for what it was – a piece of journalism that fossilized a unique moment in modern culture. The piece gave readers a guide to all of the trendiest restaurants, shops, bars, nightclubs, galleries and casinos in the city, and walked them through the rudiments of the new English, as spoken by *Ready Steady Go!* presenter Cathy McGowan, including flip terms such as 'super', 'fab', 'groovy', 'gear', 'close' and 'with-it'.

But it was more social analysis than travelogue. Through a storyboard of Swinging London scenes, she offered the magazine's largely conservative readership an insight into life in a city that had thrown off the old Establishment of 'the financial city of London, the church and Oxbridge' and was now led by a 'swinging meritocracy' of actors, photographers, singers, admen, TV executives and writers, most of them, terrifyingly, still in their early twenties. She wrote about London as the capital of a country that had 'recovered a lightness of heart lost during the weighty centuries of world leadership' and where working-class men were now 'sporting their distinct, regional accents like badges'. Other foreign news magazines, including *Stern* and *Paris-Match,* sent reporters to London to pan the same waters. Mark Palmer had so many media outlets looking to photograph him and the rest of London's beautiful people that he decided to set up a modelling agency, called English Boy.

Vogue was also keen to get a visual on what was happening. The magazine commissioned Michael Cooper – a twenty-five-year-old freelance photographer and friend of The Rolling Stones, who would soon find fame as the man who photographed a certain Beatles album cover – to find models for a spread on how men's clothes had become informed by women's fashion. As it happened, he knew a couple of dandies who'd make perfect models for the job: Tara Browne and Brian Jones.

They agreed to model for the magazine, as did Nicki and Anita, who were first sent on a shopping trip to dress their men for the shoot. For Tara, Nicki chose a maroon silk suit by Major Hayward, with a gold shirt by Turnbull & Asser, and a multicoloured, brocade tie. Brian wore a black double-breasted, 'gangster' suit, with red and white stripes, a bright pink shirt and scarlet handkerchief and tie, with white shoes from Carnaby Street.

Hair was by Anita Pallenberg. 'I always did it for him,' she remembered. 'He was so obsessed with his hair. He had to have three mirrors when he was getting ready to go out, so he could see it from every angle. Whereas Tara had this very easy hair-style. That was how it grew naturally. He didn't have to do a thing. Another thing he envied in Tara. Brian's hair was a nightmare.'

It was one of Tara and Nicki's last truly happy days as a married couple. 'We laughed our way through the whole thing,' Nicki remembered. 'I can't remember if we had taken acid, or if we were smoking something – maybe it was neither or maybe it was both. But the five of us, Michael included, just laughed and laughed and laughed. You never knew it at the time, of course, but it was one of those days – and there were lots of them in the

Sixties – that you look back on and you wish it could have stayed like that forever.'

•

If Piri Halasz had waited another week or two to file her feature, she might have added another scene to her storyboard. It would have started with a Caravelle passenger jet, leased for the day, sitting on the runway at Heathrow Airport, fuelled and ready to bring a hundred or so young groovers to Ireland for a twenty-first birthday party, where The Lovin' Spoonful, one of the hottest pop acts in America at that moment, would play at the court of England's switched-on youth.

Christopher Gibbs remembered walking across the tarmac at Dublin Airport and looking over his shoulder at this vision of Swinging London on an away day. 'All sorts of people got off that plane,' he said. 'I just remember this mass of androgynous youth moving towards the terminal building and I remember thinking how times had changed. There was a group of bohemian types there – I don't know what their connection was to Tara, but someone must have known them – and they were carrying bottles of Guinness, which I thought was a bit odd, bringing Guinness to a party that was being thrown by the Guinness family. And they said it wasn't for drinking, it was for washing their hair. It was that kind of weekend.'

Before they boarded the flight, Nicki, Anita and Brian dropped a pane of acid each. A chauffeur collected them at Dublin Airport and drove them, tripping, through the city, then deep into the Wicklow Mountains, where a hole suddenly opened up in the Earth. At the bottom of it was a stout-black lake, rimmed by a beach of white sand, as fine as flour. They stared out the windows as they descended towards the house, at the bleak, brown hills around them, and they listened to the quiet susurration of the wind in the hollow of the valley. And that's when Brian announced that he needed to pee.

'We told the driver to stop,' Anita remembered, 'and we all got out of the car. We were looking out at this beautiful countryside, all of us tripping, while Brian was having a pee at the top of this hill, then he went, "Aaaggghhh!" or he made some incredible noise. So we went to the top of the hill and Brian had found this dead goat.'

At the time, he had developed an obsession with the legend of Pan, an ancient Greek god with the hindquarters and horns of a goat, who was worshipped for his powers of fertility. A prolific sire himself, Brian believed that Pan encapsulated the spirit of rock and roll, according to his friend Stash de Rola. Who knows what images flashed through his mind as he stared, tripping on acid, at the animal's skeletal remains? He started laughing. Michael Cooper, who was in the car with them, grabbed his camera and took photographs of all of them, standing around on the barren Wicklow hillside.

'We got hysterical looking at this dead goat,' Anita remembered. 'It was hysterical laughter. It was totally the wrong reaction, but it's the reaction you get when you're on acid. We arrived at the party completely out of it.'

Behind them on the road were John Sebastian, Joe Butler, Zal Yanovsky and Steve Boone, the members of The Lovin' Spoonful, who had just played the Marquee Club in London, watched by John Lennon and George Harrison. They hadn't taken anything, but were equally blown away by the scene.

'We saw the cottages on the property while we were approaching the castle,' remembered Joe Butler, the drummer and vocalist. 'It was like *Return of the Native*. All this stuff I read about as a kid. Robin Hood. *The Count of Monte Cristo*. *Ivanhoe*. That's what I was thinking about. Anything with a castle in it. I remember entering the main hall and seeing the paintings. It was a time trip more than anything. And it remains that way in my mind. I know there were cars there, but I was able to expunge them out of my dream of the place.'

Tara, in his favourite black velvet suit, greeted them at the door. 'He gave us each a thumb of hash and a pipe. And that's when the party started.'

It was Saturday, 23 April 1966, seven weeks after his birthday, but Tara had chosen the date to fit around the band's touring and recording schedule. Oonagh paid them $10,000, more than twice what the average American worker was taking home in a year, for the private concert.

The party guests started to arrive in the middle of the afternoon in a fleet of cars and also from a second Caravelle that arrived from Paris. They were a cross-section of the eclectic mix that made up Tara's social circle, a happy jumble of aristocracy, popocracy, Chelsea bohemia, Gaelic tradition, motor world and underworld, all getting along famously in a marijuana mist under the roof of David Mlinaric's exquisitely decorated marquee.

'When we arrived, I think I was probably thinking the same as the other guys in the band,' said John Sebastian, the lead singer of The Lovin' Spoonful. 'Which was, okay, how did we end up here? We were impressed that someone in this almost royal atmosphere was interested in us. This was a guy who could have had The Beatles and the Stones over to his house anytime he wanted. He didn't want them to play his twenty-first birthday party – he wanted us. Why, I don't know. Perhaps there was an exotic quality to us. But it was like nothing any of us had ever experienced before or experienced since. A dangerous number of irresponsible, young people in the grandeur of this old castle in the middle of the Irish countryside. It was extraordinary.'

Brian and Anita, suddenly ravenous, attacked the buffet, while Mike McCartney, Mick Jagger and the art collector Sir Alfred Beit giggled at the cleaning job that a maid had done on the surrealist artwork hanging in the dining room. 'I've heard of Arthur Guinness,' Mike shouted across the room to Tara, 'but I've never heard of 'Alf a Magritte.'

David Mlinaric, wearing a fur coat indoors, shot the breeze with Tara and David Dimbleby about Sybilla's, a new London nightclub, which he'd been hired to decorate. Michael Rainey and Rupert Lycett Green talked shop, as the owners of two of London's best-known men's boutiques, while Candida Betjeman, pregnant, looked on enviously as Nicki and a group of other women in tiny skirts moved their narrow hips and their pointed elbows and Patrick Kerr offered them dancing tips.

Garech chatted to the sculptor Eddie Delaney about Nelson's Pillar, a monument on Dublin's O'Connell Street that had recently been blown up by the IRA, and Brian Jones, listening in, thought he might like to take a taxi into town to see the Admiral, fallen from his perch. Gay Kindersley tried to start an Irish ballad session, but it was far too early for 'The Mountains of Mourne'. Tara introduced Rock Brynner to his friends, the Ormsby-Gores, while John Paul Getty Jr introduced himself to the actress Siobhán McKenna.

And right in the middle of this scene sat Jimmy Scott, a Nigerian conga player whom Tara knew from the Scotch. He was dressed in native African robes and every so often he tipped Jameson onto Oonagh's lush drawing-room carpet.

'He looked magnificent,' Mike McCartney remembered. 'He kept saying "Ob-la-di, ob-la-da – I drink again, I die," then pouring the whiskey out. I said, "What the hell are you doing?" and he said, "In Africa, before you drink, you must pay homage to God and Mother Earth." And off he went again: "Ob-la-di, ob-la-da . . ." Paul met him in London then afterwards and he wrote a song about him.'

Paul sent his apologies. He wanted to be there, but The Beatles were busy, recording their new album at Abbey Road Studios. It was going to be called *Revolver*.

But all human life was there. Lords and ladies, the famous and the infamous, rich and penniless, pop stars and pipers, artists and TV personalities, ambassadors and glamour models, friends and hustlers. It was like a credits roll of the people who had played a part in Tara's life.

'There were a lot of prominent people there,' Joe Butler remembered. 'Diplomats, people like that, amid all these crazy kids who were drinking and taking drugs and having the time of their lives. And one of the things that's always stayed with me was the way they held their cigarettes – between their thumb and their forefinger, with their palm facing up. It was part of their aristocratic bearing. And everyone there was gentle – that's the other thing I remember. It wasn't like being with businessmen, where everyone's trying to sell you something, with their business voices and their hype. There was none of that. These people were sitting around and talking about – I'm not kidding you – trees and flowers!'

As evening fell on the valley, the band started their sound-check. 'It couldn't have been much of a performance. We were slaughtered. We weren't shouting drunk. But we were *drunk* drunk. We were high on hash and alcohol. Really lubricated.'

Tara and Brian sat cross-legged on the dance floor watching them, both of them tripping. 'Being very yogic,' Joe remembered. Brian had brought his sitar with him. He took it out and Tara urged him to join the band onstage. But then Zal Yanovsky asked to borrow it, tried to play it in the wild manner of Chuck Berry and managed to break it. Brian, he remembered, was suddenly not so yogic.

The band got through their set and the party stretched on through the night. Tara cut the cake while the guests sang Happy Birthday. The older ones went home or retired to bed in the house. The younger ones stayed up and kept the party going well into the following day.

Joe challenged Mick Jagger to a boat race across Lough Tay in the dark, but Mick was in the middle of an argument with Chrissie and said maybe later.

At one point, according to the following day's *Sunday Press*, a taxi was called to chauffeur an unnamed rock star the thirty miles to Dublin to 'see Nelson', or rather his pollarded remains. Three hours after depositing the man back at the party, the newspaper reported, the taxi driver was still outside the house, waiting to be paid. It was that kind of night.

More acid was taken.

'Anita and I got it into our heads that Mick Jagger was the devil,' Nicki remembered. 'We locked him into the courtyard and then we ran into the woods at the back of the house. We had these walkie-talkies, which I think had been a birthday present from someone to Tara. We were in the woods and we were talking on these things, out of our heads, and paranoid, of course, watching Mick trying to get out of the courtyard.'

Tara thought it was hilarious.

'The way my moral compass was,' said Joe Butler, 'I was interested in any oxygen-breathing female, especially in the atmosphere of that castle – the fabulous intrigue of all those tight confines. I formed a relationship there with a beautiful English girl, this gorgeous creature with a music box voice. We had the most wonderful affair. She was the first woman I ever made love to who had little tufts of hair under her arms. She was so fragrant. This delicate love child in a cotton dress. The kind of girl you wanted to feel her back to see if she was about to sprout wings.

'We made love in the middle of a field of cut grass, then we rode on horseback to some other castle to have breakfast or lunch. It was ridiculous. We saw two rainbows together at Luggala. I never saw that before. It was, like, you know, one miracle will keep you believing in God. What a time.'

13: HERE TODAY

Tara's neighbours were always driven to distraction by the comings and goings at Eaton Row. Odd-looking people showing up drunk – and worse – in the middle of the night, to say nothing of the loud music. The Sixties or not – Belgravia was still Belgravia.

They knocked on the door, sometimes forming themselves into a delegation for the job. And Tara would give them the same answer that drove Godfrey Carey and no doubt many other tutors to the ends of frustration: 'Sorrraaay.'

Then there were the cars. Tara liked to bring his work home with him. There were always two or three, clogging up the narrow laneway, maybe a Mini or an MG, jacked up on bricks, a wheel or two missing, the bonnet open, and a pair of black John Lobb Chelsea boots sticking out from under the chassis.

They couldn't get their own cars in or out. And they can't have been pleased when Tara's mother bought him another AC Cobra for his birthday, this one red, with a sleeker body and a bigger engine. He took it straight down the King's Road to see what it could do. It was a magnificent machine. Sitting at traffic lights, it purred contentedly, then you slipped it into gear and pressed the accelerator to the floor, and it roared like a waking lion.

His record player wasn't just resting on the open glovebox this time. It was incorporated into the dashboard and connected to the radio speakers. He could put 'Paint It Black' on the little turntable, or 'Sloop John B' by The Beach Boys, or 'Somebody Help Me' by The Spencer Davis Group, then turn left out of Eaton Row, past the neat Georgian terraces and gardens, towards Sloane Square, then down the King's Road, past the Saturday afternoon peacocks and the flocks of pretty flamingos with their shopping bags from

Biba and Hung On You, all the way to World's End. Or he could turn right, cutting through the Queen's back garden, as he liked to call it, past Buckingham Palace, then right onto the Mall and into Piccadilly and Leicester Square, the beating heart of the swinging city.

He loved that car, but he didn't get to enjoy it for long, because at the start of the summer of 1966 he lost his driving licence.

It happened following yet another screaming row with Nicki. He decided to blow off steam by driving to Liverpool to see Mike McCartney. But Nicki wanted to have the last word. She decided to follow him and persuaded Nicholas Gormanston to come with her.

'We travelled up to Liverpool in the back of a limo,' Nicholas remembered. 'I have absolutely no idea how we came to be in it, because we'd taken acid and we were slightly off our heads. There was an Alsatian dog with us in the back, which may have belonged to Michael Hollingshead or one of his crowd. It was one of the strangest journeys of my life.'

Nicki caught up with Tara in a bar just off Dale Street in the centre of the city. 'We were drinking in this old-fashioned pub,' Mike remembered, 'one of these no-women-allowed establishments, where men did the serious drinking. Nicki strides in, young, feisty, Irish woman, right across the bar, right up to Tara and she starts letting him have it. And all these men who'd been safe in this environment for a million years saw this madness walking into their lives, their comfort zone blown away. Their mouths just dropped as she went at him. I've never seen barmen move so quickly in my life. They were over the counter: "Madam, how are you?" and they got hold of her and walked her very quickly out to the street.'

Tara and Nicki left Liverpool in the Cobra. They hadn't travelled very far when they were pulled over for speeding. 'He came off the motorway at sixty miles per hour instead of fifty miles per hour,' Nicki remembered. 'He was ten miles over the limit and the cops caught him. And because he was a young one and driving an expensive car, they didn't like that, so they booked him and it was three points and you're out in those days.'

In court, Tara was represented by Max Mosley, who was then a newly qualified barrister and a racing car enthusiast, as well as a half-brother to Tara's cousin, Desmond Guinness. Max drove up to Liverpool for the case, but he could do nothing to prevent Tara having his licence suspended for six months.

For Tara, not being allowed to drive was a particularly cruel purgatory. 'I used to have to drive him around,' Glen Kidston said. 'His Cobras and everything. This brand-new car – an incredible car – and he wasn't allowed to get behind the wheel. You can't imagine how frustrating that was for him.'

Tara decided that if he couldn't drive it, he'd have fun with it in some other way. One day, he and Glen were in the garage when a truck turned up, its container painted with a multicoloured mural. It was an LSD lorry. Tara loved it. 'He turned to me,' Glen remembered, 'and he said, "I'm going to do that to the Cobra."'

Gerard Campbell had told him about three young artists from up north who had started out painting furniture in unusually bright colours and were now doing the same thing to cars. One of them had worked, briefly, at Hobbs and Bates, the same agency where Gerard worked; he had designed an ad for Spangles sweets that the client didn't like and he was given his cards. As it happened, Gerard was about to meet him and the two artists he worked with to put a business proposal to them.

One of the most interesting by-products of the shake-up in the British class system in the late 1950s and early 1960s was that art – for so long the preserve of bohemian types or the gallery-going rich – became of interest to the working classes. By the early 1960s most of Britain's major cities had art colleges full of young kids whose parents couldn't tell the difference between a Magritte and half of one. Socially and culturally, the effect was revolutionary – without realizing it, Britain had bred a generation of young people from the wrong side of the tracks who could talk their way around the Tate – in a Liverpudlian or a Mancunian or a Brummie accent. It would play a major part in shaping the Sixties. Amongst the notable alumni of the country's suddenly burgeoning art colleges were John Lennon, Keith Richards, Ray Davies, Eric Clapton, Eric Burdon, Pete Townshend, Jimmy Page – and three members of a pop-art collective who turned Tara's new AC Cobra into a piece of art on wheels.

Dudley Edwards, Douglas Binder and David Vaughan were three working-class lads from West Yorkshire and Lancashire who moved to London in the early 1960s, following the path laid down by David Hockney, who was Bradford born-and-bred. The three started off as Teddy Boys, became mods in art college and, by 1966, were well on their way to becoming hippies – and pioneering hippies at that, thanks to their early efforts in the area of what became recognized as psychedelic art.

'I was born in Halifax,' said Dudley. 'I grew up on a farm, a smallholding. It was always my job to look after the pigs. The school I went to was notorious. I remember one of the teachers had two bulldogs sitting beside his desk for protection. Every year, the Cock of the School, who was the best fighter, had to take on the gym master on the last day. We'd all crowd around the gym, peering through the windows, waiting for the lad to go in and have a go at him.

'I was always interested in art. That was my way out. Luckily, I had a decent art teacher who took me under his wing. When I finished school, he asked to see my dad. The old man went in and he said, "The lad's talented. He needs to go to art school." My dad said, "Well, he's fifteen now. We're looking forward to getting a wage out of him. He'll be going in the mills or down the mines like the rest of his mates." But my art teacher talked him out of it.

'So I did two years at Halifax Art School, then I went to art college in Bradford – a further three years. And that's where I met Doug and Dave. Doug was brought up in Bradford with a similar background to myself. Dave was from Manchester. He'd done twelve months in Strangeways – for nicking carpets, I think. He showed a bit of artistic talent while he was in there and Bradford was the only place that would take him when he was released.'

Douglas was a couple of years older than the other two and went to London in 1962 to further his education at the Royal College of Art. Dudley arrived shortly after graduating in 1964 and got a job with Hobbs and Bates, the advertising and public relations company where Gerard Campbell worked. Dudley and Douglas shared a flat on Gloucester Avenue. Dave had a newborn daughter, who grew up to be the actress Sadie Frost. He turned up on the doorstep one day and insinuated himself into their world. 'I wasn't that close to him in college,' Dudley said. 'But he knew where I lived and he sort of thrust himself upon us. So that was how the three of us ended up together.'

The flat they shared needed brightening up. They couldn't afford new furniture, so they decided to paint what they had – wardrobes, chairs, chests of drawers – in what became recognized as their signature style. 'Psychedelic art wasn't around when we started off. The early stuff we did had nothing to do with LSD because we hadn't had it. All our stuff came from fairgrounds – from our memories of going to the fair as kids. Bright colours. Sharp angles. We associated it with joy, from our childhoods, because the streets were dull and grey, like other major cities, until the fair rolled into town.

'Then another major influence was the Pakistani doorways in Bradford. A lot of Asians came over after the war and they settled in Yorkshire and they painted their doorways these bright colours. In Bradford, you'd walk down these dull stone terraces, then you'd come across a house where a Pakistani family lived and it'd be multicoloured. It looked magical.

'So we arrived in London with this urge to paint everything the same way. We'd have liked the commission to paint the whole of London if it'd been possible – streets, pavements, everything. There wasn't a great deal of intellectual sophistication about our art. We just wanted everything to be colourful and happy.'

But their first priority was to make the rent, which became more difficult after Dudley lost his job at the advertising firm. As it happened, their Gloucester Avenue flat was just across the road from the home of David Bailey.

'We thought if we maybe left a piece of painted furniture on his doorstep, he'd come out of the house one morning and fall over it and maybe want to keep it. In the middle of the night, we carried one of these things across the road – it was a chest of drawers – and left it on the doorstep. The next morning, his cleaner came round and she said, "David's had to go out, but he wants that chest of drawers. If one of you comes across later, there'll be a cheque for you."

'We were all a bit nervous. I don't know if we drew straws or whatever, but I finished up having to go across for the cheque. Catherine Deneuve answered the door in her negligée – handed me the first money we ever earned as Binder, Edwards and Vaughan.'

After that, success came quickly. Lord Snowdon, Princess Margaret's husband, ordered a chest of drawers from them, which generated some publicity in the national newspapers. Then the orders started to roll in: custom jobs, at first, often for rich clients living in Chelsea bedsits, a great many of whom had 'turned on' and had an urge to see the world in as many colours as possible. Henry Moore bought one of their pieces. Then they got their first major order, from Woolland Brothers, the upmarket department store in Knightsbridge, for two dozen painted chests of drawers, which they sold for between £20 and £30 per piece.

In January 1966, *House Beautiful* magazine ran a feature on their work, showcasing how they could beautify dull pine tables and chairs with a few licks of a paintbrush. David Vaughan, who had a particular gift for generating publicity, told the *London Evening Standard* that they'd been asked to paint the dome of the recently cleaned St Paul's Cathedral canary yellow and the brand-new Post Office Tower bordello red.

Gerard phoned Dudley one day and told him he wanted to introduce them to his friend, Tara Browne. 'He said, "I mentioned you to him. I think he'll love you and what you're doing," so, a few days later, he took us around to his mews house in Eaton Row.'

It was the first week in August and London was buzzing. England had just won the World Cup, beating West Germany at Wembley, thanks to a Geoff Hurst goal that may or may not have been. It seemed almost inevitable that the Russian linesman would rule that the ball had, indeed, crossed the goal line. The momentum of the pendulum swing was still with England. Bobby Moore held up the Jules Rimet trophy one-handed and London must have felt like the good times were never going to end.

Tara took Dudley, Douglas and Dave to his garage to show them the Cobra and they set about painting it immediately, all the colours of the rainbow incorporated into a flash design. It took them two weeks to finish the job, working mostly at night and into the early hours of the morning, then going back to Eaton Row to listen to music. In a six-week period that summer, three albums were released that still feature in the top ten of most serious All-Time Greatest polls – *Pet Sounds* by The Beach Boys, *Revolver* by The Beatles and *Blonde on Blonde* by Bob Dylan. The era of the album had well and truly arrived.

Tara played those records all night round at Eaton Row. Especially *Pet Sounds*. 'The Beach Boys were the reason he bought the Cobra in the first place,' Dudley remembered. 'There was something about that lifestyle that he liked. The whole California thing. The car fitted in with that.'

The heartbreaking wistfulness of songs like 'God Only Knows' and 'Don't Talk (Put Your Head On My Shoulder)' may also have had a special appeal to Tara that summer, when his marriage to Nicki was reaching its end. To all intents and purposes, they were already separated. Nicki had spent much of the summer in Marbella, where she was now clearly intent on living, whether Tara was part of her future or not. She had rented a 400-year-old whitewashed cottage in Orange Tree Square that she was hoping to turn into a boutique and hairdressing salon. The children were mostly with Oonagh in London or Paris. Tara was footloose – and free to restart his affair with Amanda Lear.

•

Amanda tried to stay away from Tara, but she couldn't. When she returned to London that summer, they picked up where they left off in Marbella. Tara would take afternoons off from the garage and call round to her flat in Chelsea. Occasionally, with Nicki away, they would go to Eaton Row. She remembered Tara playing *Revolver* for her there – he loved 'Here, There and Everywhere' and 'Tomorrow Never Knows' – while she stared at the cover artwork and realized that her feelings for him were something she could no longer control.

'I was madly in love with him,' she said. 'But at the same time I was feeling terribly guilty, because Nicki had treated me as her friend and I was doing this behind her back.

'But it was not my fault that the marriage went bad. He was not very happy with Nicki. He wanted a different kind of relationship. Nicki was into going out, taking drugs, meeting famous people – she was very wild.'

The affair went on for most of the summer. It was the talk of the town. Tara ceased to care who knew about it. He was infatuated with Amanda. It was inevitable that word of her husband's affair would reach Nicki in Marbella. Her pride wounded, perhaps it suited her to pretend that she had put the two of them together as a birthday wheeze and it had unexpectedly developed into something more serious and lasting.

Amanda was full of guilt. The man for whom she'd fallen was married and had two children. For the second time, she decided she had to remove herself from the situation, which meant getting out of London altogether. In August, she took a modelling job in Paris in the hope that the relationship might cool off. But not even distance could separate them.

With Amanda off the London scene, Tara looked for things to distract him. Again, he began to consider becoming a racing car driver. He wrote again to Gore Taylor, his postman friend back in Ireland, offering him the job they'd discussed before. Gore wrote back, agreeing to become his full-time mechanic and racing manager, starting in January 1967.

Then Tara decided to follow Michael Rainey and Nigel Waymouth into the rag trade. What he really wanted was a boutique on the King's Road right at the heart of where the action was, a place where young men and women could go to buy the latest clothes they'd seen on *Ready Steady Go!* or *Top of the Pops* or just hang out like they did at Hung On You and Granny Takes a Trip.

Through Christopher Gibbs, Tara had met John Crittle, a gregarious twenty-three-year-old Australian who had arrived in London from Sydney in 1964. 'John was the archetypal Australian rogue,' according to Alan Holsten, a friend and colleague for several years. 'He was fantastic. Wicked smile. I think his father was a policeman in Sydney and he had a brother [Peter] who played rugby for Australia and another brother who was in the army. But John was definitely the black sheep of the family. He'd been a bit of a bad boy, so they shipped him out and he came to live in London.'

Michael Rainey, one of the first men in London to employ him, remembered him as a man of ingratiating charm. 'The kind of charm that people like Jimi Hendrix, who was around London at that time, were amused by. He once asked John Lennon if he could borrow his car. John, at that time, was driving that Rolls Royce painted rather like Tara's car. He said, "Okay, take the keys." The next thing, Crittle was driving down the King's Road smashed out of his brains. The police stopped him. They said, "Where'd you get this from?" and he said, "What, this? Oh, my friend John Lennon lent it to me." Of course he got arrested.'

Early in 1966 he had used his charm to blag himself a job at Hung On You. 'He walked in off the street one day. He had a pretty girlfriend with him. He said he'd moved to England and was looking for work. I said, "Well, as it happens, I need this changing room wallpapered. If you can do that for me, then maybe we'll see what else you can do." Anyway, he did a fantastic job – wallpapered it and put a curtain up. I said, "Okay, hang around for a week and we'll see how good you are with customers." It turned out he was very good at selling.'

But John had ambitions far beyond serving as Michael Rainey's mere lackey. 'He got into his head that he could do it for himself. And he could, because he'd seen me doing it. He knew how I wanted my jackets – velvet on the collars, velvet on the sleeves. And he thought, "I could do that."'

What John wanted was to colonize the King's Road in the

same way that John Stephen had taken over Carnaby Street. He spent six months at Hung On You, learning every aspect of how the business worked, in the shop and out on the road. When Michael asked him to collect fabric from a supplier and deliver it to one of the tailors he used, John was only too happy to oblige. He was taking note of everything, while building up his own relationships.

Michael Rainey's most important supplier was Foster Tailoring, on Brewer Street in Soho, who made the jackets and suits that were Hung On You's biggest sellers. For Pop and Cliff Foster, the father and son team that ran the business, there simply weren't enough hours in the day – by the summer of 1966 they had regular orders from at least two dozen shops and new ones were approaching them every day. John decided he wanted a piece of the business. Unfortunately, he didn't have any capital. That was where Tara came in.

'John's girlfriend at the time managed to earn a wage modelling,' Michael said. 'That's how he became ensconced in the Chelsea set. They were suddenly meeting a lot of influential people. Christopher Gibbs took him under his wing a bit. So that was how he met Tara, whose involvement at that point was in motor cars.'

In the beginning, John hoped to use Tara to get to Paul McCartney or one of the other Beatles. But when he found out that Tara had access to Guinness money, he knew he'd found his new business partner. 'Tara wanted to be a backer of enterprises,' said Martin Wilkinson. 'There was very much a mood for that type of thing at the time. The Beatles did the same thing with Apple. Also, he knew something about clothes. His mother used to take him to all the fashion shows in Paris from the time he was a child – Balenciaga, Chanel, all those. So it was an area he was interested in.'

John persuaded Tara to buy a chunk of Pop Foster's business. Then he gave his notice to Michael Rainey. In August 1966, Foster Tailoring became Foster and Tara, with premises on Brewer Street and now also a lock-up garage on Gloucester Avenue, not far from Brian and Anita's house. Alan Holsten, a teenager who worked in

Woollands in Knightsbridge and who knew John from trendy clubs like Blaises and The Speakeasy, became their first employee.

'We worked out of this tiny little mews garage,' Alan remembered. 'It was deadly quiet and completely empty. We started from nothing, just building stock up. John would go up to Berwick Street Market in Soho to buy fabric and take it across London to the tailors to get a few jackets or suits knocked together, which we then supplied to the shops.'

The real plan, though, was to open a shop of their own, modelled on Hung On You, where they would sell exclusive Foster and Tara designs. 'The interesting thing for me about Tara,' said Paul Gorman, an expert on the fashion of the era, 'is that he seems to have been one of those people who knew clothes really well. You know, you think about these wonderful gadabouts and they looked great. But when you investigate it, they actually did have an aesthetic. They had a critique with which they framed everything. And it was no surprise that he opened this tailoring business with this quite established father-and-son firm. So he could say, "No, the trousers must be tapered like that." See, we often think of the Sixties as a series of accidents. But these people meant it that way.'

Tara had found the perfect unit for a clothes shop at 161 King's Road, a ground-floor space that was just below the Chelsea Methodist Church. It was available at a reasonable rent from its owners. He came up with a suitably foppish name for the place – Dandie Fashions.

While he was trying to get the business off the ground, he was also having fun with the Cobra, even though he was still forbidden from driving it. Lord Snowdon happened to see it and had an idea: to take the car to Westminster, along with a painted Buick owned by Binder, Edwards and Vaughan, to photograph them in front of the Houses of Parliament, juxtaposing old order and new.

They arranged to do it on 29 September. Dudley and the others brought along five members of an up-and-coming Birmingham band with whom they were friendly called The Move. They were led by a singer named Roy Wood, had a residency in the Marquee and knew the value of a good publicity stunt. Banned from driving, Tara sat in the back of the Buick, looking like a sixth member of the band, against the backdrop of the House of Lords, where his father had a seat.

After that, they took them up to Primrose Hill, on the northern side of Regent's Park, where Lord Snowdon wanted to capture them – the funky cars, the hot new band and the Honourable mod, Tara Browne – with the skyline of the swinging city behind them. And that's when they had a brush with authority that made the day so memorable for everyone.

'Snowdon,' the *Daily Express* reported the following day, 'was halfway up a ladder in one of the royal parks in London yesterday when a formidable blue-clad figure moved in front of his wide-angled lens. "You're not allowed to do this," said the park-keeper, Margaret Blackman, well versed in the regulations of Primrose Hill Park.

'Lord Snowdon lowered his camera and replied, in level terms, "As a member of the public, I can take pictures wherever I want. All you can do is to tell the cars to move." Snowdon walked down the path accompanied by WPK Blackman. He climbed into his Aston Martin parked outside.

'A spokesman for the Ministry of Public Buildings and Works, which controls the royal parks, said: "The woman park-keeper was mainly concerned with the cars being there, although strictly speaking special permission should have been obtained for the ladder."'

Dudley remembered laughing until it hurt. 'It was like something out of an Ealing Comedy,' he said. 'A while after, we each got a letter from the Ministry of Works or something, saying that, on such and such a date, you contravened these regulations to do with the royal parks. However, on this occasion, we're prepared to overlook it – obviously because they weren't going to bring the Queen's brother-in-law to court for having a stepladder in a royal park.'

Robert Fraser had spotted the Cobra being driven up the King's Road one afternoon, with Glen at the wheel and Tara in the passenger seat. People were running out onto the street to gawp at it as it made its way towards Sloane Square. It was so perfectly of the moment, Robert thought. He asked Tara if he could exhibit it in his gallery. Tara figured that if he couldn't enjoy the car fully then others should be allowed to.

On Saturday, 3 September 1966, the car was driven to the Fraser Gallery on Duke Street. The front window of the gallery had to be removed to get the car inside. Robert, a man who rarely missed a trick, especially where money was concerned, persuaded Tara's three artist friends to cover the cost of removing and refitting the window. After all, he was offering them a month-long showcase of their work in the city's hippest gallery. There was newspaper and TV interest. Even Pathé News wanted to film the moment for posterity.

'He said the window was part of the deal,' Dudley remembered, 'so we said we'd cover the cost of taking it out and putting it back in. But Dave got it into his head that we shouldn't have to pay full price for this. "I'll sort this out," he said, then he drove up to Notting Hill, went into some pub up there, which was full of people pissed out of their heads on a weekend afternoon. Dave went in and he said, "Does anyone want to earn a fiver?" So he got all these guys down who hadn't taken out a window before. It was a massive window. But they did a fair job, because they got it out – and they were pissed, remember.'

Once the window was removed, they placed long planks of wood down to form two ramps, one inside and one outside the gallery. Then, with Tara steering, but the engine switched off, they pushed it up one ramp, then down the other and into the exhibition space. Then Dave's half-slaughtered hirelings turned to the job of putting the window back.

'So Doug and I are standing there,' Dudley remembered, 'watching this, fretting. But they managed to get the window in place. Suddenly, there's only inches left to go and we're saying, "He's done it! The bugger's gone and done it!" Then one of the blokes gave it a nudge with his shoulder for some reason and that was it – thirty feet of window, smashed. Of course, Dave, who exploited and conned his way out of everything, got Tara to pay for the damaged window.'

On Monday, Tara's fantastically coloured sports car became the newest attraction at the Robert Fraser Gallery. Tara made a brief speech at the unveiling that night, waxing poetic and invoking the spirit of the Bright Young People era in his description of the car.

'It is the world that the Thirties promised and never fulfilled,' he said. 'All trace of smoke, oil and grease are gone, the depressing wastes of industry long since vanished. There remains a Perspex city, uninhabited, silent, built without human labour and coloured by the rays of the sun.'

The French TV station ORTF became interested in the car and its owner. They sent a documentary crew to London to make a short film about a day in the life of a member of the Swinging London set. The seven-minute, black-and-white film was entitled *Une Journée Avec L'Honorable Tara Browne* and featured Tara in some of his favourite spots, set to a backing track of 'Love You To' and 'Good Day Sunshine' from *Revolver*.

He was filmed sharing a joke with a coquettish-looking Marianne Faithfull at the Fraser Gallery, trying on a coat and a trilby in Lord John on Carnaby Street, then chatting to the singer Spencer Davis, who had become a regular visitor to Eaton Row. They captured him strolling up the King's Road; kicking back in the mews house, flicking through a pile of albums that included *Rubber Soul* and *Blonde on Blonde*; then dancing in Blaises, a popular basement nightclub in Queen's Gate. In perfectly accented French, he talked about his friendship with Brian Jones and The Rolling Stones, his garage and his love of clothes, his children and his teenage years in Paris. Significantly, there was no mention of his wife.

They filmed him getting into the multicoloured AC Cobra, despite his driving ban, then taking off with the top down and the wind in his hair. The car was then filmed passing a number of London landmarks, including Trafalgar Square, Buckingham Palace, Big Ben, the House of Lords and Piccadilly Circus, although they cheated with these shots. 'That was actually me at the wheel,' said Glen Kidston. 'I had to do all the driving, because Tara didn't have his licence.'

In truth, Tara's London – that part of the capital that was setting the agenda for the rest of Britain and, indeed, the rest of the planet – was a tight and incestuous world that comprised no more than a few hundred people. And, as with their spiritual antecedents, the Bright Young People, the media were keen to put names and faces on this new generation of fast, young, pleasure-seekers, whose influence was being felt all over the world, especially in America.

In September 1966, the New York-based men's fashion magazine *Gentleman's Quarterly* published a photograph of Tara and four of his friends, standing on the banks of the Thames, cool and unsmiling, in their finest Carnaby Street clobber. The image looked like it could have been taken from a record cover, except the five friends happened to be members of the British nobility who had never produced as much as a note of music between them.

The fact that Britain's young aristocrats were swanning around dressed like pop stars caused ripples on the other side of the pond. 'My colleagues in America report that this picture has been received there with incredulity,' ran an article in the *Daily Mail*, published under the pseudonymous by-line of Charles Greville. 'I am not surprised. It is headed, "Dandies on the Thames", and looks like a large pop group. In fact, it shows five aristocrats in their normal gear.

'They are Christopher Gibbs, 27, antique dealer and nephew of Sir Humphrey Gibbs, Governor of Rhodesia; Sir Mark Palmer, 24, son of Mrs Henriette Abel Smith, an extra Woman of the Bedchamber to the Queen; The Hon. Tara Browne, 20, car enthusiast, father of two, and son of Lord Oranmore and Browne; Nicholas Gormanston, 26, artist and premier Viscount of Ireland; and The Hon. Julian Ormsby-Gore, 25, son of Lord Harlech, former Ambassador to Washington.

'The American magazine *Gentleman's Quarterly* . . . says in a sentence that should weaken sterling a little more: "That the peacock mod of young England today is not confined to the sons of working-class blokes what shop on Carnaby Street should be apparent from the dandified flourish of these aristocratic gentlemen – all of the establishment, past and contemporary."'

The photograph was taken by Willy Rizzo of *Paris Match*, who ran into Tara and his friends one night and asked if he could take their picture. 'It isn't my fault these young aristocrats look like that,' Rizzo told the *Mail* when he was asked if he got them to dress up for the shot. 'I just took the pictures. If you don't wish your aristocrats to look like that, you should tell them what to wear.'

It was all fun, but all too fleeting. The car, the documentary, the clothes shop, the garage, the exhibition, the photograph in the American fashion magazine, the putative return to motor racing – they all took his mind off Nicki temporarily. But by the early autumn of 1966, Tara realized that he had to do something about the mess that had become of his marriage.

•

The separation from Amanda didn't take. He went to Paris to visit her regularly, sometimes every weekend, between August and the beginning of October.

They spent long, romantic evenings talking about the future. They slept together in the new apartment that Tara's mother had bought on boulevard Suchet when she split from Miguel.

Her relationship with Tara had Oonagh's full consent, according to Amanda. On those weekends when she too happened to be there, she even brought them breakfast in bed.

'The way she behaved with me was amazing,' she said. 'I was sleeping with Tara in her flat in Paris while she was also there. This was while he was still married to Nicki. She would come into the room in the morning to bring us breakfast. She would say, in her very nice voice, "Hello, Amanda, how are you today?"'

But somewhere in between Tara's regular visits to Paris, he began to feel a distance open up between them, owing to her friendship with the Spanish surrealist painter Salvador Dali.

According to Amanda, Tara was actually present the night she first met him. Tara showed up in Paris one weekend in September, with Brian Jones and Donald Cammell, the Scottish film-maker who had insinuated himself into the Stones circle and would go on to write and direct a famous bedroom scene between Anita Pallenberg and Mick Jagger in his movie, *Performance*. 'I was doing a show for Paco Rabane,' Amanda remembered. 'It was in the afternoon, so I was fully made-up, with eyelashes and everything else, which was nice because I wanted to be pretty for Tara.'

They had a romantic dinner together, then went to meet Brian and Donald in Chez Castel, a nightclub on the city's Left Bank. Dali was at a nearby table with a group of people whom he treated in the manner of courtiers. 'Tara and Brian were dressed in these lace and velvet suits. They were very dandy and they really stood out. Dali discovered that one of them was a Rolling Stone and he said, "I must meet him!"'

He introduced himself as The Divine Dali and he kissed Amanda's hand. 'I was very skinny. He said to me, "You have the most beautiful skeleton I have ever seen." I got the impression that he was making fun of us all. I found him terribly obnoxious, but Tara, Brian and Donald thought he was hilarious.'

Dali was wearing a bronze-coloured velvet suit with a gold lamé waistcoat, and his moustache was waxed and twisted upwards in its familiar fashion. Brian and Donald couldn't stop laughing, especially at the comical way he rolled his 'r's. 'It is nice to meet a Rrrolling Stone,' he said. 'But which Rrrolling Stone are you?'

'Brian Jones,' was the reply.

Then he turned to Tara. 'And you are a lord, yes?'

'No,' Tara said, 'my father is a lord.'

Dali seemed disappointed. He invited them to join him. 'We've never had an Amanda at court,' he said. 'We have had a Saint Sebastian, a Red Guard, a Unicorn and a Cardinal.'

Dali rarely used people's names. He found them too prosaic, according to Amanda. Instead, he ascribed people with generic labels. All blondes were 'Ginesteae' after a plant with a yellow flower that grows mostly in the Mediterranean. Thin people were 'Saint Sebastian', pale people were 'Christ' and people of good breeding – like Tara – were 'Fillet of Sole'.

He gestured to a woman sitting at his table. She was middle-aged, blonde and dripping in jewellery. 'Sit down beside Louis XIV,' Dali told Amanda. 'I beg you. She speaks excellent English. Did you know that Louis XIV spoke English in New York with Greta Garbo?'

Tara, Brian and Donald could barely contain their laughter. The conversation continued in this bizarre manner for about an hour before Dali announced that he was going home to bed. His wife, Gala, didn't like him to stay out late. He invited them all to lunch the following day, at the upmarket Restaurant Lasserre on the avenue Franklin D. Roosevelt. 'One o'clock,' he told them. 'On the dot.'

Then he left, with a flower behind his ear, while a member of his court, whom he introduced as The Virgin, walked behind him carrying another flower in her cupped hands.

'He's crazy, man,' Brian said. 'He's completely crazy.'

Tara and Amanda slept that night at Oonagh's flat. The following morning, Tara was keen to go to Lasserre. He thought it might be fun. Amanda dressed up in a violet silk mini-dress and knee-high boots. They arrived late. Tara always had trouble being on time for anything. Brian and Donald never showed up at all.

Dali was already sitting at a long table by the window with John and Dennis Myers, identical twins from England who regularly modelled for him and who would later appear in *Performance*. There was also the woman he called Louis XIV and another whom he introduced as the Avocatesse.

Dali, who was wearing the same clothes as the night before, told them he'd taken the liberty of ordering ortolans for everyone.

Tara began to have second thoughts about the lunch, since the artist was clearly smitten by his girlfriend. He didn't speak to Tara once during the lunch, according to Amanda, and referred to him only as 'your friend'.

His conversation was as surreal as anything he ever committed to canvas. He announced to the table that he was impotent. He said his favourite drug was mineral water. He asked Amanda if she was Chinese. He talked at length about her skull. Then he asked her, apropos of nothing, if she was a lesbian. 'All girls have a bit of lesbian in them,' he told her, 'just as all boys have a little bit of the homosexual. I bet your friend here likes boys, like all well-bred, young Englishmen.'

Tara laughed nervously, but he couldn't wait for the lunch to be over. He realized now that he had a problem. Dali wanted Amanda for a courtier and Amanda – who was interested in the world of art and artists – was clearly flattered by his attention.

●

Nicki knew of her husband's regular visits to Paris and suspected the affair was still going on. At the start of October, she returned home from Marbella. 'I stopped off in Paris on the way home,' she remembered, 'and I met up with Amanda – because we were good friends ourselves, remember. I had to go to the boulevard Suchet flat for something, so I said, "Come with me."

'And, of course, Amanda had to go through the whole rigma-role of pretending she'd never been there before, that she didn't even know where Oonagh lived. The building had four floors and you needed a special, three-digit code to operate the lift up to Oonagh's flat. I went to press the buttons, but Amanda got there before me. One, two, three. And then I knew. I took a flight straight back to London.'

She confronted Tara and he admitted everything. According to Nicki, he promised to end it the next time he was in Paris, although this would have been an unusual commitment, given that he had already made up his mind to leave Nicki and file for divorce. 'The way that it was explained to me,' recalled Garech, 'was that even though he really liked Nicki – he had nothing against her whatso-ever – he just couldn't bear another minute of being married to her.'

On Monday, 10 October, Nicki walked into the mews to find

Tara not at home. 'I realized that his music system was gone,' she remembered. 'Then I went upstairs and his clothes were gone as well. Everything else was still there, except his music and clothes and him. And that was the day we split, or rather that was the day they moved him out.'

There was a further sting in the tail for her. Oonagh had been looking after Dorian and Julian at Luggala while her daughter-in-law was in Marbella and her son was gadding about London. It's clear that Oonagh was as dismayed by Tara's performance as a father as she was by Nicki's as a mother. By the time the children's holiday in Ireland was over, she had made up her mind that she wasn't giving them back.

On Tuesday 11 October, Tara called around to the mews to tell Nicki that he was staying at the Ritz. 'We were supposed to be going to Ireland to pick up the children,' she remembered. 'Oonagh had them at Luggala while I was in Marbella, closing up the rental house. I said to Tara, "What's going on? Remember, the flight is at 2.30 p.m."

'He said, "I'm sorry, my mother has taken the children off somewhere and she's going to try to get custody of them in Ireland." I was shocked that she'd organized this coup against me. Tara was upset, too. They'd manipulated and got him. As long as Tara's mother controlled the purse strings, she knew that she could control everything.

'I said to him, "Tara, we need to go and get the children back right now. They're our children – not hers," and that's when he said the strangest thing to me. He said, "What's the point? I'm not going to live very long anyway." Then he said he had to go and see the trustees to sort some things out.'

Nicki flew to Ireland alone, but when she arrived at Luggala, there was no one home. 'I was told by a member of the staff that they had gone away,' she said. 'They were all staying at the Shelbourne Hotel, as it happened. Oonagh thought it was great fun: "Let's all play a game with Nicki."'

She returned to London and tried to contact Tara at the Ritz. He wasn't there. 'Divorce was just an accepted thing in their family,' she said. 'Tara had seen his mother go through it. She had Gay and Tessa – that's one lot. Then she married again and had Garech and Tara. I think Tara thought that was how it went. You get married, you have some kids, you get divorced, then you have another lot with someone else.'

Nicki decided she needed a lawyer and she turned to the best in the business. On Wednesday 12 October, she took a taxi to Pall Mall to see David Jacobs, Britain's leading showbusiness solicitor, whose clients included Brian Epstein, Judy Garland and Liberace. He also represented Donovan, who had recently become the first name to be busted for drugs as part of an Establishment backlash against the pop groups of the time. Nicki claimed that her mother-in-law had 'snatched' her children. Jacobs took her straight to the High Court and sought an order for the return of her children. Her counsel, Harold Law, told the court: 'One does not fear any physical danger. It is just the refusal by the grandmother to allow the mother to see the children. She has, in fact, spirited them away.'

However, the judge, Mr Justice Pennycuick, refused to make the order without first hearing her husband's side of the dispute. He adjourned the case until the following Tuesday, when evidence from Tara could be presented to the court. But Tara was reportedly missing. That night, Dublin's *Evening Press* led with the headline: 'Guinness Heir Sought by Police.'

The story said: 'Police throughout Britain were alerted to look for a 21-year-old Irishman, heir to a million pounds, and his two young children . . . The police said they wanted to question Guinness heir, the Honourable Tara Browne, about the whereabouts of his two children, Dorian (3) and Julian (1½).'

In a staged photograph, Nicki appeared in the following morning's *Daily Express*, looking at pictures of her children while 'waiting for the phone to ring'. She claimed the breakdown of her marriage had come as a bolt out of the blue. 'I just want to know where my babies are and what it's all about,' she said. 'We haven't rowed.'

Several journalists knocked on Tara's father's door in nearby

Eaton Place to ask Dom if he knew of his son's whereabouts. He told them he hadn't seen him since Wednesday and he didn't know where he was staying. Oonagh, meanwhile, had made an application to the High Court in Dublin for care and control of Dorian and Julian.

Tara finally surfaced that weekend, snapped by a photographer as he flew into Dublin. 'I can't tell you anything,' he said, before leaving in a taxi to meet with his solicitor. On Tuesday, 18 October, he was back in London for the hearing in front of Mr Justice Pennycuick. It took place in camera. Tara's counsel sought a ten-day adjournment, pending the outcome of the Dublin proceedings. The adjournment was granted.

Nicki attempted to enlist the support of Oonagh's first husband, Philip Kindersley. 'I phoned him up,' she said. 'He told me he couldn't think of a worse person to be in charge of two young children than Oonagh. I said, "Well, she's got my two." He said he wished he could help, but he couldn't.'

The following weekend, in between court appearances and meetings with solicitors, Tara flew to Paris to see Amanda. But any plans he might have had for a romantic weekend were quickly dashed when Dali phoned to invite her for dinner at Ledoyen, one of the finest restaurants in the city, on the Champs-Elysées. Amanda told Tara that he should come along, too. Tara debated whether or not he should go. He didn't like Dali. He was jealous of the influence he had over Amanda but he also wanted to be there should something develop.

He also had an ulterior motive for being in Paris that weekend. He told Amanda that he was planning to divorce Nicki and he asked her to sign a statement saying that Nicki was, in her view, a neglectful mother. Amanda agreed, although she claimed later that she regretted it.

Tara decided to go to the dinner after all. Dali escorted Amanda into the restaurant on his arm with Tara following behind. They were joined at the table by Leanor Fini, the Argentine surrealist painter, who was wearing a floor-length ballgown with a magician's cape over it and carrying a wand.

It was the beginning of what would be a miserable evening for Tara. Dali announced that he only really liked mournful music and insisted that the pianist play Bizet's *Les Pêcheurs de Perles*, while a paparazzo took endless photographs of them, and Fini, who was bisexual, stared lustfully across the table at Amanda, occasionally whispering approving comments about her to Dali out of the corner of her mouth.

Before the evening ended, Dali told Amanda that he wanted to paint her. Amanda asked Tara if he'd mind and Tara said she didn't need his permission to do anything. He knew he was losing her. Amanda was clearly infatuated with Dali, if only in a platonic way. That weekend, they also hung out with the artist at the Hotel Lambert, then he invited them to a residence in the suburbs, where they were greeted at the door by a woman holding a bullwhip. Inside, an orgy was in full swing. According to one witness, Tara felt uncomfortable and he and Amanda disappeared into a room alone. It was a peculiar weekend, even for someone who had experienced most things and wasn't easily shocked. Tara returned to London the following day. He and Amanda never saw each other again.

'A week or two later,' Amanda said, 'he phoned me to say he was coming to Paris tomorrow. I went to meet him at the airport but he didn't show up. I phoned him and he said we had to stop seeing each other because Nicki knew about us and this was going to make things very difficult in court. And that was the end. I never saw my beautiful Tara again.'

Oonagh's application for care and control of her grandchildren came before the High Court in Dublin. With the agreement of both parties, the case was heard in private. Nicki flew to Ireland. Unable to afford a hotel, she stayed with Rock Brynner in his rented mews off Pembroke Square. 'We were followed everywhere,' he later recalled, 'by private investigators, obviously trying to prove that Nicki was being unfaithful, which she certainly wasn't, by the way. She loved Tara, despite everything that was going on. She was penniless and I was just trying to be a friend.

She was completely on her own. And she'd gone up against the Guinnesses in Ireland. Good luck with that!'

Nicki argued that the children should be with her. Oonagh made the case that her daughter-in-law was an unfit mother. The judge ruled in Oonagh's favour. She was granted custody of Dorian and Julian. Nicki returned to London without her children but still believing that she could win custody as part of the divorce settlement. In the weeks that followed, as the date of their divorce hearing approached, the relationship between Tara and Nicki dissolved into bitterness and recrimination.

On 11 November, Tara drew up a will, cutting his wife out of everything. Nicki, meanwhile, was threatening to use her husband's affair with Amanda against him. Suddenly, her claim that she put Tara and Amanda together in the first place sounded all too plausible to her mother-in-law. 'Oonagh thought I did it so that I could prove adultery,' Nicki said, 'and take half of Tara's fortune. In response to that, they tried to get people to say that I'd slept with John Crittle. They even asked him if he would say it. John said, "What do you think I am? She's my friend's wife."'

But Tara suspected there was substance to the story.

•

Nicki had another issue to deal with as the date of the divorce hearing approached. She had no money. There were bills due and there was no food in the house. She went to see Oonagh's older sister, Maureen, one of the Guinness trustees, with whom Oonagh had always had a difficult relationship. Not surprisingly, Nicki got a sympathetic hearing from the woman who was once described by Cecil Beaton as 'the biggest bitch in London'.

'I had no money at all,' Nicki said. 'I didn't know how I was going to eat. So I went to see Maureen and she took out a pen and a piece of paper to figure out what I should be given to live on now that Tara and I were about to be formally separated. I think she was being nice to me just to get at Oonagh. It was, "Three pounds for manicures, twelve pounds for the hairdresser, eight pounds for clothes." I said, "Maureen, this is very generous – overly generous

– but there's also a thing called eating and paying the telephone bill." It never occurred to them that people would need money for such things because they had no idea where food came from or who paid the bills. They just thought, "What do women want? Well, they want nice hair and nice nails and, oh, nice clothes." So I said this thing about food and this friend of Maureen's, who happened to be sitting there, listening to all of this, said, "I think fifteen pounds a week is perfectly fine for a girl of your station." Can you believe that? I've never heard the likes of it outside of a Victorian play!'

14: A DAY IN THE LIFE

Tara's life was in chaos. His marriage was unspooling in a very messy and public way. His children were in Ireland. He'd lost Amanda. And he found himself going into business with a man whom he suspected was sleeping with his wife. Lonely, he had moved out of the Ritz at the end of October and moved in with his friends Gerard Campbell and Theodora Brinckman, on the Fulham Road. 'He was in a state of absolute turmoil,' Gerard remembered.

The separation of one of Swinging London's most popular couples presaged the end of the city's golden age. By the second half of the year, there were signs that England's time as the happy capital of the world was coming to an end – if you cared to see them. Three news stories from 1966 offended the happy narrative of young, fun-loving Britons changing the world with their cheery positivity. In April, two young lovers, Ian Brady and Myra Hindley, the so-called Moors Murderers, were convicted of the torture and killing of three children in Greater Manchester. In August, three policemen were shot dead in Shepherds Bush, West London, in what became known as the Massacre of Braybrook Street. And in October, 116 children and 28 adults were killed when a mountain of slurry slid down on the South Wales village of Aberfan.

Economically, the country was in deep trouble. In July, the government had attempted to tackle soaring inflation by declaring a freeze on wages. An era of austerity had begun, even if the people didn't quite realize it. The *New York Times* commented upon the fin de siècle feel to the city in the summer of 1966. 'The atmosphere in London can almost be eerie in its quality of relentless frivolity,' it reported. 'There can rarely have been a greater contrast between a country's objective situation and the mood of its people.'

The West End went on swinging, as if in denial. But the serendipitous orgy of mutual good feeling that made London the most exciting city in the world had gone. Spontaneity was replaced by calculation. Suddenly, it was all too self-aware and self-regarding. Tara was intuitive enough to understand that the happy times were coming to an end – and not just for him and Nicki. 'I remember being on the King's Road with him in the fall of 1966,' Rock Brynner remembered. 'We were both very silent. There's a good chance we were stoned. And he said to me, "This is not what we meant." By that, I think he was saying that the spontaneity had gone out of it. The whole thing had become contrived and commercialized.'

Tara spent most evenings at the Scotch or London's newest, most exclusive member's club, Sybilla's. Occasionally, he sought the consolation of a warm body. He had a one-night stand with Marianne Faithfull at some point between her split with John Dunbar and the start of her relationship with Mick Jagger.

'We had a little scene together,' she remembered. 'It was just one night in a hotel in London. Like Tara, I married too young. I had just broken up with John and I didn't know what I wanted to do next. So I was just checking things out, just as Tara was coming out of his marriage and also checking things out.

'What more can I say? It was a wonderful little fling. We liked each other very much, even though we didn't want to get involved in something so serious again. But I do think sometimes how my life might have been different had something developed between us. I think I could have loved him.'

Tara tried to stay busy. The opening of Dandie Fashions was scheduled for Christmas week. John Crittle had managed to secure the lease on the ground floor, as well as the basement below the Methodist chapel on the King's Road.

In November, Tara asked Dudley, Douglas and Dave to paint the exterior and interior of the shop to match his car. They set to work immediately, working mostly through the night, as they did with the Cobra. The final coat was barely dry when they suffered a near-disaster.

'With Dave,' Dudley remembered, 'it was like living with a time bomb. You never knew when it was going to go off. Doug and I had been working away till two, three, four in the morning, painting away. Dave would often be, like, stood around twiddling his thumbs. And that was when he was at his most dangerous. But what you didn't want him to say was, "I'll pick up a paintbrush and help you, lads," because he'd make a complete arse of it. We'd have to go over it, you know, without trying to offend him.

'On this particular night, he was hanging around. He said, "Shall I go and get some teas from the pie and tea stall down at Sloane Square?" We said, "Great idea, Dave." Anything to keep him occupied. So he shot off in the Buick. Doug and I are quietly working away, thinking, "Thank Christ for that – he's off out of the way."

'Anyway, it must have been about an hour later, or whatever, the Buick comes screeching to a halt outside. He comes racing through the door, going, "Douse the lights! Grab an 'ammer! Douse the lights! Grab an 'ammer!"

'And what had happened, it transpired, was that he'd gone to the pie stall, and, as was his wont, he got into a row with the next guy in the queue. Dave, when he got served, must have got hold of his pie and shoved it in this bloke's face.

'Then he noticed the guy run back to his car, which was full of about three or four other guys. They'd got the boot up and they were grabbing hold of jemmies and whatever. So Dave jumps in the Buick and shoots off. But instead of, like, trying to lose them, down side streets, he drives back to Tara's shop – driving the most conspicuous car in London, by the way.

'He shoots in through this narrow doorway, shouting this thing: "Douse the lights! Grab an 'ammer!" And the next thing we hear this other car screech up and all these big blokes come racing towards this entrance. As it happened, they couldn't get through more than one person at a time. I noticed the first bloke who got through had got bits of food all over his face. But Dave was stood waiting for him. And he threw the scalding hot teas in his face. So we heard this scream. The bloke shot back to the car and the car shot off.

'They must have only gone around the block, because the next thing they came back and they started throwing all these bricks at the shop front. Tara never knew anything about it. Just by a miracle, the stones hit all the bits on the corners and never broke any of the work we'd done.'

While the shop was being painted and fitted out, Tara and the man he suspected of cuckolding him were busy building up stock. John took care of business in his office in the basement, while Tara popped in, usually around lunchtime, before he started work at the garage, to check on progress.

'John would go and buy the fabric,' Alan Holsten remembered, 'then bring it up to Soho or to someone in the East End to get it turned into something. Before the shop opened and we had a cash flow, all the bills got sent to Tara, who wrote out cheques to settle everything, because he never carried cash.

'Tara's role was really as a backer, but they both knew the kind of clothes they wanted to sell – things like Regency jackets; red velvet jackets with stand-up collars, semi-bolero style. John ordered jackets in the same fabric as the trousers that the wine waiters in the Dorchester wore. We did jackets and suits in flannel cloth – all these different-coloured stripes. Jackets with ruffles and lace and all that kind of thing, which you could dress down by wearing a T-shirt underneath. And then we were going to do stuff to order. You could have a shirt with cuffs or a jacket with lapels that could be any colour you wanted.'

If it all sounded familiar, then there was a good reason. Dandie Fashions would be a shop that followed more than it led, offering almost identical styles to those Michael Rainey was selling on nearby Cale Street, but for a lower price. 'It did have its own aesthetic,' according to Paul Gorman, author of *The Look: Adventures in Rock and Pop Fashion*. 'But there's no doubt that what they were doing was very similar to – and some would say a cheap imitation of – Hung On You.'

Dandie's, as it quickly became known, was a combination of Michael Rainey's stolen vision, John Crittle's cynical opportunism and front, and Tara's access to enormous amounts of Guinness money. It broke Michael Rainey's heart – and, eventually, his will. 'They nicked my suppliers,' he said, 'my tailors, my manufacturers, everything. Foster's was my jacket and trousers maker. Then I had a shirt-maker in Soho, very close to the French Club. I had worked with these people for six months. I taught them how to cut things just the way I liked them. So Tara and John were stepping into a ready-made scene. While he was working for me, John had been filtering a lot of clothes out of my shop and they copied all my designs.'

Michael eventually took the disastrous decision to move from Cale Street to World's End. *Time* magazine had named Hung On You as one of the must-see locations in Swinging London. Suddenly, no one knew where it had gone. 'It was a mistake. I thought the King's Road was where it was happening but I went down the wrong end. I wasn't particularly ambitious – not like John Crittle was – but I was upset that I had this little shop that I loved and suddenly I felt like I'd been chased down the street by a pack of wolves.

'We didn't fall out, Tara and I. It wasn't Tara who planned it. I fell out with John, though. The suppliers were assuring me, "Don't worry, we'll never let them copy your stuff," and, "We'll continue to make stuff for you." But in the end, I gave it up. I said, "I don't think there's enough for two of us in this." John had Guinness money behind him. I couldn't compete with that. So I got out of the clothes business and went into carpets.'

The arrival of Dandie Fashions would mark the moment when the King's Road began to follow down the same commercial path as Carnaby Street. As Alan put it: 'By the time we opened, everyone was just plagiarizing everyone else.'

Dandie's would lack the personality of Granny's. Joss sticks would be the nearest things it had to a gimmick. 'But it had everything going for it. It was in the right location. We were right smack bang in the middle of the King's Road. The shop looked the business from the outside, with the mural and everything. Then when you went in, it actually felt like a shop. Those other places, they were doing their own thing, but they were a bit, I don't know, not upper-class snooty, but you were either "in" or you weren't. And they seemed to have very little to sell. Some of it was antique, some of it was new – it was whatever they got their hands on. Dandie Fashions would be more of a commercial environment. We were going to do it right.'

•

Tara wasn't alone in feeling confused and a little lost that autumn. The Beatles were exhausted at the end of what had been for them a turbulent summer.

Revolver revealed a group of musicians who were thrilling to the technical possibilities of the studio, experimenting with tape loops, backward guitar parts and varispeeding to create sounds that had never been heard on a record before.

Thematically, the album had broken all manner of taboos. 'Tomorrow Never Knows' was the band's most overtly drug-themed song yet, in which John Lennon attempted to render the experience of taking LSD in a three-minute song.

Musically, the album had everything. George was allowed to indulge his growing obsession with Indian music in 'Love You To' and Paul his penchant for classical string arrangements in the strange and ethereal 'Eleanor Rigby'. John managed to work Peter Fonda's trippy assertion that he knew what it was like to be dead into 'She Said She Said', one of three tracks with a clear drug theme. Acid, politics, love, spiritualism – and even Ringo's 'Yellow Submarine' thrown in for the kiddies. Yet it still sounded like a coherent body of work put together by four musicians who were all on the same page creatively.

But their transition into grown-up, independent-minded Beatles and heralds of a new consciousness had not been with-out growing pains. In July, they'd been attacked in the Philippines – and kicked, quite literally, onto the plane home – after refusing an invitation to meet the country's First Lady, Imelda Marcos. They were lucky to escape without serious injury.

A month later, while touring America, there was trouble of a different colour when John Lennon's philosophical musings on the popularity of The Beatles in comparison to Jesus Christ got him in trouble. When a five-month-old *London Evening Standard* interview was regurgitated in the American press, it triggered a fortnight of anti-Beatles hysteria. Radio stations banned their records. Religious fundamentalists burned them. Even the Ku Klux Klan managed to steal the moral high ground from the once 'cute' Beatles.

At a press conference, convened to try to take the heat out of the story, John – against his better judgement – apologized for what he said. But the whole absurd charade confirmed in the minds of The Beatles what they'd been discussing amongst themselves for a year: the Fab Four thing was a beaten docket.

On 29 August, after playing Candlestick Park in San Francisco, they announced that they were taking a break. When they returned to London, the four Beatles did their own thing for the first time since becoming famous. John went to Spain to play Musketeer Gripweed in Richard Lester's black comedy, *How I Won the War*. George went to India with Patti, for sitar tuition from his musical guru, Ravi Shankar. Paul stuck around England, working with Beatles producer George Martin on the score for the British film *The Family Way*.

The wholesome, fun-loving Beatles disappeared from public view, eventually to be replaced by four serious-minded cultural subversives; long-haired, drug-savvy avatars for the world's 'turned-on' youth. Tara saw a bit of Paul in London that September. Paul was growing a Pancho Villa-type moustache to try to conceal his scarred lip from the moped accident. When he saw Tara's painted Cobra, he was beside himself with excitement. 'He said he wanted the same thing done to his piano,' remembered Dudley Edwards. 'So Tara took us around to his house and introduced us to him.'

The following week, Dudley and Douglas Binder painted Paul's upright piano with an almost identical colour scheme to

Tara's car. It was the piano on which he would write the song 'Getting Better', part of a new concept album, the idea for which was starting to percolate in his head that autumn. In November, he went on holiday to Kenya with Jane Asher, but he was straining to get back to the studio. *Revolver* had been a great effort. But *Pet Sounds*, in his view, had raised the bar. And now he had an idea for something that was even better.

•

Tara, normally so self-contained, so effortlessly cool, found himself, for the first time in his life, overwhelmed by a weight of worries as December approached. The divorce. The children. His broken love affair with Amanda. Long meetings with solicitors and trustees. And Oonagh in the background, dictating matters.

His friends began to notice an unfamiliar sense of doom about him. 'I remember one night I was having a trip with him in Theodora's house,' said Martin Wilkinson. 'We were playing chess and the acid started working. And suddenly he looked at me and I was sure he was having some kind of premonition that something was going to happen.

'I'd had a very serious accident about a year before in a Lotus Elan that belonged to him. I was in Cornwall and I hit a wall and I ended up upside-down in the thing. I was very lucky that I wasn't killed. But I still had the scar and that's what Tara was staring at and he obviously saw something or developed some sense and was really frightened. He said to me, "Don't look at me like that," and Tara wasn't normally like that on acid.

'It probably had something to do with his emotional state at the time. I know he used to tell people that he wasn't going to live a long life. Then he had all these problems with Nicki and the children. I think he was disturbed at the time.'

It probably didn't help that he was spending a lot of time with Brian Jones, who was going through his own dark agonies. The Rolling Stones were adding the finishing touches to their new album, *Between the Buttons*, in London in November that December. For a whole variety of reasons, some of them chemical, Brian was playing far less of a role in the studio than he had in the recording of *Aftermath*. While his confidence reached a new low point, Mick had developed a clear sense of his own sexual potency. He was in the process of jettisoning Chrissie Shrimpton, his girlfriend from the days before he was famous, who now found herself, like the subject of 'Out of Time', old-fashioned, out of touch and obsolete, especially compared to the exotic and free-spirited Marianne, who was now sharing his bed.

Brian still showed flashes of the old brilliance, colluding with Keith to write 'Ruby Tuesday', which Marianne regarded as his final, heroic effort to regain his place as the leader of the band he founded. But The Rolling Stones was now clearly Mick and Keith, which left Brian plenty of downtime to indulge his insecurity, jealousy and full gamut of dark thoughts. He became a difficult presence around the studio, petulant, uncommunicative, drunk, or drugged.

'People always say that Mick and Keith took over the band because Brian couldn't write,' said Anita, 'but it wasn't true. Brian was very creative. He stayed up all night writing songs. But the following morning he would erase them all, because he was paranoid. He didn't want anyone to know what he was doing. And at that time, it became much worse because of the political scenario with Mick and Keith and Andrew.

'For Brian, I think his friendship with Tara was a safe haven with all that was going on in the studio, with all that antagonism. It was difficult because Brian was very sensitive and I think he recognized that Tara was sensitive, too. Brian didn't have many friendships. It was unusual that he let someone so close. In the end, he didn't have any friends at all, except people who worked for him or people who used him to procure drugs and girls. But at that time he was lucky enough to have Tara.'

Martin Wilkinson remembered calling in to see them in Courtfield Road one night that November. 'Brian answered the door,' he said. 'He invited me in. He said he was teaching Tara the chords on the guitar, or he was teaching him the blues, something like that. They were very, very close, Tara and Brian.

'The flat had a very gloomy hotel sort of feel to it. The whole Tibetan Buddhist thing was still new at the time and Brian had done a Mandala on the wall. It was like a picture of his life with all the elements represented in it. It was supposed to represent what your life meant. I remember thinking it was incredibly sinister.

'And Tara was beginning to do one as well – or he had done one. And because they were both so young, I remember thinking, how could you think your life is encapsulated in something like that? They might have seen it as an act of rebellion, writing on the walls of this ghastly flat, but I remember being worried about it. It just seemed terribly morbid.'

In the middle of November, just days before the start of the divorce case, Tara returned to Luggala for Dorian's third birthday. Brian made the trip with him. Oonagh took photographs of them in the drawing room, looking like two brothers in their matching black polo-neck jumpers and identical blond haircuts.

After the stress of the last few weeks, Tara was relieved to be home, not least because he was still permitted to drive in Ireland. He took Brian around in a Lotus Elan that he kept at Luggala and showed him the sights of Wicklow, including the trees he loved to climb as a boy and the lake where he learned to swim. On the way back to the house one day, there was an incident involving a neighbour's hens.

'I heard what sounded like a racing car coming up the hill,' remembered Thomas Webster, who sold free-range eggs from his home in Roundwood. 'The noise of the thing was unbelievable. I heard a screech, then I looked out the window and all I could see was feathers everywhere. I'd no car at the time. I was getting up on the tractor to go after him, but my wife, Noeleen, told me to forget about it. It was only two or three hens, she said. He was very attractive to the girls, you see. So I hopped down off the tractor and I said, "That lad would want to slow down." And then later, of course, I wished I had gone up after him, because maybe he would have listened to me.'

•

On Friday, 9 December, the *Daily Express* carried a short article about the forthcoming opening of Dandie Fashions. The newspaper had spoken to the Reverend Ron Hoar, the minister at the Chelsea Methodist Church, about his newest tenants. 'I don't think I shall be getting any clothes there,' he told the newspaper. 'But I will probably drop in some time to get acquainted. And my children aren't quite kinky enough. The eldest is nine.'

The official opening of the shop was less than two weeks away, but Tara was preoccupied with the divorce case. Tara and Nicki were in court almost every day to witness their lawyers argue over the custody of the children and over what settlement, if any, Nicki would receive. Alan Holsten was clearing out the lock-up garage on Gloucester Avenue one day when he found a handwritten poem in Tara's desk drawer. He presumed Tara had written it in response to his break-up with Nicki, although Martin Wilkinson thought it was more likely a song he was writing with Brian Jones. Either way, it may have offered a hint as to his emotional state at the time:

> When my heart first began to
> Crumble
> I never knew that the
> Reason for this
> Was I.
> As I watched our Real Love tumble
> I wasn't ready for
> Feelings that
> Did
> Die.
> Now I come to you ever humble
> And beg of you to
> Give love one
> More
> Try.

But reconciliation with Nicki was never on the cards, even though she later claimed they remained on good terms and in regular telephone contact, contrary to the instructions of their lawyers, throughout the court case. Tara was ready to move on, from Nicki and from Amanda. At the start of the December, he became romantically involved with one of Mark Palmer's friends, Suki Potier, a pretty, nineteen-year-old model.

Mark Palmer met her in a club on Cromwell Street when she was about seventeen. She came from a comfortable, middle-class background, he remembered, with parents who disapproved of her friends and her lifestyle. She was petite and blonde, with a painstakingly put-together look that would soon be rendered old-fashioned by the time the Summer of Love rolled around and hippie chicks like Marianne Faithfull took centre stage. She was pleasant company, according to Tara's friends, but she didn't challenge him intellectually.

'Nicki, by contrast, was bubbly and alive,' said Michael Rainey. 'She had a presence. I liked Suki a lot, but she was a bimbo really – she had a bimbo look and mind. She was basically a groupie.'

Jose Fonseca, who handled her bookings for Mark Palmer's modelling agency, English Boy, remembered her being nice if slightly scattered. 'She seemed to sort of drift through life,' she said. 'She didn't have much focus. She did the odd bit of modelling here and there and earned enough to live. But in those days, you could do two or three jobs and get by on the money for two or three months.'

Tara and Suki went out a handful of times, but nothing about the dynamic between them suggested the affair would be anything other than short and fleeting.

'She was a rebound thing for Tara,' said Martin Wilkinson. 'She was incredibly sweet, very feminine, very funny, laughed a lot. Not particularly bright. Reacted in a very light way to things, but she also had a sort of doomed quality about her. Her reaction to mishaps was always, "Oh my God, I knew that was going to happen." I would have said she was worried by life, in a way that Tara wasn't, which is why I don't think it was ever going to develop into anything serious.'

On Wednesday, 14 December, his driving licence was reinstated.

He wasted no time in getting back behind the wheel. 'He rang me the following day,' said Nicki. 'It was a Thursday. We weren't meant to be speaking to each other because we were in the middle of this court case, but we were still speaking behind everyone's back. He rang me and he said, "Guess what! I've just got my licence back!" and I said, "Oh, good!" And the last words I ever spoke to him were, "Drive carefully."'

Tara was due to fly to Ireland that Saturday afternoon to see the children, but for some reason he changed his mind. He had a big week ahead of him. On Monday, he was due back in court. On Wednesday, Dandie Fashions was opening its doors for the first time, after which he was planning to fly to Ireland to spend Christmas.

When Nicki spoke to him that week, she said he seemed 'addled'.

'I think he just saw everything going down the spout,' she said. 'His mind was distracted. He had people pulling at him from this side and that side – trustees, solicitors, Oonagh, me. You have all that going on in your mind, then you get into a car and you drive at ninety miles per hour, there's one thing that's likely to happen.'

On Saturday he slept until lunchtime, then he popped around to the garage, where he spent the afternoon servicing a light blue Lotus Elan that belonged to Glen Kidston's girlfriend, Serena. His painted Cobra was in New York and, he was tickled to hear, turning heads in Times Square. David Vaughan had taken it to America on a Cunard liner and was planning to drive it from coast to coast to drum up publicity for Binder, Edwards and Vaughan. And he was up to his old tricks, telling the *New York Times* that he was hoping to cover a skyscraper with a giant mural.

With no car of his own, Tara borrowed Serena's Lotus for the weekend. He finished work in the late afternoon, then he popped round to Courtfield Road and watched *Jukebox Jury* with Brian. He had a date that night with Suki and he was looking forward to it. He picked her up shortly before 9 p.m. and they had dinner in a restaurant on Abingdon Road. They left the restaurant just before midnight and drove off. London was festooned with

Christmas lights. They headed west in Serena's Lotus Elan, driving just for the hell of it, with no particular place to go.

'It's very dangerous if you haven't driven anything for six months to suddenly get back into a high performance car like a Lotus Elan,' said Martin Wilkinson. 'The car had a very good power-to-weight ratio. It was great, as long as you remained in control of it. But if it went away from you, because it was so light, then you really had no chance.'

Just after midnight, they were driving through Redcliffe Gardens, approaching the junction with Redcliffe Square in South Kensington, when Tara, for reasons that were never clear, lost control of the car. Neither alcohol nor drugs were a factor, as Tara had consumed less than one pint of beer, though speed may well have been a cause. Suki claimed that he wasn't going particularly fast, although that would have been wildly out of character for him. Several witnesses claimed he flew past them, accelerating and braking fast, while the car made a loud noise. Seconds later, there was a bang and the sound of the engine stopped.

According to Suki's version of events, a white car – either a Volvo or an E-type Jag – emerged unexpectedly from a side street, forcing Tara to swerve and collide with a black van that was parked nearby, before landing on the pavement a few feet away. Despite nationwide appeals, the driver of the second car was never found.

Whatever the reason for Tara's uncharacteristic loss of control, his final act in life was to pull the steering wheel to ensure that he, and not Suki, took the full impact of the collision with the van. 'A gentleman,' said Anita Pallenberg. 'To the very end.'

The car disintegrated around them. Tara suffered a fractured skull and lacerations to his brain. Suki survived with bruises and shock. She held Tara, dying in her arms, while she waited forty-five minutes for an ambulance to arrive. He was removed from the car and taken to St Stephen's Hospital in Fulham. Two hours later, he was pronounced dead.

Suki phoned Theodora, who then phoned Nicki. They both rushed to the hospital. 'Theodora got there before me,' Nicki remembered. 'When she saw me, she said, "Oh, Nicki, they've combed his hair the wrong way."'

Gay Kindersley was asleep in his farmhouse in East Garston, near Newbury, when the police rang to say that his half-brother had been killed in a car accident. They asked if he would formally identify the body. He was in such a state of shock that he didn't trust himself behind the wheel of his car. In the middle of the night, he woke his friend, the horse-trainer Billy Payne, and asked him to take him to London.

'It was the most awful thing I've ever had to do,' Gay remembered. 'I went down to this morgue and I walked through and the policeman – a very nice man – said, "Would you like a cigarette, sir?" I hadn't smoked for about twenty years. I said, "Yes, I would." And then they pulled out the drawer and there was Tara lying there, the poor chap.'

At 3 a.m., Garech, who was sleeping soundly in Woodtown Manor, his Dublin home, received a call from his mother's solicitor, James Cawley, who told him that his brother was dead. 'You expect to see your parents die,' Garech said. 'That's part of life. But you don't expect your younger brother to die – not before his time. It seemed so stupid, so pointless.'

Still numb, he drove to Luggala in the middle of the night to break the news to his mother. Oonagh was up, feeding Desmond and Manuela. 'I said to her, "I have something urgent I have to tell you," and she said, "Sit down and wait until I've finished feeding the babies." It was hell. I had to sit there while she fiddled with bottles, with this thing in my head.'

Oonagh broke down when she heard the news. Afterwards, Garech returned to Woodtown Manor. At 7 a.m. he phoned his father and broke the news to him. Dom, who had lost his own parents in a car accident forty years earlier, had lost his youngest son in similar circumstances. 'He just couldn't take it in,' Garech remembered.

He was far from alone. The following morning the news broke with the dawn. 'It was like a death knell sounding over London,' remembered Marianne Faithfull. 'I think it was a definite turning point for a lot of us. It was the end of the Sixties for many people. To have someone who was so full of life and so full of joy suddenly taken from you, it made you very pessimistic and cynical about the world, which is what we'd all been trying so hard not to be.'

Later that morning, Suki's father, Gilbert, paid tribute to Tara's actions in saving his daughter's life. 'It was a very gallant act,' he said. 'It's tragic that it should have cost him his life.'

At Courtfield Road, Brian Jones was doorstepped by a reporter, who broke the news of his friend's death to him. He wept uncontrollably. 'I am numbed,' he said. 'It's ghastly. He was so full of life.'

That night, guitar in hand, he showed up at the mews house in Eaton Row, where he'd spent so many happy nights, playing with Tara's Scalextric cars, smoking dope and listening to The Beach Boys. Nicki invited him in. He sat down and, without uttering a single word, she said, he played soothing guitar to her for two hours until she fell asleep.

Three days later, in the middle of Christmas week, Tara was laid to rest in the grounds of Luggala, on the shore of Lough Tay, under a simple granite slab that carried his name, the Browne family's coat of arms and the two dates – 1945 and 1966 – that bore out the tragedy of a life cut short.

Eight months after celebrating his twenty-first birthday, on a night that would remain for many of them the high watermark of the Swinging Sixties, his friends returned to his home at the bottom of a valley in the Wicklow Mountains to say goodbye to him. It rained so heavily that a hydraulic pump had to be employed to prevent the grave from filling up with water. Between forty and fifty of Tara's young friends, decked out in the fashions of the day, stood around in the rain, openly weeping, as if they instinctively understood that his death represented something more than just the end of a life.

'We felt immortal,' said Anita Pallenberg. 'We thought we were indestructible. But then Tara died – the first of us to go. Something changed that day. For everyone. The Sixties weren't the Sixties anymore.'

EPILOGUE: AND THOUGH
THE NEWS WAS RATHER SAD

On the morning of Monday, 19 December 1966, the day after Tara's death and still three days before he was buried, his mother and widow had a date to keep at the High Court in London. The divorce case had been finalized in the most tragically unforeseen way, but the question of who would raise Dorian and Julian was even more important now that their father was gone. Nicki and Oonagh appeared in front of Mr Justice Cross, who said he would make an order on the issue of the custody of the children in the New Year.

Everyone had an utterly miserable Christmas.

On 16 January 1967, Justice Cross upheld the decision of the Dublin court, ruling that Dorian and Julian should stay with Oonagh, although he said that every effort should be made to ensure that their mother played an increasing role in their lives.

Nicki left the court in a daze, then went back to Eaton Row and cried for four hours. 'I had no chance,' she said, 'taking on the Guinness family with all their money.'

The following day, John Lennon was sitting at his upright piano at the EMI recording studios on Abbey Road in London. He was blocked. The Beatles had been in the studio since the last week in November, laying down songs for a concept album in which they would play the part of a fictional band. Hiding behind musical alter egos would allow them to experiment creatively with different song forms and sounds. At least that was how Paul sold it to the others, since *Sergeant Pepper's Lonely Hearts Club Band* was his creative vision.

By the second week in January, the sessions had yielded three songs, whose conceptual link was that they were all nostalgic compositions inspired by their Liverpool childhoods: John's 'Strawberry Fields Forever' and Paul's 'Penny Lane' and 'When I'm Sixty-Four'. Only the last of these would make it onto the final album.

John, like George and Ringo, wasn't enjoying himself. He was, in his own words, 'very out of it then', taking enormous amounts of acid in an effort to counter the boredom of his suburban life with a wife and child. By contrast, Paul was happily gadding about London, living the life of a bachelor while his girlfriend, Jane Asher, was away in America. Creatively, he was on a roll. This was his record – his idea, his personality, his drive. *Sergeant Pepper* marked the moment when Paul became the dominant creative force in the band. Tighter with producer George Martin than any of the others, he began to assert more and more control in the studio over how their music was recorded.

Every day, he was presenting the others with new ideas for the album, whereas John was worried that he'd already shot his bolt with 'Strawberry Fields Forever'. He knew that unless he started coming up with material, every song on the record would be written by Paul.

But then he hated working this way, writing songs to order, instead of allowing inspiration to arrive. He did what he'd always done when he was bereft of ideas. He picked up a newspaper, looking to find something in the morning's headlines that might serve as inspiration. He propped a copy of the *Daily Mail* on the music stand in front of him and turned over the front page. There, in the middle of page three, was an article headlined: 'Guinness Heir Babies Stay with Grandmother'.

John had heard about Tara's death. He and Paul had just been discussing whether or not Tara would have inherited his father's seat in the House of Lords had he lived. Paul said no, that his father had a son from his first marriage, who was in line to become the next Lord Oranmore and Browne.

John touched the piano keys and out came the opening line of a song about a lucky man who made the grade, but died in a traffic accident. In John's fictionalized account of the accident, Tara was tripping on acid and failed to notice that a traffic light had turned red. He muses on how the dissemination of news trivializes things that happen, as a crowd of people gather at the scene, recognize his face and wonder if he was a member of the House of Lords.

John wrote two more verses, inspired by a report in the same morning's *Daily Express* about potholes in Blackburn and his recent experiences filming *How I Won the War*.

John played the song to Paul, who loved it, then offered him a middle section that he originally wrote for another song, about smoking pot on the upper deck of a bus and slipping off into a dope-fuelled reverie. Together, they happened upon the line about turning someone on to drugs. Paul – who was first 'turned on' by Tara – looked at John and the same thought passed between them. They couldn't say that in a song, could they?

•

While The Beatles were locked away in the studio, Tara's friends gathered for a memorial service in his honour in St Paul's Roman Catholic Church in Kensington, one mile from the scene of the accident. Despite the January cold and rain, almost all of the girls there were in miniskirts, the *Daily Sketch* reported, while most of the men were decked out in bell-bottomed trousers and multi-coloured Regency jackets.

Gerard Campbell, who had put Tara up in the final weeks of his life, was shocked to discover that his friend had left him £1,000 in his will. 'I went out and bought a new suit,' he said. 'Loud – the kind of thing he would have appreciated.'

Father Dennis, the Franciscan friar who conducted the service, said of Tara: 'He touched life fully.'

After the service, Nicki ran from the church in tears and was driven away, it was reported, with her face buried in the fur of her pet white poodle.

It was said that Oonagh was never the same after Tara's death. She already knew the tragedy of losing a child before its time but the loss of her youngest son broke her. 'She moved out of Luggala,' said Greta Fanning, who worked as a nanny to the children, 'and into Luttrelstown Castle [her sister Aileen's home]. Then we all went to Paris. Being at Luggala just reminded her of what she'd lost.'

Similarly, for his brother, Garech, Tara's death would be a scar on his life. Though their interests were very different, Tara idolized his older brother and they were just reaching the point in their lives where the six-year age gap no longer felt like a generation separating them.

'As the older brother,' Garech said, 'I was very protective of him. But in a strange way, later on, he was very protective of me, too. I remember him taking me around the bits of London that I didn't know. So that's what was most upsetting to me. I had one brother who I thought I could always talk to, who would be my relative and pal for life.'

Nicki couldn't bear to be in London anymore. Too many old ghosts. Just days after the order awarding custody of her children to her mother-in-law, she moved to Marbella, making a permanent home for herself in Orange Tree Square, in the whitewashed cottage where she had hoped that she and Tara would one day live.

'I'm going by myself,' she said before she left, 'just to pick up my life again and sort things out. I shall make a new home for myself there . . . I want to install a fountain and plant thousands and thousands of flowers.'

Despite the judge's stated wish that she should play a role in Dorian and Julian's lives, it didn't work out as anyone would have wished. It was neither a tidy nor a happy arrangement and would lead to years of hurt and estrangement between Nicki and her two sons.

While John Lennon was immortalizing Tara in song, Anita Pallenberg paid her own private tribute to him in the movie *A Degree of Murder*. 'I couldn't grieve for Tara properly because straight after he died I had to go to Germany to make this film,' she said. 'But I had this amethyst ring that Tara had lent to me. In the film, I threw it across the room – when you watch the film, you can see it flying through the air – and that was my little ode to Tara.'

Sergeant Pepper's Lonely Hearts Club Band was released in June 1967 and immediately hailed by many as the greatest music album of the twentieth century – as it still is by many critics, almost fifty years after it was first recorded. If there was a cultural gravitational point that the 1960s had been pulling towards, then this was it, a record that managed to capture the unique energy of the times. Almost everything about it was revolutionary, from its original concept, to its songwriting, to its cover art, to its use of studio trickery to achieve sounds never heard before on vinyl.

Its *pièce de résistance* was 'A Day in the Life', with John singing in a disembodied, almost spectral voice and taking licence with the details of Tara's death to provide the album with its haunting coda.

The cover photograph, taken by Tara's friend and twenty-first-birthday-party chronicler Michael Cooper, remains the most enduring image of the psychedelic era. The diorama of cut-out figures from history included, at John's suggestion, George Bernard Shaw, author of *Pygmalion*.

The album became the soundtrack for the season of hope and upheaval that was 1967's Summer of Love, when it suddenly seemed conceivable that young people really could change the world with their happy thoughts. It also represented the last hurrah for the era of Swinging London. You could almost make the case that the dying piano chord at the end of 'A Day in the Life' – a sound created by all four Beatles, plus George Martin and roadie Mal Evans, simultaneously hitting three pianos – was the moment when the essential energy of the Sixties shifted from England to the west coast of America.

The later, counterculture Sixties were about hippies in Haight-Ashbury and Vietnam War protests and civil-rights marches that turned bloody and Hells Angels turning murderous at a Rolling Stones concert at Altamont Freeway and drugs – the 'bad' kind. It was the Sixties that Tara never lived to see, which is why his death, coming when it did, became for many of his friends a historical marker.

'For me, the day that Tara died was the end of the Sixties,' said Hugo Williams, who had his eyes opened to the world by this confident little man-child in Paris in the late 1950s. 'His death was the point from which things started to go bad. While he was alive, it was the miniskirt and the Twist and "I Wanna Hold Your Hand". And after he died, it was more about long hair and drugs and psychedelia and Altamont and horrible things like that. His was a rock and roll death really. Because he stood for something in our lives. And suddenly the party was over and we all had to grow up and get married and get on with our lives. It really did stunt my youth, the way he died. I think a lot of people have a death that stands out for them in that same way.'

•

There was a perceptible change in mood in Britain in the early weeks of 1967. London was still swinging but the momentum had started to slow. The old Establishment – as represented by elements in the police and press – decided that everyone had had more than enough fun and began to assert their might.

These working-class singers and musicians, most of them still in their twenties, were buying up the stately homes that the old aristocracy could no longer afford to live in, were openly flaunting the drug laws and holding themselves out to be role models for the nation's youth. They had to be stopped. And top of the Establishment's hit-list were The Rolling Stones.

'We were all so young,' Anita Pallenberg remembered. 'That's why they were so envious. We were all young kids, especially Brian, who was driving around in a big Rolls Royce and he could barely see over the steering wheel. Can you imagine an old geezer seeing a young kid with long hair driving a Rolls? They said, "What the fuck? Why should they have that?" That's why we had to be stopped.'

Brian was devastated by Tara's death and his behaviour became increasingly reckless. In January 1967 he spoke openly about his use of illegal drugs to an undercover reporter from the *News of the World*, which had decided to wage war on The Rolling Stones on behalf of the moral majority. The reporter thought he'd just heard a confession from Mick Jagger, rather than Brian Jones.

When the newspaper ran the story, Mick immediately sued, thus bringing the weight of the police, with whom the newspaper worked hand in glove, crashing down on all of their heads. On Friday, 10 February, Mick, Keith Richards, Marianne Faithfull and Donovan were among the crowd gathered in the studio on Abbey Road to see The Beatles and a group of classical musicians work on the orchestral crescendo in 'A Day in the Life'. That weekend, Keith was entertaining guests at Redlands, his fifteenth-century home in West Wittering, West Sussex, when the bobbies arrived at the door. There, they discovered various members of the London scene sitting around, including Mick, Keith, Christopher Gibbs, Michael Cooper, Robert Fraser and Marianne, wrapped in a rug, but otherwise in a state of undress. George Harrison and Patti Boyd had just left.

They turned the place over looking for drugs but would have been disappointed with their haul. On Mick, they found four amphetamine pills that he claimed had been prescribed in Italy for travel sickness. On Robert, they found a small amount of heroin and eight capsules of methylamphetamine hydrochloride. They were both charged with possession of drugs, while the remnants of a single joint found in an ashtray meant they could charge Keith with allowing his premises to be used for the smoking of marijuana.

Anyone familiar with the hedonistic lifestyle of the Stones and their aristocratic hangers-on couldn't believe that was all the police could lay their hands on. It sounded like they were having a quiet night in.

Robert pleaded guilty to drug possession and received a six-month prison sentence with hard labour. While he was in prison, his gallery was put into receivership. It eventually closed in the summer of 1969. Mick was sentenced to three months' imprisonment, amended to a conditional discharge on appeal. Keith was sentenced to a year in prison, later overturned. William Rees-Mogg, the traditionally conservative editor of *The Times*, wrote a leader article criticizing the harshness of the sentences and the Victorian brutality brought to bear on those involved.

Soon, pinning drug charges on pop stars became the almost exclusive preserve of Norman Pilcher, the crooked drug-squad detective who was accused by many – including John Lennon and George Harrison – of bringing his own drugs to a raid in case of disappointment.

It was almost certainly Pilcher who ordered the raid on Dandie Fashions in the summer of 1967. The shop had opened, as planned, in Christmas week and was doing good business. Jimi Hendrix, The Bee Gees and Procol Harum had all bought clothes in there, while Andy Warhol had strayed in from the street once and had a look around. But John Crittle had managed to make an enemy of the local police. 'He used to really get up their noses,' remembered Alan Holsten. 'He used to park on the pavement outside the police station. When they'd tell him to move, he'd tell them to fuck off. So they decided to stitch him up.'

Amanda Lear happened to be in the shop, trying on a dress, when the police arrived. John later told the press that there were ten police officers involved in the raid. They arrested a number of people, including Amanda and John, and seized various pills and substances for analysis.

'They busted him for drugs,' Alan said. 'I was a witness at the trial and I didn't exactly help matters. I was nervous. They asked me what I did for a living and I told them I worked in a shit shop. I meant to say shirt shop. But of course shit was slang for drugs.'

John received a relatively light sentence of three weeks, while the charges against Amanda were dropped when the police confirmed that her pills were prescribed for a medical condition. But news of the raid had been splashed across the newspapers. The Guinness trustees didn't care much for the publicity and withdrew their money. They eventually sold the business to Apple Tailoring, one of the philanthropic companies established by The Beatles. And that was the end of Dandie Fashions.

It was open season on Britain's young musical stars. Brian Jones was busted separately from Mick and Keith. While they were waiting for their cases to come to trial, The Rolling Stones exiled themselves. In the summer of 1967, Brian, Anita, Keith and Christopher Gibbs went on holiday to Tangiers in Morocco. It was there one night, while Brian was hospitalized with pneumonia, that Keith, who had developed feelings for Anita, made his move. And Anita slipped from the life of one Stone and into the life of another.

'He was devastated by Tara's death,' according to Amanda Lear, who became close to him around that time. 'He also felt completely rejected by the group. He was very difficult to control because of all the drugs he was taking. He kept telling me he was going to go solo, make an album. He felt lost and rejected. He had no friends, just hangers-on. Tara, I think, was the last true friend he had.'

After his break-up with Anita, he became romantically involved with Suki Potier, the girl who survived the crash that killed his friend, but all they ever had in common was Tara and a certain doomed quality that they both shared. 'Suki was completely broken up by what happened to Tara,' said Jose Fonseca from English Boy. 'She told me once that she went to see a psychic, who told her that she would witness the deaths of three important men in her life,' a line that would prove spookily prophetic. She spent a great deal of time with Brian as he pirouetted towards his own sad demise. Then, in 1981, she was killed alongside her husband, Hong Kong-born casino heir Bob Ho, in a car crash in Portugal.

In 1969, Brian bought Crotchford Farm, the house where *Winnie the Pooh* author A. A. Milne once lived. But his heavy drug intake, mounting legal problems and ostracism from the band he still considered his own meant he couldn't find peace. It was all leading up to what happened on 3 July 1969, when, shortly after he was finally sacked by The Rolling Stones, he was discovered motionless at the bottom of his swimming pool. The coroner's report called it death by misadventure, noting that his liver and heart were unusually enlarged due to drug and alcohol abuse.

'Brian definitely went downhill after Tara died,' said Marianne Faithfull. 'I'm not saying that was the reason it happened. I know there were other things going on. But a lot of people like Brian, who loved Tara, mourned him in very dangerous ways. And that was understandable. Because a bit of the idealism of the 1960s died with him.'

•

In 1969, three years after his death, Tara's name was disinterred from history in the most bizarre circumstances. A silly-season conspiracy theory, which started among students on a university campus in Iowa, claimed that Paul McCartney was dead. Fans – or 'freaks' as Lennon would describe them in a later song – began to study the covers of all of the band's albums from *Sergeant Pepper* onwards for clues to support the theory that he had died in a road accident years earlier and it had been covered up. One claim, which was no less ridiculous than all the rest, was that Paul was killed when he crashed his moped on Boxing Day 1965 and he was replaced by a lookalike – Tara Browne.

'They said Tara had had cosmetic surgery to make him look like Paul,' Nicki remembered. 'I always thought that Tara would have been very amused by that story.'

John Lennon wasn't the only artist to immortalize Tara in music. The Pretty Things, who had been regular callers to the house in Eaton Row, wrote a song about him called 'Death of a Socialite'.

The Irish composer Seán Ó Riada composed *In Memoriam Tara Browne*, inspired by 'sekundenzeiger,' a poem by Hans Arp, to be accompanied on the piano. But it was as John Lennon's lucky man who made the grade that his memory would be preserved.

In the new spirit of puritanism, the BBC announced that it was banning the song 'A Day in the Life' because it 'could be considered to have drug-taking implications'. But it only added to the song's peculiar allure.

Fifty years after it was written, the track that closes arguably the best and most influential album of all time still exerts a fascination like no other Beatles song. In 2011, *Rolling Stone* magazine listed what its writers considered to be the 100 Greatest Songs by the band in order of preference. 'A Day in the Life' was number one. In 2010, the lyrics that John Lennon scribbled down after reading about Nicki and Oonagh's custody case sold for £800,000 when they went under the hammer at Sotheby's in New York.

Meanwhile, people whose lives Tara touched, however briefly, remembered him in their own ways. In 1976, Anita Pallenberg and Keith Richards had a baby, who died tragically after just ten months from Sudden Infant Death Syndrome. For the short time that he lived, his name was Tara Richards. In 1968, John Paul Getty Jr and his wife, Talitha, had a son, whom they named Tara Gabriel Gramophone Galaxy Getty. And back in Ireland, Larry Mooney, who talked Tara through the twists and turns of the course before his first and only car race, remembered him fondly enough to name his son after him, too.

In the decades after his death, all the principals in the story got on with their lives as best they could. Amanda Lear was a muse to Salvador Dali for sixteen years, living with him on and off. In the early 1970s, she became David Bowie's lover and, at a time when sexual ambiguity became highly fashionable, appeared on the cover of Roxy Music's *For Your Pleasure* album in a leather bodice, holding a black panther on a leash. In the 1980s she reinvented herself as a Disco Queen. Suki Potier survived one car crash only to die in another fifteen years later, while several of Tara's other friends also died young, including Julian Ormsby-Gore and Michael Cooper, both by suicide. John Lennon was murdered in New York in 1980.

Nicki spent the rest of her life in Spain. Soon after her husband's death, she became involved with a twenty-two-year-old Spanish racing driver named Rodrigo Dominguez. More than a few people remarked upon his resemblance to Tara. Later, she had a romance with the actor Oliver Tobias and starred alongside him in a production of the hippie musical *Hair* in Tel Aviv.

She and Amanda became friends again. What happened between Amanda and Tara suddenly seemed unimportant. 'Looking back,' Nicki said of the affair, 'I'm just glad he got in as many interesting and funny and colourful experiences in his short life as he did.'

Nicki and Oonagh never mended their differences and Nicki never forgave her mother-in-law for – as she saw it – 'taking my children away from me'. Oonagh spent most of her latter years in Guernsey – a financial exile after Miguel Ferreras drove her close to ruin. She died in 1995, at the age of eighty-five. After a funeral service in London, her ashes were scattered on Lough Tay in the presence of her children, Garech, Gay and Desmond.

Miguel surfaced briefly in 1997, in an interview piece in *Harpers & Queen*, in which he denied that he was ever José Maria Ozores Laredo, the Nazi soldier. There was no happy-ever-after for Miguel and Flor Trujillo. They married but divorced after seven years. He was living with his fourth wife, Felice, on New York's Upper East Side, not far from the Drake Hotel where he and Oonagh were married forty years earlier. He died in 1999.

In 2001, six years after Oonagh's death, Nicki telephoned Garech out of the blue. She asked if she and Anita Pallenberg could come to Luggala to visit Tara's grave. Garech said of course they could. In the final years of her life, she became a regular visitor to the house and a friend to her brother-in-law. She said that every time she returned to Ireland, a little bit of Tara was returned to her.

In 2012, she died from cancer at her home in Spain. Her body was cremated and, in accordance with her final wishes, her ashes were scattered on the water of Lough Tay by her sons, Dorian and Julian, just yards from where their father was laid to rest.

Fifty years after his death, the man immortalized in the opening lines of 'A Day in the Life' continues to represent, for many of those who knew him, everything that was happy and confident and fun about the 1960s.

'He wanted to be Peter Pan,' Nicki said in the final weeks of her life. 'Forever young. But he knew his time wasn't going to be long. He often said it. He epitomized the spirit of the Sixties, which was: try everything once; make the world a little bit better for other people if you can; try not to hurt anyone if you can avoid it; wear pretty clothes; and, most importantly, live your life.'

He did all of these things. Lucky man.

Select Bibliography

Anderson, Christopher. *Mick: The Wild Life and Mad Genius of Jagger* (Gallery Books, 2013)

Ashley, April, and Fallowell, Duncan. *April Ashley's Odyssey* (Arrow Books, 1982)

Barnes, Suzanne. *When Our Plane Hit the Mountain* (New Island Books, 2005)

Beatles, The. *The Beatles: Anthology* (Cassell, 2000)

Bence-Jones, Mark. *Burke's Guide to Country Houses, Volume 1 – Ireland* (Burke's Peerage/Pergamon, 1978)

Bockris, Victor. *Keith Richards: The Biography* (Da Capo Press, 2003)

Breward, Christopher; Gilbert, David; and Lister, Jenny. *Swinging Sixties* (V & A Publications, 2006)

Brynner, Rock. *Yul: The Man Who Would Be King* (Simon and Schuster, 1989)

Crampton, David, and Neligan, David. *St Stephen's School: 1946–1963. An Anthology* (2010)

Creasy, Martin. *Beatlemania: The Real Story of the Beatles' UK Tours 1963–1965* (Omnibus Press, 2011)

Cronin, Anthony. *Dead as Doornails* (Dolmen Press, 1976)

Davies, Hunter. *I Read the News Today Oh Boy. The Beatles Lyrics: The Stories Behind the Music* (Little, Brown and Company, 2014)

Davies, Hunter. *The Beatles* (W. N. Norton, 2010)

Decharne, Max. *King's Road* (Phoenix, 2006)

De Courcy, Anne. *1939: The Last Season* (Weidenfeld & Nicolson, 2012)

DiLello, Richard. *The Longest Cocktail Party: An Insider Account of The Beatles & the Wild Rise and Fall of Their Multi-Million Dollar Apple Empire* (Alfred Publishing, 2014)

Diski, Jenny. *The Sixties* (Profile Books, 2010)

Doggett, Peter. *There is a Riot Going On: Revolutionaries, Rock Stars and the Rise and Fall of the 60s* (Canongate US, 2000)

Ellis, A. E. *The Rack* (Penguin, 1958)

Emerick, Geoff. *Here, There and Everywhere: My Life Recording the Music of The Beatles* (Avery, 2007)

Espaillat, General Arturo. *Trujillo: The Last Great Caesar* (Henry Regnery, 1963)

Etherington-Smith, Meredith. *Persistence of Memory: A Biography of Dali* (Da Capo Press, 1995)

Everett, Walter. *The Beatles as Musicians* (Oxford University Press, 1999)

Faithfull, Marianne. *Memories, Dreams and Reflections* (Harper Perennial, 2008)

Gardiner, Juliet. *The Thirties* (Harper Press, 2011)

Gioia, Ted. *The History of Jazz* (Oxford University Press, 2011)

Godfrey, John, Lord Kilbracken. *Living Like a Lord* (Victor Gollancz, 1955)

Golon, Sergeanne. *Angelique in Love* (Opera Mundi, 1962)

Gorman, Paul. *The Look: Adventures in Rock and Pop Fashion* (Adelita, 2006)

Gould, Jonathan. *Can't Buy Me Love: The Beatles, Britain and America* (Three Rivers Press, 2008)

Granados, Stefan. *Those Were the Days: An Unofficial History of The Beatles' Apple Organization 1967–2002* (Cherry Red Books, 2002)

Green, Jonathon. *All Dressed Up: The Sixties and the Counterculture* (Pimlico, 1999)

Green, Shirley. *Rachman* (Littlehampton Book Services, 1981)

Greig, Geordie. *Breakfast with Lucian* (Jonathan Cape, 2013)

Hannigan, Dave. *Behan in the USA* (Ballpoint Press, 2014)

Hattersley, Roy. *Borrowed Time: The Story of Britain Between the Wars* (Abacus, 2008)

Helvik, James, aka Claud Cockburn. *Beat the Devil* (JB Lippincott, 1951)

Heylin, Clinton. *The Act You've Known For All These Years* (Canongate UK, 2008)

Hollingshead, Michael. *The Man Who Turned On the World* (Abelard-Schuman, 1974)

Huston, John. *An Open Book* (Knopf, 1980)

Jackson, Laura. *Brian Jones: The Untold Life and Mysterious Death of a Rock Legend* (Piatkus Books, 2009)

Joyce, James. *Ulysses* (Shakespeare and Company, 1922)

Joyce, Joe. *The Guinnesses* (Poolbeg Press, 2009)

Kee, Robert. *A Sign of the Times* (Eyre & Spottiswoode, 1955)

Kindersley, Gay. *Flings Over Fences* (Quiller Press, 1994)

Kindersley, Philip. *For You the War is Over* (Baton Press, 1982)

Lear, Amanda. *My Life with Dali* (Virgin Books, 1985)

Levy, Shawn. *Ready, Steady, Go!* (Fourth Estate, 2002)

Lowell, Ivana. *Why Not Say What Happened?* (Bloomsbury, 2011)

MacCarthy, Fiona. *Last Curtsey: The End of the Debutantes* (Faber & Faber, 2006)

MacDonnell, Randal. *The Lost Houses of Ireland* (Weidenfeld & Nicolson, 2002)

McDonald, Ian. *Revolution in the Head: The Beatles' Records and the Sixties* (Chicago Review Press, 2007)

Miles, Barry. *London Calling: A Countercultural History of London Since 1945* (Atlantic Books, 2010)

Miles, Barry, with McCartney, Paul. *Many Years from Now* (Vintage, 1998)

Montague, John. *Company* (Gerald Duckworth, 2001)

Montague, John. *The Pear is Ripe* (Liberties Press, 2007)

Mosley, Charlotte, ed. *The Letters of Nancy Mitford and Evelyn Waugh* (Hodder & Stoughton, 1996)

Mosley, Max. *Formula One and Beyond* (Simon & Schuster, 2015)

Mount, Ferdinand. *Cold Cream* (Bloomsbury, 2009)

Mullally, Frederick. *Silver Salver: The Story of the Guinness Family* (Granada, 1981)

Norman, Philip. *John Lennon* (Ecco, 2009)

Norman, Philip. *Mick Jagger* (Ecco Press, 2012)

O'Byrne, Robert. *Luggala Days* (CICO Books, 2012)

Ó Faoláin, Seán. *Eamon de Valera* (Penguin, 1939)

Oldham, Andrew Loog. *Stoned* (Vintage, 2001)

O'Sullivan, Michael. *Brendan Behan* (Roberts Rinehart Publishers, 2000)

Patterson, R. Gary. *The Walrus Was Paul: The Great Beatle Death Clues* (Prentice Hall & IBD, 1998)

Paudras, Francis. *Dance of the Infidels: A Portrait of Bud Powell* (Da Capo Press, 1998)

Perez, Lois A. *On Becoming Cuban: Identity, Nationality and Culture* (The University of North Carolina Press, 2009)

Pochna, Marie-France. *Christian Dior* (Gerald Duckworth, 2010)

Pugh, Martin. *We Danced All Night: A Social History of Britain Between the Wars* (Vintage, 2009)

Quant, Mary. *Quant by Quant* (Cassell, 1966)

Ramsey, Guthrie P. *Amazing Bud Powell* (University of California Press, 2013)

Rawlings, Terry. *Who Killed Christopher Robin?* (Helter Skelter Publishing, 2004)

Reed, Jeremy. *The King of Carnaby Street: A Life of John Stephen* (Haus Publishing, 2010)

Reising, Russell. *Every Sound There Is* (Ashgate Popular and Folk Music Series, 2002)

Richards, Keith. *Life* (Back Bay Books, 2011)

Rolling Stones, The. *According to The Rolling Stones* (Chronicle Books, 2009)

Sandbrook, Dominic. *Never Had It So Good: A History of Britain from Suez to The Beatles* (Little, Brown, 2006)

Sandbrook, Dominic. *White Heat: A History of Britain in the Swinging Sixties* (Abacus, 2007)

Saunders, James. *Nightmare: The Ernest Saunders Story* (Huchtinson, 1989)

Savage, Jon. *1966: The Year the Decade Exploded* (Faber & Faber, 2016)

Sheff, David. *Last Interview: John Lennon and Yoko Ono* (Sidgwick & Jackson, 2000)

Schoenberger, Nancy. *Dangerous Muse: A Life of Caroline Blackwood* (Da Capo Press, 2002)

Schreuders, Piet; Lewisohn, Mark; and Smith, Adam. *The Beatles' London* (Interlink Books, 2008)

Sinclair, Andrew. *A View of the Sixties* (Sinclair-Stevenson, 1994)

Sperber, A. M., and Lax, Eric. *Bogart* (Weidenfeld & Nicolson, 1997)

Taylor, D. J. *Bright Young People: The Rise and Fall of a Generation, 1918–1940* (Farrar, Straus and Giroux, 2010)

Trynka, Paul. *Brian Jones: The Making of a Rolling Stone* (Plume, 2015)

Turner, Steve. *A Hard Day's Write – the Stories Behind Every Beatles Song*. (It Books, 2005)

Turner, Steve. *The Gospel According to The Beatles* (Westminster John Knox Press, 2006)

Tynan, Kathleen. *The Life of Kenneth Tynan* (Methuen, 1988)

Vyner, Harriet. *Groovy Bob: The Life and Times of Robert Fraser* (Faber and Faber, 2001)

Waugh, Evelyn. *Brideshead Revisited* (Chapman and Hall, 1945)

Waugh, Evelyn. *Vile Bodies* (Chapman and Hall, 1930)

Wells, Simon. *The Great Rolling Stones Drug Bust* (Omnibus Press, 2012)

Unpublished sources

Visitors' book, Luggala

Oonagh, Lady Oranmore and Browne's photograph albums

Newspapers

Autosport
The Bystander
Daily Express
Daily Mail
Daily Mirror
Daily Telegraph
Dublin Evening Mail

Fortune
Gentleman's Quarterly
Guardian
Harpers & Queen
House Beautiful
Independent
Irish Independent
Irish Press
Irish Times
London Evening Standard
London Life
London Magazine
Melody Maker
New York Herald Tribune
New York Sunday Mirror
New York Times
Observer
Paris Match
The Pilot
Rolling Stone
Sketch
Sunday Dispatch
Sunday Express
Sunday Independent
Sunday Pictorial
Tatler
Time
The Times
Victoria Colonist
Women's Wear Daily

Other sources

www.autosport.com
www.britishpathe.com

www.historicalracing.com
www.thelotusforums.com
www.thepeerage.com

Films and movies

Art on Wheels, British Pathé News, 1966
Beatles Anthology, 1995
Blow Up, 1966
Cheer Up, 1936
Dangerous Moonlight, 1941
It Was 20 Years Ago Today, BBC, 1987
The Real John Betjeman, Channel 4, 2000
Performance, 1970
Une Journée Avec L'Honorable Tara Browne, 1966

Sources and Notes

PROLOGUE

2 – '. . . paid $10,000 to fly them to Ireland from New York . . .' Figure confirmed by Bob Cavallo, manager of The Lovin' Spoonful.

5 – '. . . said her husband never expected to live for long . . .' Author interview with Nicki Browne, by telephone, 2010.

'"He appeared in our lives almost fully formed, as if from an egg . . ."' Author interview with Martin Wilkinson, Newport, 2011.

6 – '"If you asked me to sum up the Sixties in a single moment . . ."' Author interview with Joe Butler, by telephone, 2011.

'. . . while a young Mick Jagger shares a large, pink armchair with his soon-to-be ex-girlfriend on the night when, she later remembered, their relationship began to go off the rails . . .' Chrissie Shrimpton's account as quoted in *Mick Jagger* by Philip Norman (Harper Collins, 2012) p. 202.

7 – '"While he was alive," said his friend the poet Hugo Williams, "it was the miniskirt and the Twist . . ."' Author interview with Hugo Williams, London, 2011.

1: GUINNESS FOR STRENGTH

10 – '"What do you expect? I'm an Edwardian!"' Author interview with Dominick Browne, Lord Mereworth, London, 2014.

'"Our father," recalled Judith Haslam, a daughter from his first marriage, "was what they called NSIT . . ."' Author interview with Judith Haslam, by telephone, 2014.

'"The country never wanted men of your constitutional principles more than it does at present."' Extract from a letter written by Daniel O'Connell to Dominick Browne, 1830, reproduced in *Burke's Guide to Country Houses, Volume 1 – Ireland* by Mark Bence-Jones (Burke's Peerage/Pergamon, 1978), p. 50. The letter includes the line: 'I do assure you that it

gave me most sincere pleasure to have any opportunity, however trivial . . . of showing you how anxious I am to evince to you my strong sense
of the manly independence of your Parliamentary conduct.'

11 – 'According to family legend, Dom's father had shown great kindness to a young footman who became an IRA commander . . .' Author
interview with Garech Browne, Wicklow, 2006.

'He wrote in his diary: "I don't think it will ever be possible to go
back and live at home."' Letter quoted in *Luggala Days* by Robert O'Byrne
(CICO Books, an imprint of Ryland Peters & Small Ltd, 2012), p. 93.'"He
was thrown out for having too good a time . . ."' Author interview with
Dominick Browne, Lord Mereworth, London, 2014.

12 – '"He was what they call bowler-hatted out . . ."' Ibid.

'Their chauffeur-driven Daimler was involved in a collission with a
bus . . .' Account of crash from contemporary newspaper reports. The crash
occurred on 8 June 1927. Harry Vine, the couple's chauffeur, who survived
the accident, told the subsequent inquest that he braked to avoid road works,
which he saw too late, because of 'Scotch mist'. The greasy road surface
caused the car to swerve into an oncoming bus. Dr Noel Martin, who conducted the post-mortem on Lady Oranmore and Browne's body, noted that
one of her lungs had been punctured by a rib and that she was dead by the
time he arrived on the scene, approximately ten minutes after the accident.
Lord Oranmore and Browne was injured 'about the legs', according to contemporary reports in *The Times*. He died from his injuries on 30 June. For
Dom, the tragedy of his parents' death was compounded by the series of
bizarre accidents that attended their two, seperate funerals. First, the motor
hearse carrying his mother's body caught fire. 'They had to take her coffin
out of the hearse on the side of the road and send for another one,' according to Garech, whose father told him the story shortly before he died. 'Then,
before my grandfather's funeral, the undertaker told my father that it was
traditional for members of the House of Lords to be buried in lead coffins.
Which wasn't actually true. It's kings and queens who are buried in lead.
Father agreed. They put my grandfather's body in the lead coffin and discovered that it was too heavy to carry down the stairs. So they put it in the
service lift. The ropes broke and the coffin came crashing down.'

'"He didn't fancy spending his life hanging about with other Old
Etonians . . ."' Author interview with Dominick Browne, Lord Mereworth,
London, 2014.

'Cosgrave gave him the assurance he sought . . .' Author interview
with Garech Browne, Wicklow, 2014.

13 – '. . . the big house and all it represented was "rather in the
lurch"' . . . 'The Stately Homes of England' was a song written by Noel

Coward in 1932 and was a particular favourite among the dispossessed upper classes.

13 – '"There were huge greenhouses . . ."' Author interview with Philomena Flatley, Mayo, 2010.

'"There were horses here as well . . ."' Ibid.

15 – '"With contemptuous pity, I dismiss the Guinnesses."' From *The Pilot*, 7 August, 1837.

'"The Guinnesses," he said, summing up an age-old paradox, "are the only English aristocrats who have remained truly Irish."' Brendan Behan, quoted in the *Daily Mail*, 12 September, 1958.

'Porter was first produced in Shoreditch in the East End of London in 1722 . . .' *The Guinnesses*, by Joe Joyce (Poolbeg, 2009) pp. 9–10.

'The second was to brew it so well that porter and Guinness would come to mean one and the same thing . . .' Ibid, p. 52.

'. . . immortalized as the Cunning Brothers in James Joyce's *Ulysses* . . .' *Ulysses* by James Joyce (Shakespeare and Company, 1922).

16 – '. . . earning somewhere in the region of £100,000 per year at a time when only 4,000 people in Britain had an annual income of over £5,000 . . .' From *The Guinnesses*, by Joe Joyce (Poolbeg, 2009), p. 147. Sir Edward had investments worth approximately £2.5m, including a stretch of Fifth Avenue in New York. He also purchased Farmleigh, a spectacular Georgian mansion on the west side of Dublin's Phoenix Park, to complement Iveagh House, the residence he inherited on St Stephen's Green in Dublin. He later gifted both houses to the Irish state – the latter is now occupied by the Department of Foreign Affairs.

17 – '. . . the KLG spark plug, which he had invented.' Ibid, pp. 246–7.

'"The sisters are all witches . . ."' Quote from *An Open Book* by John Huston (New York: Knopf, 1980), p. 218.

18 – 'Homework, Oonagh would later tell Tara's eldest son, Dorian . . .' Author interview with Dorian Browne, Surrey, 2011.

'"My mother told me that if she was sick . . ."' Author interview with Garech Browne, Wicklow, 2009.

'In 1922, however, while holidaying in Ireland, they were witnesses to one of the defining moments of the Irish Civil War . . .' Ibid.

'. . . she was the model for Osbert Lancaster's Maudie Littlehampton cartoons.' Obituary, *Independent*, 22 May 1998.

'"Oonagh . . . was a strange mixture of very spoiled and very sweet and very fucked-up . . ."' Author interview with Martin Wilkinson, Newport, 2011.

19 – '"My father and mother weren't suited at all . . ."' Author interview with Gay Kindersley, East Garston, 2011.

21 – '"... idle young men living in Mayfair mewses ..."' From *Bright Young People – The Rise and Fall of a Generation: 1918–1940* by D. J. Taylor (Vintage, 2007), p. 2.

'In his 1930 satirical novel, *Vile Bodies* ...' *Vile Bodies* by Evelyn Waugh (Chapman & Hall, 1930).

'... Stanley Baldwin, the Prime Minster, whose daughter Betty was a member of the set.' Betty Baldwin, a friend of Evelyn Waugh, appears in *Vile Bodies* as Miss Brown, the daughter of the Prime Minister, who invites members of the Bright Young People back to 10 Downing Street for supper. *Bright Young People – The Rise and Fall of a Generation: 1918–1940* by D. J. Taylor (Vintage, 2007), p. 28.

'"I don't understand them and I don't want to ..."' *Vile Bodies* by Evelyn Waugh (Chapman & Hall, 1930).

22 – '... surrounded by fellow revellers wearing pyjamas, false beards, public school blazers, top hats, shorts with garters and Harrow caps.' *Tatler*, 21 June, 1933.

'It was the Guinnesses, *Fortune*, the global business magazine reported, who started the fashion of driving to Cuckoo Weir ... and Kenelm Lee Guinness – the brewery director and racing driver – who drove a steamroller over an enormous pile of tin cans to find out how it would sound.' *Fortune*, December 1930.

'According to Gay, his father remained faithful to his mother for barely a year of their married life ...' Author interview with Gay Kindersley, East Garston, 2011.

23 – 'In her divorce petition, Dom's first wife, Mildred, suggested that it started early in 1934.' From *Luggala Days* by Robert O'Byrne (CICO Books, an imprint of Ryland Peters & Small Ltd, 2012), p. 104.

'By then, Valsie had already divorced her husband, who was in serious financial difficulty as a result of his gambling debts.' In 1934, he was forced to sell his home, Brougham Hall, to pay off his debts, many of which were as a result of his love of gambling. In 1952, he was declared bankrupt.

24 – '"It suited everyone ..."' Author interview with Garech Browne, Wicklow, 2013.

'*The Bystander* began to refer to Valsie rather pointedly as Oonagh's "erstwhile friend."' *The Bystander*, 30 March 1935.

'"Far be it from us to take sides, as we like them both enormously, but we consider the present situation constitutes one more instance of the close proximity of fire when we see a lot of smoke."' *The Bystander*, 15 January 1935.

'"The one with whom we sympathize deeply is the boyfriend's wife. She seems to have had very little fun."' Ibid.

24 – '"She was absolutely devastated . . ."' Autor interview with Dominick Browne, Lord Mereworth, London, 2014.

25 – 'However, the hotel manager refused to give evidence to support Philip's petition for divorce . . .' An account of this story features in *Flings Over Fences – The Ups and Downs of Gay Kindersley* by Gay Kindersley with Robin Rhoderick-Jones (Quiller Press Ltd, 1994), p. 6.

'The *Daily Express* reported that they made three unsuccessful attempts to leave the registry office . . .' *Daily Express*, 30 April 1936.

'"Luggala has been given to me by my kind father."' Visitors' book, Luggala.

2: WAR BABY

27 – 'Despite her one-time ambivalence towards outdoor pursuits, the new Lady Oranmore and Browne appeared to settle happily into country life . . .' Contemporary issues of *The Sketch*.

28 – 'They were also at the wedding of William Somerset Maugham's daughter, Elizabeth, and the reopening of the famous Ciro's Club in London . . .' Contemporary issues of *Tatler*.

'"He was a very debonair dresser . . ."' Author interview with Judith Haslam, by telephone, 2014.

29 – 'Their arguments were famous . . .' Author interview with Gay Kindersley, East Garston, 2011.

'"Oonagh's father," Judith recalled, "used to call him the Stallion."' Author interview with Judith Haslam, by telephone, 2014.

'"At first it was difficult to go back to Castle Mac Garrett . . ."' Author interview with Dominick Browne, Lord Mereworth, London, 2014.

30 – 'A recruiting officer told him that his energies would be more productively spent farming his land . . .' Author interview with Garech Browne, Wicklow, 2014.

31 – 'On Christmas Day 1942, Philip was captured by the Germans near Tunis . . .' An account of Philip Kindersley's war experiences is featured in *For You the War is Over* by the Honorable Philip Kindersley (Hippocrene Books Inc., 1984).

'Through the English courts, Sir Robert applied successfully for custody of his grandson . . .' Contemporary newspaper reports of the case.

'An application was then made to the High Court in Dublin, where Oonagh was ordered to hand over her son in time to start at Eton in September 1942 . . .' Contemporary newspaper reports of the case.

"'My mother's lawyers advised her that she couldn't lose . . .'" Author interview with Garech Browne, Wicklow, 2014.

"'. . . take the boy from a country at peace to a country engaged in a life and death struggle . . .'" Various newspaper reports of the court case, 6 December 1943.

'In July 1943, the High Court in Dublin decided that the wishes of Gay's father must be ascertained . . .' Contemporary newspaper reports of the court case.

32 – 'Philip, he said, had a deep loathing of the Irish.' Author interview with Gay Kindersley, East Garston, 2011.

"'. . . Application for release of Gay to enter Eton," the message said, "has my full knowledge and approval."' Details of the letter reported in several newspapers on 12 November 1943.

"'It is really wonderful for you to have done this for me, as I had visions of Gay being educated as a Sinn Feiner.'" Letter read into the court record on 12 November 1943 and reported in all of the main British and Irish newspapers on 13 November 1943.

"'. . . nothing other than a genuine love for her son and regard for his safety and welfare . . .'" Reported in all of the main British and Irish newspapers on 15 December 1943.

"'He was almost stillborn . . .'" Author interview with Garech Browne, Wicklow, 2009.

33 – "'I remember Dom, my stepfather, leading me out of the court . . .'" Author interview with Gay Kindersley, East Garston, 2011.

"'She caught it coming home from school . . .'" Author interview with Judith Haslam, by telephone, 2014.

34 – "'One of the reasons," according to Garech, "was of course that she'd lost a baby and she wanted another child desperately . . .'" Author interview with Garech Browne, Wicklow, 2009.

"He was going to be Fiach [mac Aodha Ó Broin] . . .'" Author interview with Garech Browne, Wicklow, 2014.

35 – 'The following day's newspapers carried photographs of Oonagh standing next to her thirteen-year-old daughter and her pony, Brown Jack, looking every inch the proud mother . . .' From contemporary Irish newspapers.

"'She said, 'I'm afraid your sister has died . . .' '" Author interview with Gay Kindersley, East Garston, 2011.

36 – '. . . according to Gay, he was there to visit one of his mistresses.' *Flings Over Fences – The Ups and Downs of Gay Kindersley* by Gay Kindersley with Robin Rhoderick-Jones (Quiller Press Ltd, 1994), p. 17.

36 – 'For the rest of his life, it was said, he carried the burden of guilt around with him . . .' According to Gay Kindersley, interviewed by the author, East Garston, 2011.

'A post mortem revealed that Tessa's death was due to cardiac arrest brought on by anaphylactic shock . . .' Contemporary newspaper reports from 5 to 9 August 1946.

'"She loved all of her children," according to Garech, "but if there was a favourite, then it probably was Tara."' Author interview with Garech Browne, Wicklow, 2011.

37 – 'On his death, almost half of his fortune went to the Irish exchequer.' *The Guinnesses*, by Joe Joyce (Poolbeg, 2009), p. 299.

'"It was my worst subject at Eton . . ."' Author interview with Gay Kindersley, East Garston, 2011.

38 – '"We could have been the British Rockefellers or Rothschilds . . . But we lost our way."' Quote attributed to Benjamin Guinness, the third Earl of Iveagh, by Ernest Saunders in *Nightmare: The Ernest Saunders Story* by James Saunders (Huchtinson, 1989), p.140.

'. . . at a charity preview screening of the romantic fantasy movie *A Matter of Life and Death* . . .' It was the first ever Royal Film Performance attended by both the King and Queen, as well as Princesses Elizabeth and Margaret, to raise money for the Cinematograph Trade Benevolent Fund.

'He was immediately smitten and soon he would be openly declaring his love to his "darling girleen" . . .' Author interview with Charles Doble, film archivist and an authority on the life and career of Sally Gray, Ashbrittle, 2014.

39 – '. . . Fred Astaire, who gave her private dancing lessons during breaks in performances.' Obituary, *Daily Telegraph*, 29 September 2006.

'. . . it was her romantic involvement with another married man . . . which brought about her mental collapse.' Author interview with Charles Doble, Ashbrittle, 2014.

40 – '". . . It didn't bother my father either. What a naughty man."' – Author interview with Dominick Browne, Lord Mereworth, London, 2014.

'"They rowed out into the middle of the lake . . ."' Author interview with Garech Browne, Wicklow, 2010.

'"They were just so in love. You can tell from the way they looked at each other. So, so in love."' Ibid.

'"I remember being taken from school by my father . . ."' Ibid.

3: OONAGHLAND

41 – "'I remember Oonagh giving a very big dinner party one night . . .'" Author interview with Kenneth Rose, by telephone, 2013.

42 – 'When asked to account for the time missing from their lives, they explained that they'd been "Luggala-ed".' Author interview with Nicholas Gormanston, London, 2014.

"'Whenever I pass between those gateposts . . .'" *Living Like a Lord*, by John Godfrey, Lord Kilbracken (Victor Gollancz Ltd, 1955), pp. 211–12.

43 – 'Where else could you find the Duke of Brissa . . .' As quoted in *Luggala Days* by Robert O'Byrne (CICO Books, an imprint of Ryland Peters & Small Ltd, 2012), p. 141.

"'She had a wicked sense of where to place people . . .'" Author interview with John Montague, by telephone, 2011.

'Brendan Behan, who was skilled in all three areas, once wrote that Luggala was a house where you could say anything you liked, "provided you were witty and didn't take too long about it".' As quoted in *Brendan Behan: A Life* by Michael O'Sullivan (Roberts Rinehart Publishers, 1999), p. 197.

44 – '. . . which in the era of the Irish showband days was Tommy Kinsman and his Orchestra.' Music was one of Gay's great passions. When he finished racing, he set up a group called the Valley Minstrels, a vocal trio with a tea-chest base and guitar. In January 1966, they performed on Ireland's *Late Late Show* ahead of a tour of Ireland. From *Flings Over Fences – The Ups and Downs of Gay Kindersley* by Gay Kindersley with Robin Rhoderick-Jones (Quiller Press Ltd, 1994), pp. 115–16.

'The Spanish Ambassador and the United States Chargé d'Affairs were among the guests who watched . . .' Author interview with Garech Browne, Wicklow, 2012.

"'When I think about Oonagh now . . .'" Author interview with Martin Wilkinson, Newport, 2011.

"'Lots of people were in love with her . . .'" Author interview with Desmond Guinness, Kildare, 2012.

45 – "'Sometimes," recalled Garech, "the telegram would simply say, 'Goodnight, Darling'.'" Author interview with Garech Browne, Wicklow, 2009.

"'I would say he was quite lonely . . .'" Author interview with Rabea Redpath, by telephone, 2011.

46 – "'My mother knew Oonagh through the social round . . .'" Ibid.

"'We ran up and down the corridors of Claridge's banging on people's doors . . .'" Ibid.

46 – '"I used to get flown off at weekends to Luggala, aged seven . . ."' Ibid.

'"There was, in the background, this sadness in him . . ."' Ibid.

47 – '"He'd have bouts where he liked one particular thing . . ."' Ibid.

'"At home, I'd been made to go to bed at seven o'clock every night . . ."' Ibid.

48 – 'He was immediately mesmerized by this shy, twenty-one-year-old aristocratic beauty . . .' Caroline Blackwood and Lucian Freud were introduced by Ann Fleming, the wife of James Bond creator, Ian Fleming. Like Oonagh, she was a celebrated hostess with her own collection of artists, writers and intellectuals. An account of their first meeting is featured in, amongst other books, *Dangerous Muse: The Life of Lady Caroline Blackwood* by Nancy Schoenberger (Da Capo Press, 2002) and *Why Not Say What Happened?* by Ivana Lowell (Vintage, 2011).

'In a letter to the writer Nancy Mitford, Evelyn Waugh wrote, "Poor Maureen's daughter made a runaway match with a terrible Yid."' *The Letters of Nancy Mitford and Evelyn Waugh*, edited by Charlotte Mosley (Hodder & Stoughton, 1996), p. 335.

'"Caroline always said she regretted that our mother wasn't her mother . . ."' Author interview with Garech Browne, Wicklow, 2011.

'She fantasized about this very thing in "How You Love Our Lady" . . .' *How You Love Our Lady* by Caroline Blackwood was first published in *London Magazine* in 1970.

49 – '. . . he had recently written a potboiler thriller called *Beat the Devil*.' *Beat the Devil* by James Helvik, aka Claud Cockburn, was published by J. B. Lippincott Company in 1951.

'"He badly needed the money that a motion-picture sale would give him."' *An Open Book* by John Huston (Knopf, 1980), p. 245.

50 – '. . . the director persuaded Truman Capote, who was then living in Rome, to produce a script from Cockburn's book.' An interesting account of the making of *Beat the Devil* is contained in *Bogart* by A. M. Sperber & Eric Lax (Weidenfeld & Nicolson, 1997), pp. 469–80.

'Tara was mesmerized by the sight of Bogart arm-wrestling the eccentric, velvet-suit-wearing and flamboyantly homosexual Capote for money . . .' – 'I couldn't go to Italy,' Garech recalled in an interview with the author, 'as I was in boarding school. I was terribly envious, because I was fourteen years old at the time and hopelessly in love with Gina Lollobrigida. But Tara brought me back a photograph of her and he'd asked her to autograph it for me.'

51 – '. . . in which she starred alongside the American actor George Raft, whom she hated intensely.' Obituary, *Independent*, 2 October 2006.

'. . . turning down a reported million-dollar contract offer from RKO Pictures in Hollywood . . .' Interview with Charles Doble, Ashbrittle, 2014.

52 – '"Tara and I watched the parade from a shop window . . ."' Author interview with Garech Browne, Wicklow, 2010.

'"I think she felt terribly guilty about taking our father away from us," said Garech.' Ibid.

'"Tara hated Sally . . ."' Author interview with Judith Haslam, by telephone, 2014.

'"He would say, 'Oh, my mother said I don't have to go to bed until eleven o'clock' ".' Ibid.

'"We used to play roulette . . ."' Author interview with Dominick Browne, Lord Mereworth, London, 2014.

'"There was a very elderly West of Ireland lady whose job it was to bath him . . ."' Author interview with Nicki Browne, by telephone, 2010.

53 – '"We each had our own greenhouse at Castle Mac Garrett . . ."' Author interview with Garech Browne, Wicklow, 2009.

'"That was when the work on the farm stopped . . ."' Author interview with Philomena Flatley, Mayo, 2010.

'"There was always a dance in the garage at Christmas for all the workers . . ."' Author interview with Garech Browne, Wicklow, 2010.

54 – '"When we were supposed to be asleep . . ."' Ibid.

'"The problem for us," said Garech, "was that these schools didn't teach any of the things that we wanted to learn . . ."' Author interview with Garech Browne, Wicklow, 2008.

55 – '"It didn't last long," Garech recalled, "because I ran away again."' Ibid.

'. . . he ended up staying the night with the driver and his wife in Salisbury, Wiltshire . . .' – 'The driver rang the headmaster,' Garech recalled in an interview with the author, 'I think with the intention of telling them that I was safe and that they were going to try to talk me into going back. But he said he'd never spoken to a bigger fool in his life and he didn't blame me for running away. I tried to ring my mother, who was on holiday in Brighton with Robert Kee. The reason I couldn't find her was because she was staying in the hotel under the name Mrs Kee. I went into hiding in London. Occasionally I'd ring my father, who thought he had to be strict, and he'd say, "You have to go back to school," and I'd say, "Toodle-oo – talk to you next week!"'

'. . . memorably characterized by the poet Seán Ó Faoláin as a "dreary Eden".' *Eamon de Valera* by Sean Ó Faoláin (Penguin, 1939), p. 180.

56 – '"It was an extraordinary little place . . ."' Author interview with Neale Webb, Dublin, 2011.

56 – 'The vast majority of the school's 120 students were boarders.' One of Tara's schoolmates was William Taft, the great-grandson of the former US president of the same name. Young William's father, who was also William, was the American ambassador to Ireland at the time.

'"There weren't terribly many cars on the road in Ireland at that point . . ."' Author interview with Neale Webb, Dublin, 2011.

'"He told me that he never, ever wanted to go to school . . ."' Author interview with Nicki Browne, by telephone, 2009.

57 – '"We knew that when he left school, it was to go back to this fairyland castle . . ."' Author interview with Neale Webb, Dublin, 2011.

'"The invitation would arrive and there would be a coronet on the envelope . . ."' Author interview with Michael Steen, Dublin, 2011.

'"He looked like a boy soprano, or a cherub . . ."' Author interview with Gordon Ledbetter, Dublin, 2011.

58 – '. . . about a headless coachman that he liked to tell Lucy Hill.' The poem was reproduced in *St Stephen's School: 1946–1963. An Anthology*, an oral history of the school, compiled and published by David Crampton, the well-known Irish building contractor, and David Neligan, the former Irish ambassador to Japan, who were both past pupils of the school. It is reproduced here with the kind permission of the Honorable Garech Browne.

'. . . from their days as Bright Young People on the London social scene.' John Betjeman had served as Press Attaché at the British Embassy in Dublin during the Second World War.

'"I remember once I told him that I'd climbed Djouce Mountain the previous weekend . . ."' Author interview with Neale Webb, Dublin, 2011.

59 – '. . . Robert Kee's new book, *A Sign of the Times*, a darkly comic, post-apocalyptic novel that was widely praised by the literary critics.' *A Sign of the Times* by Robert Kee (Eyre & Spottiswoode, 1955).

'"We had to reach him from the other side of the house . . ."' Author interview with Maura Byrne, by telephone, 2011.

60 – 'He was preparing to ride his horse, Sandymount, in the 1956 Grand National at Aintree . . .' The 1956 Grand National would become famous for the collapse of Devon Loch, the Queen Mother's horse, while five lengths clear in the closing straight. As it happened, Sandymount didn't even make it to starter's orders. Gay was forced to withdraw his 100–1 shot on the eve of the race because of a problem with a gland in the horse's tongue.

'Philip disapproved of the match, as did Gay's stepmother, Valsie.' Author interview with Gay Kindersley, East Garston, 2011.

'"I was discussing hunting," Gay recalled . . .' Ibid.

'The following day, after drinking two bottles of wine with lunch at the Savoy, Gay and Magsie made up their minds to get married in defiance of Philip and Valsie's wishes.' *Flings Over Fences – The Ups and Downs of Gay Kindersley* by Gay Kindersley with Robin Rhoderick-Jones (Quiller Press Ltd, 1994), p. 62.

61 – '"Her Ladyship," the *Daily Mail* reported, "with long blonde hair in a scarf, and a mink coat over her nightdress, sat on an old oak dining chair directing operations."' *Daily Mail*, 26 January 1956.

'The fire brigade arrived on the scene too late to save the house.' Three units were dispatched from Greystones, Rathdrum and Bray, according to contemporary newspaper reports, but they had difficulty reaching the house on the treacherously icy approach roads. All three fire engines slid into ditches and had to be dug out using shovels. Eventually, branches were laid down in front of the wheels of the vehicles to form a track over which they could make their tortuously slow progress towards the burning house.

'"My son went to stay with his mother in Ireland at the beginning of the week . . ."' *Daily Express*, 1 February 1956.

62 – 'Oonagh had taken Tara out of school for the day . . .' *Tatler*, 3 February 1960.

'"I ended up smoking quite a lot . . ."' Author interview with Michael Steen, Dublin, 2011.

'"Around the time that he boarded . . ."' Ibid.

63 – '"He was a real ringleader . . ."' Author interview with Neale Webb, Dublin, 2011.

'"He clearly learned the trick from me . . ."' Author interview with Garech Browne, Wicklow, 2009.

'"It was in a house called Cludy . . ."' Author interview with Penny Guinness (nee Cuthbertson), Kildare, 2012.

64 – '. . . though Oonagh chose purple rather than the original blue colour to match the heather in the valley.' David Mlinaric, the society designer, was very impressed by what he saw when he first visited the house in the 1960s. 'It was one of the first houses I visited that was "decorated" as they all are now,' he told Robert O'Byrne, the author of *Luggala Days*. 'Nobody then had imaginative wallpapers or colour schemes. People had very plain houses.'

4: THE TROUBLE WITH MIGUEL

65 – '"He said to me one day, 'Oh, your hair looks really pretty,' and I remember being surprised . . ."' Author interview with Rabea Redpath, by telephone, 2011.

65 – '"He got a grasp on the world pretty quickly . . ."' Ibid.

66 – '"He was one of the most important adult figures in Tara's life . . ."' Author interview with Nicki Browne, by telephone, 2010.

'. . . who considered him an English Marcel Proust.' – 'A work of somber power, or soaring comedy . . . Mr Ellis, a Proust, a Leopardi of the sanatorium.' As quoted on the jacket of the 1988 reprint of his only novel, written under the pseudonym A. E. Ellis, *The Rack* (Penguin).

'Deacon had just finished writing *The Rack* . . .' *The Rack* by A. E. Ellis (Heinemann, 1958).

'. . . immediately proclaimed a modern classic.' Graham Greene said of it: 'There are certain books which we call great for want of a better term, that rise like monuments above the cemeteries of literature: *Clarissa Harlowe*, *Great Expectations*, *Ulysses*. *The Rack*, to my mind, is in this company.' As quoted on the jacket of the 1988 Penguin reprint.

'. . . who once described him as "an expensive limited edition of a curious object".' *The Life of Kenneth Tynan* by Kathleen Tynan (William Morrow and Company Inc, 1987), p. 85.

'. . . described Deacon as "deeply pessimistic and a recluse" in her biography of her husband, *The Life of Kenneth Tynan* . . ."' Ibid, p. 85.

'". . . did not extend to himself, nor to life in principle."' Ibid, p. 26.

67 – '"He was going to be the great man," wrote another university friend, the writer Kingsley Amis . . .' Ibid, p. 85.

'"He was a great raconteur of death . . ."' *In Love and Anger – A View of the Sixties* by Andrew Sinclair (Sinclair-Stevenson, 1994), p. 102.

68 – '. . . as a man whose weary pessimism was perfectly suited to "the temper of the times under the mushroom cloud".' Ibid, p. 103.

'"I met Tara for the first time in Venice . . ."' Author interview with Lucinda Lambton, Hedgerley, 2011.

69 – '"He seemed to have no end of money . . ."' Ibid.

'. . . Caroline Blackwood, who had tired of Lucian Freud's serial unfaithfulness and left him for good in 1956 . . .' An authoritative account of the marriage between Caroline Blackwood and Lucian Freud is contained in the book *Dangerous Muse: The Life of Lady Caroline Blackwood* by Nancy Schoenberger (Da Capo Press, 2002).

70 – 'According to his own account of his life, he was born in Cuba in 1928 . . .' Miguel appeared to offer several sometimes conflicting accounts of his early life. This, however, was the one he told most consistently. Interview with Nicholas Farrell, *Harpers & Queen*, September 1997.

71 – '"She was very vulnerable at that point of her life . . ."' Author interview with Garech Browne, Wickow, 2010.

'"Oonagh told me her first two husbands did not give her any pleasure . . ."' Miguel Ferreras quoted in an interview with Nicholas Farrell,
Harpers & Queen, September 1997.

'"I think she was trying to wish this image of him as a dashing,
Spanish bullfighter figure into reality . . ."' Author interview with Garech
Browne, Wicklow, 2010.

72 – '. . . uncovered by White & Case, Oonagh's international lawyers . . .' Documents seen by the author.

73 – '. . . working odd jobs and supplementing his earnings through
looting and petty crime during the years of the Spanish Civil War.' An alternative account of Miguel's life was put together by investigators working for
Whyte & Case. The documents have been seen by the author.

74 – 'In a sworn affidavit obtained by Oonagh's lawyers . . .' Seen by the
author.

75 – 'In 1961, in an interview with the *New York Times*, James would
speak dismiss his former protégé's ambitions as a couturier . . .' *New York
Times*, 31 July 1961.

'He bragged, for instance, that he had designed a maternity dress
for Elizabeth Taylor . . .' It was reported widely over a number of years that
Miguel had made clothes for Elizabeth Taylor, though this could not be
verified.

76 – 'In September 1957, it was reported that an outfit he designed for
singer Lena Horne for the Broadway opening of the musical *Jamaica* left her
unable to move . . .' Reported in a number of US newspapers in September
1957.

'After the wedding, he told the New York press that he and his wife
would live between London and Paris, where he would be setting up his own
couture house.' Reported in several contemporary newspapers.

'"He was a real bad hat – loathsome, absolutely awful . . ."' Author
interview with Kenneth Rose, by telephone, 2013.

'. . . his mother ought to keep her new man "chained to the bedpost".' *Flings Over Fences – The Ups and Downs of Gay Kindersley* by Gay
Kindersley with Robin Rhoderick-Jones (Quiller Press Ltd, 1994), p. 69.

77 – '"The lad who appeared to eat most," the *Daily Mail* reported, "and
to dance most, was thirteen-year-old Tara Browne, wearing a heavy white
homespun suit with a red jumper, clay pipe and clogs."' *Daily Mail*,
5 May 1958.

'"Our mother had lovers from time to time . . ."' Author interview
with Garech Browne, Wicklow, 2010.

'A photograph from the party, taken by Tara, shows him looking
almost comically ill at ease in an Aran sweater and flat cap, while, beside

him, Oonagh appears brimming with happiness in her black hooded Munster cloak.' Featured in a number of British and Irish newspapers, May 1958.

77 – 'Now, according to the newspapers, he was "one of America's leading dress designers" and had a salon on Fifth Avenue . . .' *Daily Mail*, 12 May 1958.

"'I think Donegal tweed, in particular, should be better known around the world," he said.' Ibid.

"'This is a heavenly place . . .'" Ibid.

78 – 'In 1958, she gave an interview to the *Daily Mail* in which she spoke candidly about the loneliness of living in an empty castle in the wilds of County Mayo.' *Daily Mail*, 20 September 1958.

"'She was no more a country girl than I was a Norwegian . . .'" Author interview with Judith Haslam, by telephone, 2014.

79 – "'My father sent her to London," he said, "to have electro-shock treatment . . .'" Author interview with Dominick Browne, Lord Mereworth, London, 2014.

"'Even the town of Claremorris . . .'" Author interview with Garech Browne, Wicklow, 2015.

"'They were an unusual sight . . .'" Author interview with Brid Ni Dhonnchadha, by telephone, 2013.

80 – "'Tara helped me with the buttons . . .'" Author interview with Garech Browne, Wicklow, 2015.

82 – "'He thought he should have been Lord Somebody . . .'" Author interview with Garech Browne, Wicklow, 2012.

"'I don't recall us ever once calling him our stepfather . . .'" Author interview with Garech Browne, Wicklow, 2011.

"'When we were at Luggala, my place in Ireland, he was always running down the Irish, offending both my friends and my servants.'" *Sunday Express*, 7 September 1958.

83 – "'He was spending $2,000 each month . . .'" *Daily Sketch*, 11 September 1958.

'. . . dubbed by one newspaper as "society's reputed freest teenage spender".' *Sunday Dispatch*, 28 September, 1958.

'Brendan Behan loved it so much, he wrote about it in the *Irish Press*.' – 'An electric light inside his bow tie, which went on and off to the terror of his slightly nervous elders. I'd say that's a thing to remember, wouldn't you? That's a thing to keep up. No house in the land should be without one.' *Irish Press*, 29 December 1958.

84 – "'I remember feeling that there was something indecent about being the lover of your friend's mother . . .'" Author interview with Kenneth Rose, by telephone, 2013.

"'. . . he hated me . . .'" Ibid.

"'Tara took an enormous amount of baggage with him . . .'" Ibid.

"'The boat was a great disappointment . . .'" Ibid.

"'We came very close to capsizing . . .'" Ibid.

85 – "'She went back to Miguel shortly after that . . .'" Ibid.

"'I didn't want to go to Eton . . .'" *Sunday Dispatch*, 28 September 1958.

"'Tara doesn't want to conform to pattern . . .'" Ibid.

'. . . Garech was creating newspaper headlines of his own, having reportedly "run away" with one of his mother's parlour maids . . .' Reports in several British and Irish newspapers in September 1958.

86 – "'Since then," he told the *Sunday Pictorial*, "we have been going really steady.'" *Sunday Pictorial*, 7 September 1958.

"'. . . Several respectable British middle-class ladies could not conceal their horror.'" *Daily Express*, 20 October 1958.

87 – "'I think she was very much in love with Miguel in the physical sense . . .'" Author interview with Kenneth Rose, by telephone, 2013.

"'It was well after midnight . . .'" Author interview with Garech Browne, Wicklow, 2008.

88 – "'Lady Veronica had brought along a friend of hers . . .'" Author interview with Garech Browne, Wicklow, 2015.

'. . . the "formidable little bull", as his old friend the poet John Montague, remembered him . . .' *Company: A Chosen Life* by John Montague (Gerald Duckworth & Co Ltd, 2001), p. 51.

89 – 'During the months that followed, the period of his greatest success, his life continued to spiral out of control.' A full account of Brendan Behan's tragic descent is contained in *Brendan Behan: A Life* by Michael O'Sullivan (Roberts Rinehart Publishers, 1999) and *Behan in the USA: The Rise and Fall of the Most Famous Irishman in New York* by Dave Hannigan (Ballpoint Press Limited, 2014).

"'Tara was delighted to see him," said Garech, "as he always was . . .'" Author interview with Garech Browne, Wicklow, 2013.

90 – 'Thirty carloads of reporters followed him to the airport . . .' As described in *Brendan Behan: A Life* by Michael O'Sullivan (Roberts Rinehart Publishers, 1999), p. 254.

"'. . . He told him that the IRA would kill him.'" Interview with Garech Browne, Wicklow, 2014.

"'Brendan came to dinner . . .'" Ibid.

91 – 'She asked Alan Hope, the architect who oversaw the rebuilding of the house after the fire, to draw up plans for an elegant pavilion . . .' The architectural plans for the pavilion are reproduced in *Luggala Days* by

Robert O'Byrne (CICO Books, an imprint of Ryland Peters & Small Ltd, 2012), p. 170.

5: LA VIE EST BELLE

92 – '. . . between leaving second-level education and entering society.' Two very authoritative accounts of the debutant age are contained in *Last Curtsey: The End of the Debutantes* by Fiona MacCarthy (Faber and Faber, 2007) and *1939: The Last Season* by Anne De Courcy (Weidenfeld & Nicolson, 2003).

93 – '"I spent a year in Paris . . ."' Author interview with Lucinda Lambton, Hedgerley, 2011.

'"So we went and I discovered that Lucy hadn't exaggerated him at all . . ."' Author interview with Michael Boyle, London, 2011.

94 – '"It was, 'Come to dinner,' then it was, 'Come to lunch,' a constant flow of invitations . . ."' Ibid.

'One day, early in 1960, Lucy brought Judith Keppel . . .' Tara and Judith were distantly related.

'"I remember talking to him once . . ."' Author interview with Judith Keppel, London, 2009.

95 – '. . . Lady Frances Eliot, the daughter of the ninth Earl of St Germans.' Tara and Lady Frances Eliot were distantly related.

'"At a time when I was learning about life for the first time, he was very, very influential on my development . . ."' Author interview with Hugo Williams, London, 2011.

96 – '"Most girls in those days were told that they might as well get a little job until they got married . . ."' Author interview with Judith Keppel, London, 2009.

'"It was a wonderful moment in our lives between school and reality . . ."' Author interview with Hugo Williams, London, 2011.

'"Eden Roc was an extremely glamorous place . . ."' Ibid.

'"He sort of led us in a way because he knew so much more about the world than we did . . ."' Author interview with Judith Keppel, London, 2009.

97 – '"He had a very developed aesthetic sense . . ."' Author interview with Hugo Williams, London, 2011.

'"He wasn't at all macho . . ."' Ibid.

'"He would look at you very seriously . . ."' Author interview with Michael Boyle, London, 2011.

'"There was something about him being not quite a gentleman . . ."' Author interview with Hugo Williams, London, 2011.

98 – '"At the time, nobody knew they existed . . ."' Letter from Peregrine Eliot, tenth Earl of St Germans, to the author.

'"He took it everywhere . . ."' Ibid.

99 – '"I thought of him as one of my best friends . . ."' Author interview with Michael Boyle, London, 2011.

100 – '. . . from his bedroom window overlooking the Rue de l'Université.' Author interview with Nicki Browne by telephone, 2009.

'"He was always on the wrong side of the road . . ."' Author interview with Garech Browne, Wicklow, 2010.

'"He tried it on with me . . ."' Author interview with Hugo Williams, London, 2011.

101 – '"She was very coquettish around him . . ."' Author interview with Lucinda Lambton, Hedgerley, 2011.

'"Tara would have been completely uninterested in what was going on with Miguel . . ."' Author interview with Michael Boyle, London, 2011.

102 – '"Miguel was unavoidable really . . ."' Author interview with Prince Stanislaus Klossowski de Rola, aka Stash de Rola, by telephone, 2009.

'"He got him down quite easily . . ."' Interview with John Montague, by telephone, 2011.

'"She viewed the entire thing, as she did most things, with a certain detachment . . ."' Ibid.

'Miguel claimed that Brendan had been "interfering with children", implying that he had made sexual advances towards Tara . . .' The story of Brendan Behan's alleged sexual assault of Tara was related in two previous books: *Brendan Behan: A Life* by Michael O'Sullivan (Roberts Rinehart Publishers, 1999), p. 139; and *Silver Salver: The Story of the Guinness Family* by Frederick Mullally (Granada, 1981), p. 148. The latter book gives the story more credence than the former. However, in another book, the author Anthony Cronin mentions a similar 'misunderstanding' involving the fourteen-year-old son of a painter and novelist whom Brendan was accused of molesting while he was alone with him during a house party. In that case, according to the book, Brendan's claim that the boy was upset because they had been having an intense discussion about the existence of God was accepted at face value. *Dead as Doornails* by Anthony Cronin (Dolmen Press, 1976), pp. 16–17.

103 – '. . . was the type he had met at borstal – "clean-skinned fresh lads" . . .' *Brendan* by Ulick O'Connor (Hamish-Hamilton, 1970), p. 96.

'"The real reason he beat Brendan up was that Brendan had told him to get out of Ireland . . ."' Author interview with Garech Browne, Wicklow, 2010.

103 – 'Paris had ceased to be the style capital of the world . . .' The story of Christian Dior from *Christian Dior: The Biography* by Marie-France Pochna (Overlook Duckworth, 2009).

104 – 'By 1949, Dior's international empire was so big that it accounted for 5 per cent of France's total export revenue.' Ibid.

'"He saw himself as the head of a major fashion house . . ."' Author interview with Desmond Guinness, Wicklow, 2012.

105 – '"He tended to steer clear whenever Miguel was around." according to Garech . . .' Author interview with Garech Browne, Wicklow, 2013.

'"Oonagh was a patient of my father . . ."' Author interview with Godfrey Carey, London, 2011.

106 – '"I had agreed a plan with Oonagh . . ."' Ibid.

'"I cannot remember any day in Paris when the programme was carried out . . ."' Ibid.

'Mark couldn't believe his confidence, how nothing appeared to faze him . . .' Author interview with Mark Palmer, Cheltenham, 2015.

'. . . friends remember him opening in Paris was *Angelique* . . .' *Angelique: Marquis of the Angels* (Hachette, 1956) was the first of ten Angelique books published under the name Sergeanne Golon, a portmanteau representing the names of Anne Golon, who did the writing, and her husband, Sergeïvich Goloubinoff, who did the historical research.

'"I went to her and I said, quite honestly, 'You're wasting your money . . .""' Author interview with Godfrey Carey, London, 2011.

108 – '"The new plan was that we were to take up residence in two adjoining suites in the Drake Hotel . . ."' Ibid.

'"I stayed, enjoying the New York social scene for two weeks . . ."' Ibid.

109 – '"He was this charming, very young-looking, rather frail-looking child . . ."' Author interview with Christopher Gibbs, London, 2010.

'. . . That summer, she was trying her hand at modelling.' She was photographed by Cecil Beaton. Charmian, who would go on to make her name as a children's portraitist, drew a sketch of Tara in profile on Claridge's notepaper while they had tea one afternoon.

'. . . when the IRA had seriously considered murdering him for being a spy.' In April 2000, a Channel 4 documentary, *The Real John Betjeman*, revealed that, in 1967, Diarmuid Brennan, the IRA council's head of civilian intelligence, wrote to the poet to tell him how his life had been spared. In 1941, he said, he was approached by two gunmen from the second battalion of the Dublin IRA – known within the organization as the Edward

Gees, after the actor Edward G. Robinson, who was famous for his gangster roles – and asked to provide a photograph of Betjeman. 'I got communications describing you as "dangerous" and a person of menace to us all,' he wrote to the intended victim. 'In short, you were depicted in the blackest of colours.' However, having read some of Betjeman's poetry, he decided to let him off the hook. 'I came to the conclusion that a man who could give such pleasure with his pen couldn't be much of a secret agent. I could be wrong.'

'"Tara and I immediately clicked . . ."' Author interview with Candida Betjeman, Uffington, 2011.

110 – '"I don't remember him having any what we called liaisons around that time . . ."' Ibid.

'"My mother used to embarrass me incredibly . . ."' Ibid.

112 '"They were being mobbed by fans . . ."' Author interview with Lucinda Lambton, Hedgerley, 2011.

113 – '. . . who wanted her son to enjoy some of the experiences she had when she sailed around the world with her father and sisters as a thirteen-year-old girl.' In 1923, Ernest took his daughters on a year-long, round the world trip on *Fantôme II*, a luxury yacht he had recently purchased from the Duke of Westminster. *Belem*, as it was originally known, was a three-masted barque that first saw service as a cargo ship, transporting sugar, cocoa and coffee from the West Indies, Brazil and French Guiana to France. The Duke of Westminster bought it and had it converted into a pleasure yacht, before selling it to Oonagh's father in 1921. A keen sailor all his life, Ernest had the ship's interior reshaped and its six state rooms redecorated, then installed a bar and an upright piano, to create a new home for his family during the twelve months they would spend circumnavigating a world still recovering from the ravages of the First World War. On 29 March 1923, they sailed from Southampton to Seville. From there, the journey took them to the Canary Islands, then across the Atlantic to St Vincent and Trinidad in the Caribbean and to Venezuela. They travelled on through the Panama Canal to see the Galapagos Islands, with their abundant and exotic wildlife, then spent several months exploring the tropical paradises of the South Pacific, from the Marquesas Islands, to Tahiti, Tonga and Fiji, then on to the Caroline and Solomon Islands. From there, they sailed to Japan, whose main island, they discovered on their arrival, had been hit by a catastrophic earthquake just weeks earlier. The Great Kanto Earthquake of September 1923 was the most powerful ever to hit the region at that time, killing an estimated 150,000 people and devastating the cities of Tokyo and Yoko-hama. They left for Hong Kong and China, then sailed on to Singapore, Malaysia and Sarawak, where they stayed as guests of Charles Vyner Brook, the last White Rajah of Sarawak, and where Oonagh had her first teenage

romance. 'My mother was found hugging a sailor on the beach at the age of fourteen,' Garech says, 'and was confined to the palace for the rest of her stay.' From Sarawak, they sailed homeward via Sri Lanka, Yemen and the Suez Canal to Egypt, Crete and Gibraltar, before arriving – 360 days and 31,129 miles later – back in England.

113 – '"He got a nail on the door – a writ to pay a bill . . ."' Author interview with Garech Browne, Wicklow, 2010.

'". . . to once again announce Miguel's coming-out as a couturier."' Reported in the *New York Sunday Mirror*, 17 July 1960.

114 – '. . . planned to open a *maison de couture* in the centre of Paris in September.' Ibid.

'"The de Ribes is one of those slinky, sloe-eyed, beautifully-boned types who is forever in a Dior . . ."' Ibid.

'. . . for what the social commentator Nigel Dempster called "a wild, Rabelaisian week of total drunkenness".' *Last Curtsey: The End of the Debutantes* by Fiona MacCarthy (Faber and Faber, 2007), p. 167.

'Desmond Guinness and his then German princess wife, Mariga, regularly threw open the doors of their home, Leixlip Castle, to more than one hundred guests . . .' Author interview with Desmond Guinness, Kildare, 2012.

'"My guests can come and go as they wish . . ."' *Daily Mail*, August 1960.

115 – '"From the moment she heard that I'd become friends with Tara . . ."' Author interview with Candida Betjeman, Uffington, 2011.

'The guests included Brendan Behan, who appeared in Oonagh's photographs smoking a large cigar, with a pink carnation in his button hole . . .' From Oonagh, Lady Oranmore and Browne's personal photograph collection, viewed by the author with kind permission of Garech and Dorian Browne.

'Brendan was temporarily on the wagon, having determined to stay sober ahead of the opening of *The Hostage* in New York later in the year . . .' *Brendan Behan: A Life* by Michael O'Sullivan (Roberts Rinehart Publishers, 1999), pp. 260–2.

'"We all sat on the floor of the drawing room listening to him telling stories . . ."' Author interview with Candida Betjeman, Uffington, 2011.

116 '"He kept walking around," remembered Desmond Guinness, who was also on the trip . . ."' Author interview with Desmond Guinness, Kildare, 2012.

'"I remember one day," he recalled, "my father said . . ."' Author interview with Hugo Williams, London, 2011.

6: ALL THAT JAZZ

117 – "'I was with them and we were walking down the rue Saint-Dominique . . .'" Author interview with John Montague, by telephone, 2011. The shop, according to Garech Browne, was most likely Petrossian, on the Rue de l'Université.

'Mark remembered Glen as being withdrawn . . .' Interview with Mark Palmer, Cheltenham, 2015.

118 – 'Glen's first impression of Tara was . . .' Author interview with Glen Kidston, by telephone, 2015.

"'He was like a king in his own terrain . . .'" Ibid.

"'Glen was the essence of cool . . .'" Author interview with Hugo Williams, London, 2011.

"'He always slouched around school . . .'" Author interview with Rupert Lycett-Green, Uffington, 2011.

119 – "'They could be freer here . . .'" Author interview with Glen Kidston, by telephone, 2015.

120 – 'Clubs sprouted up everywhere . . .' A highly illuminating account of the post-war jazz scene in Paris is offered in *Dance of the Infidels: A Portrait of Bud Powell* by Francis Paudras (Da Capo Press, 1998).

"'I saw Lionel Hampton's Big Band at the Olympia in Paris . . .'" Author interview with Glen Kidston, by telephone, 2015.

"'Glen became a kind of guru to him . . .'" Interview with Serena Connell (nee Gillilan), by telephone, 2011.

121 – "'He started off with Dave Brubeck . . .'" Author interview with Glen Kidston, by telephone, 2015.

122 – "'It was the most exotic thing I'd ever seen in my life . . .'" Author interview with Melissa North, London, 2011.

"'He never proposed having sex with me . . .'" Ibid.

"'He liked a lot of black musicians that I didn't know . . .'" Ibid.

123 – '. . . kept him locked up in a drugged-out state of dependence in the home they'd made for themselves in the Hotel La Louisiane.' *Dance of the Infidels: A Portrait of Bud Powell* by Francis Paudras (Da Capo Press, 1998).

"'He'd be playing the most wonderful piano any of us had ever heard . . .'" Author interview with Melissa North, London, 2011.

"'One is a baronet and page to the Queen and the other is the son of a member of the House of Lords . . .'" Ibid.

124 – "'Oonagh would take us out for dinner at the George V . . .'" Ibid.

"'In his own way, he thought it was funny, too . . .'" Ibid.

124 – "'One just felt that because you had to spend hours admiring his clothes . . .'" Ibid.

125 – "'He takes my body with him everywhere he goes . . .'" *Daily Mirror*, 22 June 1961.

"'I couldn't say whether she was in love with him . . .'" Author interview with Melissa North, London, 2011.

'. . . Miguel outlined his ambitious plans to *Women's Wear Daily* . . .' *Women's Wear Daily*, October 1960.

'At around the same time, he told the *Sunday Express* that his wife was "not involved in the new venture, either financially or in any other way".' *Sunday Express*, 2 October 1960.

'. . . in which his wife had a five-million-dollar holding.' Author interview with Garech Browne, Wicklow, 2010.

'She stood beside him, beaming proudly, while he announced to the American press that Maison Ferreras would present its first collection in the spring of 1961.' From contemporary newspaper reports.

126 – 'He had fallen off the wagon in spectacular fashion in New York . . .' A full account of Brendan Behan's time in New York is featured in *Behan in the USA: The Rise and Fall of the Most Famous Irishman in New York* by Dave Hannigan (Ballpoint Press Limited, 2014).

127 – "'At Luggala, you had a very straightforward formal dinner with his mother and everybody sitting down in dinner jackets . . .'" Author interview with Nicholas Gormanston, London, 2010.

"'He introduced me to Durban Poison . . .'" Ibid.

128 – "'The movie started and very quickly he discovered that he didn't like it very much . . .'" Author interview with Dorian Browne, Surrey, 2011.

'. . . advice he would continue to ignore for another four years.' Gay had already reached the high-point of his career when he won the amateur jockeys' championship in 1959–60, riding 22 winners from 100 rides, almost all on his own horses. The fall at Hurst Park was the second time he broke his back, after an earlier fall at Stratford in 1955. He ignored medical advice to quit racing and fulfilled his lifetime ambition of riding in the Aintree Grand National in 1965, although his horse, the 100-1 shot Ronald's Boy, fell at the third fence. He continued to ride in Flat races until 1969.

"'It was referred to as being sacked . . .'" Author interview with Melissa North, London, 2011.

130 – 'At the back of the salon, she installed an indoor tropical garden, behind whose fronds – according to a *New York Times* article – "women sew to music".' *New York Times*, 31 July 1961.

'A photographer from the weekly magazine *Paris Match* captured several images of Tara . . .' Photographs from the private collection of

Oonagh, Lady Oranmore and Browne, seen by the author by kind permission of Garech Browne and Dorian Browne.

'Miguel was on hand to remind them . . .' *New York Herald Tribune*, 6 July 1961.

'"Society women who spend several hundred dollars on a ready-made dress . . ."' *New York Times,* 31 July 1961.

'A girl should not expect a boy to court her when she's wearing blue jeans.' Quoted in Canada's *Victoria Colonist*, BC, 27 September 1961.

131 – '. . . a gesture to the woman who was, after all, paying for all of this.' – 'Brown and green will be the colours,' Miguel said, 'with Irish interest well emphasized.' Quoted in the *Sunday Independent*, 23 July 1961.

'"In those days, the general opinion was that the Bateaux Mouches destroyed the Seine . . ."' Author interview with Garech Browne, Wicklow, 2009.

'"For which she got no benefit or pleasure," he added.' Ibid.

132 – '"The thing about Tara was that you never thought about how old he was . . ."' Author interview with Glen Kidston, by telephone, 2015.

'"He used to cross the bay in the dark . . ."' Author interview with Serena Connell (née Gillilan), by telephone, 2011.

133 – '"We saw Ray Charles play . . ."' Author interview with Nicholas Gormanston, London, 2014.

'. . . dancing the Walls of Limerick.' *Dublin Evening Mail*, 8 August 1961.

'". . . resplendent in tight trousers, an electric blue shirt and a maroon tie . . ."' Ibid.

'. . . Camilla Wigan, an English aristocrat and debbie girl.' Camilla's older sister, Lola, had been the cult star of the debs circuit in 1958, the final year of presentations at court, when she was photographed by Anthony Armstrong Jones – the future husband of Princess Margaret – for the cover of *Harpers & Queen*. The photograph, featuring a suggestive flash of bare shoulder, defined the image of the reluctant debutante and was a sort of precursor to the waif look that would be popularised by models like Jean Shrimpton in the coming years. *Last Curtsey: The End of the Debutantes* by Fiona MacCarthy (Faber and Faber, 2007), pp. 39–40.

'"I'm not particularly worried," Tara told London's *Evening Standard*, before the three headed off into the night . . .' *London Evening Standard*, 8 August 1961.

'"It was always this mix of people . . ."' Author interview with David Mlinaric, London, 2009.

134 – '"We smoked a joint . . ."' Author interview with Candida Betjeman, Uffington, 2011.

134 – 'The suite that Oonagh booked for the event was so full . . .' Contemporary newspaper reports.

135 – "'He came around one day to see someone else . . .'" Author interview with Jacquetta Lampson, London, 2011.

"'He just said, 'Oh, you like it? You can have it,' and he just gave it to me . . .'" Ibid.

"'Which was absolutely not allowed . . .'" Ibid.

136 – "'They would have these tremendously passionate rows . . .'" Ibid.

"'A bottle of Haig Dimple whisky a day . . .'" Author interview with John Montague, by telephone, 2011.

"There was also the problem that she couldn't prove adultery . . .'" Author interview with Garech Browne, Wicklow, 2009.

137– "'Oonagh clearly adored Tara," she said . . .' Author interview with Jacquetta Lampson, London, 2011.

"'It was in cloud cuckoo land they lived . . .'" Author interview with Nicki Browne, by telephone, 2010.

7: VENUS IN BLUE JEANS

138 – "'You'd see houses that were blown wide open . . .'" Author interview with David Mlinaric, London, 2009.

"'I remember buses being abandoned on Oxford Street . . .'" Author interview with Michael Rainey, by telephone, 2011.

139 – '. . . economically frozen out of the Europe it helped to liberate . . .' Britain was still not a member of the European Economic Community, which was founded in 1957 with the stated aim of bringing about a common European market. French President Charles de Gaulle would twice block the country's application for membership, in 1963 and in 1967.

"'It was the whole end of empire thing . . .'" Author interview with David Mlinaric, London, 2009.

'The economic roots of Swinging London . . .' *Never Had it So Good: A History of Britain from Suez to The Beatles* by Dominic Sandbrook (Abacus, 2005) offers a fascinating insight into the post-war era in Britain.

'". . . horizontal city with a skyline dominated by Mary Poppins chimney pots . . ." From a feature in *Time* magazine, 15 April 1966, by Piri Halasz, entitled 'Great Britain: You Can Walk on It Across the Grass'.

140 – "'At the start of the Sixties, London had this cloak of dullness about it . . .'" Author interview with Michael Rainey, by telephone, 2011.

'. . . After the war, the Italian government allowed young men to defer their military service until the age of thirty-six, on condition that they could find work abroad.' An interesting account of the change in the military culture in post-war Italy and how it helped shape London's coffee-bar scene is featured in *Ready, Steady, Go!* by Shawn Levy (Fourth Estate, 2002), p. 52.

141 – '"We hired a pastry chef," remembered Dominick . . .' Author interview with Dominick Browne, London, 2014.

'They despised the drinkers . . .' Author interview with Mark Palmer, Cheltenham, 2015.

142 – 'John Stephen, a gay, former welder's apprentice from Glasgow . . .' The definitive account of John Stephen's life and times is contained in *The King of Carnaby Street: A Life of John Stephen* by Jeremy Reed (Haus Publishing, 2010).

'. . . Mohair sweaters, fashioned from a rug – when they sold one to Cliff Richard, they couldn't deal with the sudden demand.' A fascinating and highly authoritative insight into the fashion of the era is offered by *The Look: Adventures in Rock and Pop Fashion* by Paul Gorman (Adelita Limited, 2006).

143 – 'At twenty-eight, the career and reputation of the woman . . .' The story of Mary Quant, Bazaar and the miniskirt is related, in her own words, in *Quant by Quant* by Mary Quant (Cassell, 1966).

144 – 'While they were there, they watched a young man from Cheltenham . . .' *Life* by Keith Richards (Weidenfeld & Nicolson, 2010), pp. 89–90.

'Dick Rowe, the head of A&R at the label, reportedly told Brian Epstein . . .' This is the most popular account of the band's Decca audition and its aftermath. While Dick Rowe has gone down in history as the man who turned down The Beatles, some accounts have suggested that his role may have been exaggerated by Brian Epstein. Author Paul Trynka has claimed that the decision to pass on The Beatles was actually taken by Rowe's assistant, Mike Smith. As it happened, The Beatles never held a grudge. In fact, it was George Harrison who suggested to Rowe that he check out The Rolling Stones, which he did, before signing them to his label. *Brian Jones: The Making of a Rolling Stone* by Paul Trynka (Viking, 2014), pp. 99–100.

145 – 'The music newspaper *Melody Maker* had carried a feature about the new American dance . . .' *Melody Maker*, 16 December 1962.

146 – '"She flew this chap over from New York . . ."' Author interview with Nicholas Gormanston, London, 2011.

'"He was a frightful man . . ."' Ibid.

'"There was a club called the Roaring Twenties . . ."' Ibid.

147 – "'He was a mix of French and American cool . . .'" Ibid.

"'She took one look at it . . .'" Author interview with Glen Kidston, by telephone, 2015.

148 – "'The first night he got it . . .'" Ibid.

"'He came around to our house in Montpelier Square . . .'" Author interview with Jacquetta Lampson, London, 2011.

149 – "'At one point, he grew quite melancholy . . .'" Ibid.

"'She was the runaway daughter of an Irish-born postman . . .'" Nicki was always referred to by the press as the daughter of a farmer from County Down. Her father, Seán (whose name was usually pronounced 'Shane') MacSherry, did own land in Ireland and later retired to live on a farm in Carrickmacross, County Monaghan. But in the 1960s, he worked for the Post Office in London. The confusion may have been a deliberate effort by Nicki to cover up her working-class roots. Describing her father as simply a famer would have given no indication as to her family's financial circumstances. Tara's father was also a farmer.

"'She had a kind of slightly androgynous quality . . .'" Author interview with Christopher Gibbs, London, 2010.

150 – '. . . and she'd given her up for adoption.' She confided this information in at least two friends, who did not wish to be named.

"'The bank thought that was a very good idea . . .'" Author interview with Nicki Browne, by telephone, 2010.

"'This flatmate of mine said Michael was calling around . . .'" Ibid.

151 – "'He wanted to show me the boat . . .'" Ibid.

152 – "'Tara was very sweet . . .'" Ibid.

"'He knew she wouldn't approve . . .'" Ibid.

"'From that point on,' she said, "we were inseparable . . .'" Ibid.

"'He outgrew us really . . .'" Author interview with Hugo Williams, London, 2011.

153 – "'He used to say to me, 'I know they're hustlers . . .'" Author interview with Michael Boyle, London, 2011.

"'He was with Nicki at the time and I think things were already difficult . . .'" Author interview with Rabea Redpath, by telephone, 2011.

154 – "'He got his motto from that record . . .'" Author interview with Hugo Williams, London, 2011.

"'His father had told him there was no way he was taking the car . . .'" Author interview with Nicki Browne, by telephone, 2009.

"'We heard a siren . . .'" Ibid.

"'I think Tara and Nicki were the first couple I ever understood to be incredibly sexually in love . . .'" Author interview with Melissa North, London, 2011.

156 – '. . . the *Daily Express* carried a photograph of Tara on the dance floor . . .' *Daily Express*, 6 August 1962.

'"In the morning, towards eleven . . ."' *Cold Cream – My Early Life and Other Mistakes* by Ferdinand Mount (Bloomsbury Publishing PLC, 2009), p. 196.

157 – '"I was still in love with Tara . . ."' Author interview with Melissa North, London, 2011.

'All she owned of any real value, she remembered . . .' Author interview with Nicki Browne, by telephone, 2011.

'"She seemed so much older than us . . ."' Author interview with Melissa North, London, 2011.

'"Oh, I was a gold digger . . ."' Author interview with Nicki Browne, by telephone, 2011.

'"We were never happier than we were at that time . . ."' Ibid.

8: ONE PLUS ONE MAKES THREE

160 – '. . . with no one prepared to brave the drifts . . .' From contemporary newspaper reports.

161 – '"Tara could hardly write . . ."' Author interview with Nicki Browne, by telephone, 2011.

'"He said I'm not going unless I can bring my girlfriend with me . . ."' Ibid.

162 – '"The clubs in Wardour Street tended to be full of gangsters," she recalled . . .' Ibid.

163 – '"There was a time that winter when I was very pale . . ."' Ibid.

'"We discussed a termination . . ."' Ibid.

'"Except he said, 'We've got a problem here . . .' " ' Ibid.

164 – '. . . the first of which, 'How Do You Do It?', had been passed over by The Beatles.' The Beatles did record the song, which was written by Mitch Murray, but chose not to release it as a single, preferring 'Love Me Do' instead. Their version appears on the 1995 Beatles retrospective album, *Anthology*. Their lack of enthusiasm for the song is quite apparent in the recording.

165 – '*Melody Maker* pronounced in June 1963 . . .' *Melody Maker*, 8 June 1963.

166 – 'And, of course, those ever-northward-inclining hemlines.' The question of who 'invented' the miniskirt remains the subject of much debate. In 1958, Mary Quant raised the length of her skirts to above the knee for the first time. But as author Paul Gorman points out, she was actually

continuing a trend started by Cristóbal Balenciaga seven years earlier, when he invented the first free-form dress, meaning hemlines could be raised without affecting the line. Author interview with Paul Gorman, London, 2011.

166 – "'I remember being hit over the head with umbrellas . . .'" Author interview with Victoria Ormsby-Gore, Dublin, 2009.

167 – "'He used to drive through Piccadilly . . .'" Author interview with Melissa North, London, 2011.

"'Tara appeared in my life fully formed . . .'" Author interview with Martin Wilkinson, Newport, 2011.

168 – "'I wanted to be a racing driver from very early on . . .'" Ibid.

169 – "'Unlike our parents and our grandparents . . .'" Ibid.

'Michael Beeby had started going out with . . . Lady Henrietta Guinness.' Lady Henrietta Guinness was the daughter of Major Arthur Onslow Guinness, Viscount Elveden, who was killed in a rocket strike in Holland in the final year of the war (*The Guinnesses*, by Joe Joyce (Poolbeg, 2009), p. 296), and Lady Elizabeth Cecilia Hare. Her grandfather was Rupert Guinness, the second Earl of Iveagh.

"'Mike was the most dangerous driver I met . . .'" Author interview with Glen Kidston, by telephone, 2015.

170 – "'We decided that we were going to go to see it . . .'" Author interview with Tchaik Chassay, London, 2011.

"'We had breakfast in the SKR with the car ticking over outside . . .'" Ibid.

'Now, her solicitor husband was suing him . . .' From contemporary newspaper reports.

171 – "'What she wanted me to do . . .'" Author interview with Nicki Browne, by telephone, 2011.

"'He told her he loved me . . .'" Ibid.

"'All she wanted was to legitimize the child . . .'" Ibid.

"'I didn't give a damn if I was married or not . . .'" Ibid.

172 – "'. . . he told us we couldn't do it there because we weren't resident nearby . . .'" Ibid.

173 – '. . . Henrietta committed suicide by jumping off an aqueduct in the town of Spoleto.' On 6 January 1969, she had been granted the rank of an earl's daughter. After rejecting her society life, she married Luigi Marinori on 3 February 1978 and went by the name Henrietta Marinori until her death three months later at the age of thirty-five. Source: The Peerage.

"'They didn't know she was married . . .'" Family friend who didn't wish to be named.

174 – "'We had a lovely day . . .'" Author interview with Nicki Browne, by telephone, 2011.

'"We didn't need one . . ."' Ibid.

'"It was such a long labour . . ."' Ibid.

'. . . So we called him Dorian Clifford Browne.' Ibid.

'Garech said they couldn't understand why Irish people . . .' Author interview with Garech Browne, Wicklow, 2011.

'"They were standing in the drawing room . . ."' Author interview with Garech Browne, Wicklow, 2011.

9: SPEED

178 – '. . . they held the top five positions in the US chart.' In the week of 4 April 1964, The Beatles held the top five positions in the US Billboard Chart with 'Can't Buy Me Love' (1), 'Twist and Shout' (2), 'She Loves You' (3), 'I Want to Hold Your Hand' (4) and 'Please Please Me' (5). At the same time, they had seven further singles in the top 100: 'I Saw Her Standing There' (31); 'From Me To You' (41); 'Do You Want to Know a Secret' (46); 'All My Loving' (58); 'You Can't Do That' (65); 'Roll Over Beethoven' (68); and 'Thank You Girl' (79).

'. . . and George Harrison and Ringo Starr, the band's two single-tons, in a bachelor pad in William Mews, near Knightsbridge.' *The Beatles' London* by Piet Schreuders, Mark Lewisohn and Adam Smith (Interlink Books, 2008).

179 – '"I barely saw them . . ."' Author interview with Mary Fanning, by telephone, 2010.

'. . . And life, or at least the social aspect of it, began to revolve around a nightclub called the Ad Lib.' A very interesting account of the life and times of the Ab Lib is featured in *Ready, Steady, Go!* by Shawn Levy (Fourth Estate, 2002), pp. 159–62. According to author Levy, George Harrison was the first Beatle to discover the Ad Lib in early 1964. It was likely while the band was in London filming *A Hard Day's Night*, the 1964 satirical comedy about the new phenomenon of screaming fandom.

180 – '"I wouldn't say it was a mutual, made-in-heaven arrangement . . ."' Author interview with Michael Rainey, by telephone, 2011.

'"He didn't court attention . . ."' Author interview with Martin Wilkinson, Newport, 2011.

'"He was absolutely central to it . . ."' Author interview with Jane Ormsby-Gore, London, 2010.

181 – '"Paul McCartney liked being around people he thought he could learn something from . . ."' Author interview with Nicholas Gormanson, London, 2011.

181 – ". . . a member of an aspiring comedy musical hall act called The Scaffold.' In 1968, The Scaffold scored a UK number one with 'Lily the Pink'. They had two other top ten hits: 'Thank U Very Much', which reached number four in 1967, and 'Liverpool Lou', written by Dominic Behan, a brother of Brendan, which reached number seven in 1974.

"'I first knew him as just a guy on the scene . . .'" Author interview with Mike McCartney, Liverpool, 2008.

182 – 'Before the 1960s . . .' Ibid.

183 – "'Quad 303 amplification . . .'" Author interview with Glen Kidston, by telephone, 2015.

'Over dinner, he told Mike some of his Brendan stories.' Author interview with Mike McCartney, Liverpool, 2008. Interestingly, one of the stories Tara told him involved being groped by Brendan, not as a child, but as an adult. 'Tara said he'd be driving Brendan home from Luggala,' Mike recalled, 'and Brendan would make a grab for him, drunk out of his mind, thinking he was a woman with the blond hair.'

184 – "'He ordered a brandy . . .'" Ibid. The brandy was probably Hine cognac, according to Garech.

"'People used to say, 'Be careful driving over the bridge to Annamoe . . . ' " ' Author interview Monsignor Tom Stack, Wicklow, 2011.

"'He drove it . . .'" Author interview with Nicholas Gormanston, London, 2010.

185 – "'We were going to Bray . . .'" Author interview with Nicki Browne, by telephone, 2009.

"'Oonagh was worried about the way he drove . . .'" Author interview with Nicki Browne, by telephone, 2011.

"'Tara took it out for a test drive . . .'" Author interview with Glen Kidston, by telephone, 2015.

"'Clark was a humble fellow . . .'" Ibid.

186 – "'I drove it one night . . .'" Author interview with Hugo Williams, London, 2011.

"'They arrived in pieces in a series of crates . . .'" Author interview with Nicholas Gormanston, London, 2010.

'. . . started to take an interest in the story of Sir Algernon Lee Guinness and his younger brother, Kenelm . . .' An account of the lives of the two racing Guinness brothers is featured on the website historicracing.com.

187 – 'Algy told the subsequent inquest . . .' Contemporary newspaper reports of the inquest.

"'I think he was going to do Formula Three first . . .'" Author interview with Martin Wilkinson, Newport, 2011.

"'I remember one time we were going to Ireland . . .'" Author interview with Glen Kidston, by telephone, 2015.

188 – "'I was aware that two grand-uncles of his . . .'" Author interview with Larry Mooney, Dublin, 2009.

189 – "'The handicaps were worked out very scientifically . . .'" Ibid.

"'I took it out for him . . .'" Ibid.

'. . . *Autosport* magazine reported . . .' *Autosport*, 20 June 1964.

'. . . while the *Irish Times* reported that he had driven "faultlessly" . . .' *Irish Times*, 1 June 1964.

"'I was in quite a slow car . . .'" Author interview with Rosemary Smith, Dublin, 2009.

"'It was pretty clear to everyone that he had a gift . . .'" Author interiew with Larry Mooney, Dublin, 2009.

190 – "'It was a fabulous place . . .'" Author interview with Rosemary Smith, Dublin, 2009.

"'Every week or so . . .'" Author interview with Nicki Browne, by telephone, 2011.

191 – "'A sixteen-year-old girl from a tiny village . . .'" Author interview with Mary Fanning, by telephone, 2010.

192 – 'Nicki was far less prepared for a lifetime of stay-at-home fidelity than Tara . . .' In interviews with the author, Nicki often responded to questions about marital infidelity with the line, 'It was the Sixties!'

"'He once made me beans on toast . . .'" Email from Douglas Binder to the author, 2010.

"'She had lost her baby to me . . .'" Author interview with Nicki Browne, by telephone, 2011.

193 – "'. . . a reaction to her loss of control over Tara . . .'" Author interview with Nicki Browne, by telephone, 2011.

194 – "'There was another fellow who came to dinner . . .'" Author interview with Michael Rainey, by telephone, 2011.

"'She also went to Denmark . . .'" Author interview with Nicki Browne, by telephone, 2011.

195 – "'In a few months," she told the *Irish Independent* . . .' *Irish Independent*, 14 August 1964.

'. . . Rafael Trujillo, who was assassinated after robbing the tiny Caribbean country blind for years.' *Trujillo: The Last Caesar* by General Arturo Espaillat (Henry Regnery, 1963) is a fascinating account of Trujillo's time as leader of the Dominican Republic by a former intelligence officer.

196 – '. . . then decamped to Flor's more impressive suite on a higher floor.' Miguel acknowledged an overlap in the two relationships in his September 1997 interview with Nicholas Farrell of *Harpers & Queen*.

196 – '"He told Oonagh, 'I have to go back to France to get my collection together' . . ."' Author interview with Nicki Browne, by telephone, 2011.

'. . . whom Miguel claimed was his brother, signed an affidavit, admitting the subterfuge.' Document seen by the author.

'A solicitor even found the real Miguel's mother, selling newspapers in Madrid.' The solicitor confirmed the story to the author but did not wish to be named.

'"Under English, Irish and French law . . ."' Author interview with Garech Browne, Wicklow, 2010.

'"He remembered what I had told him years earlier . . ."' Author interview with Hugo Williams, London, 2011.

197 – '. . . Garech agreed that the figure of £6 million . . .' This is the figure most often quoted as the cost of Oonagh Guinness' marriage to Miguel Ferreras. Garech estimated that the business cost her £5 million and his extravagant lifestyle a further £1 million.

'"I know he wasn't God's gift to humanity . . ."' Author interview with Nicki Browne, by telephone, 2011.

'While his wife reverted to her former name of Oonagh, Lady Oranmore and Browne . . .' According to Garech Browne, Oonagh had no intention of emulating her sister, who called herself Maureen, Marchioness of Dufferin and Ava during her two subsequent marriages. So Oonagh consulted Dom, who agreed to her reverting to her old title having seen the evidence suggesting her marriage to Miguel was invalid.

'Within weeks, the *New York World-Telegram* reported that he was planning to marry Flor . . .' From contemporary American newspaper reports.

'. . . Miguel told the the *New York Daily Mirror* that he would continue "dressing the very rich" . . .' Ibid.

198 – '"The thing that people often forget about the Sixties . . ."' Author interview with Marianne Faithfull, by telephone, 2011.

199 – 'Marianne Faithfull once characterized him as someone who would "attend dinners given by any silly thing with a title and a castle".' As quoted in *Ready, Steady, Go!* by Shawn Levy (Fourth Estate, 2002), p. 202.

'"A lot of these aristocratic kids had a lot going on in their heads . . ."' Author interview with Marianne Faithfull, by telephone, 2011.

'"They were very alike . . ."' Author interview Jane Ormsby-Gore, London, 2010.

200 – '"I don't know if you believe in astrology . . ."' Author interview with Nicki Browne, by telephone, 2010.

'"Tara was such a mellow kind of person . . ."' Author interview with Anita Pallenberg, London, 2015.

'. . . Even by Tara's standards, Brian had lived what could be described as a full and interesting life.' From several biographies of Brian Jones, especially *Brian Jones: The Making of a Rolling Stone* by Paul Trynka (Viking, 2014); *Brian Jones: The Untold Life and Mysterious Death of a Rock Legend* by Laura Jackson (Smith Gryphon, 1992); and *Who Killed Christopher Robin?: The Murder of a Rolling Stone* by Terry Rawlings (Helter Skelter Publishing, 1994).

201 – '"Brian was the grown-up one . . ."' Author interview with Anita Pallenberg, London, 2015.

202 – 'By then, Mick and Keith were starting to find their stroke as songwriters . . .' They also came up with 'My Only Girl', another ballad that Gene Pitney released in America under the title 'That Girl Belongs to Yesterday'. It was a top ten single in the UK, but it failed to break into the top 40 in the US.

'"Tara wasn't trying to get on any trip . . ."' Author interview with Michael Rainey, by telephone, 2011.

203 – '"He was obsessed with engines . . ."' Author interview with Nicki Browne, by telephone, 2010.

204 – '"She thought she'd get me married to Tara to legitimize Dorian . . ."' Ibid.

'Tara chatted to a reporter from the *Daily Express* about their forthcoming arrival . . .' *Daily Express*, 19 October 1964.

'"People in London thought he was mad . . ."' Author interview with Nicholas Gormanston, London, 2010.

'"The plan was to start at the bottom . . ."' Author interview with Nicki Browne, by telephone, 2011.

205 – '. . . Roman Polanski . . . was another regular caller.' Dudley Edwards remembered one such occasion. He told the author: 'Tara was very excited. He said, "Polanski's coming around." And then not long afterwards he arrived. He shoved his head around the door, said, "Looks like a conspiracy to me!" then shut the door and went off again.'

'"The house was always strewn with bodies . . ."' Author interview with Nicki Browne, by telephone, 2011.

'"Her intention . . . was to keep an eye on things . . ."' Author interview with Garech Browne, Wicklow, 2015.

10: FULL SWING

206 – '"Someone told us that you could induce labour . . ."' Author interview with Nicki Browne, by telephone, 2010.

206 – 'He told her that his name was Rock Brynner . . .' Rock Brynner was Yul's son from his first marriage, to the actress Virginia Gilmore. They divorced in 1960 when Rock was fourteen.

207 – '"Nicki was from – I think – an Irish farming background . . ."' Author interview with Rock Brynner, by telephone, 2009.

'"We came from different social backgrounds . . ."' Ibid.

208 – 'She was described as "indisposed" . . .' *Daily Mail*, 29 March 1965.

209 – '"Everyone in London wondered . . ."' Author interview with Nicholas Gormsanton, London, 2010.

210 – '"I know people will hate me for this . . ."' David Bailey quoted in *Ready, Steady, Go!* by Shawn Levy (Fourth Estate, 2002), p. 176.

'"They wanted their cars turned into getaway cars . . ."' Author interview with Nicki Browne, by telephone, 2010.

211 – '"We will piss anywhere, man!"' Contemporary newspaper reports of the subsequent court case.

'"Just because you have reached an exalted height in your profession . . ."' Ibid.

212 – '"At Shea Stadium . . . I saw the top of the mountain . . ."' John Lennon reportedly said this to Sidney Bernstein, the producer of the show.

213 – '"There will be a growth in album sales . . ."' Interestingly, Goddard Lieberson was once a visitor to Luggala. His connection to Oonagh Guinness may have been John Huston. He apparently loved the Luggala morning ritual of Bloody Marys for breakfast. For many years after his visit, he would send a crate of V8 tomato juice to Oonagh each Christmas with his best wishes.

'". . . a rhythm and blues Angus Steakhouse"'. As quoted in *Ready, Steady, Go!* by Shawn Levy (Fourth Estate, 2002), p. 244.

214 – '"He made me laugh . . ."' Author interview with Gerard Campbell, by telephone, 2010.

215 – '"You could see it was going wrong . . ."' Author interview with Martin Wilkinson, Newport, 2011.

216 – '"He wasn't a Dartford lad or whatnot . . ."' Author interview with Anita Pallenberg, London, 2015.

'"The first night I was with him . . ."' Ibid.

'"Anita was this sophisticated, exotic, international creature . . ."' Author interview with Prince Stanislaus Klossowski de Rola, aka Stash de Rola, by telephone, 2009.

11: LONDON TAKES A TRIP

218 – '. . . described by Richard Nixon as "the most dangerous man in America".' Obituary, *New York Times*, 1 June 1996.

'. . . At the climax of the evening, Leary would be introduced to the crowd as the High Priest of the psychedelic movement.' From *The Man Who Turned on the World* by Michael Hollingshead (Abelard-Schuman Ltd, 1973), pp. 144–5.

219 – '"Hollingshead was the only source of LSD in London at the time . . ."' Author interview with Martin Wilkinson, Newport, 2011.

'. . . as "intelligent" and "profound".' *The Man Who Turned on the World* by Michael Hollingshead (Abelard-Schuman Ltd, 1973), p. 158.

'"It was a period when people paid attention . . ."' *The Man Who Turned on the World* by Michael Hollingshead (Abelard-Schuman Ltd, 1973).

220 – '"One evening, I was with Martin Wilkinson and Tara had managed to get his hands on some LSD . . ."' Interview with Gerard Campbell, by telephone, 2010.

'"You took acid and you actually thought you were very close to God . . ."' Author interview with Jane Ormsby-Gore, London, 2010.

'"This rather strange, cosmic explosion . . ."' Author interview with Christopher Gibbs, London, 2010.

221 – 'It belonged to Joseph Bonnano, the boss of one of the New York Mafia's Five Families . . .' Author interview with Nicholas Gormanston, London, 2015.

'"She was living right on top of us . . ."' Author interview with Nicki Browne, by telephone, 2011.

222 – '"She had already made up her mind what she was going to do . . ."' Ibid.

'"She led an absolute campaign against Nicki . . ."' Author interview with Rock Brynner, by telephone, 2009.

'"By then, I was sick of London . . ."' Author interview with Nicki Browne, by telephone, 2011.

223 – '"When we got there . . . it was cold and wet . . ."' Interview with Gerard Campbell, by telephone, 2010.

'"Anyway, while we were there . . ."' Ibid.

224 – '"I was jealous . . ."' Author interview with Nicki Browne, by telephone, 2010.

'She was photographed leaving court . . .' *Daily Express*, 30 June 1965.

224 – '"I think she was French-Vietnamese . . ."' Author interview with Nicki Browne, by telephone, 2010.

225 – '"Dali and I built the Amanda Lear persona" . . .' Interview by Christa D'Souza, *Daily Telegraph*, 23 January 2001.

'In her book, *April Ashley's Odyssey*, she claimed that Amanda was originally a man . . .' *April Ashley's Odyssey* by Duncan Fallowell and Apirl Ashley (Jonathan Cape, 1982), pp. 69–70, pp. 178–180.

'"People don't want normality. They want people from Mars . . ."' Interview by Christa D'Souza, *Daily Telegraph*, 23 January 2001.

'. . . the kind of people who, according to the writer Jonathan Meades, "once shared a line with someone who shared a line with a Rolling Stone".' Quoted by Andrew Anthony in the *Observer*, Sunday, 24 December 2000.

'"She caught me staring at her . . ."' Author interview with Nicki Browne, by telephone, 2010.

226 – '"One evening . . . I was in the Marbella Club . . ."' Author interview with Amanda Lear, by telephone, 2010.

'"I said to Tara that I should leave . . ."' Ibid.

227 – 'A day or two after Tara left, an article appeared in the *Daily Express* . . .' *Daily Express*, 18 November 1965.

'. . . as he watches over Julian and Dorian in their playpen.' *Daily Express*, 22 November 1965.

'"Tara said to me, 'You have to have a go of it, Michael . . . ' " ' Author interview with Mike McCartney, Liverpool, 2008.

228 – 'In December, Tara wrote to him, offering him a full-time job . . .' Gore Taylor died in August 2003 and his papers were subsequently destroyed. However, he showed his letters from Tara to several people who were interviewed by the author.

'"He would have had to modify his lifestyle . . ."' Author interview with Glen Kidston, by telephone, 2015.

'"As an alliance between two people . . ."' Author interview with Christopher Gibbs, London, 2010.

229 – '"There was a lot of yahoo, yobbo kind of catcalls . . ."' Author interview with Nigel Waymouth, London, 2010.

'"They were piling up everywhere . . ."' Ibid.

'"We were really making it up as we went along . . ."' Ibid.

230 – '"Then we started designing our own stuff . . ."' Ibid.

231 – '"Tara had an extraordinary visual sense . . ."' Author interview with Martin Wilkinson, Newport, 2011.

232 – '"I had no background in the rag trade . . ."' Author interview with Michael Rainey, by telephone, 2011.

'The shop had something of a wild reputation . . .' *The Look: Adventures in Rock and Pop Fashion* by Paul Gorman (Adelita Limited, 2006), p. 83.

'"I suppose it had an energy about it . . ."' Author interview with Michael Rainey, by telephone, 2011.

'. . . John Lennon and George Harrison had first sampled . . .' There are numerous accounts of the night that John Lennon and George Harrison had their coffee spiked with LSD, including Lennon's own account in an interview with Jann Wenner, *Rolling Stone*, 21 January 1971. The identity of the dentist was first revealed in *The Gospel According to The Beatles* by Steve Turner (WJK Press, 2006).

233 – '. . . whispering, "I know what it's like to be dead."' John Lennon interviewed in *Rolling Stone*, 21 January 1971.

'". . . because we were all a bit slightly cruel, sort of, 'We're taking it, and you're not.'" ' Ibid.

'"I think he really sneered at people from Tara's background . . ."' Author interview with Nicki Browne, by telephone, 2009.

'"John didn't say much . . ."' Author interview with Martin Wilkinson, Newport, 2011.

234 – 'Tara was taking acid on blotting paper . . .' Paul McCartney's account of his first acid trip is featured in *Many Years from Now* by Barry Miles with Paul McCartney (Vintage, 1998), pp. 380–2.

'"Because it was Paul's first time . . ."' Interview with Nicki Browne, by telephone, 2009.

'Paul stayed up all night . . .' *Many Years from Now* by Barry Miles with Paul McCartney (Vintage, 1998), pp. 380–2.

'John later said he thought Paul regretted taking it . . .' John Lennon interviewed in *Rolling Stone*, 21 January 1971

'. . . he would always have mixed feelings about what happened in Tara's house that night.' *Many Years from Now* by Barry Miles with Paul McCartney (Vintage, 1998), pp. 380–2.

235 – '"I'd spent some of my allowance . . ."' Author interview with Nicki Browne, by telephone, 2009.

236 – '"He looked like he'd been in a boxing match . . ."' Author interview with Mike McCartney, Liverpool, 2008.

'Paul recounted what really happened in *The Beatles Anthology* . . .' *The Beatles Anthology* by The Beatles (Cassell & Co, 2000), p. 236.

'"His stepmother took it . . ."' Author interview with Nicki Browne, by telephone, 2009.

12: A DAY FOR A DAYDREAM

238 – '"We had this crazy apartment . . ."' Author interview with Anita Pallenberg, London, 2015.

'"Brian loved model trains when he was a boy . . ."' Ibid.

239 – '"We had loads of affinity together . . ."' Ibid.

'"We'd get in our cars . . ."' Ibid.

240 – 'Shortly after that, Dawn Malloy . . .' From several biographies of Brian Jones, especially *Brian Jones: The Making of a Rolling Stone* by Paul Trynka (Viking, 2014); *Brian Jones: The Untold Life and Mysterious Death of a Rock Legend* by Laura Jackson (Smith Gryphon, 1992); and *Who Killed Christopher Robin?: The Murder of a Rolling Stone* by Terry Rawlings (Helter Skelter Publishing, 1994).

'"Brian was a tortured soul . . ."' Author interview with Anita Pallenberg, London, 2015.

241 – '. . . Mick, whose three-year relationship with Chrissie Shrimpton was known to be on the skids.' Chrissie Shrimpton is often cited by music historians as the inspiration for some of Mick Jagger's bitterest compositions, including 'Stupid Girl' and '19th Nervous Breakdown'.

'"That's when I met Tara for the first time . . ."' Author interview with Marianne Faithfull, by telephone, 2011.

242 – '"He'd married a village girl . . ."' Ibid.

'"All of a sudden, it was a very, very non-talking environment . . ."' Author interview with Melissa North, London, 2011.

243 – 'In March, *London Life* magazine had blown the whistle . . .' *London Life*, March 1966.

'"The cops were pretty corrupt . . ."' Author interview with Martin Wilkinson, Newport, 2011.

'"Being busted is like going bald . . ."' *The Man Who Turned on the World* by Michael Hollingshead (Abelard-Schuman Ltd, 1973), pp. 169–170.

244 – '"It seems silly now . . ."' Author interview with Michael Rainey, by telephone, 2011.

245 – '. . . when America's *Time* magazine made "the Swinging City" the subject of an era-defining cover story.' *Time*, 15 April 1966.

246 – '"I always did it for him . . ."' Author interview with Anita Pallenberg, London, 2015.

'"We laughed our way through the whole thing . . ."' Author interview with Nicki Browne, by telephone, 2009.

247 – "'All sorts of people got off that plane . . .'" Author interview with Christopher Gibbs, London, 2010.

"'We told the driver to stop . . .'" Author interview with Anita Pallenberg, London, 2015.

248 – 'At the time, he had developed an obsession with the legend of Pan . . .' An interesting account of Brian Jones' fascination with Pan is featured in *Brian Jones: The Making of a Rolling Stone* by Paul Trynka (Viking, 2014), pp. 160–1, pp. 284–5.

"'We got hysterical looking at this dead goat . . .'" Author interview with Anita Pallenberg, London, 2015.

"'We saw the cottages on the property . . .'" Author interview with Joe Butler, by telephone, 2011.

249 – "'When we arrived, I think I was probably thinking the same . . .'" Author interview with John Sebastian, by telephone, 2011.

250 – "'He looked magnificent . . .'" Author interview with Mike McCartney, Liverpool, 2008.

"'There were a lot of prominent people there . . .'" Interview with Joe Butler, by telephone, 2011.

251 – 'At one point, according to the following day's *Sunday Press* . . .' *Sunday Press*, 24 April 1966.

"'Anita and I got it into our heads . . .'" Author interview with Nicki Browne, by telephone, 2009.

252 – "'The way my moral compass was . . .'" Author interview with Joe Butler, by telephone, 2011.

13: HERE TODAY

254 – "'We travelled up to Liverpool in the back of a limo . . .'" Author interview with Nicholas Gormanston, London, 2010.

"'We were drinking in this old-fashioned pub . . .'" Author interview with Mike McCartney, Liverpool, 2008.

"'He came off the motorway at sixty miles per hour . . .'" Author interview with Nicki Browne, by telephone, 2009.

255 – 'In court, Tara was represented by Max Mosley . . .' Desmond Guinness and Max Mosley were both sons of Diana Mitford: Desmond from her first marriage to Bryan Guinness; and Max from her second marriage to Sir Oswald Mosley.

"'I used to have to drive him around . . .'" Author interview with Glen Kidston, by telephone, 2015.

255 – "'He turned to me . . . and he said, 'I'm going to do that to the Cobra.'" ' Ibid.

257 – "'I wasn't that close to him in college . . .'" Author interview with Dudley Edwards, Harrogate, 2009.

"'Psychedelic art wasn't around when we started off . . .'" Ibid.

"'We thought if we maybe left a piece of painted furniture on his doorstep . . .'" Ibid.

258 – 'In January 1966, *House Beautiful* magazine ran a feature on their work . . .' *House Beautiful*, January edition, 1966.

'David Vaughan . . . told the *London Evening Standard* that they'd been asked to paint the dome of the recently cleaned St Paul's Cathedral canary yellow . . .' Author interview with Dudley Edwards, Harrogate, 2009.

"'He said, 'I mentioned you to him. I think he'll love you and what you're doing . . .' " ' Author interview with Dudley Edwards, Harrogate, 2009.

259 – "'The Beach Boys were the reason he bought the Cobra . . .'" Ibid.

260 – "'I was madly in love with him . . .'" Author interview with Amanda Lear, by telephone, 2010.

261 – "'John was the archetypal Australian rogue . . .'" Author interview with Alan Holsten, London, 2010.

"'The kind of charm that people like Jimi Hendrix . . .'" Author interview with Michael Rainey, by telephone, 2011.

262 – "'John's girlfriend at the time managed to earn a wage modelling . . .'" Ibid.

"'Tara wanted to be a backer of enterprises . . .'" Author interview with Martin Wilkinson, Newport, 2011.

263 – "'We worked out of this tiny little mews garage . . .'" Author interview with Alan Holsten, London, 2010.

"'The interesting thing for me . . .'" Author interview with Paul Gorman, London, 2009.

264 – "'Snowdon . . . was halfway up a ladder . . .'" *Daily Express*, 30 September 1966.

"'It was like something out of an Ealing Comedy . . .'" Author interview with Dudley Edwards, Harrogate, 2009.

265 – '. . . Even Pathé News wanted to film the moment for posterity.' The film is available to view at www.britishpathe.com/video/art-on-wheels.

"'He said the window was part of the deal . . .'" Author interview with Dudley Edwards, Harrogate, 2009.

"'So Doug and I are standing there . . .'" Ibid.

266 – "'It is the world that the Thirties promised . . .'" Tara quoted in several newspaper reports on 7 September 1966.

'The seven-minute, black-and-white film was entitled *Une Journée Avec L'Honorable Tara Browne . . .*' Seen by the author.

"'That was actually me at the wheel . . .'" Author interview with Glen Kidston, by telephone, 2015.

267 – 'In September 1966, the New York-based men's fashion magazine *Gentleman's Quarterly . . .*' *Gentlemen's Quarterly*, September 1966.

268 – ' " ' . . . all of the establishment, past and contemporary.' " ' Ibid.

"'The way she behaved with me was amazing . . .'" Author interview with Amanda Lear, by telephone, 2010.

269 – "'I was doing a show for Paco Rabane . . .'" Ibid.

"'Tara and Brian were dressed in these lace and velvet suits . . .'" Ibid. A fuller account of this story is featured in *My Life with Dali* by Amanda Lear (Virgin Books, 1985), pp. 9–18.

"'I was very skinny . . .'" Ibid.

271 – "'I stopped off in Paris on the way home . . .'" Author interview with Nicki Browne, by telephone, 2010.

"'The way that it was explained to me . . .'" Author interview with Garech Browne, Wicklow, 2010.

"'I realized that his music system was gone . . .'" Author interview with Nicki Browne, by telephone, 2010.

272 – "'We were supposed to be going to Ireland . . .'" Ibid.

"'I was told by a member of the staff that they had gone away . . .'" Ibid.

"'Divorce was just an accepted thing in their family . . .'" Ibid.

273 – '. . . she took a taxi to Pall Mall to see David Jacobs . . .' In 1959, David Jacobs helped formulate the strategy for Liberace's successful libel suit against the *Daily Mirror* for suggesting that he was gay. Jacobs committed suicide in 1968. See also: 'The Mystery of David Jacobs, the Liberace Lawyer', an article by Mick Brown, *Daily Telegraph*, 3 June 2013.

'Jacobs took her straight to the High Court . . .' Contemporary newspaper reports of the court case.

'Her counsel, Harold Law, told the court . . . .' Contemporary newspaper reports.

'That night, Dublin's *Evening Press* led with the headline: "Guinness Heir Sought by Police".' *Evening Press*, 13 October 1966.

"Nicki appeared in the following morning's *Daily Express . . .*" *Daily Express*, 15 October 1966.

"'I just want to know where my babies are . . .'"Ibid.

274 – '"I can't tell you anything . . ."' *Daily Express*, 17 October 1966.

'"I phoned him up . . ."' Author interview with Nicki Browne, by telephone 2010.

'The following weekend . . . Tara flew to Paris to see Amanda . . .' A full account of this story is featured in *My Life with Dali* by Amanda Lear (Virgin Books, 1985), pp. 18–23.

'Amanda agreed, although she claimed later that she regretted it . . .' Author interview with Amanda Lear, by telephone, 2010.

275 – '"A week or two later . . . he phoned me to say he was coming to Paris tomorrow . . ."' Ibid.

'"We were followed everywhere . . ."' Author interview with Rock Brynner, by telephone, 2009.

276 – '"Oonagh thought I did it so that I could prove adultery . . ."' Author interview with Nicki Browne, by telephone, 2010.

'. . . the woman who was once described by Cecil Beaton as "the biggest bitch in London".' Maureen told the writer Hugo Vickers that Cecil Beaton had introduced her thus at a dinner party in 1935. Obituary, *Independent*, 22 May 1998.

'"I had no money at all . . ."' Author interview with Nicki Browne, by telephone, 2010.

14: A DAY IN THE LIFE

278 – '"He was in a state of absolute turmoil . . ."' Author interview with Gerard Campbell, by telephone, 2010.

'. . . The *New York Times* commented upon the fin de siècle feel to the city . . .' *New York Times*, 8 June 1966.

279 – '"I remember being on the King's Road with him . . ."' Author interview with Rock Brynner, by telephone, 2009.

'"We had a little scene together . . ."' Author interview with Marianne Faithfull, by telephone, 2011.

280 – '"On this particular night, he was hanging around . . ."' Author interview with Dudley Edwards, Harrogate, 2009.

281 – '"John would go and buy the fabric . . ."' Author interview with Alan Holsten, London, 2010.

'"It did have its own aesthetic . . ."' Author interview with Paul Gorman, London, 2011.

282 – '"They nicked my suppliers . . ."' Author interview with Michael Rainey, by telephone, 2011.

"'It was a mistake. I thought the King's Road was where it was happening . . .'" Ibid.

"'By the time we opened, everyone was just plagiarizing everyone else . . .'" Author interview with Alan Holsten, London, 2010.

"'But it had everything going for it . . .'" Ibid.

284 – "'He said he wanted the same thing done to his piano . . .'" Author interview with Dudley Edwards, Harrogate, 2009. Dudley Edwards and Paul McCartney became fast friends. In fact, while Jane Asher was in America pursuing her career as an actress, Paul invited Dudley to move into his house and paint a mural. 'I don't think I took a lid off a paint tin,' Dudley said. 'I'd be ready to start work and he'd say, "Come to the pub," or, "Come to the studio." I think he was just lonely for company. When Jane came back, I moved out and Ringo asked me to move in with him and paint him a mural. He got his mural, though.'

285 – "'I remember one night I was having a trip with him in Theodora's house . . .'" Author interview with Martin Wilkinson, Newport, 2011.

286 – '. . . He became a difficult presence around the studio, petulant, uncommunicative, drunk, or drugged.' From several biographies of Brian Jones, especially *Brian Jones: The Making of a Rolling Stone* by Paul Trynka (Viking, 2014); *Brian Jones: The Untold Life and Mysterious Death of a Rock Legend* by Laura Jackson (Smith Gryphon, 1992); and *Who Killed Christopher Robin?: The Murder of a Rolling Stone* by Terry Rawlings (Helter Skelter Publishing, 1994).

"'For Brian, I think his friendship with Tara was a safe haven . . .'" Author interview with Anita Pallenberg, London, 2015.

"'Brian answered the door . . .'" Author interview with Martin Wilkinson, Newport, 2011.

287 – "'I heard what sounded like a racing car . . .'" Author interview with Thomas Webster, Wicklow, 2009.

288 – "'I don't think I shall be getting any clothes there . . .'" Quoted in the *Daily Express*, 9 December 1966.

'When my heart first began . . .' Reproduced with the kind permission of the Honorable Garech Browne.

289 – 'She came from a comfortable, middle-class background, he remembered . . .' Author interview with Mark Palmer, Cheltenham, 2015.

"'Nicki, by contrast, was bubbly and alive . . .'" Author interview with Michael Rainey, by telephone, 2011.

"'She seemed to sort of drift through life . . .'" Author interview with Jose Fonseca, by telephone, 2010.

"'She was a rebound thing for Tara . . .'" Author interview with Martin Wilkinson, Newport, 2011.

290 – '"He rang me the following day . . ."' Author interview with Nicki Browne, by telephone, 2009.

'"I think he just saw everything going down the spout . . ."' Ibid.

291 – '"It's very dangerous if you haven't driven anything for six months . . ."' Author interview with Martin Wilkinson, Newport, 2011.

'Seconds later, there was a bang . . .' From contemporary newspaper reports of the accident, quoting eye-witnesses.

'"A gentleman," said Anita Pallenberg . . .' Author interview with Anita Pallenberg, London, 2015.

292 – '"Theodora got there before me . . ."' Author interview with Nicki Browne, by telephone, 2010.

'"It was the most awful thing I've ever had to do . . ."' Author interview with Gay Kindersley, East Garston, 2011.

'"You expect to see your parents die . . ."' Author interview with Garech Browne, Wicklow, 2006.

'"I said to her, 'I have something urgent I have to tell you.'"' Author interview with Garech Browne, Wicklow, 2016.

'"It was like a death knell sounding over London . . ."' Author interview with Marianne Faithfull, by telephone, 2011.

293 – '"It was a very gallant act . . ."' Gilbert Potier, quoted in several newspapers, 19 December 1966.

'"I am numbed . . ."' Brian Jones, quoted in several newspapers, 19 December 1966.

'"We felt immortal . . ."' Author interview with Anita Pallenberg, London, 2015.

EPILOGUE: AND THOUGH THE NEWS WAS RATHER SAD

294 – 'Nicki and Oonagh appeared in front of Mr Justice Cross . . .' From several contemporary newspaper reports.

'. . . every effort should be made to ensure that their mother played an increasing role in their lives.' Ibid.

'"I had no chance . . ."' Author interview with Nicki Browne, by telephone, 2010.

295 – 'He was, in his own words, "very out of it then" . . .' John Lennon interviewed in *Rolling Stone*, 21 January 1971.

296 – '"I went out and bought a new suit . . ."' Author interview with Gerard Campbell, by telephone, 2010.

'"She moved out of Luggala . . ."' Author interview with Greta

Fanning, Wicklow, 2009. Greta is a sister of Mary Fanning, who went to London to work as a nanny for Tara and Nicki.

297 – '"As the older brother . . ."' Author interview with Garech Browne, Wicklow, 2006.

'"I'm going by myself . . ."' As quoted in several contemporary newspapers.

'"I couldn't grieve for Tara properly . . ."' Author interview with Anita Pallenberg, London, 2015.

299 – '"For me, the day that Tara died was the end of the Sixties . . ."' Author interview with Hugo Williams, London, 2011.

'"We were all so young . . ."' Author interview with Anita Pallenberg, London, 2015.

300 – '. . . thought he'd just heard a confession from Mick Jagger, rather than Brian Jones.' Various sources, including *Butterfly on a Wheel: The Great Rolling Stones Drug Bust* by Simon Wells (Omnibus Press, 2012).

301 – '. . . a leader article criticizing the harshness of the sentences and the Victorian brutality brought to bear on those involved.' Paraphrasing Alexander Pope's poem *Epistle to Dr Arbuthnot*, William Rees-Mogg asked, 'Who breaks a butterfly on a wheel?' *The Times*, 1 July 1967.

'"He used to really get up their noses . . ."' Author interview with Alan Holsten, London, 2010.

'"They busted him for drugs . . ."' Ibid.

302 – 'Keith, who had developed feelings for Anita, made his move . . .' Various accounts, especially *Life* by Keith Richards (Weidenfeld & Nicolson, 2010).

'"He was devastated by Tara's death . . ."' Author interview with Amanda Lear, by telephone, 2010.

'"Suki was completely broken up by what happened . . ."' Author interview with Jose Fonseca, by telephone, 2010.

303 – '"Brian definitely went downhill after Tara died . . ."' Author interview with Marianne Faithfull, by telephone, 2011.

'A silly-season conspiracy theory, which started among students on a university campus in Iowa . . .' *The Walrus was Paul: The Great Beatle Death Clues* by R. Gary Patterson (Prentice Hall & IBD, 1998) is a fascinating account of the Paul is Dead hoax.

'"They said Tara had had cosmetic surgery to make him look like Paul . . ."' Author interview with Nicki Browne, by telephone, 2011.

304 – '. . . the 100 Greatest Songs by the band in order . . .' *Rolling Stone*, special edition, 19 September 2011.

305 – '"Looking back," Nicki said of the affair . . .' Author interview with Nicki Browne, by telephone, 2010.

306 – '"He wanted to be Peter Pan . . ."' Author interview with Nicki Browne, by telephone, 2012.

PICTURE CREDITS

Acknowledgements

My interest in the short but fascinating life of the Honourable Tara Browne stretches back to 2006 and a feature article I was commissioned to write for the magazine of the now sadly defunct *Sunday Tribune*. It was published in December 2006 in the week of the fortieth anniversary of his death in a car crash in London. Though I interviewed his brother, the Honorable Garech Browne, and several of his friends, I was disappointed with the final piece, knowing that it did scant justice to his extraordinarily colourful life and times. Over the months that followed, I couldn't help feeling that his story required a fuller telling, which is when my decade-long quest to find out everything I could about Tara Browne began.

This book would not have been possible without the agreement and kind help of Garech, who has become a dear friend to me since my first of what must now be seventy visits to Luggala since 2006. Garech has inherited his mother's extraordinary gift for hospitality and the warmth of the welcome I have always received when visiting the house, whether alone to work, or with my wife for dinner, will never be forgotten.

Garech gave me access to the Luggala visitors' book and his mother's enormous collection of photographs and newspaper clippings, which proved invaluable in piecing together the story of Tara's life. He asked for permission to read the manuscript before it was published but promised only to correct facts and not my interpretation of events. While some of the story was undoubtedly difficult for him to read, he was true to his word, asking for nothing to be amended or removed, apart from my occasional spelling mistakes or errors relating to my lack of knowledge of the aristocratic tradition. For that and the friendship that has come as a happy by-product of my work on this book, I am forever grateful.

I never got to meet Tara's widow, Nicki, before her death in 2012, which saddens me greatly. Twice I was due to travel to Spain to interview her, but both times she was forced to cancel owing to illness. We spoke many times on the phone over the course of several years and she shared a great many details of her story with me, painful though some of our conversations were for her. It pleased me enormously to receive a post-card from her shortly before her death, featuring a cartoon of a frog sitting on a lily pad, casting a line into a pond. On the reverse side, she had written, 'Keep fishing. Nicki.'

I am also hugely grateful to Tara's sons, Dorian and Julian. While they were too young at the time of their father's death to have formed any strong and lasting memories of him, their support and interest in the project was a great help, as were the family albums that Dorian kindly allowed me to see. I would also like to thank Julian's wife, Tanja, for the generous welcome that she and her husband extended to me when we met at Luggala. And Dorian's wife, Alison, and their sons, Sebastian and Gabriel, for the hospitality and regular refreshments they offered me when I spent an entire weekend in their dining room poring over volumes of old photos.

It is a rare and happy thing as a biographer to find a subject who was as universally loved as Tara Browne. Almost all of his friends whom I approached were delighted to share their memories of him with me and I enjoyed the experience of meeting most of them face to face while pursuing the story all over Ireland and Britain.

For their wonderful reminiscences, I would especially like to thank Michael Boyle; Dominick Browne, Lord Mereworth; Rock Brynner; Joe Butler; Sean Byrne; Maura Byrne; Gerard Campbell; Godfrey Carey; Tchaik Chassay; Serena Connell; Dudley Edwards; Marianne Faithfull; Greta Fanning; the late Desmond Fitzgerald, the Knight of Glin; Jose Fonseca; Christopher Gibbs; Nicholas Gormanston; Desmond Guinness; Penny Guinness; Judith Haslam; Alan Holsten; Catheryn Huntley; Judith Keppel; Glen Kidston; the late Gay Kindersley; Kim Kindersley; Robin Kindersley; Prince Stanislaus Klossowski de Rola; Amanda Lear; Lady Lucinda Lambton; Jacquetta Lampson; Gordon Ledbetter; the late Candida Lycett Green; Rupert Lycett Green; Mike McCartney; John Medlycott, David Mlinaric; Paddy Moloney; John Montague; Larry

Mooney; Max Mosley; Brid Ni Dhonnchadha; Melissa North; Lady Jane Ormsby-Gore, Lady Victoria Ormsby-Gore; Sir Mark Palmer; Anita Pallenberg; Mary Quain; Michael Rainey; Rabea Redpath; the late Kenneth Rose; Peregrine St Germans; John Sebastian; Rosemary Smith; Monsignor Tom Stack; Michael Steen; Nigel Waymouth; Neale Webb; Thomas Webster; Noeleen Webster; Martin Wilkinson; and Hugo Williams.

I owe an enormous debt of thanks to Philomena Flatley, the former secretary to Lord Oranmore and Browne, who gave up an entire day to show me around the empty rooms of Castle Mac Garrett in County Mayo. It was of considerable help in gaining a picture of the early years of Tara's boyhood.

I am also grateful to Charles Doble for sharing his knowledge of the life and times of Sally Gray with me, for his hospitality when I visited him at his home in Ashbrittle and for the day we spent watching her movies. I am hugely grateful, too, to Paul Gorman for the fascinating insight he gave me into the fashion of the 1960s; Robert O'Byrne for both his knowledge and his wonderful book on the history of Luggala; and to Joe Joyce for his brilliant history of the Guinness family.

The staff of Luggala were not only helpful but very welcoming every time I visited, especially Frances Gillespie, Kristina Jambrovich, John Welsby and the late Nicholas Myers.

For assisting in other valuable ways, I would like to thank Stuart Bell, Douglas Binder, Tony Boylan, Bob Cavallo, James Cawley, Clive Chapman, Adam Cooper, Richie Conroy, David Crampton, Michael de las Casas, Michael Fanning, Nicholas Farrell, Mary Finnegan, Brian Foley, Christopher Haslam, Harry Havelin, Tom Heatley, Sarah Janson, Philippa Kindersley, Chloe Lonsdale, Ivana Lowell, Robin McNeill, Peter MacSherry, Roderic O'Connor, Gordon Orenbuch, Robin Rhoderick-Jones, Mark St John, Mildred Trail, Gabriel Waddington, Miles Wilkins and Susan Wylie-Roberts.

I am very grateful to the staff of the British Library's newspaper archive in Colindale and the National Library in Dublin for their help in finding newspapers, and to Sean McCarthy and Richard Howard for conducting additional research for me.

But research is only part of the job of producing a book like this.

This story would not have been told were it not for the encouragement and support of my agent, Faith O'Grady, and the belief of Paul Baggaley of Picador, whose enthusiasm for the subject from the very beginning happily matched my own. It has been a pleasure to work with Paul and the rest of the Picador team, especially Kris Doyle, Luke Brown and Nicole Foster, who all worked on the manuscript and made excellent suggestions. Sincere thanks to my brother, Vincent Howard, who proofread the manuscript and made many valued comments.

I would like to say a huge thank you to my superb solicitors, John Whelan and Alison Quinn of A&L Goodbody. And I am grateful to former *Sunday Tribune* editor Noirin Hegarty and magazine editor Fionnuala McCarthy for commissioning the original feature about Tara Browne.

Lastly, I would like to thank my wife, Mary McCarthy, who for ten years has borne my obsession with telling this story with good cheer and who kept me going with encouraging words and excellent breakfasts. Mary, I am sorry for all the times I was absent, either physically or mentally, while writing this book. For your patience and your understanding, there are no words, other than I love you.

Index